Programming Logic and Design, Comprehensive,

Second Edition

Joyce Farrell

University of Wisconsin

Stevens Point

**COURSE
TECHNOLOGY**
—✦—
THOMSON LEARNING

Australia • Canada • Mexico • Singapore • Spain • United Kingdom • United States

COURSE TECHNOLOGY
TM
THOMSON LEARNING

Programming Logic and Design, Comprehensive, Second Edition
By Joyce Farrell

Product Manager:
Tricia Boyle

Managing Editor:
Jennifer Locke

Senior Editor:
Jennifer Muroff

Development Editor:
Lisa Ruffolo

Editorial Assistant:
Janet Aras

Production Editor:
Karen Jacot

Cover Designer:
Betsy Young

Compositor:
GEX Publishing Services

Manufacturing Coordinator:
Alexander Schall

Disclaimer
Course Technology reserves the right t revise this publication and make changes from time to time in its conte without notice.

ISBN 0-619-06315-7

BRIEF

Contents

TABLE OF
Contents

CHAPTER FOURTEEN
Program Design   391

CHAPTER FIFTEEN
System Modeling With UML   411

APPENDIX A   A-1
A Difficult Structuring Problem

APPENDIX B   B-1
Using a Large Decision Table

INDEX   I-1

Preface

Programming Logic and Design, Comprehensive, Second Edition, provides the beginning programmer with a guide to developing structured program logic. This textbook assumes that students have no programming language experience. The writing is nontechnical and emphasizes good programming practices. The examples are business examples; they do not assume mathematical background beyond high school business math. Additionally, the examples illustrate one or two major points; they do not contain so many features that students become lost following irrelevant and extraneous details.

The examples in *Programming Logic and Design, Comprehensive, Second Edition,* have been created to provide students with a sound background in logic no matter what programming languages they might eventually use to write programs. This book can be used in a stand-alone logic course that students take as a prerequisite to a programming course, or as a companion book to an introductory programming text using any programming language.

ORGANIZATION AND COVERAGE

Programming Logic and Design, Comprehensive, Second Edition, introduces students to programming concepts, enforcing good style and logical thinking. General programming concepts are introduced in Chapter 1. Chapter 2 discusses the key concepts of structure including what structure is, how to recognize it, and, most importantly, the advantages to writing structured programs. Chapter 3 extends the information on structured programming to the area of modules. By Chapter 4 students can write complete, structured business programs. Chapters 5 and 6 explore the intricacies of decision making and looping. Students learn to develop sophisticated programs that use control breaks and arrays in Chapters 7 and 8.

In Chapter 9 students use arrays in more sophisticated ways by exploring sorting techniques. Chapter 10 focuses on the special issues involved in writing interactive programs that allow users to make menu selections from both single- and multiple-level menus. Chapter 11 covers the intricacies of sequential file merging, matching, and updating. In Chapter 12, students learn valuable modularization techniques, including the differences between local and global variables and how to pass variables to and from modules. Chapter 12 also provides clear explanations of the sometimes confusing terminology associated with object-oriented programming. In Chapter 13, students learn the vocabulary associated with event-driven programming and how to incorporate GUI objects into programs. Chapter 14 brings together all the concepts that students have learned so far by addressing issues of good program design—including reducing coupling and increasing cohesion. Chapter 15 provides an introduction to UML, a powerful graphic tool for designing object-oriented systems.

Programming Logic and Design, Comprehensive, Second Edition, combines text explanation with flowcharts and pseudocode examples to provide students with alternative means of expressing structured logic. Numerous detailed, full-program exercises at the end of each section illustrate the concepts explained within the section and reinforce students' understanding and retention of the material presented.

Programming Logic and Design, Comprehensive, Second Edition, distinguishes itself from other programming logic language books in the following ways:

- It is written and designed to be non-language specific. The logic used in this book can be applied to any programming language.

- The examples are everyday business examples; no special knowledge of mathematics, accounting, or other disciplines is assumed.

- The concept of structure is covered earlier than in many other texts. Students are exposed to structure naturally, so they will automatically create properly designed programs.

- Text explanation is interspersed with both flowcharts and pseudocode so students can become comfortable with both logic development tools and understand their interrelationship.

- Complex programs are built through the use of complete business examples. Students see how an application is built from start to finish instead of studying only segments of programs. Students learn the difference between local and global variables, and how to pass their values to and from modules.

- Object-oriented terminology is thoroughly explained. This feature is absent from many other programming logic books.

- Event-driven GUI programs are presented. Students enjoy working with the graphical objects. Few texts explore the logic behind them.

- Students gain an appreciation for good program design, and learn to recognize poor design.

- Students learn about UML, a powerful object-oriented design tool.

FEATURES

New to this edition of the text is the use of camel casing for naming variables and methods, and the addition of parentheses to method names. These improvements expose students to variable and method names that closely resemble those they will be most likely to use in introductory programming classes in C++, Java, Visual Basic or Pascal. To improve students' comprehension of the decision-making process, endif has been added to the pseudocode in all decision examples. Additional end-of-chapter exercises are included so students have more opportunities to practice concepts as they learn them.

Programming Logic and Design, Comprehensive, Second Edition, is a superior textbook because it also includes the following features:

- **Objectives** Each chapter begins with a list of objectives so the student knows the topics that will be presented in the chapter. In addition to providing a quick reference to topics covered, this feature provides a useful study aid.

- **Tips** These notes provide additional information—for example, an alternative method of performing a procedure, another term for a concept, background information on a technique, or a common error to watch out for.

- **Summaries** Following each section is a summary that recaps the programming concepts and techniques covered in the section. This feature provides a concise means for the student to recap and check understanding of each chapter's main points.

- **Exercises** Each chapter section concludes with meaningful programming exercises that provide students with additional practice of the skills and concepts they learned in the lesson. These exercises increase in difficulty and are designed to allow students to explore logical programming concepts.

TEACHING TOOLS

The following supplemental materials are available when this book is used in a classroom setting. All of the teaching tools available with this book are provided to the instructor on a single CD-ROM.

Electronic Instructor's Manual. The Instructor's Manual that accompanies this textbook includes:

- Additional instructional material to assist in class preparation, including suggestions for lecture topics.
- Solutions to all end-of-chapter materials.

ExamView®. This textbook is accompanied by ExamView, a powerful testing software package that allows instructors to create and administer printed, computer (LAN-based), and Internet exams. ExamView includes hundreds of questions that correspond to the topics covered in this text, enabling students to generate detailed study guides that include page references for further review. The computer-based and Internet testing components allow students to take exams at their computers, and also save the instructor time by grading each exam automatically.

PowerPoint Presentations. This book comes with Microsoft PowerPoint slides for each chapter. These are included as a teaching aid for classroom presentation, to make available to students on the network for chapter review, or to be printed for classroom distribution. Instructors can add their own slides for additional topics they introduce to the class.

Solution Files. Solutions to end-of chapter exercises are provided on the Teaching Tools CD-ROM and may also be found on the Course Technology Web site at **www.course.com**. The solutions are password protected.

Distance Learning. Course Technology is proud to present online courses in WebCT and Blackboard, as well as at MyCourse.com, Course Technology's own course enhancement tool, to provide the most complete and dynamic learning experience possible. When you add online content to one of your courses, you're adding a lot: self tests, links, glossaries, and, most of all, a gateway to the 21st century's most important information resource. We hope you will make the most of your course, both online and offline. For more information on how to bring distance learning to your course, contact your local Course Technology sales representative.

Acknowledgments

I would like to thank all of the people who helped to make this book a reality, especially Lisa Ruffolo, Development Editor, whose hard work, attention to detail, and perceptive appreciation for the methodology required to teach this subject matter have made this a quality textbook. Thanks also to Kristen Duerr, Vice President and Publisher; Tricia Boyle, Product Manager; Jennifer Locke, Managing Editor; Jennifer Muroff, Senior Editor; Margarita Donovan, Senior Product Manager; Karen Jacot, Production Editor; Janet Aras, Editorial Assistant; and Beverly Jackson, Quality Assurance Tester. I am grateful to be able to work with so many fine people who are dedicated to producing quality instructional materials.

I am grateful to the many reviewers who provided helpful and insightful comments during the development of this revision, including R. Scott Cost, University of Maryland at Catonsville; Bob Husson, Craven Community College; Cathleen Kennedy, College of San Mateo; Marilyn D. Moore, Morehead State University; George Novotny, Ferris State University; Steve Prettyman, Chattahoochee Technical Institute; and Pamela Silvers, Asheville-Buncombe Technical Community College.

Thanks, too, to my husband, Geoff, who acts as friend and advisor in the book-writing process. This book, as was its previous edition, is dedicated to him and to my daughters, Andrea and Audrey.

Joyce Farrell

1

AN OVERVIEW OF COMPUTERS AND LOGIC

After studying Chapter 1, you should be able to:

♦ Understand computer components and operations

♦ Describe the steps involved in the programming process

♦ Describe the data hierarchy

♦ Understand how to use flowchart symbols and pseudocode statements

♦ Use and name variables

♦ Use a sentinel, or dummy value, to end a program

♦ Use a connector symbol

♦ Assign values to variables

♦ Recognize the proper format of assignment statements

♦ Describe data types

UNDERSTANDING COMPUTER COMPONENTS AND OPERATIONS

The two major components of any computer system are its hardware and its software. **Hardware** is the equipment, or the devices, associated with a computer. For a computer to be useful, however, it needs more than equipment; a computer needs to be given instructions. The instructions that tell the computer what to do are called **software**, or programs, and are written by programmers. This book focuses on the process of writing these instructions.

Together, computer hardware and software accomplish four major operations:

1. Input

2. Processing

3. Output

4. Storage

Hardware devices that perform input include keyboards and mice. Through these devices, **data**, or facts, enter the computer system. Processing data items may involve organizing them, checking them for accuracy, or performing mathematical operations on them. The piece of hardware that performs these sorts of tasks is the **Central Processing Unit,** or **CPU**. After data have been processed, the resulting information is sent to a printer, monitor, or some other output device. Often, you also want to store the output information on hardware, such as magnetic disks or tapes. Computer software consists of all the instructions that control how and when the data are input, how they are processed, and the form in which they are output or stored.

Computer hardware by itself is useless without a programmer's instructions or software, just as your stereo equipment doesn't do much until you provide music on a CD or tape. You can enter instructions into a computer system through any of the hardware devices you use for data: for example, a keyboard or disk drive.

You write computer instructions in a computer **programming language** such as Visual Basic, Pascal, COBOL, RPG, C#, C++, Java, or Fortran. Just as some humans speak English and others speak Japanese, programmers also write programs in different languages. Some programmers work exclusively in one language, while others know several and use the one that seems most appropriate for the task at hand.

No matter which programming language a computer programmer uses, the language has rules governing its word usage and punctuation. These rules are called the language's **syntax**. If you ask, "How the get to store do I?" in English, most people can figure out what you probably mean even though you have not used proper English syntax. However, computers are not nearly as smart as most humans; with a computer you might as well have asked, "Xpu mxv ot dodnm cadf B?" Unless the syntax is perfect, the computer cannot interpret the programming language instruction at all.

Every computer operates on circuitry that consists of millions of on-off switches. Each programming language uses a piece of software to translate the specific programming language into the computer's on-off circuitry language, or **machine language**. The language translation software is called a **compiler** or **interpreter**, and it tells you if you have used a programming language incorrectly. Therefore, syntax errors are relatively easy to locate and correct. If you write a computer program using a language such as C++, but spell one of its words incorrectly or reverse the proper order of two words, the translator lets you know it found a mistake as soon as you try to run the program.

 Although there are differences in how compilers and interpreters work, their basic function is the same—to translate your programming statements into code the computer can use.

For a program to work properly, you must give the instructions to the computer in a specific sequence, you must not leave any instructions out, and you must not add extraneous instructions. By doing this, you are developing the **logic** of the computer program. Suppose you instruct someone to make a cake as follows:

```
Stir
Add two eggs
Add a gallon of gasoline
Bake at 350 degrees for 45 minutes
Add three cups of flour
```

Even though you have used the English language syntax correctly, the instructions are out of sequence, some instructions are missing, and some instructions belong to procedures other than baking a cake. If you follow these instructions, you are not going to end up with an edible cake, and you may end up with a disaster. Logical errors are much more difficult to locate than syntax errors; it is easier for you to determine whether *eggs* is spelled incorrectly in a recipe than it is for you to tell if there are too many eggs or they are added too soon.

Just as baking directions can be given correctly in French, German, or Spanish, the same logic of a program can be expressed in any number of programming languages. This book is almost exclusively concerned with the logic development process. Because it is not concerned with any specific language, this book could have been written in Japanese, C++, or Java. The logic is the same in any language. For convenience, the book uses English!

Once instructions have been input to the computer and translated into machine language, a program can be **run** or **executed**. You can write a program that takes a number (an input step), doubles it (processing), and tells you the answer (output) in a programming language such as Pascal or C++, but if you were to write it in English, it would look like this:

```
Get inputNumber
Compute calculatedAnswer as inputNumber times 2
Print calculatedAnswer
```

The instruction to `Get inputNumber` is an example of an input operation. When the computer interprets this instruction, it knows to look to an input device to obtain a number. Computers often have several input devices, perhaps a keyboard, a mouse, a CD drive, and two or more disk drives. When you learn a specific programming language, you learn how to tell the computer which of those input devices to access for input. For now, however, it doesn't really matter which hardware device is used as long as the computer knows to look for a number. The logic of the input operation—that the computer must obtain a number for input, and that the computer must obtain it before multiplying it by two—remains the same regardless of any specific input hardware device.

 Many computer professionals categorize disk drives and CD drives as storage devices rather than input devices. Such devices actually can be used for input, storage, and output.

Processing is the step that occurs when the mathematics is performed to double the `inputNumber`; the statement Compute `calculatedAnswer` as `inputNumber` times 2 represents processing. Mathematical operations are not the only kind of processing, but they are very typical. After you write a program, the program can be used on computers of different brand names, sizes, and speeds. Whether you use an IBM, Macintosh, or UNIX operating system, and whether you use a personal computer that sits on your desk or a mainframe that costs hundreds of thousands of dollars and resides in a special building in a university, multiplying by two is the same process. The hardware is not important; the processing will be the same.

In the number doubling program, the Print `calculatedAnswer` statement represents output. Within a particular program, this statement could cause the output to appear on the monitor, which might be a flat panel screen or a cathode ray tube, or the output could go to a printer, which can be laser or inkjet. The logic of the process is the same no matter what hardware device you use.

Besides input, processing, and output, the fourth operation in any computer system is storage. Storage comes in two broad categories. All computers have **internal storage**, probably referred to more often as **memory**, **main memory**, or **primary memory**. This storage is inside the machine and is the type of storage most often discussed in this book. Computers also have **external storage**, which is permanent storage outside the main memory of the machine on a device such as a floppy disk, hard disk, or magnetic tape. In other words, external storage is outside of the main memory, not necessarily outside the computer. Both programs and data sometimes are stored on each of these kinds of media.

To use computer programs, you must first load them into memory. You might type a program into memory from the keyboard, or you might use a program that has already been written and stored on a disk. Either way, a copy of the instructions must be placed in memory before the program can be run.

A computer system needs both internal memory and external storage. Internal memory is needed to run the programs, but internal memory is **volatile**—that is, its contents are lost every time the computer loses power. Therefore, if you are going to use a program more than once, you must store it, or **save** it, on some nonvolatile medium. Otherwise, the program in main memory is lost forever when the computer is turned off. External storage (usually disks or tape) provides a nonvolatile medium.

 Even though a hard disk drive is located inside your computer, the hard disk is not main, internal memory. Internal memory is temporary and volatile; a hard drive is permanent, nonvolatile storage.

Once you have a copy of a program in main memory, you must also place any data that the program requires into memory. For example, after you place the following program into memory and start to run it, you need to provide an actual `inputNumber`—for example, 8—that you also place in main memory.

```
Get inputNumber
Compute calculatedAnswer as inputNumber times 2
Print calculatedAnswer
```

The `inputNumber` is placed in memory in a specific memory location that the program will call `inputNumber`. Then, and only then, can the `calculatedAnswer`, in this case 16, be calculated and printed.

 Computer memory consists of millions of numbered locations where data can be stored. The memory location of `inputNumber` has a specific numeric address, for example, 48604. Your program associates `inputNumber` with that address. Every time you refer to `inputNumber` within a program, the computer retrieves the value at the associated memory location.

UNDERSTANDING THE PROGRAMMING PROCESS

A programmer's job involves writing instructions (such as the three instructions in the doubling program in the preceding section), and can be broken down into six **programming steps**:

1. Understand the problem.

2. Plan the logic.

3. Code the program.

4. Translate the program into machine language.

5. Test the program.

6. Put the program into production.

Understand the Problem

Professional computer programmers write programs to satisfy the needs of others. For example: the Human Resources department that needs a printed list of all employees, the Billing department that wants a list of clients who are 30 or more days overdue in their payments, and the office manager who would like to be notified when specific supplies reach the reorder point. Because programmers are providing a service to these users, programmers must first understand what it is the users want.

Suppose the director of Human Resources says to a programmer, "Our department needs a list of all employees who have been here over five years because we want to invite them to a special thank-you dinner." On the surface this seems like a simple enough request. An experienced programmer, however, will know that he or she may not yet understand the whole problem. Does the director want a list of full-time employees only, or a list of full- and part-time employees together? Does she want people who have worked for the company on a month-to-month contractual basis over the past five years, or regular employees only? Do the listed employees need to be working for the organization for five years as of today, as of the date of the dinner, or is some other date to be used as a cutoff? What about an employee who worked three years, took a two-year leave of absence, and has been back for three years? Does he or she qualify? The programmer cannot make any of these decisions; the user is the one who must address these questions.

More decisions still might be required. For example, what does the user want the report of five-year employees to look like? Should it contain both first and last names? Social Security numbers? Phone numbers? Addresses? Is all this data available? Several pieces of documentation are often provided to help the programmer understand the problem. This documentation includes print layout charts and file specifications, which you will learn about in Chapter 3.

Really understanding the problem may be one of the most difficult aspects of programming. On any job, the description of what the user needs may be vague; worse yet, the user may not even really know what it is he or she wants. A good programmer is often part counselor, part detective!

Plan the Logic

The heart of the programming process lies in planning the program's logic. During this phase of the programming process, the programmer plans the steps to the program, deciding what steps to include and how to order them. You can plan the solution to a problem in many ways. The two most common tools are flowcharts and pseudocode. Both tools involve writing the steps of the program in English, much as you would plan a trip on paper before getting into the car or plan a party theme before going shopping for food and favors.

You may hear programmers refer to planning a program as "developing an algorithm." An algorithm is the sequence of steps necessary to solve any problem.

You will learn more about flowcharts and pseudocode later in this chapter.

The programmer doesn't worry about the syntax of any particular language at this point, just about figuring out what sequence of events will lead from the available input to the desired output. You will learn more about planning the logic later; in fact, this book focuses on this step almost exclusively.

Code the Program

Once the programmer has developed the logic of a program, only then can he or she write the program in one of more than 400 programming languages. Now the programmer can worry about each command being spelled correctly and all of the punctuation getting into the right spots—in other words, using the correct *syntax*.

Some very experienced programmers can successfully combine the logic planning and the actual instruction writing, or **coding** of the program, in one step. This may work for planning and writing a very simple program, just as you can plan and write a post-card to a friend using one step. A good term paper or a Hollywood screenplay, however, needs planning before writing, and so do most programs.

Which step is harder, planning the logic or coding the program? Right now, it may seem to you that writing in a programming language is a very difficult task, considering all the spelling and grammar rules you must learn. However, the planning step is actually more difficult. Which is more difficult, thinking up the twists and turns to the plot of a best-selling mystery novel or writing a translation of an already written novel from English to Spanish? And who do you think gets paid more, the writer or the translator?

Translate the Program into Machine Language

Even though there are many programming languages, each computer knows only one language, its machine language, which consists of many 1s and 0s. Computers understand machine language because computers themselves are made up of thousands of tiny electrical switches, each of which can be set in either the on or off state, which is represented by a 1 or 0, respectively.

Languages like Java or Visual Basic are available for programmers to use because someone has written a translator program (a compiler or interpreter) that changes the English-like **high-level language** in which the programmer writes into the **low-level machine language** that the computer understands. If you write a programming language statement incorrectly, (for example by misspelling a word, using a word that doesn't exist in the language, or using illegal grammar), the translator program doesn't know what to do and issues an error message. You receive the same response when you speak nonsense to a human language translator. Imagine trying to look up a list of words in a Spanish-English dictionary if some of the listed words are misspelled—you can't complete the task until the words are spelled correctly. Although making errors is never desirable, syntax errors are not a major concern to programmers because the compiler or translator catches every syntax error, and the computer will not execute a program that contains them.

If you could use an English compiler and submit the sentence `The grl go to school`, the compiler would point out two syntax errors to you. The second word, `grl`, is illegal because it is not part of the English language. Once you corrected the word `girl`, the compiler would find another syntax error on the third word, `go`, because it is the wrong verb form for the subject `girl`. This doesn't mean `go` is necessarily the wrong word.

Maybe `girl` is wrong; perhaps the subject should be `girls`, in which case `go` is right. Compilers don't always know exactly what you mean, nor do they know what the proper correction should be, but they do know when something is wrong with your syntax.

Test the Program

A program that is free of syntax errors is not necessarily free of **logical errors**. For example, the sentence `The girl goes to school`, although syntactically perfect, is not logically correct if the girl is a baby or a drop-out.

Once a program is free from syntax errors, the programmer can test it—that is, execute it with some sample data to see whether or not the results are logically correct. Recall the number doubling program:

```
Get inputNumber
Compute calculatedAnswer as inputNumber times 2
Print calculatedAnswer
```

If you provide the value 2 as input to the program and the answer 4 prints out, you have executed one successful test run of the program.

However, if the answer 40 prints out, maybe it's because the program contains a logical error. Maybe the second line of code was mistyped with an extra zero so that the program reads:

```
Get inputNumber
Compute calculatedAnswer as inputNumber times 20
Print calculatedAnswer
```

The error of placing 20 instead of 2 in the multiplication statement caused a logical error. Notice that nothing is syntactically wrong with this second program—it is just as reasonable to multiply a number by 20 as by 2—but if the programmer intends only to double the `inputNumber`, then a logical error has occurred.

Programs should be tested with many sets of data. For example, if you write the program to double a number and enter 2 and get an output value of 4, it doesn't mean you have a correct program. Perhaps you have typed this program by mistake:

```
Get inputNumber
Compute calculatedAnswer as inputNumber plus 2
Print calculatedAnswer
```

An input of 2 results in an answer of 4, but it doesn't mean your program doubles numbers—it actually only adds 2 to them. If you test your program with additional data—for example using a 3 and you get an answer of 5, you know there is a problem with your code.

Selecting test data is somewhat of an art in itself, and it should be done carefully. If the Human Resources department wants a list of the names of five-year employees, it would be a mistake to test the program with a small sample file of only long-term employees. If no new employees are part of the data being used for testing, you don't really know if the program would have eliminated them from the five-year list. Many companies don't know that their software has a problem until an unusual circumstance occurs; for example, the first time an employee has more than nine dependents, the first time a customer orders more than 999 items at a time, or when, in an example that has been well documented in the popular press, a new century begins.

Put the Program into Production

Once the program is tested adequately, it is ready for the organization to use. Putting the program into production might mean simply running the program once if it was written to satisfy a user's request for a special list. However, the process might take months if the program will be run on a regular basis, or if it is one of a large system of programs being developed. Perhaps data entry people must be trained to prepare the input for the new program, users must be trained to understand the output, or existing data in the company must be changed to an entirely new format to accommodate this program. **Conversion**, the entire set of actions an organization must take to switch over to using a new program or set of programs, can sometimes take months or years to accomplish.

You might consider maintaining programs as a seventh step in the programming process. After programs are put into production, making required changes is called maintenance. Maintenance is necessary for many reasons. For example, new tax rates are legislated, the format of an input file is altered, or the end user requires additional information not included in the original output specifications.

You might consider retiring the program as the eighth and final step in the programming process. A program is retired when it is no longer needed by an organization—usually when a new program is in the process of being put into production.

UNDERSTANDING THE DATA HIERARCHY

Some very simple programs require very simple data. For example, the number doubling program requires just one value as input. Most business programs, however, use much more data—inventory files list thousands of items, personnel and customer files list thousands of people. When data are stored for use on computer systems, they are often stored in what is known as a **data hierarchy**, where the smallest usable unit of data is the character. **Characters** are letters, numbers, and special symbols such as "A", "7", and "$". Anything you can type from the keyboard in one keystroke (including a space or a tab) is a character. Characters are made up of smaller elements called bits, but just as most humans can use a pencil without caring whether atoms are flying around inside it, most computer users can store characters without caring about these bits.

Computers also recognize characters you cannot enter from the keyboard, such as foreign alphabet characters like φ or Σ.

Characters are grouped together to form a field. A **field** is a single data item such as `lastName`, `streetAddress`, or `annualSalary`. For most of us, an "S", an "m", an "i", a "t", and an "h" don't have much meaning individually, but if the combination of characters makes up your last name, "Smith", then as a group the characters have useful meaning.

Related fields are often grouped together to form a record. **Records** are groups of fields that go together for some logical reason. A random name, address, and salary aren't very useful, but if they're your name, your address, and your salary, then that's your record. An inventory record might contain fields for item number, color, and price; a student record might contain ID number, grade point average, and major.

Related records in turn, are grouped together to form a file. **Files** are groups of records that go together for some logical reason. The individual records of each student in your class might go together in a file called CLASS. Records of each person at your company might be in a file called PERSONNEL. Items you sell might be in an INVENTORY file.

Some files can have just a few records; others, like the file of credit card holders for a major department store chain or policyholders of an insurance company, can have thousands or even millions of records.

Finally, many organizations use database software to organize many files. A **database** holds a group of files, often called **tables**, that together serve the information needs of an organization. This book will not discuss database management; instead, it will concentrate on programs that use files for both input and output.

In summary, you can picture the data hierarchy as shown in Figure 1-1.

```
Database
    File
        Record
            Field
                Character
```

Figure 1-1   The data hierarchy

A database contains many files. A file contains many records. Each record in a file has the same fields; each record's fields contain different data items that consists of one or more stored characters in each field.

As an example, you can picture a file as a set of index cards as shown in Figure 1-2. The stack of cards is the EMPLOYEE file, where each card represents one employee record. On each card, each line holds one field—`name`, `address`, or `salary`. Almost all the program examples in this book will use files that are organized in this way.

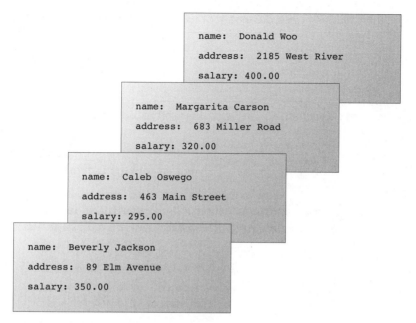

```
                    name:  Donald Woo

                    address:  2185 West River

                    salary: 400.00

              name:  Margarita Carson

              address:  683 Miller Road

              salary: 320.00

        name:  Caleb Oswego

        address:  463 Main Street

        salary: 295.00

  name:  Beverly Jackson

  address:  89 Elm Avenue

  salary: 350.00
```

Figure 1-2   A file of employee records

USING FLOWCHART SYMBOLS AND PSEUDOCODE STATEMENTS

When programmers plan the logic for a solution to a programming problem, they often use one of two tools, **flowcharts** or **pseudocode** (pronounced "sue–dough–code"). A flowchart is a pictorial representation of the logical steps it takes to solve a problem. Pseudocode is an English-like representation of the same thing. *Pseudo* is a prefix that means false, and to *code* a program means to put it in a programming language; therefore *pseudocode* simply means "false code," or sentences that appear to have been written in a computer programming language but don't necessarily follow all the syntax rules of any specific language.

You have already seen pseudocode earlier in this chapter, and there is nothing mysterious about it. The following three statements constitute a pseudocode representation of a number doubling problem:

```
get inputNumber
compute calculatedAnswer as inputNumber times 2
print calculatedAnswer
```

Using pseudocode involves writing down all the steps you will use in a program. Some professional programmers prefer writing pseudocode to drawing flowcharts, because using pseudocode is more similar to writing the final statements in the programming language. Others prefer using flowcharts to represent the logical flow, because they can more easily visualize how the program statements will connect. Especially for beginning programmers, flowcharts are an excellent tool to help you visualize how the statements in a program are interrelated.

Almost every program involves the steps of input, processing, and output, as in the following program:

```
get inputNumber
compute calculatedAnswer as inputNumber times 2
print calculatedAnswer
```

Therefore, most flowcharts need some graphical way to separate these three steps. When you create a flowchart, you draw geometric shapes around the individual statements and connect them with arrows.

When you draw a flowchart, you use a parallelogram to represent an **input** operation. You write an input statement, in English, inside the parallelogram, as shown in Figure 1-3.

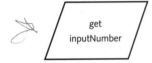
get
inputNumber

Figure 1-3   Input symbol

Arithmetic operation statements are examples of **processing**. In a flowchart you use a rectangle to represent a processing statement as shown in Figure 1-4.

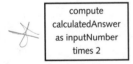
compute
calculatedAnswer
as inputNumber
times 2

Figure 1-4   Processing symbol

To represent an **output** statement, you use the same symbol as you do for input statements—the parallelogram, as in Figure 1-5.

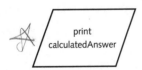
print
calculatedAnswer

Figure 1-5   Output symbol

To show the correct sequence of these statements, you use arrows, or **flowlines**, to connect the steps. Whenever possible, most of a flowchart should read from top to bottom or from left to right on a page. That's the natural way we read English, so when flowcharts follow this convention, they are easier to understand.

To be complete, a flowchart should include two more elements: a **terminal** or start/stop symbol at each end. Often, you place a word like "start" or "begin" in the first terminal symbol and a word like "end" or "stop" in the other. The standard terminal symbol is shaped like a racetrack. Figure 1-6 shows a complete flowchart for the program that doubles a number, and the pseudocode for the same problem.

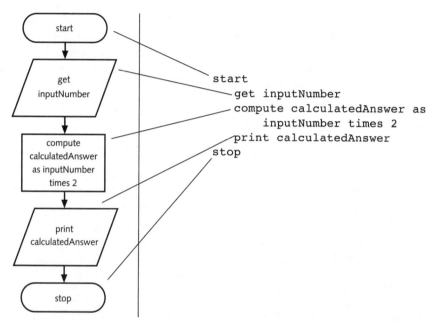

Figure 1-6   Flowchart and pseudocode of program that doubles a number

 In the pseudocode in Figure 1-6, the words start and stop are aligned in the left margin; the actual program statements are indented. This style is not required when you write pseudocode, but as you develop more complex programs, indenting the program statements within the start-stop pair will help you to see the beginning and ending points in program segments.

 Programmers seldom create both pseudocode and a flowchart for the same problem. You usually use one or the other.

The logic for the program represented by the flowchart and pseudocode in Figure 1-6 is correct no matter what programming language the programmer eventually uses to write the corresponding code. After the flowchart or pseudocode has been developed, the programmer needs only to buy a computer, learn a language, code the program, compile it, test it, and put it into production.

"Whoa!" you are probably saying to yourself. "This is simply not worth it! All that work to create a flowchart, and *then* all those other steps? For five dollars I can buy a pocket calculator that will double any number for me!" You are absolutely right. If this were a real computer program, it simply would not be worth all the effort. Writing a computer program would be worth the effort only if you had many, let's say 10,000, numbers to find the double of in a limited amount of time, let's say the next two minutes. Then it would be worth your while to create a computer program.

Unfortunately, the number-doubling program represented in Figure 1-6 does not double 10,000 numbers; it doubles only one. You could execute the program 10,000 times, of course, but that would require you to sit at the computer telling it to run the program over and over again. You would be better off with a program that could process 10,000 numbers, one after the other.

One solution is to write the program as shown in Figure 1-7 and execute the same steps 10,000 times. Of course, writing this program would be very time consuming; you might as well buy the calculator.

```
start
     get inputNumber
     compute calculatedAnswer as inputNumber times 2
     print calculatedAnswer
     get inputNumber
     compute calculatedAnswer as inputNumber times 2
     print calculatedAnswer
     get inputNumber
     compute calculatedAnswer as inputNumber times 2
     print calculatedAnswer
     . . . and so on
```

Figure 1-7   Inefficient pseudocode for program that doubles 10,000 numbers

A better solution is to have the computer execute the same set of three instructions over and over again as shown in Figure 1-8. With this approach, the computer gets a number, doubles it, prints out the answer, and then starts over again with the first instruction. The same spot in memory, called **inputNumber**, is reused for the second number and for any subsequent numbers. The spot in memory named **calculatedAnswer** is reused each time to store the result of the multiplication operation.

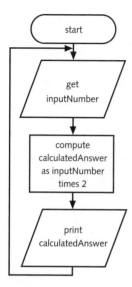

Figure 1-8 Flowchart of infinite number-doubling program

USING AND NAMING VARIABLES

Programmers commonly refer to the locations in memory called `inputNumber` and `calculatedAnswer` as variables. **Variables** are memory locations, whose contents can vary or differ over time. Sometimes `inputNumber` can hold a 2 and `calculatedAnswer` will hold a 4; other times `inputNumber` can hold a 6 and `calculatedAnswer` will hold a 12. It is the ability of memory variables to change in value that makes computers and programming worthwhile. Because one memory location can be used over and over again with different values, you can write program instructions once and then use them for thousands of separate calculations. One set of payroll instructions at your company produces each individual's paycheck, and one set of instructions at your electric company produces each household's bill.

The number-doubling example requires two variables, `inputNumber` and `calculatedAnswer`. These can just as well be named `userEntry` and `programSolution`, or `inputValue` and `twiceTheValue`. As a programmer, you choose reasonable names for your variables. The language interpreter then associates the names you choose with specific memory addresses.

Every computer programming language has its own set of rules for naming variables. Most languages allow both letters and digits within variable names. Some languages allow hyphens in variable names, for example `hourly-wage`. Others allow underscores, as in `hourly_wage`. Still others allow neither. Some languages allow dollar signs or other special characters in variable names, for example `hourly$`; others allow foreign alphabet characters like π or Ω.

Different languages put different limits on the length of variable names, although in general, newer languages allow longer names. For example, in some very old versions of BASIC, a variable name could consist of only one or two letters and one or two digits. You could have some cryptic variable names like `hw` , `a3` , or `re02`. In other languages, variable names can be very long. COBOL, for example, allows up to 30 characters in its variable names, so names like `AMOUNT-OF-SALE` and `TOTAL-FOR-JANUARY` are common. In addition, COBOL allows hyphens in its variable names for better readability.

Many modern languages, such as C++, C#, and Java, allow more than two hundred characters in a variable name. Variable names in these languages usually consist of lowercase letters, don't allow hyphens, but do allow underscores, so you can use a name like `price_of_item`. These languages are case sensitive, so `HOURLYWAGE`, `hourlywage`, and `hourlyWage` are considered three separate variable names, although the last example, in which the new word begins with an uppercase letter, is easiest to read. Most programmers who use the more modern languages employ the format in which multiple-word variable names are run together, and each new word within the variable name begins with an uppercase letter. This format is called **camel casing**, because such variable names, like `hourlyWage`, have a "hump" in the middle. The variable names in this text are shown using camel casing.

Even though every language has its own rules for naming variables, when designing the logic of a computer program, you should not concern yourself with the specific syntax of any particular computer language. The logic, after all, works with any language. The variable names used throughout this book follow only two rules:

1. *Variable names must be one word.* The name can contain letters, digits, hyphens, underscores, or any other characters you choose, with the exception of *spaces*. Therefore `r` is a legal variable name, as is `rate`, as is `interestRate`. The variable name `interest rate` is not allowed because of the space. No programming language allows spaces within a variable name. If you see a name such as `interest rate` in a flowchart or pseudocode, you should assume that the programmer is discussing two variables, `interest` and `rate`, each of which individually would be a fine variable name.

 When you write a program, your compiler may show variable names in a different color from the rest of the program. This visual aid helps your variable names stand out from words that are part of the programming language.

2. *Variable names should have some appropriate meaning.* This is not a rule of any programming language. When computing an interest rate in a program, the computer does not care if you call the variable `g`, `u84`, or `fred`. As long as the correct numeric result is placed in the variable, its actual name doesn't really matter. However, it's much easier to follow the logic of a program with a statement in it like `compute finalBalance as equal to initialInvestment times interestRate` than one with a statement

in it like `compute someBanana as equal to j89 times myFriendLinda`. You might think you will remember how you intended to use a cryptic variable name within a program, but six years later when a program requires changes, you, and other programmers working with you, will appreciate clear, descriptive, variable names.

Notice that the flowchart in Figure 1-8 follows these two rules for variables: both variable names, `inputNumber` and `calculatedAnswer`, are one word, and they have some appropriate meaning. Some programmers have fun with their variable names by naming them after friends or creating puns with them, but such behavior is unprofessional and marks those programmers as amateurs.

 Another general rule in all programming languages is that variable names may not begin with a digit, although usually they may contain digits. Thus in most languages budget2003 is a legal variable name, but 2013Budget is not.

ENDING A PROGRAM BY USING SENTINEL VALUES

Something is still wrong with the flowchart for doubling numbers shown in Figure 1-8. It never ends! If, for example, the input numbers are being entered at the keyboard, the program will keep accepting numbers and printing out doubles forever. Of course, the user could refuse to type in any more numbers. But the computer is very patient, and if you refuse to give it any more numbers, it will sit and wait forever. When you finally type in a number, the program doubles it, prints the result, and waits for another. The program cannot progress any farther while it is waiting for input; meanwhile, the program is occupying computer memory and tying up operating system resources. Refusing to enter any more numbers is not a practical solution. Another way to end the program is to simply turn the computer off! That'll fix it! But again, it's neither the best nor an elegant way to bring the program to an end.

A superior way to end the program is to set a predetermined value for `inputNumber` that means "Stop the program!" For example, the programmer and the user could agree that the user will never need to know the double of zero, so the user could enter a zero when he or she wants to stop. The program could then test any incoming value for `inputNumber` and, if it is a zero, stop the program. Testing a value is also called making a **decision**.

You represent a decision in a flowchart by drawing a **decision symbol** or a diamond. The diamond usually contains a question, the answer to which is either yes or no. All good computer questions have two mutually exclusive answers like yes and no or true and false. For example, "What day of the year is your birthday?" is not a good computer question because there are 366 possible answers. But "Is your birthday June 24?" *is* a good computer question because for everyone in the world, the answer is either yes or no.

The question to stop the doubling program should be "Is the `inputNumber` just entered equal to zero?" or "`inputNumber = 0`?" for short. The complete flowchart will now look like the one shown in Figure 1-9.

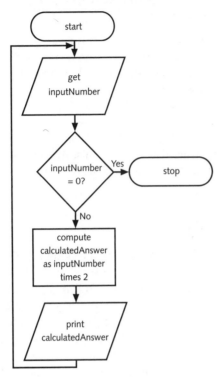

Figure 1-9 Flowchart for number-doubling program with sentinel value of zero

One drawback to using zero to stop a program, of course, is that it won't work if the user *does* need to find the double of zero. In that case, some other data entry value that the user never will need, such as 999 or −1 could be selected to signal that the program should end. A preselected value that stops the execution of a program is often called a **dummy value** because it does not represent real data, but just a signal to stop. Sometimes such a value is called a **sentinel value** because it represents an entry or exit point like a sentinel that guards a fortress.

Not all programs rely on user data entry from a keyboard; many read data from an input device such as a disk or tape drive. When organizations store data on a disk or tape, they do not commonly use a sentinel value to signal the end of the file. For one thing, an input record might have hundreds of fields, and if you store a dummy record in every file, you are wasting a large quantity of storage on "non-data." Additionally, it is often difficult to choose sentinel values for fields in a company's data files. Any `balanceDue`, even a zero or negative one, can be a legitimate value, and any `customerName`, even "ZZ" could be someone's name. Fortunately, programming languages can recognize the end of data in a file automatically, without a sentinel value, through a code that is stored at the end of the data. Many programming languages use the term **eof** (for "end of file") to talk about this marker. This book therefore uses `eof` to indicate the end of data, regardless of whether it is a special disk marker or a dummy value such as zero from the keyboard. Therefore, the flowchart now looks like the one in Figure 1-10.

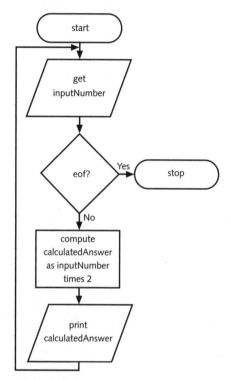

Figure 1-10   Flowchart using eof

USING THE CONNECTOR

By using just the input, processing, output, decision, and terminal symbols, you can represent the logic for many diverse applications. This book uses only one other symbol, the **connector**. A connector will be used when limited page size forces you to continue the flowchart on the following page. If a flowchart has six processing steps and a page provides room for only three, you might represent the logic as shown in Figure 1-11.

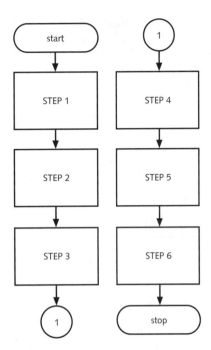

Figure 1-11   Flowchart using the connector

The circle at the bottom of the left column tells someone reading the flowchart that there is more to the flowchart. The circle should contain a number or letter that can then be matched to another number or letter somewhere else, in this case on the right. If a large flowchart needs more connectors, new numbers or letters would be assigned in sequence (1, 2, 3... or A, B, C...) to each successive pair of connectors.

When you are creating your own flowcharts, you should avoid using the connector if at all possible; flowcharts are more difficult to follow when they do not fit on a page. Your instructor or future programming supervisor may require that long flowcharts be redrawn so you don't need to use the connector. However, when continuing on a new page is unavoidable, the connector provides the means.

ASSIGNING VALUES TO VARIABLES

When you create a flowchart or pseudocode for a program that doubles numbers, you can include the statement `compute calculatedAnswer as inputNumber times 2`. This statement incorporates two actions. First, the computer computes the arithmetic value of `inputNumber` times 2. Second, the computed value is stored in the `calculatedAnswer` memory location. Most programming languages allow a shorthand expression for these **assignment statements** such as `compute calculatedAnswer as inputNumber times 2`. The shorthand takes the form `calculatedAnswer = inputNumber * 2`.

In Pascal, the same expression is `calculatedAnswer := inputNumber * 2`. You type a colon followed by an equal sign to create the assignment symbol. Java, C++, C#, Visual Basic, and COBOL all use the equal sign for assignment.

According to the rules of algebra, a statement like `calculatedAnswer = inputNumber * 2` should be exactly equivalent to the statement `inputNumber * 2 = calculatedAnswer`. To most programmers, however, `calculatedAnswer = inputNumber * 2` means "multiply `inputNumber` by 2 and store the result in the variable called `calculatedAnswer`." Whatever operation is performed to the right of the equal sign results in a value that is placed in the memory location to the left of the equal sign. Therefore, the statement `inputNumber * 2 = calculatedAnswer` means to take the value of `calculatedAnswer` and store it in a location called `inputNumber * 2`. A location called `inputNumber` is valid, but there can't be a location called `inputNumber * 2`. For one thing, `inputNumber * 2` can't be a variable because it has spaces in it. For another, a location can't be multiplied. Its contents can be multiplied, but the location itself cannot be. The statement `inputNumber * 2 = calculatedAnswer` contains a syntax error, no matter what programming language you use; a program with such a statement will not execute.

 When you create an assignment statement, it may help to imagine the word "let" in front of the statement. Thus, you can read the statement `calculatedAnswer = inputNumber * 2` as "Let calculatedAnswer equal inputNumber times two." The BASIC programming language allows you to use the word "let" in such statements.

Computer memory is made up of millions of distinct locations, each of which has an address. Fifty years ago, programmers had to deal with these addresses and had to remember, for instance, that they had stored a salary in location 6428 of their computer. Today we are very fortunate that high-level computer languages allow us to pick a reasonable "English" name for a memory address and let the computer keep track of where it is. Just as it is easier for you to remember that the president lives in the White House than at 1600 Pennsylvania Avenue, Washington, D.C., it is also easier for you to remember that your salary is in a variable called `mySalary` than at memory location 6428.

Similarly, it does not usually make sense to perform mathematical operations on memory addresses, but it does make sense to perform mathematical operations on the *contents* of memory addresses. If you live in `blueSplitLevelOnTheCorner`, you can't add 1 to that, but you certainly can add 1 person to the number of people already in that house. For our purposes, then, the statement `calculatedAnswer = inputNumber * 2` means exactly the same thing as the statement `move inputNumber * 2 to calculatedAnswer`, which also means exactly the same thing as the statement `multiply inputNumber times 2 resulting in calculatedAnswer`. None of these statements, however, is equivalent to `inputNumber * 2 = calculatedAnswer`, which is an illegal statement.

Many programming languages allow you to create constants. A constant is a named memory location, similar to a variable, except its value never changes during a program. If you are working with a programming language that allows it, you might create a constant for a value like `pi = 3.14` or `countySalesTaxRate = .06`.

UNDERSTANDING DATA TYPES

Computers deal with two basic types of data—character and numeric. When you use a specific numeric value, like *43*, within a program, you write it using the digits and no quotation marks. A specific numeric value is often called a **numeric constant**, because it does not change—a 43 always has the value 43. When you use a specific character value, or **string** of characters, like "Chris," you enclose the string or **character constant** within quotation marks.

 Some languages require single quotes surrounding character constants while others require double quotes. Many languages, like C++, C#, Java, and Pascal, reserve single quotes for a single character such as 'C', and double quotes for a character string such as "Chris".

Similarly, most computer languages allow at least two distinct types of variables. One type of variable can hold a number and is often called a **numeric variable**. In the statement `calculatedAnswer = inputNumber * 2` both `calculatedAnswer` and `inputNumber` are numeric variables; that is, their intended contents are numeric values such as 6 and 3, 150 and 75, or −18 and −9.

Most programming languages have a separate type of variable that can hold letters of the alphabet and other special characters such as punctuation marks. Depending on the language, these variables are called **character**, **text**, or **string variables**. If a working program contains the statement `lastName = "Lincoln"` then `lastName` is a character or string variable.

Programmers must distinguish between numeric and character variables because computers handle the two types of data differently. Therefore, means are provided within the syntax rules of computer programming languages to tell the computer which type of data to expect. How this is done is different in every language; some languages have different rules for naming the variables, but with others you must include a simple statement (called a **declaration**) telling the computer which type of data to expect.

Some languages allow for several types of numeric data. Languages like Pascal, C++, C#, and Java distinguish between **integer** or whole number numeric variables, and **floating-point** or fractional numeric variables that contain a decimal point. Thus, in some languages the numbers 4 and 4.3 would have to be stored in different types of variables.

Some programming languages allow even more specific variable types, but the character versus numeric distinction is universal. For the programs you develop in this book, assume each variable is one of the two broad types. If a variable called `taxRate` is supposed to hold a value of 2.5, assume that it is a numeric variable. If a variable called `inventoryItem` is supposed to hold a value of "monitor," assume that it is a character variable.

 Values like "monitor" and 2.5 are called constants or literal constants because they never change. A variable value *can* change. Thus, inventoryItem can hold "monitor" at one moment during the execution of a program, and later you can change its value to hold "modem".

By convention, this book encloses character data like "monitor" within quotation marks to distinguish the characters from yet another variable name. Also, by convention, numeric data is not enclosed within quotation marks. According to these conventions, then, `taxRate = 2.5` and `inventoryItem = "monitor"` are both valid statements. The statement `inventoryItem = monitor` is a valid statement only if monitor is also a character variable. In other words, if `monitor ="color"`, and subsequently `inventoryItem = monitor`, then the end result is that `inventoryItem = "color"`.

Every computer and every computer application handles text or character data differently from the way it handles numeric data. Every programming language requires that you distinguish variables as to their correct type and that you use each type of variable appropriately. (For example, you cannot perform arithmetic calculations with string data.) Identifying your variables correctly as numeric or character is one of the first steps you have to take when writing programs in any programming language.

CHAPTER SUMMARY

❑ Together, computer hardware (equipment) and software (instructions) accomplish four major operations: input, processing, output, and storage. You write computer instructions in a computer programming language that requires specific syntax; the instructions are translated into machine language by a compiler or interpreter. When both the syntax and logic of a program are correct, you can run or execute the program to produce the desired results.

❑ A programmer's job involves understanding the problem, planning the logic, coding the program, translating the program into machine language, testing the program, and putting the program into production.

❑ When data are stored for use on computer systems, they are stored in a data hierarchy of character, field, record, and file.

❑ When programmers plan the logic for a solution to a programming problem, they often use flowcharts or pseudocode. When you draw a flowchart, you use parallelograms to represent input and output operations and rectangles to represent processing.

❑ Variables are named memory locations, the contents of which can vary. As a programmer, you choose reasonable names for your variables. Every computer programming language has its own set of rules for naming variables; however, all variable names must be written as one word without embedded spaces, and should have appropriate meaning.

❑ Testing a value involves making a decision. You represent a decision in a flowchart by drawing a diamond-shaped decision symbol which contains a question, the answer to which is either yes or no. You can stop a program's execution by testing a sentinel value with a decision.

❑ A circular connector symbol is used to continue a flowchart that does not fit on a single page.

❑ Most programming languages allow the equal sign to assign values to variables. Assignment always takes place from right to left.

❑ Programmers must distinguish between numeric and character variables because computers handle the two types of data differently. A variable declaration tells the computer which type of data to expect. By convention, character data is included within quotation marks.

EXERCISES

1. Match the definition with the appropriate term.

   1. Computer system equipment   a. compiler
   2. Another word for programs   b. syntax
   3. Language rules   c. logic
   4. Order of instructions   d. hardware
   5. Language translator   e. software

2. In your own words, describe the steps to writing a computer program.

3. Consider a student file that contains the following data:

LAST NAME	FIRST NAME	MAJOR	GRADE POINT AVERAGE
Andrews	David	Psychology	3.4
Broederdorf	Melissa	Computer Science	4.0
Brogan	Lindsey	Biology	3.8
Carson	Joshua	Computer Science	2.8
Eisfelder	Katie	Mathematics	3.5
Faris	Natalie	Biology	2.8
Fredricks	Zachary	Psychology	2.0
Gonzales	Eduardo	Biology	3.1

Would this set of data be suitable and sufficient to use to test each of the following programs? Explain why or why not.

1

a. A program that prints a list of Psychology majors

b. A program that prints a list of Art majors

c. A program that prints a list of students on academic probation—those with a grade point average under 2.0

d. A program that prints a list of students on the dean's list

e. A program that prints a list of students from Wisconsin

f. A program that prints a list of female students

4. Suggest a good set of test data to use for a program that gives an employee a $50 bonus check if the employee has produced more than 1,000 items in a week.

5. Suggest a good set of test data for a program that computes gross paychecks (that is, before any taxes or other deductions) based on hours worked and rate of pay. The program computes gross as hours times rate unless hours are over 40. Then the program computes gross as regular rate of pay for 40 hours, plus one and a half times the rate of pay for the hours over 40.

6. Suggest a good set of test data for a program that is intended to output a student's grade point average based on letter grades (A, B, C, D, or F) in five courses.

7. Suggest a good set of data for a program for an automobile insurance company that wants to increase its premiums by $50 a month for every ticket a driver receives in a three-year period.

8. Assume a grocery store keeps a file for inventory where each grocery item has its own record. Two fields within each record are the name of the manufacturer and the weight of the item. Name at least six more fields that might be stored for each record. Provide an example of the data for one record. For example, for one product the manufacturer is DelMonte, and the weight is twelve ounces.

9. Assume a library keeps a file with data about its collection, one record for each item the library loans out. Name at least eight fields that might be stored for each record. Provide an example of the data for one record.

10. Match the term with the appropriate shape.

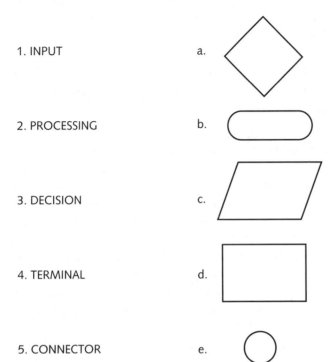

1. INPUT   a.

2. PROCESSING   b.

3. DECISION   c.

4. TERMINAL   d.

5. CONNECTOR   e.

11. Which of the following names seem like good variable names to you? If a name doesn't seem like a good variable name, explain why not.

    a. c
    b. cost
    c. costAmount
    d. cost amount
    e. cstofdngbsns
    f. costOfDoingBusinessThisFiscalYear
    g. cost2004

12. If myAge and yourRate are numeric variables, and departmentCode is a character variable, which of the following statements are valid assignments? If a statement is not valid, explain why not.

    a. myAge = 23
    b. myAge = yourRate
    c. myAge = departmentCode
    d. myAge = "departmentCode"

e. 42 = myAge

f. yourRate = 3.5

g. yourRate = myAge

h. yourRate = departmentCode

i. 6.91 = yourRate

j. departmentCode = Personnel

k. departmentCode = "Personnel"

l. departmentCode = 413

m. departmentCode = "413"

n. departmentCode = myAge

o. departmentCode = yourRate

p. 413 = departmentCode

q. "413" = departmentCode

13. a. Draw a flowchart to represent the logic of a program that allows the user to enter a value. The program multiplies the value by 10 and prints out the result.

b. Write pseudocode for the same problem.

14. a. Draw a flowchart to represent the logic of a program that allows the user to enter two values. The program prints the sum of the two values.

b. Write pseudocode for the same problem.

2

UNDERSTANDING STRUCTURE

After studying Chapter 2, you should be able to:
- Describe the features of unstructured spaghetti code
- Describe the three basic structures of sequence, selection, and loop
- Use a priming read
- Appreciate the need for structure
- Recognize structure
- Describe two special structures—case and do until

UNDERSTANDING UNSTRUCTURED SPAGHETTI CODE

Professional computer programs usually get far more complicated than the number-doubling program from Chapter 1, shown in Figure 2-1.

```
get inputNumber
calculatedAnswer = inputNumber * 2
print calculatedAnswer
```

Figure 2-1 Number-doubling program

Imagine the number of instructions in the computer program that NASA uses to calculate the launch angle of a space shuttle, or in the program the IRS uses to audit your income tax return. Even the program that produces a paycheck for you on your job contains many, many instructions. Designing the logic for such a program can be a time-consuming task. When you add several thousand instructions to a program, including several hundred decisions, it is easy to create a complicated mess. The popular name for snarled program statements is **spaghetti code**. The reason for the name should be obvious—it's as confusing to follow as following one noodle through a plate of spaghetti.

For example, suppose you are in charge of admissions at a college, and you've decided you will admit prospective students based on the following criteria:

- You will admit students who score 90 or better on the admission test your college gives as long as they are in the upper 75 percent of their high school graduating class. (These are smart students who score well on the admissions test. Maybe they didn't do so well in high school because it was a tough school, or maybe they have matured.)

- You will admit students who score at least 80 on the admission test if they are in the upper 50 percent of their high school graduating class. (These students score fairly well on the test, and do fairly well in school.)

- You will admit students who score only 70 on your test if they are in the top 25 percent of their class. (Maybe these students don't take tests well, but obviously they are achievers.)

Figure 2-2 summarizes the admission requirements:

Test Score	High School Rank (%)
90–100	25–100
80–89	50–100
70–79	75–100

Figure 2-2   Admission requirements

The flowchart for this program could look like the one in Figure 2-3. This kind of flowchart is an example of spaghetti code. Many computer programs (especially older computer programs) bear a striking resemblance to the flowchart in Figure 2-3. Such programs might "work," that is, they might produce correct results, but they are very difficult to read and maintain, and their logic is difficult to follow.

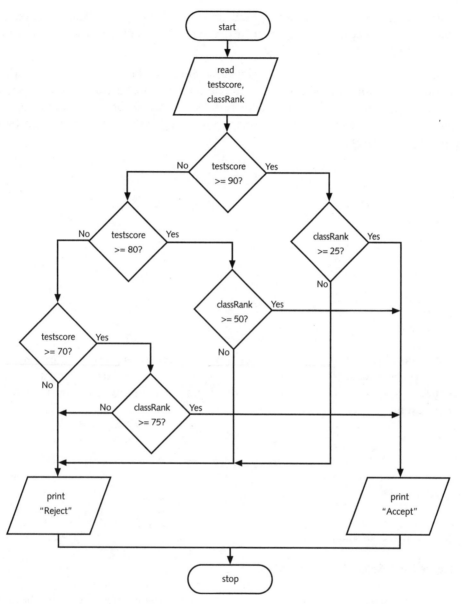

Figure 2-3   Spaghetti code example

UNDERSTANDING THE THREE BASIC STRUCTURES

In the mid–1960s, mathematicians proved that any program, no matter how complicated, can be constructed using only three sets of flowcharting shapes or structures. A **structure** is a basic unit of programming logic; each structure is a sequence, selection, or loop. With these three structures alone, you can diagram any event, from doubling a number to performing brain surgery.

The first of these structures is a sequence, as shown in Figure 2-4. With a **sequence**, you perform an action or event, and then you perform the next action in order. A sequence can contain any number of events, but there is no chance to branch off and skip any of the events. Once you start a series of events in a sequence, you must continue step-by-step until the sequence ends.

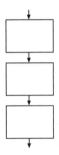

Figure 2-4   Sequence structure

The second structure is called a **selection**, or a **decision**, as shown in Figure 2-5. With this structure, you ask a question, and depending on the answer, you take one of two courses of action. Then, no matter which path you follow, you continue on with the next event.

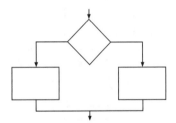

Figure 2-5   Selection structure

Some people call the selection structure an **if-then-else** because it fits the statement

```
if someCondition is true then
    do oneProcess
else
    do theOtherProcess
```

For example, while cooking you may decide

```
if we have brownSugar then
   use brownSugar
else
   use whiteSugar
```

Similarly, a payroll program might include a statement such as

```
if hoursWorked is more than 40 then
   calculate overtimePay
else
   calculate regularPay
```

Note that it is perfectly correct for one branch of the selection to be a "do nothing" branch. For example

```
if it is raining then
   take anUmbrella
```

or

```
if employee belongs to dentalPlan then
   deduct $40 from employeeGrossPay
```

The previous examples are **single–alternative ifs** and a diagram of their structure is shown in Figure 2-6. In these cases you don't take any special action if it is not raining or if the employee does not belong to the dental plan. The case where nothing is done is often called the **null case**.

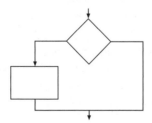

Figure 2-6   Single-alternative if structure

The third structure, shown in Figure 2-7, is a loop. You may hear programmers refer to looping as **repetition** or **iteration.** In a **loop**, you ask a question; if the answer requires an action, you perform the action and ask the original question again. If the question's answer requires that the action be taken again, you take the action and then ask the original question again. This continues until the answer to the question is such that the action is no longer required; then you exit the structure.

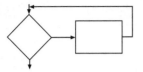

Figure 2-7   Loop structure

Some programmers call this structure a **do while** because it fits the statement

> **while testCondition** continues to be true, **do someProcess**

You encounter examples of looping every day, as in

> **while** you continue to beHungry
>
> take anotherBiteOfFood

or

> **while unreadPages** remain in the readingAssignment
>
> read another unreadPage

In a business program you can write

> **while quantityInInventory** remains low
>
> continue to orderItems

or

> **while** there are more retailPrices to be discounted
>
> compute a discount

All logic problems can be solved using only these three structures—sequence, selection, and looping. The three structures, of course, can be combined in an infinite number of ways. For example, there can be a sequence of steps followed by a selection or a loop followed by a sequence. Attaching structures end-to-end is called **stacking** structures. For example, Figure 2-8 shows a structured flowchart achieved by stacking structures and pseudocode that might follow that flowchart logic.

2

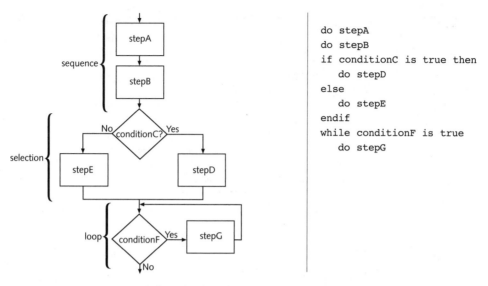

```
do stepA
do stepB
if conditionC is true then
    do stepD
else
    do stepE
endif
while conditionF is true
    do stepG
```

Figure 2-8   A structured flowchart and pseudocode

Additionally, you can replace any individual step in the preceding flowchart diagrams or pseudocode segments with another structure—any sequence, selection, or loop. For example, you can have a sequence of three steps on one side of a selection, as shown in Figure 2-9. Placing a structure within another structure is called **nesting** the structures. When you write the pseudocode for the logic shown in Figure 2-9, the convention is to indent all statements that depend on one branch of the decision as shown in the pseudocode. This shows that all three statements must execute if conditionA is not true.

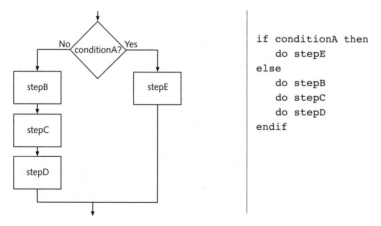

```
if conditionA then
    do stepE
else
    do stepB
    do stepC
    do stepD
endif
```

Figure 2-9   Flowchat and pseudocode for sequence within a selection

In the pseudocode in Figure 2-9, notice that the statements do stepB, do stepC, and do stepD align vertically and indent under the else. This shows that all three steps execute when conditionA is not true.

In place of one of the steps in the sequence in Figure 2-9, you can insert a selection. In Figure 2-10, stepC has been replaced with a selection structure that begins with a test of conditionF.

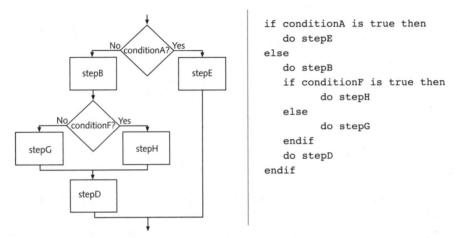

```
if conditionA is true then
    do stepE
else
    do stepB
    if conditionF is true then
            do stepH
    else
            do stepG
    endif
    do stepD
endif
```

Figure 2-10 Selection in a sequence within a selection

In the pseudocode shown in Figure 2-10, notice that do stepB, if conditionF then, else, and do stepD align vertically. This shows that they are all "on the same level." If you look at the same problem flowcharted in Figure 2-10, you see that you could draw a vertical line through the symbols with stepB, conditionF, and stepD. The flowchart and the pseudocode represent exactly the same logic. The stepH and stepG steps, on the other hand, are one level down; they are dependent on the answer to the conditionF question. Therefore, the do stepH and do stepG statements are indented one level further in the pseudocode.

Also notice that the pseudocode in Figure 2-10 has two endif statements. Each is aligned to correspond to an if. An endif always partners with the most recent if that does not already have an endif partner.

In place of do stepH on one side of the new selection in Figure 2-10, you can insert a loop. This loop, based on conditionI, appears inside the selection that is within the sequence that constitutes the "no" side of the original conditionA selection. See Figure 2-11.

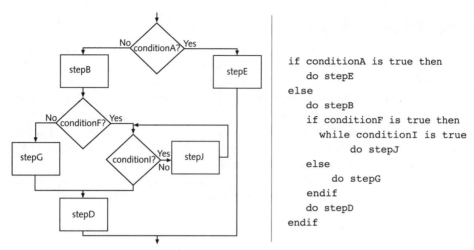

```
if conditionA is true then
    do stepE
else
    do stepB
    if conditionF is true then
        while conditionI is true
            do stepJ
    else
        do stepG
    endif
    do stepD
endif
```

Figure 2-11 Flowchart and pseudocode for loop within selection within sequence within selection

The combinations are endless, but each of a structured program's segments is a sequence, a selection, or a loop. Notice in Figure 2-12 that each structure has one entry and one exit point. One structure can attach to another only at one of these entry or exit points.

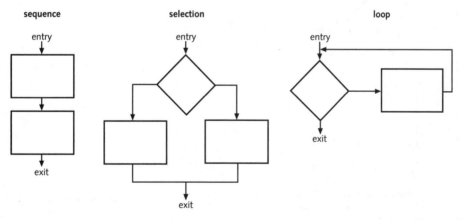

Figure 2-12   The three structures

In summary, a structured program has the following characteristics:

- A structured program includes only combinations of the three structures—sequence, selection, and loop.

- Structures connect to one another only at their entrance or exit points.

USING THE PRIMING READ

For a program to be structured and also work the way you want it to, sometimes you need to add extra steps. The priming read is one kind of added step. A **priming read** or **priming input** is the first read or data input statement in a program. If a program will read one hundred data records, you read the first data record in a statement separate from the other ninety-nine. You must do this to keep the program structured.

At the end of Chapter 1, you read about a program like the one in Figure 2-13. The program gets a number and checks for end of file. If it is not end of file, then the number is doubled, the answer is printed, and the next number is input.

Is the program represented by Figure 2-13 structured? At first, it might be hard to tell. The three allowed structures were illustrated in Figure 2-12.

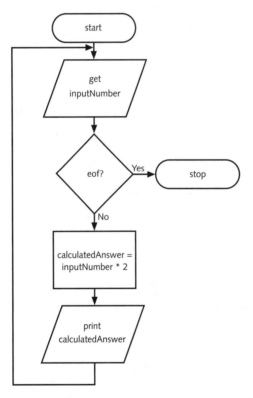

Figure 2-13   Flowchart of a number-doubling program

The flowchart in Figure 2-13 does not look exactly like any of the three shapes shown in Figure 2-12. However, because you may stack and nest structures while retaining overall structure, it might be difficult to determine whether the flowchart as a whole is structured. It's easiest to analyze the flowchart one step at a time. The beginning of the flowchart looks like Figure 2-14.

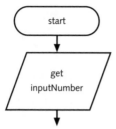

Figure 2-14   Beginning of a number-doubling flowchart

Is this portion of the flowchart structured? Yes, it's a sequence. The next part of the flow-chart looks like Figure 2-15.

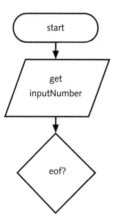

Figure 2-15   Number-doubling flowchart continued

The sequence is finished; either a selection or a loop is starting. You might not know which one, but you do know the sequence is not continuing because sequences can't have questions in them. With a sequence, each step must follow without any opportunity to branch away. Therefore, which type of structure starts with the question in Figure 2-15? Is it a selection or a loop?

With a selection structure, the logic goes in one of two directions after the question; then the flow comes back together. With a selection structure, the question is not asked a second time. In a loop, if the answer to the question results in the procedure execut-ing, then the logic returns to the question that started the loop; the question is always asked again.

In the doubling problem, if it is not eof (that is, if the end-of-file condition is not met), some math is done, an answer is printed, a new number is obtained, and the eof ques-tion is asked again. Therefore, the doubling problem contains a structure that is more like a loop than a selection.

The doubling problem *does* contain a loop, but it's not a structured loop. In a structured loop, the rules are:

1. You ask a question.

2. If the answer indicates you should perform a procedure, you do so.

3. If you perform the procedure, then you must go right back to repeat the question.

The flowchart in Figure 2-13 asks a question; if the answer is *no*, it performs more than one task: it does the arithmetic and it prints. Doing two things is acceptable because two steps constitute a sequence, and it is fine to nest a structure within another structure. However, when the sequence ends, the logic doesn't flow right back to the question. Instead, it goes *above* the question to get another number. For the loop in Figure 2-13 to be a structured loop, the logic must return to the eof question when the sequence ends.

The flowchart in Figure 2-16 shows the flow of logic returning to the eof immediately after the sequence. Figure 2-16 shows a structured flowchart, but the flowchart has one major flaw—it doesn't do the job of continuously doubling numbers.

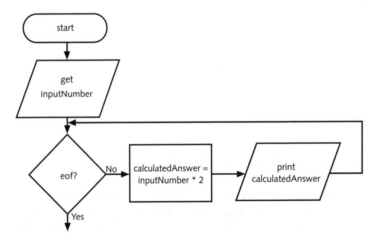

Figure 2-16   Structured, but nonfunctional, flowchart

Follow the flowchart in Figure 2-16 through a typical program run. Suppose when the program starts, the user enters a 9 for the value of inputNumber. That's not **eof**, so the number doubles, and 18 prints out as the `calculatedAnswer`. Then the question **eof?** is asked again. It can't be **eof** because the sentinel (ending) value can't be entered. The logic never returns to the `get inputNumber` step. Therefore, 9 doubles again and the answer, 18 prints again. It's still not eof, so the same steps are repeated. This goes on *forever*, with the answer 18 printing repeatedly. The program logic shown in Figure 2-16 is structured, but it doesn't work; the program in Figure 2-17 works, but it isn't structured!

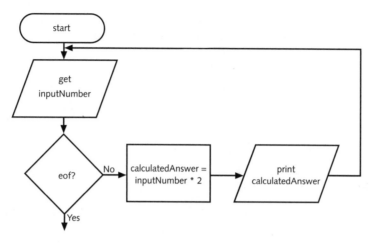

Figure 2-17   Functional, but nonstructured, flowchart

How can the number-doubling problem be both structured and work? Often, for a program to be structured, you must add something extra. In this case, it's an extra `get inputNumber` step. Consider the solution in Figure 2-18; it's structured, *and* it does what it's supposed to do! The program logic illustrated in Figure 2-18 contains a sequence and a loop. The loop contains another sequence.

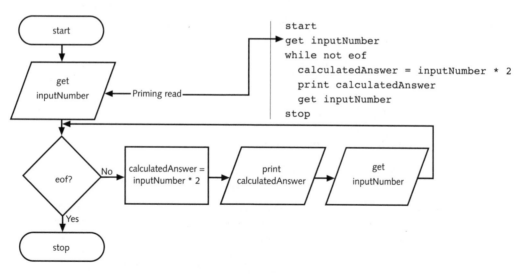

Figure 2-18   Functional, structured flowchart and pseudocode

The additional `get inputNumber` step is typical in structured programs. The first of the two input steps is the priming input, or priming read. The term *priming* comes from the fact that the read is first, or *primary* (what gets the process going, as in "priming the pump"). The purpose of the priming read step is to control the upcoming loop that begins with the eof question. The last element within the structured loop gets the next, and all subsequent input values. This is also typical in structured loops—the last step executed within the loop alters the condition tested in the question that begins the loop, which in this case is the `eof` question.

UNDERSTANDING THE REASONS FOR STRUCTURE

At this point you may very well be saying, "I liked the original doubling program just fine. I could follow it. Also, the first program had one less step in it, so it was less work. Who cares if a program is structured?"

Until you have some programming experience, it is difficult to appreciate the reasons for using nothing other than the three structures. However, staying with these three structures is better for the following reasons:

- Clarity—The doubling program is a small program. As programs get bigger, they get more confusing if they're not structured.

- Professionalism—All other programmers (and programming teachers you might encounter) expect your programs to be structured. It's the way things are done professionally.

- Efficiency—Most newer computer languages are structured languages with syntax that lets you deal efficiently with sequence, selection, and looping. Even programs written using older languages such as assembly languages, COBOL, and RPG, which were developed before the principles of structured programming, can be written in a structured form, and are expected to be written that way today. Newer languages like C++ and Java enforce structure by their syntax.

- Maintenance—In the future, you, as well as other programmers, will find it easier to modify and maintain structured programs.

- Modularity—Structured programs can be easily broken into routines that can be assigned to any number of programmers. The routines are then pieced back together like modular furniture at each routine's single entry or exit point. Additionally, often a module can be used in multiple programs, saving development time in the new project.

Most programs that you purchase are huge, consisting of thousands or millions of statements. If you've worked with a word processing program or spreadsheet, think of the number of menu options and keystroke combinations available to the user. Such programs are not the work of one programmer. The modular nature of structured programs means that work can be divided among many programmers; then the modules can be connected and a large program can be completed much more quickly. Money is often a motivating factor. The quicker you write a program and make it available for use, the sooner it begins making money for the developer.

Consider the college admission program from the beginning of the chapter. It has been rewritten in structured form in Figure 2-19. Not only is it easier to follow now, but also Figure 2-19 shows how you can simplify the main module even further by using a structured module that plugs into the main module in several locations. Figure 2-19 also shows structured pseudocode for the same problem.

 Don't be alarmed if it is difficult for you to follow the many nested ifs within the pseudocode in Figure 2-19. After you study the selection process in more detail, reading this type of pseudocode will become much easier for you.

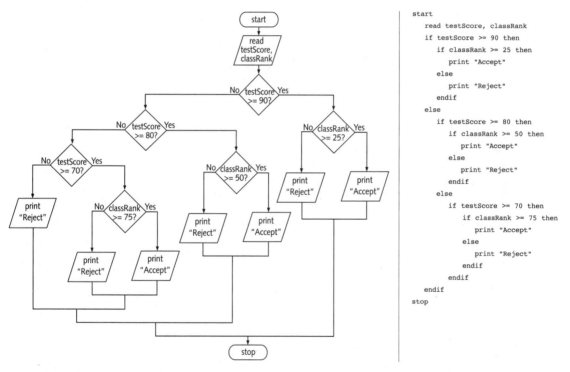

Figure 2-19: Flowchart and pseudocode of structured college admission program

RECOGNIZING STRUCTURE

When you are just learning about structured program design, it is difficult to detect whether a program's logic is structured or not. For example, is the flowchart segment in Figure 2-20 structured?

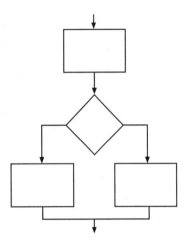

Figure 2-20   Example 1

Yes, it is. It has a sequence and a selection structure.

Is the flowchart segment in Figure 2-21 structured?

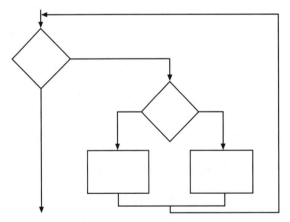

Figure 2-21   Example 2

Yes, it is. It has a loop, and within the loop is a selection.

Is the flowchart segment in Figure 2-22 structured? (The symbols are lettered so you can better follow the discussion.)

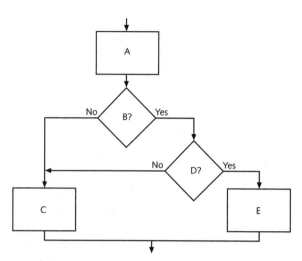

Figure 2-22 Example 3

No, it isn't; it is not constructed from the three basic structures. One way to straighten out a flowchart segment that isn't structured is to use what you can call the "spaghetti bowl" method; that is, picture the flowchart as a bowl of spaghetti that you must untangle. Imagine you can grab one piece of pasta at the top of the bowl, and start pulling. As you "pull" each symbol out of the tangled mess, you can untangle the separate paths until the entire segment is structured. For example, with the diagram in Figure 2-22, if you start pulling at the top, you encounter a procedure box, labeled A. (See Figure 2-23.)

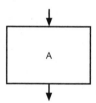

Figure 2-23 Untangling Example 3, first step

A single process like A is part of an acceptable structure—it constitutes at least the beginning of a sequence structure. Imagine you continue pulling symbols from the tangled segment. The next item in the flowchart is a question that tests a condition labeled B, as you can see in Figure 2-24.

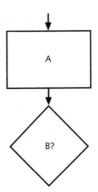

Figure 2-24   Untangling Example 3, second step

At this point, you know the sequence that was started with A has ended. Sequences never have decisions in them, so the sequence is finished; either a selection or a loop is beginning. A loop must return to the question at some later point. You can see from the original logic in Figure 2-22 that whether the answer to B is yes or no, the logic never returns to B. Therefore, B begins a selection structure, not a loop structure.

To continue detangling the logic, you pull up on the flowline that emerges from the left side (the "No" side) of Question B. You encounter C, as shown in Figure 2-25. When you continue beyond C, you reach the end of the flowchart.

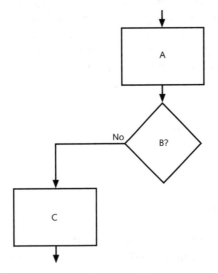

Figure 2-25   Untangling Example 3, third step

Now you can turn your attention to the *yes* side (the right side) of the condition tested in B. When you pull up on the right side, you encounter Question D. (See Figure 2-26.)

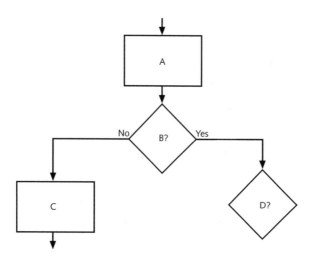

Figure 2-26   Untangling Example 3, fourth step

Follow the line on the left side of Question D. If the line is attached somewhere else, as it is (to Step C) in Figure 2-22, just untangle it by repeating the step that is tangled. (In this example you repeat Step C to untangle it from the other usage of C.) Continue pulling on the flowline that emerges from Step C, and you reach the end of the program segment, as shown in Figure 2-27.

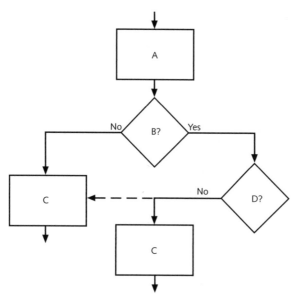

Figure 2-27   Untangling Example 3, fifth step

Now pull on the right side of Question D. Process E pops up, as shown in Figure 2-28; then you reach the end.

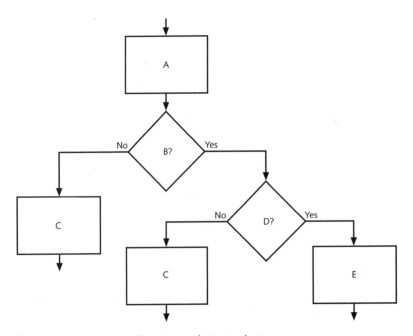

Figure 2-28   Untangling Example 3, sixth step

At this point the untangled flowchart has three loose ends. The loose ends of Question D can be brought together to form a selection structure, then the loose ends of Question B can be brought together to form another selection structure. The result is the flowchart shown in Figure 2-29. The entire flowchart segment is structured—it has a sequence (A) followed by a selection inside a selection.

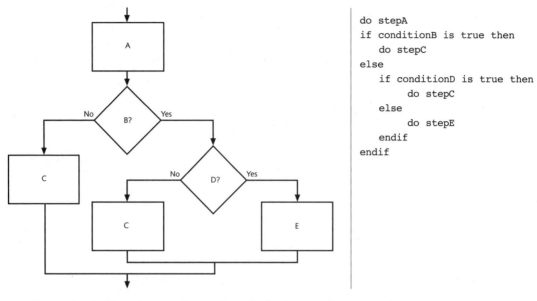

```
do stepA
if conditionB is true then
    do stepC
else
    if conditionD is true then
        do stepC
    else
        do stepE
    endif
endif
```

2

Figure 2-29 Flowchart and pseudocode for Untangling Example 3

If you would like to try structuring a very difficult example of an unstructured program, see Appendix A.

TWO SPECIAL STRUCTURES—CASE AND DO UNTIL

You can skip this section for now without any loss in continuity. Your instructor may prefer to discuss the case structure with the Decision chapter and the do until loop with the Looping chapter.

You can solve any logic problem you might encounter using only the three structures: sequence, selection, and loop. However, many programming languages allow two more structures: the case structure and the do until loop. These structures are never *needed* to solve a problem, but sometimes they are convenient. Programmers consider them both to be acceptable, legal structures.

The Case Structure

You use the **case structure** when there are several distinct possible values for a variable you are testing. Suppose you administer a school where tuition is $75, $50, $30, or $10 per credit hour, depending on whether a student is a freshman, sophomore, junior, or senior. The structured flowchart in Figure 2-30 shows a series of decisions that assign the correct tuition to a student.

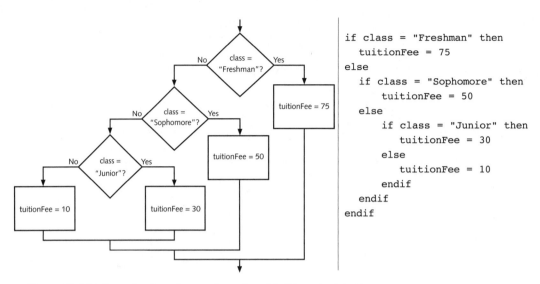

Figure 2-30 Flowchart and pseudocode of tuition decisions

This logic shown in Figure 2-30 is absolutely correct and completely structured. The `class="Junior"` selection structure is contained within the `class="Sophomore"` structure, which is contained within the `class="Freshman"` structure. Note that there is no need to ask if a student is a senior because if a student is not a freshman, sophomore, or junior, it is assumed the student is a senior.

Even though the program segments in Figure 2-30 are correct and structured, many programming languages permit a case structure as shown in Figure 2-31. When using the case structure, you test a variable against a series of values, taking appropriate action based on the variable's value. To many, these programs seem easier to read, and because you understand that the same results *could* be achieved with a series of structured selections (and thus be structured), the case structure is allowed. That is, if the first one is structured and the second one reflects the first one point by point, then the second one must be structured also.

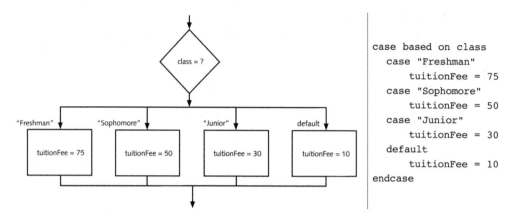

```
case based on class
    case "Freshman"
        tuitionFee = 75
    case "Sophomore"
        tuitionFee = 50
    case "Junior"
        tuitionFee = 30
    default
        tuitionFee = 10
endcase
```

Figure 2-31 Flowchart and pseudocode of case structure

The term default used in Figure 2-31 means "if none of the other cases were true." Each programming language you learn may use a different syntax for the default case.

Even though a programming language permits you to use the case structure, you should understand that the case structure is just a convenience that might make a flowchart, pseudocode, or actual program code easier to understand at first glance. When you write a series of decisions using the case structure, the computer still makes a series of individual decisions just as though you had used many if-then-else combinations. In other words, you might prefer looking at the diagram in Figure 2-31 to understand the tuition fees charged by a school, but a computer actually makes the decisions as shown in Figure 2-30—one at a time. When you write your own programs, it is always acceptable to express a complicated decision-making process as a series of individual selections.

The Do Until Loop

Recall that a structured loop (often called a do while) looks like Figure 2-32. A do until loop looks like Figure 2-33.

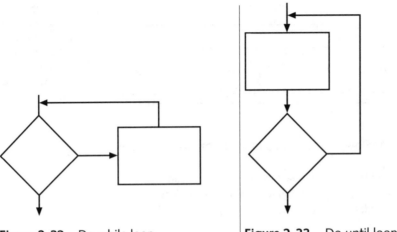

Figure 2-32 Do while loop | **Figure 2-33** Do until loop

A difference exists between these two structures. In a do while loop, you ask a question and, depending on the answer, you might never enter the loop to execute the loop's procedure. Conversely, in a **do until loop** you ensure that the procedure executes at least once; then, depending on the answer to the controlling question, the loop may or may not execute additional times.

You can duplicate the same series of events generated by any do until loop by creating a sequence followed by a do while loop. Consider the flowcharts in Figures 2-34 and 2-35.

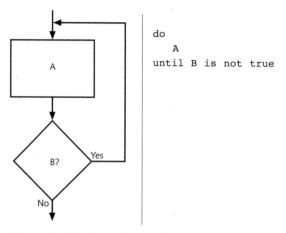

Figure 2-34 Flowchart and pseudocode for do until loop

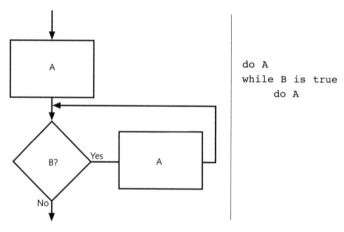

Figure 2-35 Flowchart and pseudocode for sequence followed by do while loop

In Figure 2-34, A is done, then B is asked. If B is yes, then A is done and B is asked again. In Figure 2-35, A is done, then B is asked. If B is yes, then A is done and B is asked again. Both flowcharts do exactly the same thing.

Because programmers understand that a do until can be expressed with a sequence followed by a do while, most languages allow the do until. Again, you are never required to use a do until; you can always accomplish the same events with a sequence followed by a do while.

CHAPTER SUMMARY

- The popular name for snarled program statements is spaghetti code.

- Clearer programs can be constructed using only three basic structures: sequence, selection, and loop. These three structures can be combined in an infinite number of ways by stacking and nesting them. Each structure has one entry and one exit point; one structure can attach to another only at one of these entry or exit points.

- A priming read or priming input is the first read or data input statement prior to beginning a structured loop. The last step within the loop gets the next, and all subsequent, input values.

- You use structured techniques to promote clarity, professionalism, efficiency, and modularity.

- One way to straighten a flowchart segment that isn't structured is to imagine the flowchart as a bowl of spaghetti that you must untangle.

- You can use a case structure when there are several distinct possible values for a variable you are testing. When you write a series of decisions using the case structure, the computer still makes a series of individual decisions.

- In a do while loop you ask a question and, depending on the answer, you might never enter the loop to execute the loop's procedure. In a do until loop, you ensure that the procedure executes at least once. You can duplicate the same series of events generated by any do until loop by creating a sequence followed by a do while loop.

2

Exercises

1. Match the term with the structure diagram. (Because the structures go by more than one name, there are more terms than diagrams.)

   1. sequence   5. decision
   2. selection   6. if-then–else
   3. loop   7. iteration
   4. do while

   a.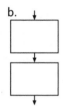

   b.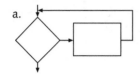

   c.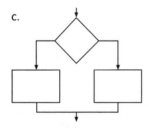

2. Match the term with the pseudocode segment. (Because the structures go by more than one name, there are more terms than pseudocode segments.)

   1. sequence   4. decision
   2. selection   5. if-then–else
   3. loop   6. iteration

   a. `while not eof`
      `    print theAnswer`

b.
```
if inventoryQuantity  >  0 then
    do fillOrderProcess
else
    do backOrderNotification
endif
```

c.
```
do localTaxCalculation
do stateTaxCalculation
do federalTaxCalculation
```

3. Is each of the following segments structured or unstructured? If unstructured, redraw it so it does the same thing but is structured.

a.
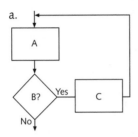

b.
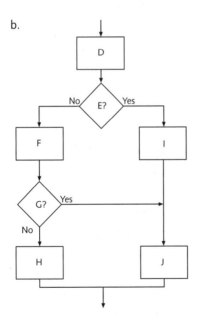

2

c.

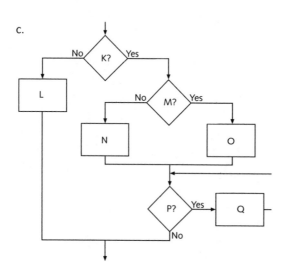

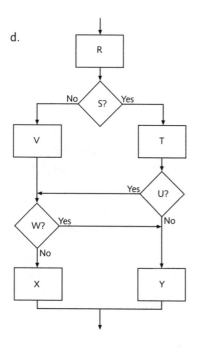

d.

e.

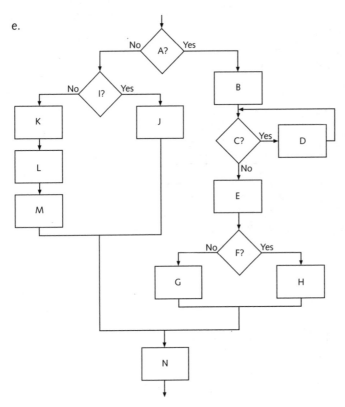

4. Write pseudocode for each example (a through e) in Exercise 3.

5. Assume you have created a mechanical arm that can hold a pen. The arm can perform the following tasks:

   ❑ lower the pen to a piece of paper

   ❑ raise the pen from the paper

   ❑ move the pen one inch along a straight line (If the pen is lowered, this action draws a one-inch line from left to right; if the pen is raised, this action just repositions the pen one inch to the right.)

   ❑ turn 90 degrees to the right

   ❑ draw a circle that is one inch in diameter

   Draw a structured flowchart or write pseudocode that would cause the arm to draw the following:

   a. a one-inch square

   b. a two-inch by one-inch rectangle

   c. a string of three beads

   Have a fellow student act as the mechanical arm and carry out your instructions.

2

6. Assume you have created a mechanical robot that can perform the following tasks:

   ◻ stand up

   ◻ sit down

   ◻ turn left 90 degrees

   ◻ turn right 90 degrees

   ◻ take a step

   Additionally, the robot can determine the answer to one test condition:

   ◻ Am I touching something?

   Place two chairs 20 feet apart, directly facing each other. Draw a structured flowchart or write pseudocode that would allow the robot to start from a sitting position in one chair, cross the room, and end up sitting in the other chair.

   Have a fellow student act as the robot and carry out your instructions.

7. Draw a structured flowchart of your preparation to go to work or school in the morning. Include at least two decisions and two loops.

8. Write structured pseudocode of your preparation to go to bed at night. Include at least two decisions and two loops.

3

MODULES, HIERARCHY CHARTS, AND DOCUMENTATION

After studying Chapter 3, you should be able to:

♦ Describe the advantages of modularization

♦ Modularize a program

♦ Understand how a module can call another module

♦ Explain how to declare variables

♦ Create hierarchy charts

♦ Understand documentation

♦ Create print charts

♦ Interpret file descriptions

♦ Understand the attributes of complete documentation

MODULES, SUBROUTINES, PROCEDURES, FUNCTIONS, OR METHODS

Programmers seldom write programs as one long series of steps. Instead, they break the programming problem down into reasonable units and tackle one small task at a time. These reasonable units are called **modules**. Programmers also refer to them as **subroutines**, **procedures**, **functions**, or **methods**.

 The name that programmers use for their modules usually reflects the programming language they use. COBOL, RPG, and BASIC programmers are most likely to use "subroutine." Pascal and Visual Basic programmers use "procedure" (or "subprocedure"). C and C++ programmers call their modules "functions," while C# and Java programmers are more likely to use "method."

You are never required to break a large program into modules, but there are at least four reasons for doing so:

- Modularization provides abstraction.

- Modularization allows multiple programmers to work on a problem.

- Modularization allows you to reuse your work.

- Modularization makes it easier to identify structures.

Modularization Provides Abstraction

One reason modularized programs are easier to understand is that they enable a programmer to see the big picture. **Abstraction** is the process of paying attention to important properties while ignoring nonessential details. Life would be tedious without abstraction. For example, you can create a list of things to accomplish today:

```
Do laundry
Call Aunt Nan
Start term paper
```

Without abstraction, the list of chores would begin:

```
Pick up laundry basket
Put laundry basket in car
Drive to laundromat
Get out of car with basket
Walk into laundromat
Set basket down
Find quarters for washing machine
…and so on.
```

You might list a dozen more steps before you finish the laundry and move on to the second chore on your original list. If you had to consider every small, **low-level** detail of every task in your day, you would probably never make it out of bed in the morning. Using a higher-level, more abstract list makes your day manageable.

Likewise, some level of abstraction occurs in every computer program. Fifty years ago, you had to understand the low-level circuitry instructions your computer used. But now, newer **high-level** programming languages allow you to use English-like vocabulary in which one broad statement corresponds to dozens of machine instructions. No matter which high-level programming language you use, if you display a message on the monitor, you are never required to understand how a monitor works to create each pixel on the screen. You write an instruction like `print message` and the details of the hardware operations are handled for you.

Modules or subroutines provide another way to achieve abstraction. For example, a payroll program can call a module named `computeFederalWithholdingTax`. You can write the mathematical details of the function later, someone else can write them, or you can purchase them from an outside source. When you plan your main payroll program, your only concern is that a federal withholding tax will have to be calculated; you save the details for later.

Modularization Allows Multiple Programmers to Work on a Problem

When you dissect any large task into modules, you gain the ability to divide the task among various people. Rarely does a single programmer write a commercial program that you buy off the shelf. Consider any word processing, spreadsheet, or database program you have used. Each program has so many options, and responds to user selections in so many possible ways, that it would take years for a single programmer to write all the instructions. Professional software developers can write new programs in weeks or months, instead of years, by dividing large programs into modules and assigning each module to an individual programmer or programming team.

Modularization Allows You to Reuse Your Work

If a subroutine or function is useful and well written, you may want to reuse it more than once within a program or in other programs. For example, a routine that checks the current month to make sure it is valid (not lower than 1 or higher than 12) is useful in many programs written for a business. A program that uses a personnel file containing each employee's birth date, hire date, last promotion date, and termination date can use the month-validation module four times with each employee record. Other programs in an organization can also use the module; these include programs that ship customer orders, plan employees' birthday parties, and calculate when loan payments should be made. If you write the month-checking instructions so they are entangled with other statements in a program, they are difficult to extract and reuse. On the other hand, if you place the instructions in their own module, the unit becomes easily used and portable to other applications.

You can find many real-world examples of **reusability**. When you build a house, you don't invent plumbing and heating systems; you incorporate systems with proven designs. This certainly reduces the time and effort it takes to build a house. Assuming the plumbing and electrical systems you choose are also in service in other houses, it also improves your house's **reliability**. Similarly, software that is reusable is more reliable, yet saves time and money. If you create the functional components of your programs as stand-alone modules and test them in your current programs, much of the work will already be done when you use the modules in future applications.

Modularization Makes It Easier to Identify Structures

When you combine several programming tasks into modules, it may be easier for you to identify structures. For example, you learned in Chapter 2 that the selection structure looks like Figure 3-1.

When you work with a program segment that looks like Figure 3-2, you may question whether it is structured. If you can modularize some of the statements and give them a more abstract group name, as in Figure 3-3, it is easier to see that the program involves a major selection and that the program segment is structured.

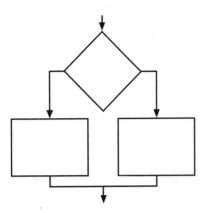

Figure 3-1   Selection structure

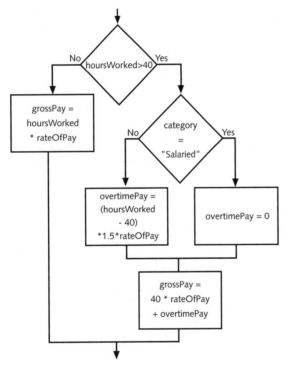

Figure 3-2   Section of logic from a payroll program

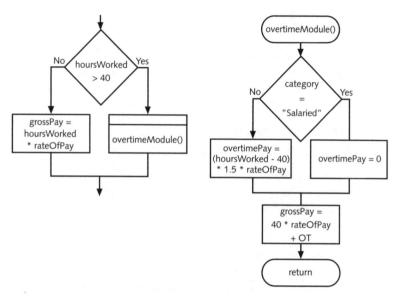

Figure 3-3   Modularized logic from a payroll program

The single program segment shown in Figure 3-2 accomplishes the same steps as the two program segments shown together in Figure 3-3; both programs are structured. The structure may be more obvious in the program segments in Figure 3-3 because you can see two distinct parts—a decision structure calls a subroutine that contains another decision structure, which is followed by a sequence. Neither of the program segments shown in Figures 3-2 and 3-3 is superior to the other in terms of functionality, but you may prefer to modularize to help you identify structures.

 As a professional programmer, you never modularize simply to *identify* whether a program is structured—you modularize for reasons of abstraction, ease of dividing the work, and reusability. However, as a beginning programmer, being able to see and identify structure is important.

MODULARIZING A PROGRAM

When you create a module or subroutine, you give the module a name. The rules for naming modules are different in every programming language, but they often are similar to the language's rules for variable names. In this text, module names will follow the same two rules used for variable names:

- Module names must be one word.

- Module names should have some meaning.

- Additionally, in this text module names will be followed by a set of parentheses. This will help you distinguish module names from variable names. This style corresponds to the way modules are named in many programming languages, such as Java, C++, C#, and Pascal.

 As you learn more about modules in specific programming languages, you will find that you sometimes place variable names within the parentheses of module names. For now, the parentheses we use at the end of module names will be empty.

 Most programming languages require that module names begin with an alphabetic character. This text will follow that convention.

When a program uses a module, you can refer to the main program as the **calling program**, because it "calls" the module's name when it wants to use the module. The flowchart symbol used to call a subroutine is a rectangle with a bar across the top. You place the name of the module you are calling inside the rectangle.

 Instead of placing only the name of the module you are calling in the flowchart, many programmers insert an appropriate verb such as "perform" or "do" before the module name.

You draw each module separately with its own sentinel symbols. The symbol that is the equivalent of the `start` symbol in a program contains the name of the module. This name must be identical to the name used in the calling program. The symbol that is the equivalent of the `end` symbol in a program does not contain "end"; after all, the program is not ending. Instead, the module ends with a "gentler," less final term such as `exit` or `return`. These words correctly indicate that when the module ends, the logical progression of statements will return to the calling program.

A flowchart and pseudocode for a program that calculates the arithmetic average of two numbers a user enters can look like Figure 3-4. Here the **main program**, or calling program, calls three modules.

The logic of the program in Figure 3-4 proceeds as follows:

1. The main program starts.

2. The main program calls the getInput() module.

3. Within the getInput()module, the prompt "Enter a number" displays.

4. Within the getInput() module, the program accepts a value into the firstNumber variable.

5. Within the getInput() module, the prompt "Enter another number" displays.

6. Within the getInput() module, the program accepts a value into the secondNumber variable.

7. The getInput() module ends, and control returns to the main calling program.

8. The main program calls the calculateAverage() module.

9. Within the calculateAverage() module, a value for the variable average is calculated.

10. The calculateAverage()module ends, and control returns to the main calling program.

11. The main program calls the printResult() module.

12. Within the printResult() module, the value of average displays.

13. Within the printResult() module, a thank-you message displays.

14. The printResult() module ends, and control returns to the main calling program.

15. The main program ends.

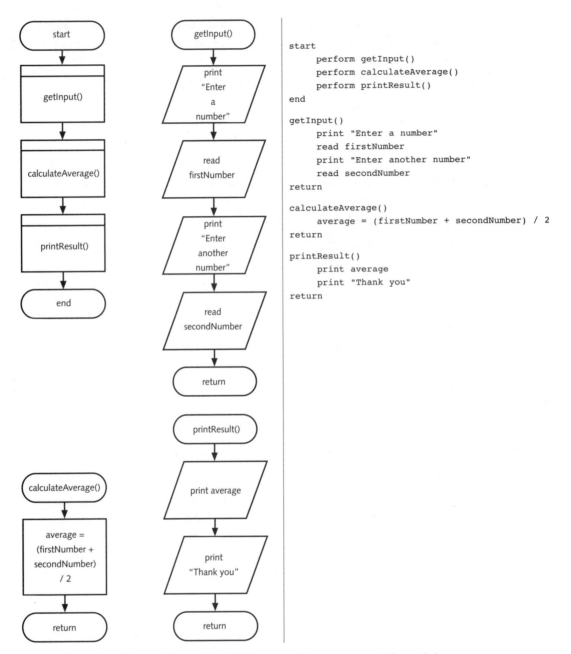

Figure 3-4   Flowchart and pseudocode for averaging program with modules

Whenever a main program calls a module, the logic transfers to the module. When the module ends, the logical flow transfers back to the main calling program and begins where it left off.

The computer keeps track of the correct memory address to which it should return after executing a module by recording the memory address in a location known as the *stack*.

MODULES CALLING OTHER MODULES

Just as a program can call a module or subroutine, any module can call another module. For example, the program illustrated in Figure 3-4 can be broken down further as shown in Figure 3-5.

After the program in Figure 3-5 begins:

1. The main program calls the `getInput()` module, and the logical flow transfers to that module.

2. From there, the `getInput()` module calls the `getFirstValue()` module, and the logical flow immediately transfers to the `getFirstValue()` module.

3. When `getFirstValue()` ends, control passes back to `getInput()` where `getSecondValue()` is called.

4. Control passes to `getSecondValue()`, and when this module ends control passes back to `getInput()`.

5. When `getInput()` ends, control returns to the main program.

6. Then `calculateAverage()` and `printResult()` execute as before.

Deciding whether to break down any particular module further into its own subroutines or submodules is an art. Programmers do follow some guidelines when deciding how far to break down subroutines or how much to put in them. Some companies may have arbitrary rules such as "a subroutine should never take more than a page," or "a module should never have more than 30 statements in it," or "never have a method or function with only one statement in it."

Rather than use such arbitrary rules, a better policy is to place together statements that contribute to one specific task. The more the statements contribute to the same job, the greater the **functional cohesion** of the module. A routine that checks the validity of a `month` variable's value, or one that prompts a user and allows the user to type in a value, would be considered cohesive. A routine that checks date validity, deducts insurance premiums, and computes federal withholding tax for an employee would be less cohesive.

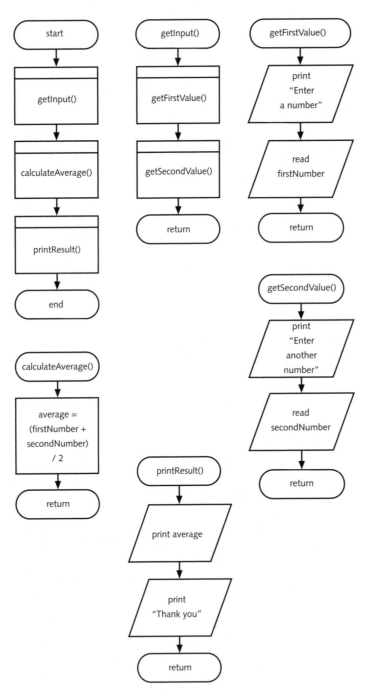

Figure 3-5   Flowchart for averaging program with submodules

DECLARING VARIABLES

The primary work of most modules in most programs you write is to manipulate data—for example, to calculate the figures needed for a paycheck, customer bill, or sales report. You store your program data in variables.

Many program languages require you to declare all variables before you use them. **Declaring a variable** involves providing a name for the memory location where the computer will store the variable value and notifying the computer what type of data to expect. Every programming language requires that you follow specific rules when declaring variables, but all the rules involve identifying at least two attributes for every variable:

- You must declare a data type.
- You must give the variable a name.

You learned in Chapter 1 that different programming languages provide different variable types, but all allow at least the distinction between character and numeric data. The rest of this book uses just two data types—num which will hold number values, and char which will hold all other values, including those that hold letters, and combinations of letters and numbers.

Remember, you also learned in Chapter 1 that variable names must not contain spaces, so this book uses statements such as `char lastName` and `num weeklySalary` to declare two variables of different types.

Some programming languages, like BASIC and RPG, do not require you to name any variable until the first time you use it. However, languages including COBOL, C++, C#, Java, and Pascal require that you declare variables with a name and a type. Some languages require that you declare all variables at the beginning of a program before you write any executable statements; others allow you to declare variables at any point, but require the declaration before you can use the variable. For our purposes, this book follows the convention of declaring all variables at the beginning of a program.

When you use many modern programming languages, variables typically are declared within each module that uses them. Such variables are known as **local variables**. As you continue your study of programming logic, you will learn how to use local variables and understand their advantages. For now, this text will use **global variables**—variables that are given a type and name once, and then used in all modules of the program.

For example, to complete the averaging program shown in Figure 3-5 so that its variables are declared, you can redraw the main program flowchart to look like Figure 3-6. Three variables are required, `firstNumber`, `secondNumber`, and `average`. The variables are declared as the first step in the program, before you use any of them, and each is correctly identified as numeric. They appear to the side of the "declare variables" step in an **annotation symbol** or **annotation box**, which is simply an attached box containing notes. You can use an annotation symbol any time you have more to write than conveniently fits within a flowchart symbol.

Many programming languages support more specific numeric types with names like int (for integers or whole numbers), float (for floating point or decimal-place values), and double (for double-precision floating point values, which means more memory space is reserved). Many languages distinguish even more precisely. For example, in addition to whole-number integers, C++, C#, and Java allow short integers and long integers, which require less and more memory, respectively.

 Many programming languages support more specific character types. Often, programming languages provide a distinction between single character variables (like an initial or a grade in a class) and string variables, like a last name, which hold multiple characters.

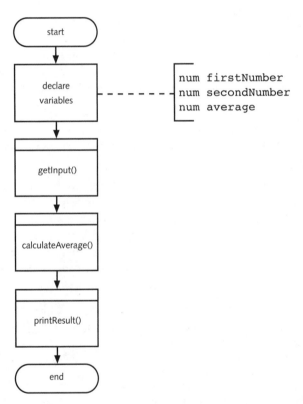

Figure 3-6   Averaging program with declared variables

Programmers sometimes create a **data dictionary**, which is a list of every variable name used in a program, along with its type, size, and description. When a data dictionary is created, it becomes part of the program documentation.

After you name a variable, you must use that exact name every time you refer to the variable within your program.

3

CREATING HIERARCHY CHARTS

When a program has several modules calling other modules, programmers often use a tool besides flowcharts or pseudocode to show the overall picture of how these modules are related to one another. You can use a **hierarchy chart** to illustrate modules' relationships. A hierarchy chart does not tell you what tasks are to be performed within a module; it doesn't tell you *when* or *how* a module executes. It tells you only which routines exist within a program and which routines call which other routines.

The hierarchy chart for the last version of the value-averaging program looks like Figure 3-7, and shows which modules call which others. You don't know *when* the modules are called or *why* they are called; that information is in the flowchart or pseudocode. A hierarchy chart just tells you which modules *are* called by other modules.

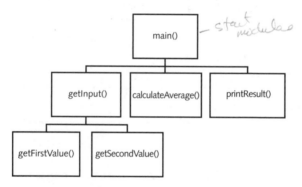

Figure 3-7   Hierarchy chart for value-averaging program

You may have seen hierarchy charts for organizations, such as the one in Figure 3-8. The chart shows who reports to whom, not when or how often they report. Program hierarchy charts operate in an identical manner.

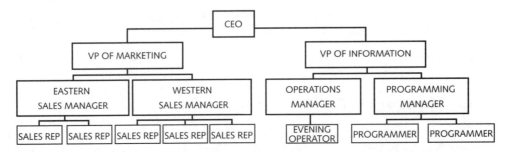

Figure 3-8 An organizational hierarchy chart

Figure 3-9 shows an example of a hierarchy chart for the billing program of a mail order company. The hierarchy chart supplies module names only; it provides a general overview of the tasks to be performed without specifying any details.

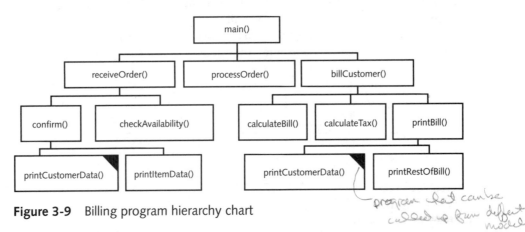

Figure 3-9 Billing program hierarchy chart

The hierarchy chart can be a useful tool when a program must be modified months or years after the original writing. For example, if a tax law changes, a programmer might be asked to rewrite the `calculateTax()` module in the billing program diagrammed in Figure 3-9. As the programmer changes the `calculateTax()` routine, the hierarchy chart shows what other dependent routines might be affected. A hierarchy chart is useful for "getting the big picture" in a complex program.

Because program modules are reusable, a specific module may be called from several locations within a program. For example, in the billing program hierarchy chart in Figure 3-9, you can see that the `printCustomerData()` module is used twice. By convention, you blacken a corner of each box representing the `printCustomerData()` module. This action alerts readers that any change to this module will affect more than one location.

Understanding Documentation

Documentation refers to all of the supporting material that goes with a program. Two broad categories of documentation are intended for the programmer and for the user. People who use computer programs are called **end users**, or **users** for short. Most likely you have been the end user of an application such as a word processing program or a game. When you purchase software that other programmers have written, you appreciate clearly written instructions on how to install and use the software. These instructions constitute user documentation. In a small organization, programmers may write user documentation, but in most organizations, systems analysts or technical writers produce end-user instructions. These instructions may take the form of a printed manual or may be presented online through a Web site or on a compact disc.

When programmers begin to plan the logic of a computer program, they require instructions known as **program documentation**. End users never see program documentation; rather, programmers use it when planning or modifying programs.

Program documentation falls into two categories: internal and external. **Internal program documentation** consists of **program comments**, or nonexecuting statements that programmers place within their code to explain program statements in English. The method for inserting comments within a program differs in each programming language, but every method provides a means for inserting illuminating comments that do not affect the running of a program. You will learn how to insert comments when you learn a specific programming language.

 In the BASIC programming language, program comments begin with the letters REM (for REMark). In C++, C#, and Java, comments can begin with two forward slashes (//). An RPG program indicates that a line is a comment if there is an asterisk (*) in the sixth typed position in the line.

External program documentation includes all the supporting paperwork that programmers develop before they write a program. Since most programs have input, processing, and output, usually there is documentation for all these functions.

Output Documentation

Output documentation is usually the first to be written. This may seem backwards, but if you're planning a trip, which do you decide first: how to get to your destination or where you're going?

Most requests for programs arise because a user needs particular information to be output, so the planning of program output is usually done in consultation with the person or persons who will be using the output. Only after the desired output is known can the programmer hope to plan the processes needed to produce the output.

Often the programmer does not design the output. Instead, the user who requests the output presents the programmer (or programming team) with an example or sketch of the desired result. Then the programmer might work with the user to refine the request, suggest improvements in the design, or clarify the user's needs. If you don't determine precisely what the user wants or needs at this point, you will write a program that the user soon wants redesigned and rewritten.

The most common type of output is a printed report. You can design a printed report on a **printer spacing chart**, which is also referred to as a **print chart** or a **print layout**. Figure 3-10 shows a printer spacing chart, which basically looks like graph paper. The chart has many boxes, and in each box the designer places one character that will be printed.

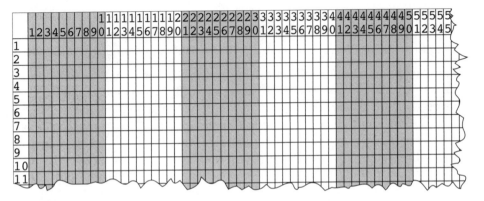

Figure 3-10   Printer spacing chart

  Besides using handwritten print charts, you can design report layouts on a computer using a word processing program or other design software.

For example, if you want to create a printed report with the title INVENTORY REPORT and you decide that the title looks best 11 spaces over from the left of the page and one line down, you would begin to create the printer spacing chart shown in Figure 3-11.

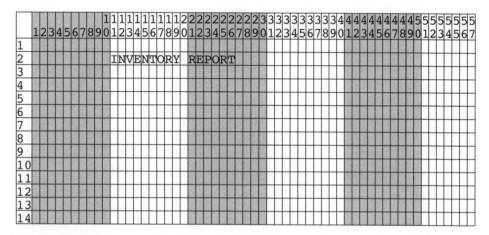

Figure 3-11 Printer spacing chart with first title

You might want to skip a line and print column headings ITEM NAME, PRICE, and QUANTITY IN STOCK, so the printer spacing chart would evolve into the one in Figure 3-12.

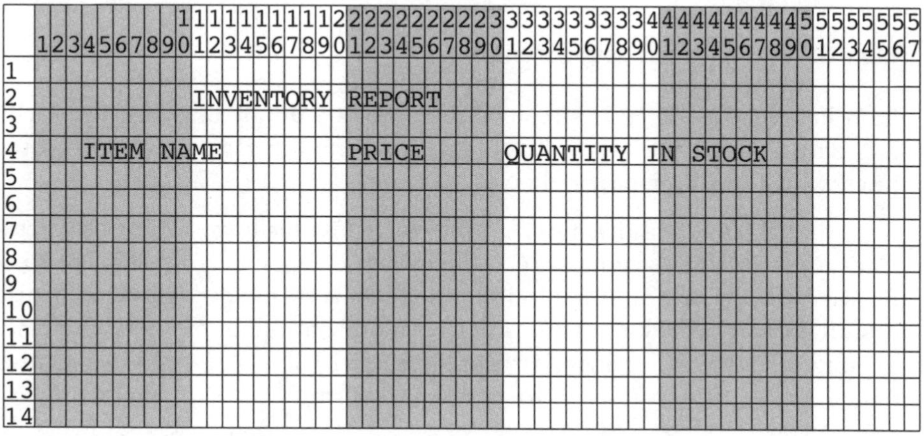

Figure 3-12 Printer spacing chart with title and column headings

The title and column headings will be **constant** on every page of the report, so they are written on the print chart literally. The exact spacing and use of upper- or lowercase make a difference. Notice that the constants used within a report do not need to follow the same rules as variable names. Within a report, constants like INVENTORY REPORT and ITEM NAME can contain spaces. These headings exist to help readers understand the information presented in the report—not for a computer to interpret.

3

A print layout typically shows how the variable data will appear on the report. Of course, the data will probably be different every time the report is run. Thus, instead of writing in actual item names and prices, the users and programmers usually use Xs to represent generic variable character data and 9s to represent generic variable numeric data. (Some programmers use Xs for both character and numeric data.) For example, Figure 3-13 shows how some data will look in the print chart.

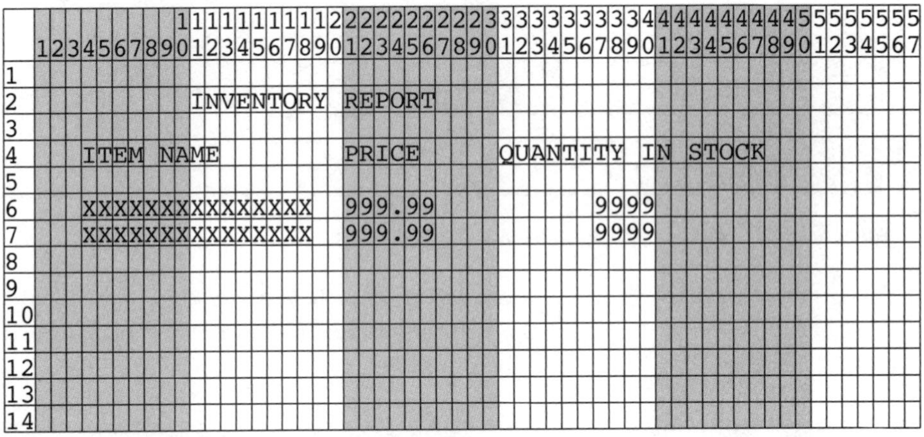

```
            1111111111222222222233333333334444444444555555555
   1234567890123456789012345678901234567890123456789012345678901234567
1
2                 INVENTORY REPORT
3
4     ITEM NAME            PRICE       QUANTITY IN STOCK
5
6     XXXXXXXXXXXXXXXX     999.99          9999
7     XXXXXXXXXXXXXXXX     999.99          9999
8
9
10
11
12
13
14
```

Figure 3-13   Print chart with generic data

Each line with its Xs and 9s representing data is a **detail line**, because it contains the data details. Detail lines typically appear many times per page, as opposed to **heading lines**, which usually appear only once per page.

Even though an actual inventory report might eventually go on for hundreds or thousands of detail lines, writing two or three rows of Xs and 9s is sufficient to show how the data will appear. For example, if a report contains employee names and salaries, those data items will occupy the same print positions on output for line after line, whether the output eventually contains 10 employees or 10,000. A few rows of identically positioned Xs and 9s are sufficient to establish the pattern.

In any report layout, then, you write in constant data (like headings) that will be the same on every run of this report. You write Xs and 9s to represent the variable data (like the items, their prices, and their quantities) that will change from run to run.

In the inventory report layout shown in Figure 3-13, the headings truly are constant, but you should not assume that all headings are completely constant. Let's say that your user decides to include the date in the inventory report heading. The report might now have a layout like Figure 3-14. Notice that now there is variable data, the date, in the report heading.

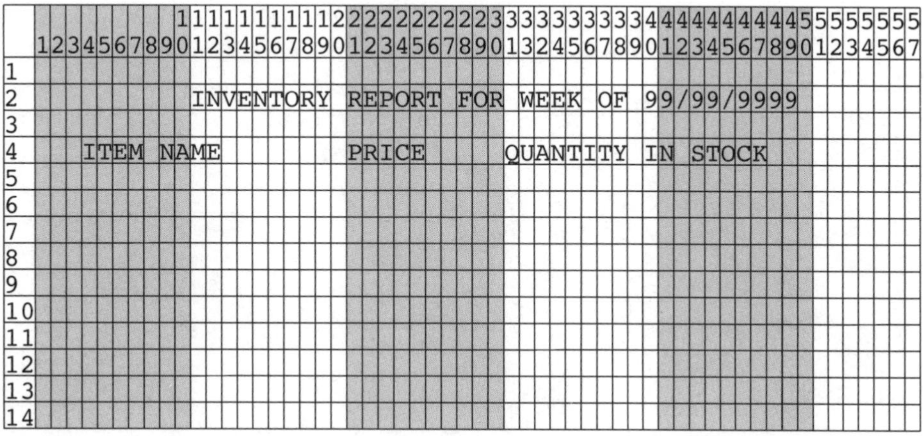

Figure 3-14   Variable data in report heading

For a long report that requires multiple pages, perhaps the user will also decide that the headings should appear at the top of every printed page, and that page numbers should also be added. Figure 3-15 shows how you might indicate page numbers.

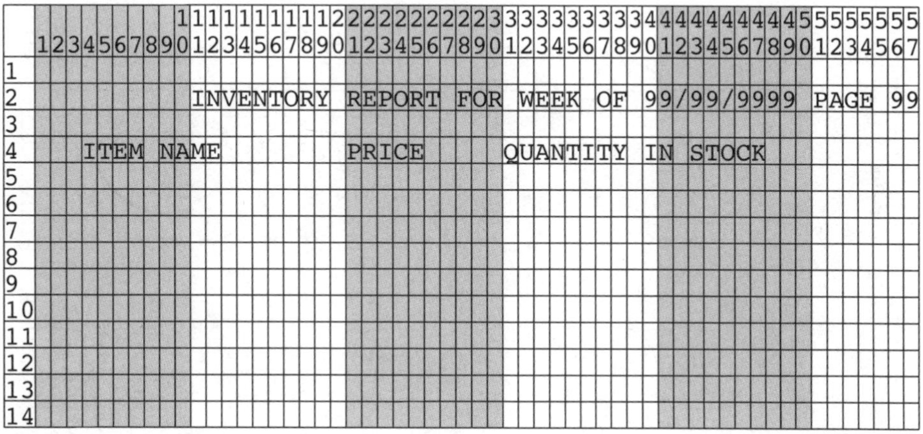

Figure 3-15   Heading with page numbers

Just as variable data might appear in a heading, constants might appear in the detail lines. For example, if the company sells all of its inventory items by the dozen, then each number in the QUANTITY IN STOCK column actually represents the number of dozens of that item. The users might choose to see the word DOZEN with each detail line. The print chart in Figure 3-16 indicates that the word DOZEN would literally appear on each line.

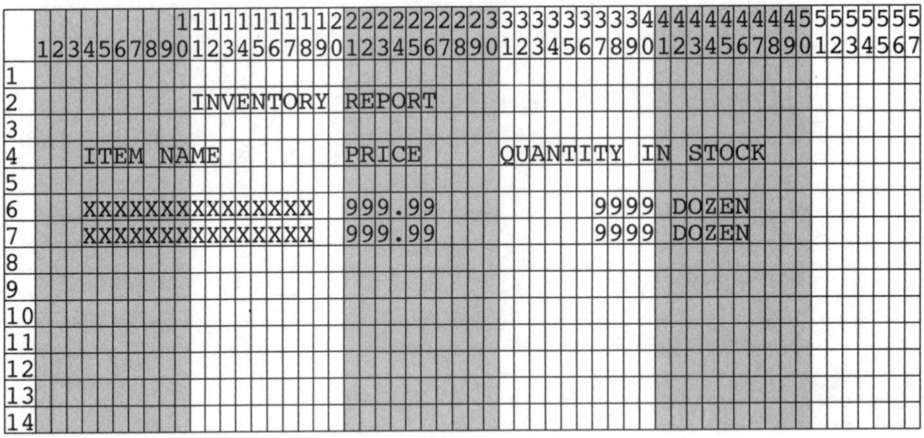

Figure 3-16   Print chart with literal in each detail line

Besides header lines and detail lines, reports often include special lines at the end of a report. These may have variable data only as in Figure 3-17, or constant data only as in Figure 3-18. Most often, however, reports will have both, as in Figure 3-19.

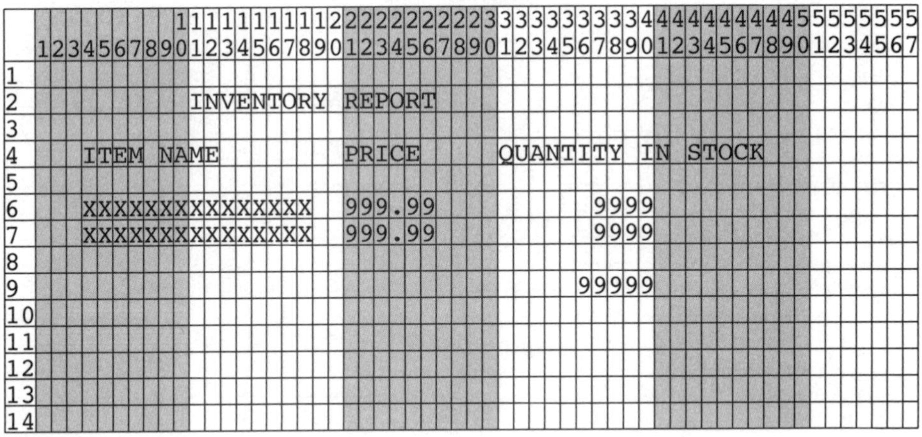

Figure 3-17   Report with variable data at end

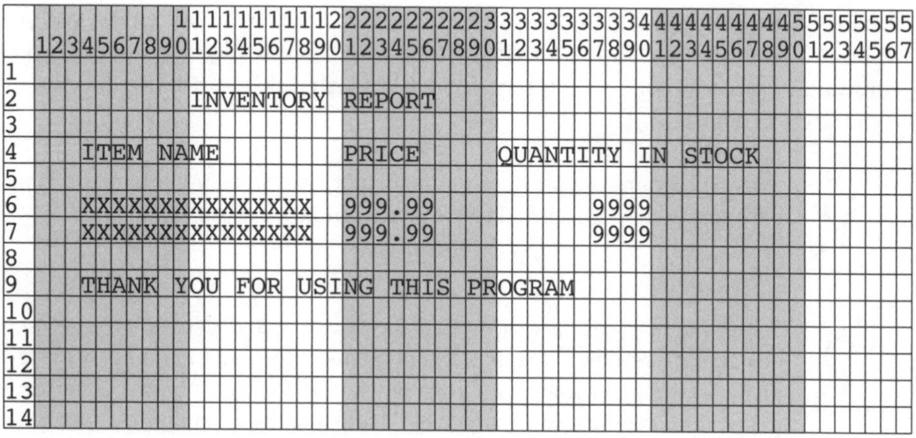

Figure 3-18   Report with constant data at end

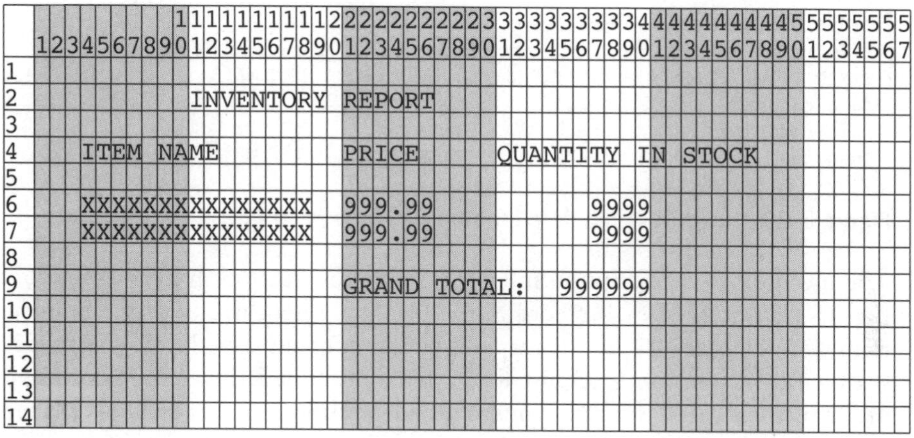

Figure 3-19   Report with combined constant and variable data at end

Even though lines at the end of a report don't always contain numeric totals, they are usually referred to generically as **total lines**.

INPUT DOCUMENTATION

Once you have planned the design of the output, you need to know what input is available to produce this output. If you are producing a report from stored data, you frequently will be provided with a **file description** that describes the data that are contained in a file. You usually find a file's description as part of an organization's information systems' documentation; physically, the description might be on paper in a binder in the Information Systems department, or it might be stored on a disk. If the file you will use comes from an outside source, the person requesting the report will have to provide you with a description of the data stored on the file. For example, Figure 3-20 shows an inventory file description for a file that could be used to produce the report described in Figure 3-13.

 Not all programs use previously stored input files. Some use interactive input data supplied by a user during the execution of a program.

 Some programs produce an output file that is stored directly on a storage device, such as a disk. If your program produces file output instead of printed report output, you will create a file description for your output. Other programs then may use your output file description as an input description for their programs.

```
INVENTORY FILE DESCRIPTION
File name: INVTRY
FIELD DESCRIPTION     POSITIONS     DATA TYPE     DECIMALS
Name of item          1–15          Character
Price of item         16–20         Numeric       2
Quantity in stock     21–24         Numeric       0
```

Figure 3-20 Inventory file description

The inventory file description in Figure 3-20 shows that each item's name occupies the first 15 characters of each record in the file. Some item names may require all 15 positions, for example "12 by 16 carpet", which contains exactly 15 characters including spaces. Other item names require fewer than the allotted 15 positions, for example "door mat". In such cases, the remaining allotted positions remain blank. Whether the item name requires all 15 positions or not, the price for each item begins in position 16 of each input record.

The price of any item in the inventory file is allowed five positions, 16 through 20. Two of the positions are reserved for decimal places. Typically, decimal points themselves are not stored in data files; they are **implied** or **assumed**. Also typically, numeric data are stored with leading zeros so that all allotted positions are occupied. Thus an item valued at $345.67 is stored as 34567, and an item valued at $1.23 is stored as 00123.

 Decimal points are implied in data files, but occupy positions on printed reports. Within data files, it is most efficient to save space. On printed reports, it is most important to represent information in a way that is easy for the reader to interpret.

Leading zeros fill numeric fields within files, but are not used on printed reports. Within data files, numeric fields must be totally numeric so spaces are not allowed within numeric fields. On printed reports, information must be easy for the reader to interpret; readers usually do not expect to see leading zeros in numeric data.

3

Typically, programmers create one program variable for each field that is part of the input file. In addition to the field descriptions contained in the input documentation, the programmer might be given specific variable names to use for each field, particularly if such variable names must agree with those other programmers working on the project are using. In many cases, however, programmers are allowed to choose their own variable names. Therefore, you can choose `itemName`, `nameOfItem`, `itemDescription`, or any other reasonable one-word variable name when you refer to the item name within your program. The variable names you use within your program need not match constants printed on the report. Thus, the variable `nameOfItem` might hold the characters that will print under the column heading NAME OF ITEM.

Recall the data hierarchy relationship introduced in Chapter 1:

- Database
- File
- Record
- Field
- Character

Whether the inventory file is part of a database or not, it will contain many records; each record will contain an item name, price, and quantity, which are fields. In turn, the field that holds the name of an item might contain up to 15 characters, for example "12 by 16 carpet", "blue miniblinds", or "diskette holder".

Organizations may use different forms to relay the information about records and fields, but the very least the programmer needs to know is:

- What is the name of the file?
- What data does it contain?
- How much room does the file and each of its fields take up?
- What type of data is each field—character or numeric?

The inventory file description in Figure 3-20 appears to contain all the information the programmer needs to create the output requested in Figure 3-13. The output lists each item's name, price, and quantity, and the input records clearly contain that data. Often, however, a file description more closely resembles the description in Figure 3-21.

```
INVENTORY FILE DESCRIPTION
File name: INVTRY
FIELD DESCRIPTION              POSITIONS      DATA TYPE      DECIMALS
Item number                   1-4            Numeric        0
Name of item                  5-19           Character
Size                          20             Numeric        0
Manufacturing cost of item    21-25          Numeric        2
Retail price of item          26-30          Numeric        2
Quantity in stock             31-34          Numeric        0
Reorder point                 35-38          Numeric        0
Sales rep                     39-48          Character
Sales last year               49-54          Numeric        0
```

Figure 3-21   Expanded inventory file description

The file description in Figure 3-21 contains nine fields. With this file description, it's harder to pinpoint the information needed for the report; but the necessary data fields are available, and you still can write the program. The input file contains more information than you need for the report you want to print, so you will ignore some of the input fields, such as item number and sales rep. These fields certainly may be used in other reports within the company. Typically, data input files contain more data than any one program requires.

However, if the input file description resembles Figure 3-22, then there is not enough data to produce the requested report.

```
INVENTORY FILE DESCRIPTION
File name: INVTRY
FIELD DESCRIPTION              POSITIONS      DATA TYPE      DECIMALS
Item number                   1-4            Numeric        0
Name of item                  5-19           Character
Size                          20             Numeric        0
Manufacturing cost of item    21-25          Numeric        2
Retail price of item          26-30          Numeric        2
Reorder point                 35-38          Numeric        0
Sales rep                     39-48          Character
Sales last year               49-54          Numeric        0
```

Figure 3-22   Insufficient inventory file description

In Figure 3-22, there is no indication that the input file contains a figure for quantity in stock. If the user really needs (or wants) the report as requested, it's out of the programmer's hands until the data can be collected from some source.

Each field printed on a report need not exist in the same format on the input file. Assume that a user requests a report in the format shown in Figure 3-23, and that the input file description is the one in Figure 3-22. In this case, it's difficult to determine whether you can create the requested report because the input file does not contain a `profit` field. However, since the input data includes the company's cost and the company's selling price for each item, you can calculate the `profit` within your program and produce the desired output.

```
                1111111111222222222233333333334444444444555555555
      1234567890123456789012345678901234567890123456789012345678901234567
 1
 2              PROFIT REPORT
 3
 4     ITEM NUMBER        PRICE      COST        PROFIT
 5
 6         9999           999.99     999.99      999.99
 7         9999           999.99     999.99      999.99
 8
 9
10
11
12
13
14
```

Figure 3-23   Requested profit report

COMPLETING THE DOCUMENTATION

When you have designed the output and confirmed that it is possible to produce it from the input, then you can plan the logic of the program, code the program, and test the program. The original output design, input description, flowchart or pseudocode, and program code all become part of the program documentation. These pieces of documentation typically are stored together in a binder within the programming department of an organization, where they can be studied later when program changes become necessary.

In addition to this program documentation, you typically must create user documentation. **User documentation** includes all the manuals or other instructional materials that nontechnical people use, as well as the operating instructions that computer operators and data-entry personnel need. It needs to be written clearly, in plain language, with reasonable expectations of the users' expertise. Within a small organization, the programmer may prepare the user documentation. In a large organization, user documentation is usually prepared by technical writers or systems analysts, who oversee programmers' work and coordinate programmers' efforts. These professionals consult with the programmer to ensure that the user documentation is complete and accurate.

The areas addressed in user documentation may include:

- How to prepare input for the program
- To whom the output should be distributed
- How to interpret the normal output

- How to interpret and react to any error message generated by the program
- How frequently the program needs to run

 Complete documentation also might include operations support documentation. This type of documentation provides backup and recovery information,
run-time instructions, and security considerations for computer center personnel who run large applications within data centers.

All these issues must be addressed before a program can be fully functional in an organization. When users throughout an organization can supply input data to computer programs and obtain the information they need in order to do their jobs well, then a skilled
programmer has provided a complete piece of work.

CHAPTER SUMMARY

- ◘ Programmers break programming problems down into smaller, reasonable units
  called modules, subroutines, procedures, functions, or methods. Modularization
  provides abstraction, allows multiple programmers to work on a problem, makes
  it easy to reuse your work, and allows you to identify structures more easily.

- ◘ When you create a module or subroutine, you give the module a name that a
  calling program uses when the module is about to execute. The flowchart symbol used to call a subroutine is a rectangle with a bar across the top; the name
  of the module that you are calling is inside the rectangle. You draw each module separately with its own sentinel symbols.

- ◘ A module can call other modules.

- ◘ Declaring a variable involves providing a name for the memory location where
  the computer will store the variable value and notifying the computer what
  type of data to expect.

- ◘ You can use a hierarchy chart to illustrate modules' relationships.

- ◘ Documentation refers to all of the supporting material that goes with a program.

- ◘ Output documentation is usually written first. You can design a printed report
  on a printer spacing chart to represent both constant and variable data.

- ◘ A file description lists the data that are contained in a file, including a description, size, and data type. Typically, numeric data are stored with leading zeros
  and without decimal points.

- ◘ In addition to program documentation, you typically must create user documentation, which includes the manuals or other instructional materials that
  nontechnical people use, as well as the operating instructions that computer
  operators and data-entry personnel may need.

EXERCISES

1. Redraw the following flowchart so that the compensation calculations are in a module.

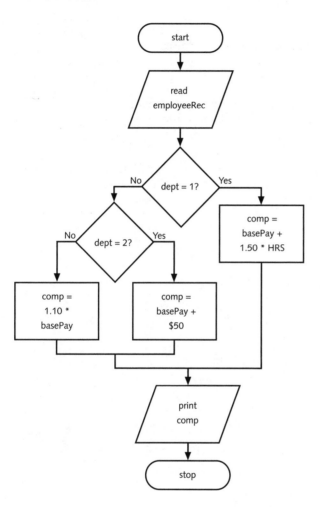

3

2. Rewrite the following pseudocode so the discount calculations are in a module.

```
start
   read customerRecord
   if quantityOrdered > 100 then
      discount = .20
   else
      if quantityOrdered > 12 then
         discount = .10
      endif
   endif
   total = priceEach * quantityOrdered
   total = total - discount * total
   print total
end
```

3. What are the final values of variables a, b, and c after the following program runs?

```
start
   a = 2
   b = 4
   c = 10
   while c > 6
       changeBAndC()
   if a = 2 then
       changeA()
   endif
   if c = 10 then
       changeA()
   else
       changeBAndC()
   endif
end

changeBAndC()
   b = b + 1
   c = c - 1
return

changeA()
   a = a + 1
   b = b - 1
return
```

4. Draw a typical hierarchy chart for a paycheck-producing program. Try to think of at least 10 separate modules that might be included.

5. Design a print chart for a payroll roster that is intended to list the following items for every employee: employee's first name, last name, and salary.

6. Design a print chart for a payroll roster that is intended to list the following items for every employee: employee's first name, last name, hours worked, rate per hour, gross pay, federal withholding tax, state withholding tax, union dues, and net pay.

7. Given the following input file description, determine if there is enough information provided to produce each of the requested reports:

```
INSURANCE PREMIUM LIST
File name: INSPREM
FIELD DESCRIPTION          POSITIONS     DATA TYPE      DECIMALS
Name of insured
     driver                1—40          Character
Birth date                41—46         Numeric          0
Gender                    47            Character
Make of car               48—57         Character
Year of car               58—61         Numeric          0
Miles driven
     per year             62—67         Numeric          0
Number of
     traffic tickets      68—69         Numeric          0
```

a. A list of the names of all insured drivers

b. A list of very high-risk insured drivers, defined as male, under 25 years old, with more than two tickets

c. A list of low-risk insured drivers, defined as those with no tickets in the last three years, and over 30 years old

d. A list of insured drivers to contact about a special premium offer for those with a passenger car who drive under 10,000 miles per year

8. Given the INSPREM file description in Exercise 7, design a print chart to satisfy each of the following requests:

a. A list of every driver's name and make of car

b. A list of the names of all insured drivers who drive more than 20,000 miles per year

c. A list of the name, gender, make of car, and year of car for all drivers who have more than two tickets

d. A report that summarizes the number of tickets held by drivers who were born in 1940 or before, from 1941–1960, from 1961–1980, and from 1981 on

e. A report that summarizes the number of tickets held by drivers in the four birth-date categories listed in Part d, grouped by gender

3

4

WRITING A
COMPLETE PROGRAM

After studying Chapter 4, you should be able to:
- Plan the mainline logic for a complete program.
- Describe typical housekeeping tasks.
- Describe tasks typically performed in the main loop of a program.
- Describe tasks performed in the end-of-job module.

UNDERSTANDING THE MAINLINE LOGICAL FLOW THROUGH A PROGRAM

You're ready to plan the logic for your first complete computer program. The output is an inventory report, as shown in Figure 4-1. The report lists inventory items along with the price, cost, and profit of each item.

```
              1111111111222222222233333333334444444444555555555566
     1234567890123456789012345678901234567890123456789012345678901
 1
 2                          INVENTORY REPORT
 3
 4     ITEM                 RETAIL PRICE    MANUFACTURING    PROFIT PER
 5     DESCRIPTION          EACH            COST EACH        ITEM
 6
 7     XXXXXXXXXXXXXXXX     999.99           999.99          999.99
 8     XXXXXXXXXXXXXXXX     999.99           999.99          999.99
 9
10
11
12
13
14
```

Figure 4-1 Print chart for inventory report

Figure 4-2 shows the input INVENTORY file description.

```
INVENTORY FILE DESCRIPTION
File name: INVENTORY
FIELD DESCRIPTION        POSITIONS       DATA TYPE       DECIMALS
Item name                1–15            Character
Price                    16–20           Numeric             2
Cost                     21–25           Numeric             2
Quantity in stock        26–29           Numeric             0
```

Figure 4-2 Inventory file description

In some systems, filenames are limited to eight characters, so INVENTORY might be an unacceptable filename.

Examine the print chart and the input file description. Your first task is to determine whether you have all the data you need to produce the report. The output requires the item name, price, and cost, and you can see that all three are data items on the input file. The output also requires a profit figure for each item; you can determine the profit by subtracting an item's cost from its selling price. The input record contains an additional field, "Quantity in stock." Input records often contain more data than an application needs, so you will ignore this field in your program. You have all the necessary data so you can begin to plan the program.

Where should you begin? It's wise to try to understand the big picture first. You can write a program that reads records from an input file and produces a printed report as a **procedural program**—that is, a program in which one procedure follows another from beginning until the end. You write the entire set of instructions for a procedural program, and when the program executes, each instruction takes place one at a time following your program's logic. The overall or **mainline logic** of almost every procedural computer program can follow a general structure that consists of three distinct parts:

1. Performing housekeeping, or initialization tasks. **Housekeeping** includes steps you must perform at the beginning of a program to get ready for the rest of the program.

2. Performing the main loop within the program. The **main loop** contains the steps that are repeated for every record.

3. Performing the end-of-job routine. The **end-of-job routine** holds the steps you take at the end of the program to finish the application.

Not all programs are procedural; some are object-oriented. A distinguishing feature of many object-oriented programs is that the user determines the timing of events in the main loop of the program by using an input device such as a mouse. As you advance in your knowledge of programming, you will learn more about object-oriented techniques.

You can write any procedural program as one long series of program language statements, but most programmers prefer to break their programs into at least three parts. The main program can call the three major modules as shown in the flowchart and pseudocode in Figure 4-3. The module or subroutine names, of course, are entirely up to the programmer.

Figure 4-4 shows the hierarchy chart for this program.

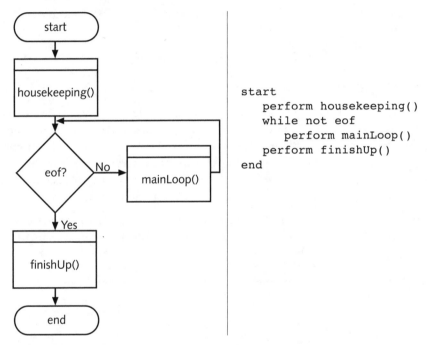

```
start
    perform housekeeping()
    while not eof
        perform mainLoop()
    perform finishUp()
end
```

Figure 4-3   Flowchart and pseudocode of mainline logic

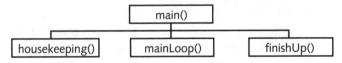

Figure 4-4   Hierarchy chart for inventory report program

Breaking down a big program into three basic procedures helps keep the job manageable, allowing you to tackle a large job one step at a time. Dividing the work into routines allows you to assign the three major procedures to three different programmers if you choose. It also helps you keep the program structured.

HOUSEKEEPING TASKS

Housekeeping tasks include all the steps that must take place at the beginning of a program. Very often, this includes four major tasks:

- You declare variables.
- You open files.
- You perform any one-time-only tasks, such as printing headings at the beginning of a report.
- You read the first input record.

Declaring Variables

Your first task in writing any program is to **declare variables**. When you declare variables, you assign reasonable names to memory locations so you can store and retrieve data there. Declaring a variable involves selecting a name and a type. When you declare a variable in program code, the operating system will reserve space in memory to hold the contents of the variable. It will use the type (`num` or `char`) to determine how to store the information; it stores numeric and character values in different formats.

For example, within the inventory report program you need to supply variable names for the data fields that appear in each input record. You might decide on the variable names and types shown in Figure 4-5.

```
char    invItemName
num     invPrice
num     invCost
num     invQuantity
```

Figure 4-5   Variable declarations for the inventory file

 Some languages require that you provide storage size in addition to a type and name for each variable. Other languages provide a predetermined amount of storage based on the variable type; for example, four bytes for an integer or one byte for a character. Also, many languages require you to provide a length for strings of characters.

You can provide any names you choose for your variables. When you write another program that uses the same input file, you are free to choose completely new variable names. Similarly, other programmers can write programs that use the same file and choose their own variable names. The variable names just represent memory positions and are internal to your program. The files do not contain the variable names; files contain only data. When you read the characters "Cotton shirt" from an input file, it doesn't matter whether you store those characters at a memory location named `invItemName`, `nameOfItem`, `productDescription`, or any other one-word variable name.

Each of the four variable declarations in Figure 4-5 contains a type (character or numeric) and a name. You can choose any one-word names for the variables, but a typical practice involves beginning similar variables with a common **prefix**, for example, `inv`. In a large program in which you eventually declare dozens of variables, the `inv` prefix will help you immediately identify a variable as part of the inventory file.

Creating the inventory report shown in Figure 4-1 involves using the `invItemName`, `invPrice`, and `invCost` fields, but you do not need to use the `invQuantity` field in this program. However, the information regarding quantity does take room on the input file. If you imagine the surface of a disk as pictured in Figure 4-6, you can envision how the data fields follow one another in the file.

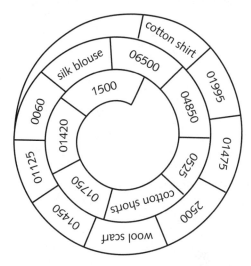

Figure 4-6   Representation of typical data for INVENTORY file

When you ask the program to read in an inventory record, four "chunks" of data will be transferred from the input device to the computer's main memory: name, price, cost, and quantity. When you declare the variables that represent the input data, you must provide a memory position for each of the four pieces of data, whether or not they all are used within this program.

 In COBOL you can use the generic name FILLER for all unused data positions. This frees you from the task of creating variable names for items you do not intend to use.

Considering that dozens of programs within the organization might access the INVENTORY file, some organizations create the data file descriptions for you. This system is efficient because the description of variable names and types is stored in one location, and each programmer who uses the file simply imports the data file description into his or her own program. Of course, the organization must provide the programmer with documentation specifying the chosen names.

In most programming languages you can give a group of associated variables a **group name**. Just as it is easier to refer to "The Andersons" than it is to list "Nancy, Bud, Jim, Tom, Julie, Jane, Kate, and John," the benefit of using a group name is the ability to reference several variables with one all-encompassing name. For example, writing `read invRecord` is simpler than writing `read invItemName, invPrice, invCost, and invQuantity`. How you assign a group name to several variables differs in each programming language. This book follows the convention of underlining any group name and indenting the group members beneath, as shown in Figure 4-7.

```
invRecord
    char    invItemName
    num     invPrice
    num     invCost
    num     invQuantity
```

Figure 4-7   Variable declarations for the inventory file including a group name

A group of variables is often called a *data structure*, or more simply, a *structure*. Some object-oriented languages refer to a group as a *class*, although a class often contains methods as well as variables.

In addition to declaring variables, sometimes you want to provide a variable with an initial value. Providing a variable with a value when you create it is known as **initialization** or **defining the variable**. For example, for the inventory report shown in Figure 4-1, you might want to create a variable named `mainHeading` and store the value "INVENTORY REPORT" in that variable. The declaration is `char mainHeading = "INVENTORY REPORT"`. This indicates that `mainHeading` is a character variable, and that the character contents are the words "INVENTORY REPORT".

Declaring a variable provides it with a name and type. *Defining* a variable provides it with a value.

In some programming languages you can declare a variable such as `mainHeading` to be constant, or never changing. Even though `invItemName`, `invPrice`, and the other fields in the input file will hold a variety of values when a program executes, the `mainHeading` will never change.

In most programming languages, if you do not provide an initial value when declaring a variable, then the value is unknown or **garbage**. Some programming languages do provide you with an automatic starting value; for example in BASIC or RPG, all numeric variables automatically begin with the value zero. However, in C++, C#, Java, Pascal, and COBOL, variables do not receive any initial value unless you provide one. No matter which programming language you use, it is always clearest to provide a value for those variables that require them.

 Be especially careful to make sure all variables you use in calculations have initial values. If you perform arithmetic with garbage values, the result also will contain garbage.

When you declare the variables `invItemName`, `invPrice`, `invCost`, and `invQuantity`, you do not provide them with any initial value. The values for these variables will be assigned when the first file record is read into memory. It would be *legal* to assign a value to input file record variables—for example, `invItemName = "Cotton shirt"`, but it would be a waste of time and might mislead others who read your program. The first `invItemName` will come from an input device and may or may not be "Cotton shirt".

The report illustrated in Figure 4-1 contains three individual heading lines. The most common practice is to declare one variable or constant for each of these lines. The three declarations are as follows:

```
char mainHeading = "INVENTORY REPORT"
char columnHead1 = "ITEM            RETAIL PRICE
    MANUFACTURING        PROFIT PER"
char columnHead2 = "DESCRIPTION  EACH
    COST EACH           ITEM"
```

Within the program, when it is time to write the heading lines to an output device, you will code:

```
print mainHeading
print columnHead1
print columnHead2
```

You are not required to create variables for your headings. Your program can contain the following statements in which you use literal strings of characters instead of variable names. The printed results are the same either way.

```
print "INVENTORY REPORT"
print "ITEM            RETAIL PRICE MANUFACTURING PROFIT PER"
print "DESCRIPTION  EACH            COST EACH      ITEM"
```

Using variable names, as in `print mainHeading`, is usually more convenient than spelling out the heading's contents, especially if you will use the headings in multiple locations within your program.

When you write a program, you type spaces between the words within column headings so the spacing matches the print chart you created for the program. For convenience, some languages provide you with a tab character. The goal is to provide well-spaced output in readable columns.

Dividing the headings into three lines is not required either, but it is a common practice. In most programming languages you could write all the headings in one statement, using a code that indicates a new line at every appropriate position. Alternatively, most programming languages let you produce a character for output without advancing to a new line. You could write out the headings one character at a time, advancing to a new one only after all the line's characters had been individually printed, although this approach seems painstakingly detailed. Storing and writing one complete line at a time is a reasonable compromise.

Every programming language provides you with a means to physically advance printer paper to the top of a page when you print the first heading. Similarly, every language provides you with a means for producing double- and triple-spaced lines of text. Because the methods differ from language to language, examples in this book assume that if a print chart shows a heading that prints at the top of the page and then skips a line, when you create a corresponding variable like `mainHeading`, it also will print in this manner. You can add the appropriate language-specific codes to implement the `mainHeading` spacing when you write the actual computer program. Similarly, if you create a print chart that shows detail lines as double-spaced, assume your detail lines will double-space when you execute the step to write them.

Often you must create dozens of variables when you write a computer program. If you are using a flowchart to diagram the logic, it is physically impossible to fit the variables in one flowchart box. Therefore, you might want to use an annotation symbol. Similarly, when writing pseudocode, it is often more convenient to place variable names off to the side. The beginning of a flowchart for the `housekeeping()` module of the inventory report program is shown in Figure 4-8.

You learned about the annotation symbol in Chapter 3.

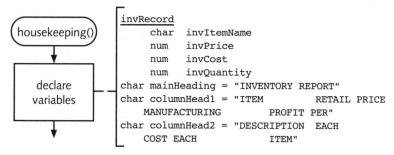

Figure 4-8   Beginning of flowchart for housekeeping() module for the inventory report program

Notice that the three heading variables defined in Figure 4-8 are not indented under `invRecord` like the `invRecord` fields are. This shows that although `invItemName`, `invPrice`, `invCost`, and `invQuantity` are part of the `invRecord` group, `mainHeading`, `columnHead1`, and `columnHead2` are not.

Opening Files

If a program will use input files, you must tell the computer where the input is coming from—for example, a specific disk drive, CD, or tape drive. This process is known as **opening a file**. Since a disk can have many files stored on it, the program also needs to know the name of the file being opened. In many languages if no input file is opened, input is accepted from a default or **standard input device**, most often the keyboard.

If a program will have output, you must also open a file for output. Perhaps the output file will be sent to a disk or tape. Although you might not think of a printed report as a file, computers treat a printer as just another output device, and if output will go to a printer, then you must open the printer output device as well. Again, if no file is opened, a default or **standard output device**, usually the monitor, is used.

When you flowchart, you usually write the command to open the files within a parallelogram. You use the parallelogram because it is the input/output symbol, and you are opening the input and output devices. You can use an annotation box to list the files that you open, as shown in Figure 4-9.

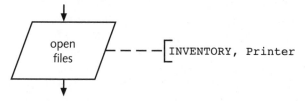

Figure 4-9   Specifying files that you open

Printing Headings

A common housekeeping task involves printing headings at the top of a report. In the inventory report example, three lines of headings appear at the beginning of the report. In this example, printing the heading lines is straightforward:

```
print mainHeading
print columnHead1
print columnHead2
```

Reading the First Input Record

The last task you execute in the housekeeping() module of most computer programs is to read the first data record in memory. When you read the four data fields for the inventory file data, you can write read invItemName, invPrice, invCost, invQuantity, but if you have declared a group name such as invRecord, it is simpler to write read invRecord. Using the group name is a shortcut to writing each field name.

When the last task within housekeeping() reads the first invRecord, the first task following housekeeping() is to check for eof on the file that contains the inventory records. An input device recognizes it has reached the end of a file when it attempts to read a record and finds no records available. Recall the mainline logic of the inventory report program from Figure 4-3—eof is tested immediately after housekeeping() ends.

If the input file has no records, when you read the first record the computer will recognize the end-of-file condition and proceed to the finishUp() module, never executing mainLoop(). More commonly, an input file does have records, and after the first read the computer will determine that the eof condition is false, and the logic will proceed to the mainLoop().

Immediately after reading from a file, the next step always should determine whether eof was encountered. Notice in Figure 4-3 that the eof question always follows both the housekeeping() module and the mainLoop() module. When the last instruction in each of these modules reads a record, then the eof question correctly follows each read instruction immediately.

Not reading the first record within the housekeeping() module is a mistake. If housekeeping() does not include a step to read a record from the input file, you must read a record as the first step in the mainLoop() as shown on the left side of Figure 4-10. In this program a record is read, a profit is calculated, and a line is printed. Then, if it is not eof, another record is read, a profit calculated, and a line printed. The program works well, reading records, calculating profits, and printing information until reaching a read command where the computer encounters the eof condition. When this last read occurs, the next steps involve computing a profit and writing a line—but there isn't any data to process. Depending on the programming language you use, either garbage data will calculate and print, or a repeat of the data from the last record before eof will print.

The figure on the right side of Figure 4-10 shows correct record-reading logic. The appropriate place for the priming record **read** is at the end of the preliminary housekeeping steps, and the appropriate place for all subsequent reads is at the end of the main processing loop.

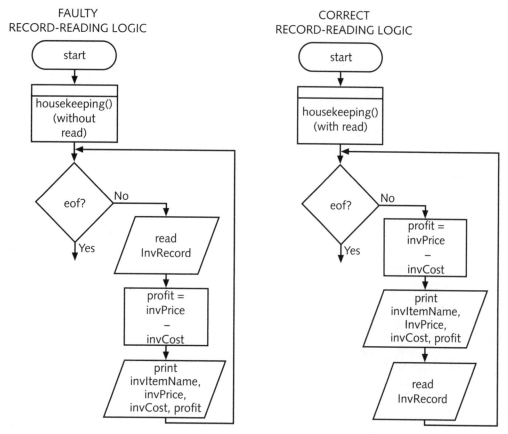

Figure 4-10   Comparing faulty and correct record-reading logic

 Reading an input record in the housekeeping() section is an example of a priming read. You learned about the priming read in Chapter 2.

 In some modern programming languages, such as Visual Basic, read commands can look ahead to determine if the *next* record is empty. With these languages, the priming read is no longer necessary. Because most languages do not currently have this type of read statement, this book will use the conventional priming read.

Figure 4-11 shows a completed housekeeping() routine for the inventory program in both flowchart and pseudocode versions.

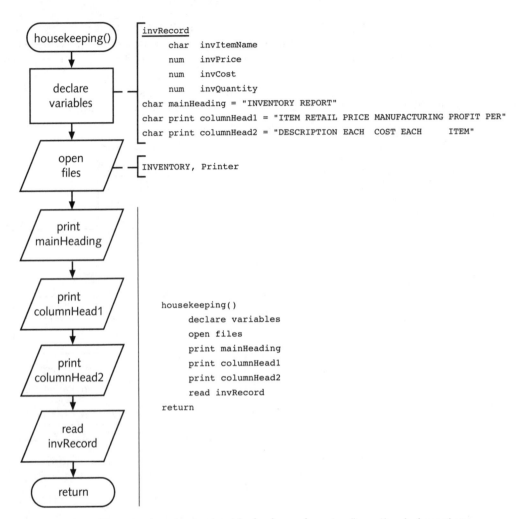

Figure 4-11 Flowchart and pseudocode for housekeeping() routine in inventory
report program

As an alternative to including `print mainHeading, print columnHead1`, and
`print columnHead2` within the `housekeeping()` module, you can place the three
heading line statements in their own subroutine. In this case, the flowchart and
pseudocode for `housekeeping()` will look like Figure 4-12, with the steps in the newly
created `headings()` module appearing in Figure 4-13. Either approach is fine; the logic
of the program is the same whether or not the heading line statements are segregated into
their own routine. The programmer can decide on the program organization that makes
the most sense.

4

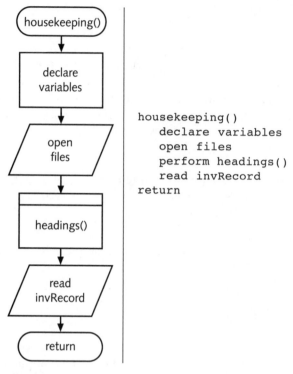

```
housekeeping()
   declare variables
   open files
   perform headings()
   read invRecord
return
```

Figure 4-12   Flowchart and pseudocode for housekeeping() with headings() module

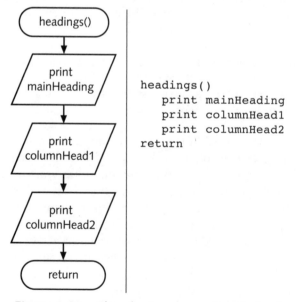

```
headings()
   print mainHeading
   print columnHead1
   print columnHead2
return
```

Figure 4-13   Flowchart and pseudocode for headings() module

WRITING THE MAIN LOOP

After you declare the variables for a program and perform the housekeeping tasks, the "real work" of the program begins. The inventory report described at the beginning of this chapter and depicted in Figure 4-1 needs just one set of variables and one set of headings, yet there might be hundreds or thousands of inventory items to process. The **main loop** of a program, controlled by the `eof` decision, is the program's "workhorse." Each data record will pass once through the main loop where calculations are performed with the data and the results printed.

 If the inventory report contains more records than fit on a page of output, you probably will want to print a new set of headings at the top of each page. You will learn how to do this in Chapter 7.

For the inventory report program to work, the `mainLoop()` module must include three steps:

1. Calculate the profit for an item.

2. Print the item information on the report.

3. Read the next inventory record.

At the end of `housekeeping()`, you read one data record into the computer's memory. As the first step in the `mainLoop()`, you can calculate an item's profit by subtracting its manufacturing cost from its retail price: `profit = invPrice - invCost`. The name `profit` is the programmer-created variable name for a new spot in computer memory where the value of the profit is stored.

 Recall that the standard way to express mathematical statements is to assign values from the right side of an equal sign to the left. That is, `profit = invPrice - invCost` assigns a value to `profit`. The statement `invPrice - invCost = profit` is an illegal statement.

Because you have a new variable, you must add `profit` to the list of declared variables at the beginning of the program. Programmers often work back and forth between the variable list and the logical steps during the creation of a program, listing some of the variables they will need as soon as they start to plan and adding others later as they think of them. Since `profit` will hold the result of a mathematical calculation, you should declare it as a numeric variable when you add it to the variable list as shown in Figure 4-14. Notice that like the headings, `profit` is not indented under `invRecord`. You want to show that `profit` is not part of the `invRecord` group; instead, it is a separate variable that you are declaring to store a calculated value.

You can declare `mainHeading`, `columnHead1`, `columnHead2`, and `profit` in any order. The important point is that none of these four variables are part of the `invRecord` group.

```
invRecord
        char    invItemName
        num     invPrice
        num     invCost
        num     invQuantity
char mainHeading = "INVENTORY REPORT"
char columnHead1 = "ITEM              RETAIL PRICE   MANUFACTURING   PROFIT PER"
char columnHead2 = "DESCRIPTION       EACH           COST EACH       ITEM"
num profit
```

Figure 4-14   Variable list for inventory report program, including profit

 Although you can give a variable any legal name, you probably do not want to begin the name for the variable that holds the profit value with the `inv` prefix, because `profit` is not part of the INVENTORY input file. Beginning `profit` with the `inv` prefix might mislead those who read your program.

After you determine an item's profit, you can write a detail line of information on the inventory report: `print invItemName, invPrice, invCost, profit`.

The last step in the `mainLoop()` module of the inventory report program involves reading in the next `invRecord`. Figure 4-15 shows the flowchart and pseudocode for `mainLoop()`.

Just as headings are printed one full line at a time, detail lines are also printed one line at a time. You can print each field separately, as in the following code, but it is clearer and most efficient to write one full line at a time.

```
print invItemName
print invPrice
print invCost
print profit
```

In most programming languages you also have the option of calculating the profit and printing it in one statement, as in the following:

```
print invItemName, invPrice, invCost, invPrice - invCost
```

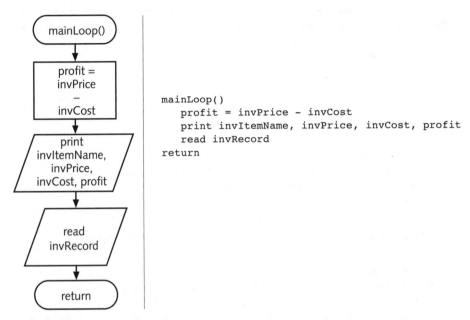

```
mainLoop()
    profit = invPrice - invCost
    print invItemName, invPrice, invCost, profit
    read invRecord
return
```

Figure 4-15   Flowchart and pseudocode for mainLoop() of inventory report program

If the language you use allows this type of statement in which a calculation takes place within the output statement, it is up to you to decide which format to use. Performing the arithmetic as part of the **print** statement allows you to avoid declaring a **profit** variable. However, if you need the **profit** figure for further calculations, then it makes sense to compute the profit and store it in a **profit** field. Using a separate **work variable** or **work field** such as **profit** to temporarily hold a calculation is never wrong, and often it's the clearest course of action.

After the detail line has been written, the last step you take before leaving the **mainLoop()** module is to read the next record from the input file into memory. When you exit the **mainLoop()**, the logic flows back to the **eof** question in the mainline logic. If it is not **eof**—that is, if an additional data record exists—then you enter the **mainLoop()** again, compute profit on the second record, print the detail line, and read the third record.

Eventually, during an execution of the **mainLoop()**, the program will read a new record and encounter the end of the file. Then when you ask the **eof** question in the main line of the program, the answer will be *yes*, and the program will not enter the **mainLoop()** again. Instead, the program logic will enter the **finishUp()** routine.

PERFORMING END-OF-JOB TASKS

Within any program, the end-of-job routine holds the steps you must take at the end of the program after all input records are processed. Some end-of-job modules print summaries or grand totals at the end of a report. Others might print a message such as "End of Report" so readers can be confident that they have received all the information that should be included. Very often, end-of-job modules must close any open files.

The end-of-job module for the inventory report program is very simple. The print chart does not indicate that any special messages, such as "Thank you for reading this report", print after the detail lines end. Likewise, there are no required summary or total lines; nothing special happens. Only one task needs to be performed in the end-of-job routine that this program calls finishUp(). In housekeeping() you opened files; in finishUp() you close them. The complete finishUp() module is flowcharted and written in pseudocode in Figure 4-16.

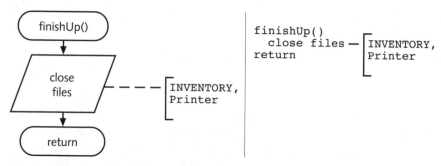

Figure 4-16   Flowchart and pseudocode of finishUp() module

Many programmers wouldn't bother with a subroutine for just one statement, but as you create more complicated programs, your end-of-job routines will get bigger and it will make more sense to see the necessary job-finishing tasks together in a module.

CHAPTER SUMMARY

- ❑ When you write a complete program, you first determine whether you have all the necessary data to produce the report. Then you plan the mainline logic, which usually includes modules to perform housekeeping, a main loop that contains the steps which repeat for every record, and an end-of-job routine.

- ❑ Housekeeping tasks include all steps that must take place at the beginning of a program. These tasks include declaring variables, opening files, performing any one-time-only tasks, such as printing headings at the beginning of a report, and reading the first input record.

❐ The main loop of a program is controlled by the eof decision. Each data record will pass once through the main loop where calculations are performed with the data and results are printed.

❐ Within any program, the end-of-job module holds the steps you must take at the end of the program after all the input records have been processed. Typical tasks include printing summaries, grand totals, or final messages at the end of a report, and closing all open files.

EXERCISES

1. A pet store owner needs a weekly sales report. The output consists of a printed report titled PET SALES. Fields printed on output are: type of animal and price. The input file description is shown below.

File name: PETS

FIELD DESCRIPTION	POSITIONS	DATA TYPE	DECIMALS
Type of Animal	1–20	Character	
Price of Animal	21–26	Numeric	2

a. Design the print chart, draw the hierarchy chart, and draw the flowchart for this program.

b. Design the print chart, draw the hierarchy chart, and write the pseudocode for this program.

2. An employer wants to produce a personnel report. The output consists of a printed report entitled ACTIVE PERSONNEL. Fields printed on output are: last name of employee, first name of employee, and current salary. The input file description is shown below.

File name: PERSONNEL

FIELD DESCRIPTION	POSITIONS	DATA TYPE	DECIMALS
Last Name	1–15	Character	
First Name	16–30	Character	
Soc. Sec. Number	31–39	Numeric	0
Department	40–41	Numeric	0
Current Salary	42–47	Numeric	2

a. Design the print chart, draw the hierarchy chart, and draw the flowchart for this program.

b. Design the print chart, draw the hierarchy chart, and write the pseudocode for this program.

3. An employer wants to produce a personnel report that shows the end result if she gives everyone a 10 percent raise in salary. The output consists of a printed report entitled PROJECTED RAISES. Fields printed on output are: last name of

employee, first name of employee, current salary, and projected salary. The input file description is shown below.

File name: PERSONNEL

FIELD DESCRIPTION	POSITIONS	DATA TYPE	DECIMALS
Last Name	1–15	Character	
First Name	16–30	Character	
Soc. Sec. Number	31–39	Numeric	0
Department	40–41	Numeric	0
Current Salary	42–47	Numeric	2

a. Design the print chart, draw the hierarchy chart, and draw the flowchart for this program.

b. Design the print chart, draw the hierarchy chart, and write the pseudocode for this program.

4. A furniture store maintains an inventory file that includes data about every item it sells. The manager wants a report that lists each stock number, description, and profit, which is the retail price minus the wholesale price. The fields include a stock number, description, wholesale price, and retail price. The input file description is shown below.

File name: FURNITURE

FIELD DESCRIPTION	POSITIONS	DATA TYPE	DECIMALS
Stock Number	1–4	Numeric	0
Description	5–29	Character	
Wholesale Price	30–35	Numeric	2
Retail Price	36–41	Numeric	2

a. Design the print chart, draw the hierarchy chart, and draw the flowchart for this program.

b. Design the print chart, draw the hierarchy chart, and write the pseudocode for this program.

5. A summer camp keeps a record for every camper including first name, last name, birth date, and skill scores that range from 1 to 10 in four areas: swimming, tennis, horsemanship, and crafts. The camp wants a printed report listing each camper's data, plus a total score that is the sum of the camper's four skill scores.

a. Design the print chart, draw the hierarchy chart, and draw the flowchart for this program.

b. Design the print chart, draw the hierarchy chart, and write the pseudocode for this program.

6. An employer needs to determine how much tax to withhold for each employee. This withholding amount computes as 20 percent of each employee's weekly pay. The output consists of a printed report entitled WITHHOLDING FOR EACH EMPLOYEE. Fields printed on output are: last name of employee, first name of

employee, hourly pay, weekly pay based on a 40-hour work week, and withholding amount per week. The input file description is shown below.

File name: EMPLOYEES

FIELD DESCRIPTION	POSITIONS	DATA TYPE	DECIMALS
Company ID	1–5	Numeric	0
First Name	6–17	Character	
Last Name	18–29	Character	
Hourly Rate	30–34	Numeric	2

a. Design the print chart, draw the hierarchy chart, and draw the flowchart for this program.

b. Design the print chart, draw the hierarchy chart, and write the pseudocode for this program.

7. A baseball team manager wants a report showing her players' batting statistics. A batting average is computed as hits divided by at-bats and is usually expressed to three decimal positions, for example .235. The output consists of a printed report entitled TEAM STATISTICS. Fields printed on output are: player number, first name, last name, and batting average. The input file description is shown below.

File name: BASEBALL

FIELD DESCRIPTION	POSITIONS	DATA TYPE	DECIMALS
Player Number	1–2	Numeric	0
First Name	3–18	Character	
Last Name	19–35	Character	
At–bats	36–38	Numeric	0
Hits	39–41	Numeric	0

a. Design the print chart, draw the hierarchy chart, and draw the flowchart for this program.

b. Design the print chart, draw the hierarchy chart, and write the pseudocode for this program.

5

MAKING DECISIONS

After studying Chapter 5, you should be able to:

- Evaluate Boolean expressions to make comparisons
- Use the logical comparison operators
- Understand AND logic
- Write AND decisions for efficiency
- Combine decisions in an AND situation
- Avoid common errors in an AND situation
- Understand OR logic
- Avoid common errors in an OR situation
- Write OR decisions for efficiency
- Combine decisions in an OR situation
- Use selections within ranges
- Understand common errors using range checks
- Use decision tables

EVALUATING BOOLEAN EXPRESSIONS TO MAKE COMPARISONS

The reason people think computers are smart lies in the computer program's ability to make decisions. A medical diagnosis program that can decide if your symptoms fit various disease profiles seems quite intelligent, as does a program that can offer you different potential vacation routes based on your destination.

The selection structure (sometimes called a decision structure) involved in such programs is not new to you—it's one of the basic structures of structured programming. See Figures 5-1 and 5-2.

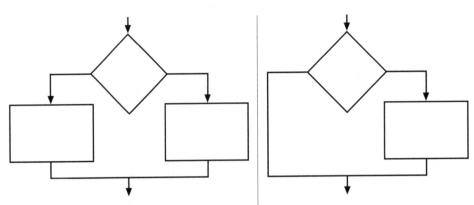

Figure 5-1   The dual-alternative selection
structure

Figure 5-2   The single-alternative selection
structure

You can refer to the structure in Figure 5-1 as a **dual-alternative** or **binary** selection because there are two possible outcomes: depending on the answer to the question represented by the diamond, the logical flow proceeds either to the left branch of the structure or to the right. The choices are mutually exclusive; that is, the logic can flow only to one of the two alternatives, never both. This selection structure also is called an **if-then-else** structure because it fits the statement:

```
if the answer to the question is yes, then
    do something
else
    do somethingElse
endif
```

The flowchart segment in Figure 5-2 represents a **single-alternative** or **unary** selection where action is required for only one outcome of the question. You call this form of the if-then-else structure an **if-then**, because no "else" action is necessary.

You can call a single-alternative decision (or selection) a *single-sided decision*. Similarly, a dual-alternative decision is a *double-sided decision* (or selection).

For example, Figure 5-3 shows the flowchart and pseudocode for a typical if-then-else decision in a business program. Many organizations pay employees time-and-a-half (one and one half times their usual hourly rate) for hours in excess of 40 per week. The logic segments in the figure show this decision.

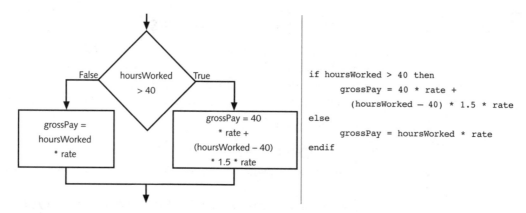

```
if hoursWorked > 40 then
      grossPay = 40 * rate +
            (hoursWorked - 40) * 1.5 * rate
else
      grossPay = hoursWorked * rate
endif
```

5

Figure 5-3   Flowchart and pseudocode for overtime decision

The typical if-then decision in Figure 5-4 shows the employee's paycheck being reduced if the employee participates in the dental plan. No action is taken if the employee is not in the dental plan.

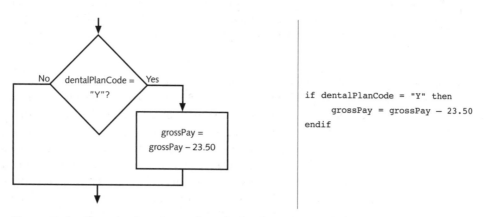

```
if dentalPlanCode = "Y" then
      grossPay = grossPay - 23.50
endif
```

Figure 5-4   Flowchart and pseudocode for dental plan decision

The expressions `hoursWorked > 40` and `dentalPlanCode = "Y"` that appear in Figures 5-3 and 5-4 are Boolean expressions. A **Boolean expression** is one that represents only one of two states, usually expressed as true or false. Every decision you make in a computer program involves evaluating a Boolean expression. True/false evaluation is "natural" from a computer's standpoint because computer circuitry consists of two-state, on-off switches, often represented by 1 or 0, so every computer decision yields a true-or-false, yes-or-no, 1-or-0 result.

George Boole was a mathematician who lived from 1815 to 1864. He approached logic more simply than his predecessors did by expressing logical selections with common algebraic symbols. He is considered the founder of symbolic logic, and Boolean (true/false) expressions are named for him.

USING THE LOGICAL COMPARISON OPERATORS

Usually, you can compare only values that are of the same type; that is, you can compare numeric values to other numeric values and character values to other characters. You can ask every programming question by using only three types of comparisons (Boolean expressions). For any two values that are the same type, you can decide whether:

- The two values are equal.

- The first value is greater than the second value.

- The first value is less than the second value.

Usually, character variables are not considered to be equal unless they are identical, including the spacing and whether or not they appear in upper- or lowercase. For example, "black pen" is *not* equal to "blackpen", "BLACK PEN", or "Black Pen".

Some programming languages allow you to compare a character to a number. If this is the case, then a single character's numeric code value is used in the comparison. For example, most microcomputers use the ASCII coding system in which an uppercase "A" is represented numerically as a 65, an uppercase "B" is a 66, and so on.

In any Boolean expression, the two values used can be either variables or constants. For example, the expression `currentTotal = 100?` compares a variable, `currentTotal`, to a constant, 100. Depending on the `currentTotal` value, the expression is true or false. In the expression `currentTotal = previousTotal?`, both values are variables, and the result is also true or false depending on the values stored in each of the two variables. Although it's legal to do this, you would never use expressions in which you compare two constants, for example `20 = 20?` or `30 = 40?`. Such expressions are considered **trivial** because each always results in the same value: true for the first expression and false for the second.

Each programming language supports its own set of **logical comparison operators**, or comparison symbols, that express these Boolean tests. For example, many languages use the equal sign (=) to express testing for equivalency, so `balanceDue = 0?` compares `balanceDue` to zero. COBOL programmers can use the equal sign, but they also can spell out the expression as in `balanceDue equal to 0?`. C#, C++, and Java programmers use two equal signs to test for equivalency, so they write `balanceDue == 0?` to compare the two values.

The reason some languages use two equal signs for comparisons is to avoid confusion with assignment statements like `balanceDue = 0`. In C++ or Java, this statement only assigns the value 0 to `balanceDue`; it does not compare `balanceDue` to zero.

Whenever you use a comparison operator, you must provide a value on each side of the operator. Comparison operators are sometimes called *binary operators* because of this requirement.

Most languages allow you to use the algebraic signs for greater than (>) and less than (<) to make the corresponding comparisons. Additionally, COBOL, which is very similar to English, allows you to spell out the comparisons in expressions like `daysPastDue is greater than 30` or `packageWeight is less than maximumWeightAllowed`. When you create a flowchart or pseudocode, you can use any form of notation you want to express "greater than" and "less than". It's simplest to use the symbols > and < if you are comfortable with their meaning.

In addition to the three basic comparisons you can make, most programming languages provide three others. For any two values that are the same type, you can decide whether:

- The first is greater than or equal to the second.

- The first is less than or equal to the second.

- The two are not equal.

Most programming languages allow you to express "greater than or equal to" by typing a greater-than sign immediately followed by an equal sign (>=). When you are drawing a flowchart or writing pseudocode, you might prefer a greater-than sign with a line under it (≥) because mathematicians use that symbol to mean "greater than or equal to." However, when you write a program, you type >= as two separate characters because no single key on the keyboard expresses this concept. Similarly, "less than or equal to" is written with two symbols, < followed by =.

The operators >= and <= are always treated as a single unit; no spaces separate the two parts of the operator. Also, the equal sign always appears second. No programming language allows => or =< as comparison operators.

Any logical situation can be expressed using just three types of comparisons: equal, greater than, and less than. You never need the three additional comparisons (greater than or equal, less than or equal, or not equal), but using them often makes decisions more convenient. For example, assume you need to issue a 10% discount to any customer whose age is 65 or greater and charge full price to other customers. You can use the greater-than-or-equal-to symbol to write the logic as follows:

```
if customerAge >= 65 then
        discount = .10
else
        discount = 0
endif
```

As an alternative, if you want to use only the three basic comparisons (=, >, and <) you can express the same logic by writing:

```
if customerAge < 65 then
        discount = 0
else
        discount = .10
endif
```

In any decision for which a >= b is true, then a < b is false. Conversely, if a >= b is false, then a < b is true. By rephrasing the question and swapping the actions taken based on the outcome, you can make the same decision in multiple ways. Asking a question so the positive or true outcome results in the unusual action is often the clearest route. When your company policy is to "provide a discount for those who are 65 and older," the phrase greater than or equal to comes to mind, so it is the most natural to use. Conversely, if your policy is to "provide no discount for those under 65," then it is more natural to use the less than syntax. Either way, the same people receive a discount.

Comparing two amounts to decide if they are *not* equal to each other is the most confusing of all the comparisons. Using "not equal to" in decisions involves thinking in double negatives and makes you prone to include logical errors in your programs. For example, consider the flowchart segment in Figure 5-5.

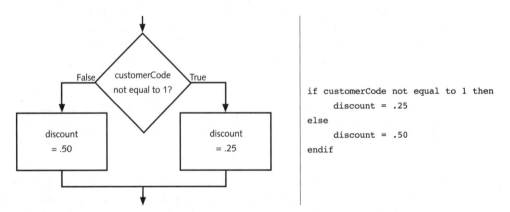

Figure 5-5   Using a negative comparison

In Figure 5-5, if the value of **customerCode** *is* equal to 1, the logical flow follows the false branch of the selection. If **customerCode** not equal to 1 is true, the **discount** is .25; if **customerCode** not equal to 1 is not true, it means the **customerCode** *is* 1, and the **discount** is .50. Even using the phrase "**customerCode not equal to 1 is not true**" is awkward.

Figure 5-6 shows the same decision, this time asked in the positive. Making the decision **if customerCode** *is* **1 then discount = .50** is clearer than trying to determine what **customerCode** is *not*.

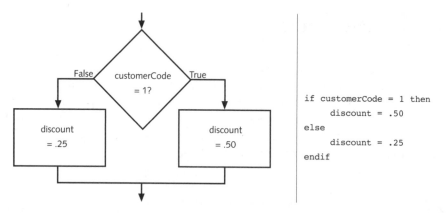

```
if customerCode = 1 then
        discount = .50
else
        discount = .25
endif
```

Figure 5-6   Using the positive equivalent of the negative comparison in Figure 5-5

Besides being awkward to use, the not equal to comparison operator is the one most likely to be different in the various programming languages you may use. COBOL allows you to write "not equal to"; Pascal uses a less-than sign followed immediately by a greater-than sign (<>); C#, C++, C, and Java use an exclamation point followed by an equal sign (!=). In a flowchart or in pseudocode, you can use the symbol that mathematicians use to mean "not equal," an equal sign with a slash through it (≠). When you program, you will not be able to use this symbol because no single key on the keyboard produces it.

 Although NOT comparisons can be awkward to use, there are times when your meaning is clearest if you use one. For example, the mainline logic of many programs, including those you have worked with in this book, includes a statement like while *not* **eof, perform mainLoop()**.

Figure 5-7 summarizes the six comparisons and contrasts trivial (both true and false) and typical examples of their use.

Comparison	Trivial True Example	Trivial False Example	Typical Example
Equal to	7 = 7?	7 = 4?	amtOrdered = 12?
Greater than	12 > 3?	4 > 9?	hoursWorked > 40?
Less than	1 < 8?	13 < 10?	hourlyWage < 5.65?
Greater than or equal to	5 >= 5?	3 >= 9?	customerAge >= 65?
Less than or equal to	4 <= 4?	8 <= 2?	daysOverdue <= 60?
Not equal to	16 <> 3?	18 <> 18?	customerBalance <> 0?

Figure 5-7   Logical comparisons

UNDERSTANDING AND LOGIC

Often you need more than one selection structure to determine whether an action should take place. For example, suppose that your employer wants a report that lists workers who have registered for both insurance plans offered by the company: the medical plan and the dental plan. This type of situation is known as an **AND** situation because the employee's record must pass two tests—participation in the medical plan *and* participation in the dental plan—before you write that employee's information on the report. An AND situation requires a **nested decision** or a **nested if**; that is, a decision "inside of" another decision. The logic looks like Figure 5-8.

 You first learned about nesting structures in Chapter 2.

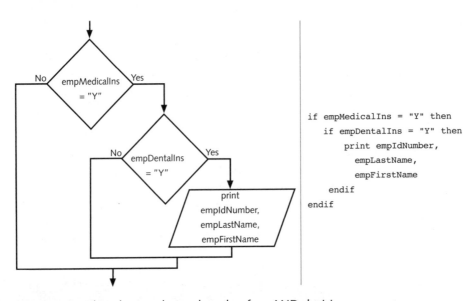

```
if empMedicalIns = "Y" then
    if empDentalIns = "Y" then
        print empIdNumber,
            empLastName,
            empFirstName
    endif
endif
```

Figure 5-8   Flowchart and pseudocode of an AND decision

The AND decision shown in Figure 5-8 is part of a much larger program. To help you develop this program, suppose your employer provides you with the employee data file description shown in Figure 5-9, and you learn that the medical and dental insurance fields contain a single character, "Y" or "N", indicating each employee's participation status. With your employer's approval, you develop the print chart shown in Figure 5-10.

```
EMPLOYEE FILE DESCRIPTION
File Name: EMPFILE
FIELD DESCRIPTION      POSITIONS      DATA TYPE      DECIMALS      EXAMPLE
ID Number              1—4            Numeric        0             1234
Last Name              5—20           Character                    Kroening
First Name             21—35          Character                    Ginny
Department             36             Numeric        0             3
Hourly Rate            37—40          Numeric        2             17.50
Medical Plan           41             Character                    Y
Dental Plan            42             Character                    N
Number of              43—44          Numeric        0             2
  Dependents
```

Figure 5-9   Employee file description

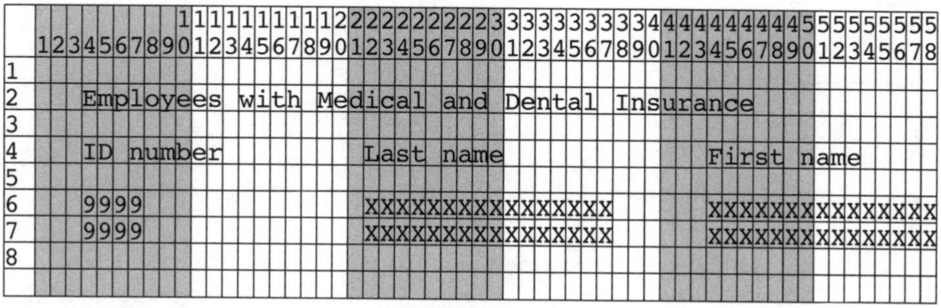

Figure 5-10   Print chart for employees participating in both insurance plans

The mainline logic and `housekeeping()` routines for this program are diagrammed in Figures 5-11 and 5-12.

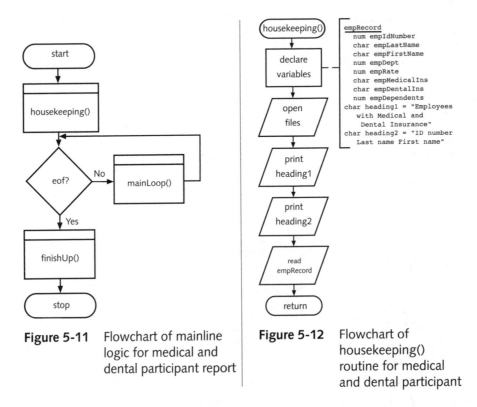

Figure 5-11 Flowchart of mainline logic for medical and dental participant report

Figure 5-12 Flowchart of housekeeping() routine for medical and dental participant

At the end of the `housekeeping()` routine, the first employee record is read into computer memory. Assuming that the `eof` condition is not yet met, the logical flow proceeds to the `mainLoop()`. Within the `mainLoop()` module of this program, you ask the questions that determine whether the current employee's record will print; if so, then you print the employee's data. Whether or not the employee meets the medical and dental insurance requirements for printing, the last thing you do in the `mainLoop()` is to read the next input record. Figure 5-13 shows the `mainLoop()` module.

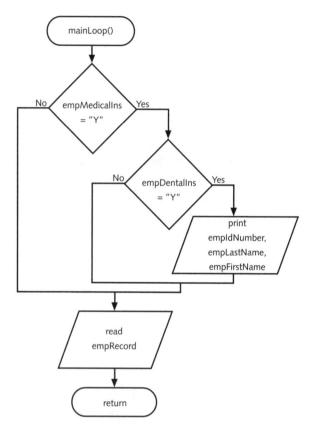

Figure 5-13   mainLoop( ) of program that lists medical and dental participants

The `mainLoop()` module works like this: If the employee has medical insurance, *then* and *only then,* test to see if the employee has dental insurance. If so, *then* and *only then,* print the employee's data. The dental insurance question is nested entirely within half of the medical insurance question structure. If an employee does not carry medical insurance, there is no need to ask about the dental insurance; the employee is already disqualified from the report. Pseudocode for the entire program is shown in Figure 5-14. Notice how the second (dental insurance) decision within the `mainLoop()` is indented within the first (medical insurance) decision. This technique shows the second question is asked only when the result of the first comparison is true.

```
start
    perform houskeeping()
    while not eof
            perform mainLoop()
    perform finishUp()
stop

housekeeping()
    declare variables ── ── ──┐
    open files
    print heading1
    print heading2
    read empRecord
return

mainLoop()
    if empMedicalIns = "Y" then
        if empDentalIns = "Y" then
            print empIdNumber, empLastName, empFirstName
        endif
    endif
    read empRecord
return

finishUp()
      close files
return
```

```
empRecord
      num empIdNumber
      char empLastName
      char empFirstName
      num empDept
      num empRate
      char empMedicalIns
      char empDentalIns
      num empDependents
char heading1 = "Employees with Medical
              and Dental Insurance"
char heading2 = "ID number    Last name
              First name"
```

Figure 5-14   Pseudocode of medical and dental participants report program

WRITING AND DECISIONS FOR EFFICIENCY

When you nest decisions because the resulting action requires that two conditions be true, you must decide which of the two decisions to make first. Logically, either selection in an AND situation can come first. However, when there are two selections, you often can improve your program's performance by making an appropriate choice as to which selection to make first.

For example, the nested decision structure in the `mainLoop()` logic of the program that produces a report of employees who participate in both the medical and dental insurance plans is written as in Figure 5-15.

```
if empMedicalIns = "Y" then
    if empDentalIns = "Y" then
        print empIdNumber, empLastName, empFirstName
    endif
endif
```

Figure 5-15   Finding medical and dental plan participants

Alternatively, you can write the decision as in Figure 5-16.

```
if empDentalIns = "Y" then
     if empMedicalIns = "Y" then
          print empIdNumber, empLastName, empFirstName
     endif
endif
```

Figure 5-16   Finding dental and medical plan participants

Examine the decision statements in the preceding figures. If you want to print employ-ees who participate in the medical AND dental plans, you can ask about the medical plan first, eliminate those employees who do not participate, and ask about the dental plan only for those employees who "pass" the medical insurance test. Or you could ask about the dental plan first, eliminate those who do not participate, and ask about the medical plan only for those employees who "pass" the dental insurance test. Either way, the final list contains only those employees who have both kinds of insurance.

Does it make a difference which question is asked first? As far as the output goes, no. Either way, the same employee names appear on the report—those with both types of insurance. As far as program efficiency goes, however, it *might* make a difference which question is asked first.

Assume you know that out of 1,000 employees in your company, about 90%, or 900, participate in the medical insurance plan. Assume you also know that out of 1,000 employees, only about half, or 500, participate in the dental plan.

Using the logic in Figure 5-15, the program asks the first question `empMedicalIns = "Y"`? 1,000 times. For approximately 90% of the employees, or 900 of the records, the answer is `true`, thus the `empMedicalIns` field contains the character "Y". So 100 employees are eliminated, and 900 proceed to the next question about dental insurance. Only about half of the employees participate in the dental plan, so 450 out of the 900 will appear on the printed report.

Using the alternative logic in Figure 5-16, the program asks the first question `empDentalIns = "Y"`? 1,000 times. Because only about half of the company's employees participate, only 500 will "pass" this test and proceed to the medical insur-ance question. Then about 90% of the 500, or 450 employees, will appear on the report. Whether you use the logic in Figure 5-15 or 5-16, the same 450 employees who have both types of insurance appear on the report.

The difference lies in the fact that when using the logic in Figure 5-15, the program must ask 1,900 questions to produce the report—the medical insurance question tests all 1,000 employee records, and 900 continue to the dental insurance question. If you use the logic in Figure 5-16 to produce the report, the program asks only 1,500 questions—all 1,000 records are tested for dental insurance, but only 500 proceed to the medical insur-ance question. By asking about the dental insurance first, you "save" 400 decisions.

The 400-question difference between the first set of decisions and the second set really doesn't take much time on most computers. But it will take some time, and if there are hundreds of thousands of employees instead of only 1,000, or if many such decisions have to be made within a program, performance time can be significantly improved by asking questions in the proper order.

In many AND situations, the programmer has no idea which of two events is more likely to occur; in that case, you can legitimately ask either question first. In addition, even though you know the probability of each of two conditions, the two events might not be mutually exclusive; that is, one might depend on the other. For example, if employees with dental insurance are significantly more likely to carry medical insurance than those who don't carry dental insurance, the order in which to ask the questions might matter less or not matter at all. However, if you do know the probabilities of the conditions, or can make a reasonable guess, the general rule is: *In an AND situation, first ask the question that is less likely to be true.* This eliminates as many records as possible from having to go through the second decision and speeds up processing time.

COMBINING DECISIONS IN AN AND SITUATION

Most programming languages allow you to ask two or more questions in a single comparison by using a **logical AND operator**. For example, if you want to select employees who carry both medical and dental insurance, you can use nested `if`s, or you can include both decisions in a single statement by writing `empDentalIns = "Y" AND empMedicalIns = "Y"?`. If the programming language you use allows an AND operator, you still must realize that the question you place first is the question that will be asked first, and cases that are eliminated based on the first question will not proceed to the second question. The computer can ask only one question at a time; even though you draw the flowchart segment in Figure 5-17, the computer will execute the logic in the flowchart in Figure 5-18.

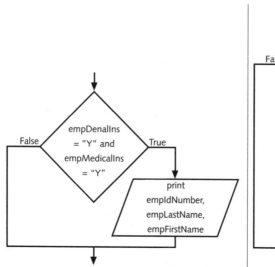

Figure 5-17   Flowchart of AND decision using an AND operator

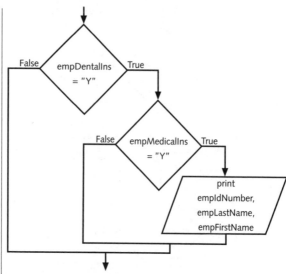

Figure 5-18   Computer logic of program containing an AND decision using an AND operator

AVOIDING COMMON ERRORS IN AN AND SITUATION

When you must satisfy two or more criteria to initiate an event in a program, you must make sure that the second decision is made entirely within the first decision. For example, if a program's objective is to print those employees who carry both medical and dental insurance, then the program segment shown in Figure 5-19 contains three different types of logic errors.

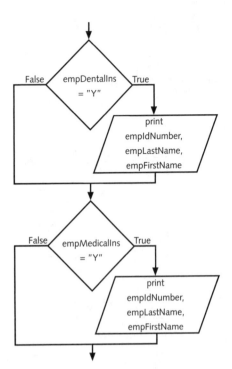

Figure 5-19   Incorrect logic to produce report with medical and dental participants

    C#, C++, C, and Java use the symbol && to represent the logical AND.

The diagram shows that the program asks the dental insurance question first. However, if an employee participates in the dental program, the employee prints immediately. The employee should not print, because the employee might not have the medical insurance. In addition, the program should eliminate an employee without dental insurance from the next selection, but every employee's record proceeds to the medical insurance question, where it might print whether the employee has dental insurance or not. Additionally, any employee who has both medical and dental insurance, having passed each test successfully, will appear twice on this report. For many reasons, the logic shown in Figure 5-19 is *not* correct for this problem.

Beginning programmers often make another type of error when they must make two comparisons on the same field while using a logical AND operator. For example, suppose you want to list employees who make between $10.00 and $11.99 per hour inclusive. You want to select employees whose **empRate** is greater than or equal to 10.00 AND whose `empRate` is less than 12.00; therefore, you need to make two comparisons on the same field. Without the logical AND operator, the comparison is:

```
if empRate >= 10.00 then
    if empRate < 12.00 then
        print empIdNumber, empLastName, empFirstName
    endif
endif
```

To check for `empRate` values that are 10.00 and greater, you can use either expression empRate > 9.99? or empRate >= 10.00?. To check for empRate values under 12.00, you can write empRate <= 11.99? or empRate < 12.00?.

The correct way to make this comparison with the AND operator is as follows:

```
if empRate >= 10.00 AND empRate < 12.00 then
    print empIdNumber, empLastName, empFirstName
endif
```

You substitute the AND operator for the `then if`. However, some programmers try to make the comparison as follows:

```
if empRate >= 10.00 AND < 12.00 then
    print empIdNumber, empLastName, empFirstName
endif
```

In most languages, the phrase `empRate >= 10.00 AND < 12.00` is incorrect. When you use a logical AND, you must use a complete Boolean expression on both sides of the AND. The expression to the right of the AND, `< 12.00`, is not a complete Boolean expression; you must indicate *what* is being compared to 12.00.

In COBOL and RPG you can write the equivalent of empRate >= 10.00 AND < 12.00? and the empRate variable is implied for both comparisons. Still, it is clearer and therefore preferable to use the two full expressions, empRate >= 10.00 AND empRate < 12.00?.

UNDERSTANDING OR LOGIC

Sometimes you want to take action when one *or* the other of two conditions is true. This is called an **OR** situation because either one condition must be met *or* some other condition must be met in order for an event to take place.

For example, suppose your employer wants a list of all employees who participate in either the medical or dental plan. Assuming you are using the same input file described in Figure 5-9, the mainline logic and `housekeeping()` module for this program are identical to those used in Figures 5-11 and 5-12. You need only to change the heading on the print chart (Figure 5-10) and change the `heading1` variable in Figure 5-12 from `heading1 = "Employees with Medical `*`and`*` Dental Insurance"` to `heading1 = "Employees with Medical `*`or`*` Dental Insurance"`. The substantial changes to the program occur in the `mainLoop()` module.

Figure 5-20 shows the possible logic for `mainLoop()` in this OR situation. As each record enters the `mainLoop()`, you ask the question `empMedicalIns = "Y"?`, and if the result is true, you print the employee data. Because the employee needs to participate in only one of the two insurance plans to be selected for printing, there is no need for further questioning. If the employee does not participate in the medical insurance plan, only then do you need to ask if `empDentalIns = "Y"?`. If the employee does not have medical insurance, but does have dental, you want this employee to print on the report.

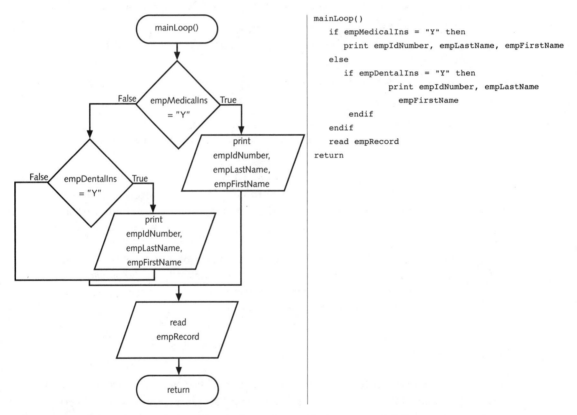

Figure 5-20   Flowchart and pseudocode for mainLoop() that prints employees who have medical or dental insurance

AVOIDING COMMON ERRORS IN AN OR SITUATION

You might have noticed that the statement `print empIdNumber, empLastName, empFirstName` appears twice in the flowchart and in the pseudocode shown in Figure 5-20. The temptation is to redraw the flowchart in Figure 5-20 to look like Figure 5-21. Logically, you can argue that the flowchart in Figure 5-21 is correct because the correct employees print. However, this flowchart is not allowed because it is not structured.

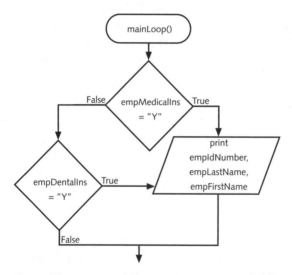

Figure 5-21   Incorrect flowchart for mainLoop() module

 If you do not see that Figure 5-21 is not structured, go back and review Chapter 2. In particular, review the example that begins at Figure 2-22.

An additional source of error that is specific to the OR situation stems from a problem with language and the way people use it too casually. When your boss needs a report of all employees who carry medical or dental insurance, she is likely to say, "I need a report of all the people who have medical insurance and all those who have dental insurance." The request contains the word "and," and the report contains people who have one type of insurance "and" people who have another. However, the records you want to print are those from employees who have medical insurance OR dental insurance OR both. The logical situation is an OR situation. As a programmer it is up to you to clarify what really is being requested, and determine that often a request for A and B means a request for A or B.

WRITING OR DECISIONS FOR EFFICIENCY

You can write a program that creates a report containing all employees who take either the medical or dental insurance by using the `mainLoop()` in either Figure 5-22 or Figure 5-23.

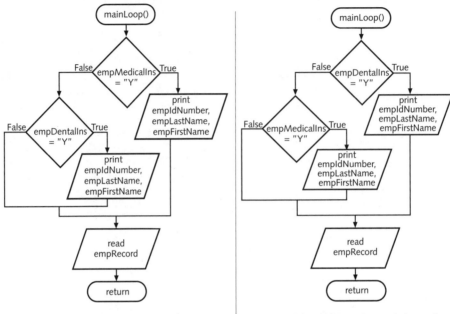

Figure 5-22   mainLoop() to select employees with medical or dental insurance

Figure 5-23   Alternate mainLoop() to select employees with medical or dental insurance

You might have guessed that one of these selections is superior to the other if you have some background information about the relative likelihood of each condition you are testing. For example, once again assume you know that out of 1,000 employees in your company, about 90%, or 900, participate in the medical insurance plan, and about half, or 500, participate in the dental plan.

When you use the logic shown in Figure 5-22 to select employees who participate in either insurance plan, you first ask about medical insurance. For 900 employees the answer is true; you print these employee records. Only about 100 records continue to the next question regarding dental insurance, where about half, or 50, fulfill the requirements to print. In the end, you print about 950 employees.

If you use Figure 5-23, you ask `empDentalIns = "Y"?`. The result is true for 50%, or 500 employees, whose names then print. Five hundred employee records then progress to the medical insurance question after which 90% or 450 of them print.

Using either scenario, 950 employee records appear on the list, but the logic used in Figure 5-22 requires 1,100 decisions while the logic used in Figure 5-23 requires 1,500 decisions. The general rule is: *In an OR situation, first ask the question that is more likely to be true.* Because a record qualifies for printing as soon as it passes one test, asking the more likely question first eliminates as many records as possible from having to go through the second decision. The time it takes to execute the program is decreased.

COMBINING DECISIONS IN AN OR SITUATION

5

When you need to take action when either one or the other of two conditions is met, you can use two separate, nested selection structures as in the previous examples. However, most programming languages allow you to ask two or more questions in a single comparison by using a **logical OR operator**—for example, `empDentalIns = "Y" OR empMedicalIns = "Y"`. When you use the logical OR operator, only one of the listed conditions must be met for the resulting action to take place. If the programming language you use allows this construct, you still must realize that the question you place first is the question that will be asked first, and cases that you eliminate based on the first question will not proceed to the second question. The computer can ask only one question at a time; even though you draw the flowchart in Figure 5-24, the computer will execute the logic in the flowchart in Figure 5-25.

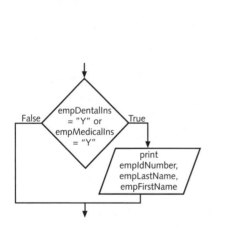

Figure 5-24   Flowchart of OR decision using an OR operator

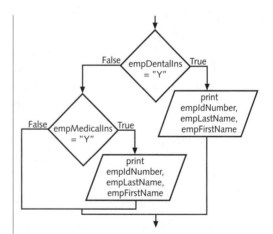

Figure 5-25   Computer logic of program containing an OR decision using an OR operator

  C#, C++, C, and Java use the symbol || to represent the logical OR.

USING SELECTIONS WITHIN RANGES

Business programs often need to make selections based on a variable falling within a range of values. For example, suppose you want to print a list of all employees and the names of their supervisors. An employee's supervisor is assigned based on the employee's department number, as shown in Figure 5-26:

```
DEPARTMENT NUMBER          SUPERVISOR
1-3                        Dykeman
4-7                        Erhardt
8-9                        Jackson
```

Figure 5-26   Supervisors by department

When you write the program that reads each employee's record, you could make nine decisions before printing the supervisor's name, such as **empDept = 1?**, **empDept = 2?**, and so on. However, it is more convenient to find the supervisor by using a range check.

To perform a **range check**, make comparisons using either the lowest or highest value in each range of values you are using to make selections. For example, to find each employee's supervisor as listed in Figure 5-26, use either the values 1, 4, and 8, which represent the low ends of each supervisor's department range, or use the values 3, 7, and 9, which represent the high ends.

The pseudocode representing the logic for choosing a supervisor name by using the high-end range values appears in Figure 5-27. You test the **empDept** value for less than or equal to the high end of the lowest range group. If the comparison evaluates as true, you know the **supervisorName**. If not, you continue checking.

```
if empDept <= 3 then
      supervisorName = "Dykeman"
else
      if empDept <= 7 then
          supervisorName = "Erhardt"
      else
          supervisorName = "Jackson"
      endif
endif
```

Figure 5-27   Using high-end values for a range check

In Figure 5-27, notice how each else aligns vertically with its corresponding if.

The flowchart for choosing a supervisor name using the reverse of this method, by seeking the low-end range values, appears in Figure 5-28. You compare empDept to the low end of the highest range first; if the empDept falls in the range, the supervisorName is known; otherwise you check the next lower group.

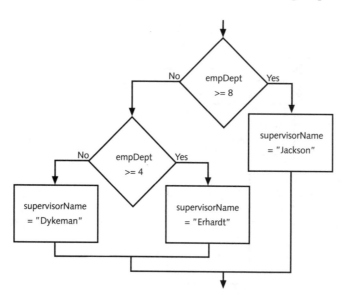

Figure 5-28   Using low-end values for a range check

COMMON ERRORS USING RANGE CHECKS

Two common errors that occur when programmers perform range checks both entail doing more work than is necessary. Figure 5-29 shows a range check in which the programmer has asked one question too many. If you know that all empDept values are positive numbers, then if the empDept is not greater than or equal to eight, and it is also not greater than or equal to four, then by default it must be greater than or equal to one. Asking whether empDept is greater than or equal to one is a waste of time; no employee record can ever travel the logical path on the far left.

Similarly, Figure 5-30 shows the beginning of an inefficient range selection. If empDept is greater than or equal to eight, "Jackson" is the supervisor. If the empDept is not greater than or equal to eight, the next question does not have to check for less than eight. The computer will never get to the second question unless the empDept is already less than eight, so you are wasting computer time asking a question that has previously been answered.

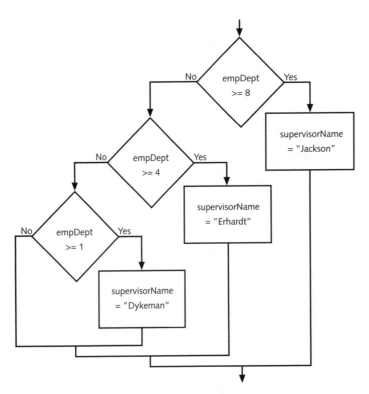

Figure 5-29   Inefficient range selection

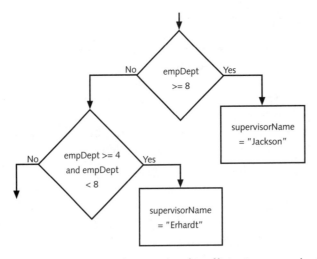

Figure 5-30   Partial example of inefficient range selection

USING DECISION TABLES

Some programs require multiple decisions to produce the correct output. Managing all possible outcomes of multiple decisions can be a difficult task, so programmers sometimes use a tool called a decision table to help organize the possible decision outcome combinations.

A **decision table** is a problem-analysis tool that consists of four parts:

- Conditions
- Possible combinations of Boolean values for the conditions
- Possible actions based on the conditions
- The actions that correspond to each Boolean value of each condition

For example, suppose a college collects input data like that shown in Figure 5-31. Each student's data record includes the student's age and a variable that indicates whether the student has requested a residence hall that enforces quiet study hours.

STUDENT FILE DESCRIPTION				
File Name: STURESFILE				
FIELD DESCRIPTION	POSITIONS	DATA TYPE	DECIMALS	EXAMPLE
ID Number	1–4	Numeric	0	5377
Last Name	5–20	Character		Bowers
First Name	21–35	Character		Laurel
Age	36–37	Numeric	0	19
Request for Hall	38	Character		Y
with Quiet Hours				

Figure 5-31   Student file description

Assume the residence hall director makes residence hall assignments based on the following rules:

- Students who are under 21 years old and who request a residence hall with quiet study hours are assigned to Addams Hall.
- Students who are under 21 years old and who do not request a residence hall with quiet study hours are assigned to Grant Hall.
- Students who are 21 years old and over who request a residence hall with quiet study hours are assigned to Lincoln Hall.
- Students who are 21 years old and over who do not request a residence hall with quiet study hours also are assigned to Lincoln Hall.

You can create a program that assigns each student to the appropriate residence hall and prints a list of students along with each student's hall assignment. The mainline logic for this program could look exactly like the mainline logic shown for the employee medical and dental benefits program in Figure 5-11, or you can choose new module names as shown in Figure 5-32. The programs are similar in that each performs start-up or housekeeping tasks, a main loop that acts repeatedly, once for each input record, and a finishing module that closes the open files. The general shape of the mainline logic modules in many computer programs look very similar; the individual module names can be any appropriate names you choose.

The **getReady()** module for the program that produces the residence hall report is shown in Figure 5-33.

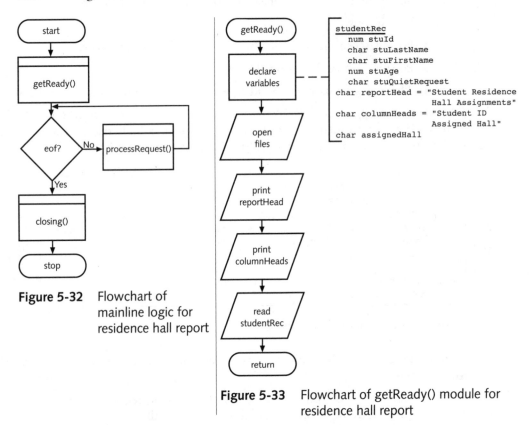

Figure 5-32 Flowchart of mainline logic for residence hall report

Figure 5-33 Flowchart of getReady() module for residence hall report

Before you draw a flowchart or write the pseudocode for the **processRequest()**, you can create a decision table to help you manage all the decisions. You can begin to create a decision table by listing all possible conditions. They are:

- stuAge < 21, or not

- stuQuietRequest = "Y", or not

Next determine how many possible Boolean value combinations exist for the conditions. In this case there are four possible combinations shown in Figure 5-34. A student can be under 21, request a residence hall with quiet hours, both, or neither. Since each condition has two outcomes and there are two conditions, there are 2 * 2 or four possibilities. Three conditions would produce eight possibilities (2 * 2 * 2); four conditions would produce 16 possible outcome combinations (2 * 2 * 2 * 2), and so on.

Condition	Outcome			
stuAge < 21	T	T	F	F
stuQuietRequest = "Y"	T	F	T	F

Figure 5-34   Possible outcomes of residence hall request conditions

Next, add rows to the decision table to list the possible outcome actions. A student might be assigned to Addams, Grant, or Lincoln Hall. Figure 5-35 shows these three possible outcomes.

Condition	Outcome			
stuAge < 21	T	T	F	F
stuQuietRequest = "Y"	T	F	T	F
assignedHall = "Addams"				
assignedHall = "Grant"				
assignedHall = "Lincoln"				

Figure 5-35   Possible outcome actions of residence hall requests

Choose one required outcome for each possible combination of conditions. As shown in Figure 5-36, place an X in the Addams Hall row when stuAge is less than 21 and the student requests a residence hall with quiet study hours.

Condition	Outcome			
stuAge < 21	T	T	F	F
stuQuietRequest = "Y"	T	F	T	F
assignedHall = "Addams"	X			
assignedHall = "Grant"				
assignedHall = "Lincoln"				

Figure 5-36   Decision table for residence hall selection, part 1 of 3

Next, place an X in the Grant Hall row under the condition when a student is under 21 but does not request a residence hall with quiet hours. See Figure 5-37.

Condition	Outcome			
stuAge < 21	T	T	F	F
stuQuietRequest = "Y"	T	F	T	F
assignedHall = "Addams"	X			
assignedHall = "Grant"		X		
assignedHall = "Lincoln"				

Figure 5-37   Decision table for residence hall selection, part 2 of 3

Finally, place Xs in the Lincoln Hall row for both situations when a student is not under 21 years old—only one residence hall is available for students 21 and over, whether they have requested a hall with quiet hours or not. See Figure 5-38.

Condition	Outcome			
stuAge < 21	T	T	F	F
stuQuietRequest = "Y"	T	F	T	F
assignedHall = "Addams"	X			
assignedHall = "Grant"		X		
assignedHall = "Lincoln"			X	X

Figure 5-38   Decision table for residence hall selection, part 3 of 3

The decision table is complete (count the Xs—there are four possible outcomes). Take a moment and confirm that each residence hall selection is the appropriate value based on the original specifications. Now you can start to plan the logic.

If you choose to use a flowchart to express the logic, you start by drawing a path to the outcome shown in the first column. This result (which occurs when **stuAge < 21** and **stuQuietRequest = "Y"**) sets the residence hall to "Addams". See Figure 5-39.

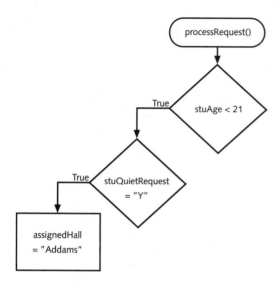

Figure 5-39   Flowchart for residence hall selection, part 1 of 5

Next, add the resulting action shown in the second column of the decision table, which occurs when **stuAge < 21** is true and **stuQuietRequest = "Y"** is false. See Figure 5-40.

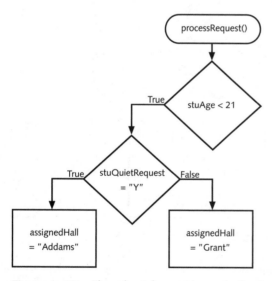

Figure 5-40   Flowchart for residence hall selection, part 2 of 5

Add the resulting action shown in the third column of the decision table, which occurs when **stuAge < 21** is false and **stuQuietRequest = "Y"** is true. See Figure 5-41.

Finally, add the resulting action shown in the fourth column of the decision table, which occurs when both conditions are false, as in Figure 5-42.

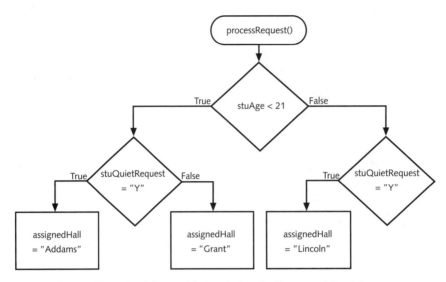

Figure 5-41   Flowchart for residence hall selection, part 3 of 5

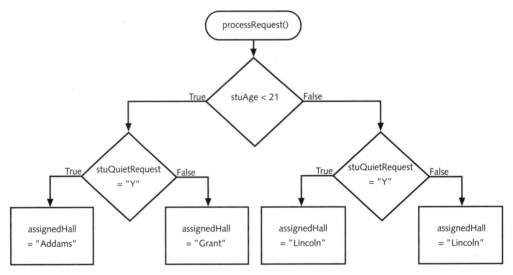

Figure 5-42   Flowchart for residence hall selection, part 4 of 5

The flowchart segment is now complete and accurately assigns each student to the correct residence hall. Just tie up the ends, print a student's ID number and residence hall assignment, and read the next record. However, if you examine the two rightmost result boxes, you see that the assigned residence hall is identical—Lincoln in both cases. When a student is not under 21, whether the **stuQuietRequest** equals "Y" or not, the residence hall assignment is the same; therefore, there is no point in asking the **stuQuietRequest** question. Additionally, many programmers prefer that the True or Yes side of a flowchart decision always appears on the right side. Figure 5-43 shows the complete program, including the `processRequest()` module with True results to the right of each selection.

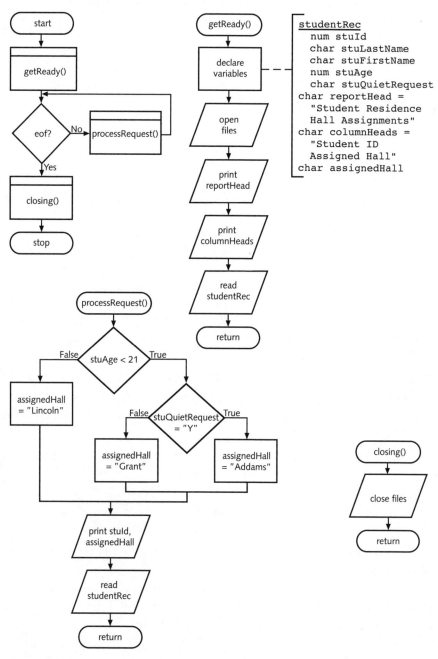

Figure 5-43   Flowchart for residence hall selection, part 5 of 5

Perhaps you could have created the final decision-making `processRequest()` module without creating the decision table first. If so, you need not use the table. Decision tables are more useful to the programmer when the decision-making process becomes more complicated. Additionally, they serve as a useful graphic tool when you want to explain the decision-making process of a program to a user who is not familiar with flowcharting symbols.

 In Appendix B, you can walk through the process used to create a larger decision table.

CHAPTER SUMMARY

- Every decision you make in a computer program involves evaluating a Boolean expression. You can use dual-alternative, binary selections, or if-then-else structures to choose between two possible outcomes. You also can use single-alternative, unary, or if-then selections when there is only one outcome for the question where action is required.

- For any two values that are the same type, you can use logical comparison operators to decide whether the two values are equal, the first value is greater than the second value, or the first value is less than the second value. The two values used in a Boolean expression can be either variables or constants.

- An AND situation occurs when two conditions must be true in order for a resulting action to take place. An AND situation requires a nested decision or a nested if.

- In an AND situation, first ask the question that is less likely to be true. This eliminates as many records as possible from having to go through the second decision and speeds up processing time.

- Most programming languages allow you to ask two or more questions in a single comparison by using a logical AND operator.

- When you must satisfy two or more criteria to initiate an event in a program, you must make sure that the second decision is made entirely within the first decision, and that you use a complete Boolean expression on both sides of the AND.

- An OR situation occurs when you want to take action when one *or* the other of two conditions is true.

- Errors occur in OR situations when programmers do not maintain structure. An additional source of errors that are particular to the OR situation stems from people using the word AND to express OR requirements.

- In an OR situation, first ask the question that is more likely to be true.

❑ Most programming languages allow you to ask two or more questions in a single comparison by using a logical OR operator.

❑ To perform a range check, make comparisons with either the lowest or highest value in each range of values you are using.

❑ Common errors that occur when programmers perform range checks include asking unnecessary and previously answered questions.

❑ A decision table is a problem-analysis tool that consists of conditions, possible combinations of Boolean values for the conditions, possible actions based on the conditions, and the actions that correspond to each Boolean value of each condition.

5

EXERCISES

1. Assume the following variables contain the values shown:

   numberRed = 100   numberBlue = 200   numberGreen = 300
   wordRed = "Wagon"   wordBlue = "Sky"   wordGreen = "Grass"

   For each of the following Boolean expressions, decide whether the statement is true, false, or illegal.

   a. numberRed = numberBlue?

   b. numberBlue > numberGreen?

   c. numberGreen < numberRed?

   d. numberBlue = wordBlue?

   e. numberGreen = "Green"?

   f. wordRed = "Red"?

   g. wordBlue = "Blue"?

   h. numberRed <= numberGreen?

   i. numberBlue >= 200?

   j. numberGreen >= numberRed + numberBlue?

2. a. A candy company wants a list of its best-selling items, including item number and name of candy. Best-selling items are those that sell over 2,000 pounds per month. Input records contain fields for the item number (three digits), the name of the candy (20 characters), the price per pound (four digits, two assumed decimal places), and the quantity in pounds sold last month (four digits, no decimals). Design the print chart, hierarchy chart, and flowchart.

   b. Write the pseudocode for the same problem.

   c. The candy company wants a list of its high-priced, best-selling items. Best-selling items are those that sell over 2,000 pounds per month. High-priced items are those that sell for $10 per pound or more. Design the print chart, hierarchy chart, and flowchart.

   d. Write the pseudocode for the same problem.

3. a. The Literary Honor Society needs a list of English majors who have a grade point average of 3.5 or higher. The student record file includes students' last names and first names (15 characters each), major (10 characters, for example "History" or "English"), and grade point average (two digits, one assumed decimal place). Design the print chart, hierarchy chart, and flowchart for this problem.

   b. Write the pseudocode for the same problem.

4. a. A telephone company charges 10 cents per minute for all calls outside the customer's area code that last over 20 minutes. All other calls are 13 cents per minute. The phone company has a file with one record for every call made in one day. (In other words, a single customer might have many such records on file.) Fields for each call include customer area code (three digits), customer phone number (seven digits), called area code (three digits), called number (seven digits), and call time in minutes (four digits). The company wants a report listing one detail line for each call, including the customer area code and number, the called area code and number, the minutes, and the total charge. Create a decision table to use with this problem.

   b. Design the print chart, hierarchy chart, and flowchart.

   c. Write the pseudocode for the same problem.

5. a. A nursery maintains a file of all plants in stock along with such data as price and characteristics. Only 20% of the nursery stock does well in shade and 50% does well in sandy soil. Create a decision table to use with this problem.

   b. Design a print chart, create an hierarchy chart, and draw the flowchart that would perform the most efficient search for a plant in a shady, sandy yard.

   c. Write the pseudocode for the same problem.

6. You have declared variables for an insurance company program as follows:

FIELD	POSITIONS	EXAMPLE
num custPolicyNumber	1–6	223356
char custLastName	7–20	Falkenburg
num custAge	21–23	25
num custDueMonth	24–25	06
num custDueDay	26–27	24
num custDueYear	28–31	2004
num custAccidents	32–34	2

   Draw the selection structures that print the custPolicyNumber and custLastName that satisfy the following requests for lists of policyholders:

   a. over 35 years old

   b. at least 21 years old

   c. no more than 30 years old

   d. due no later than March 15 any year

   e. due up to and including January 1, 2004

f. due by April 27, 2007

g. due as early as December 1, 2002

h. fewer than 11 accidents

i. no more than 5 accidents

j. no accidents

7. a. Student files contain an ID number (four digits), last and first names (15 characters each), and major field of study (10 characters). Draw the print chart, create the hierarchy chart, and draw the flowchart for a program that lists ID numbers and names for all French or Spanish majors.

b. Write the pseudocode for the same problem.

8. a. A florist wants to send coupons to her best customers, so she needs a list of names and addresses for customers who placed orders more than three times last year or spent more than $200 last year. The input file description follows:

File name: FLORISTCUSTS

FIELD DESCRIPTION	POSITIONS	TYPE	DECIMALS
Customer ID	1–3	Numeric	0
First Name	4–16	Character	
Last Name	17–30	Character	
Street Address	31–51	Character	
Orders Last Year	52–55	Numeric	0
Amount Spent Last Year	56–62	Numeric	2

(Note: To save room, don't include city or state. Assume all the florist's best customers are in town.) Design the print chart, write the hierarchy chart, and draw the flowchart for this program.

b. Write the pseudocode for the same problem.

9. a. A carpenter needs a program that computes the price of any desk a customer orders based on the following input fields: order number, desk length in inches and width in inches (three digits each, no decimals), type of wood (20 characters), and number of drawers (two digits). The price is computed as follows:

  ❑ The charge for all desks is a minimum $200.

  ❑ If the surface (length * width) is over 750 square inches, add $50.

  ❑ If the wood is "mahogany" add $150; for "oak" add $125. No charge is added for "pine."

  ❑ For every drawer in the desk, there is an additional $30 charge.

  Create a decision table to use with this problem.

b. Design the print chart, write the hierarchy chart, and draw the flowchart for this program.

c. Write the pseudocode for the same problem.

10. a. A company is attempting to organize carpools to save energy. Ten percent of the company's employees live in Wonder Lake. Thirty percent of the employees live in Woodstock. Since these towns are both north of the company, the company wants a list of employees who live in either town so it can recommend that these employees drive to work together. Create a flowchart that shows the most efficient process for selecting these employees, assuming there is a field called `empCity` in each employee's personnel record.

   b. Write pseudocode for the same process.

11. a. Create the logic to help plan your next vacation. Possible outcomes for destination are Hawaii, Grandma's house, and nowhere (stay home). If your bank balance is $1 million or more, you will go to Hawaii. If your bank balance is less than $1 million, and your boss says you must work, you will stay home. If your boss says you can go, you will go to Hawaii unless your bank account is below $2,000. In that case, you will go to Grandma's house. Assuming you have declared variables for `vacationDestination`, `vacationBossDecision`, and `vacationBankBalance`, create a flowchart that shows the decision-making process.

   b. Assuming you have declared variables for `vacationDestination`, `vacationBossDecision`, and `vacationBankBalance`, write pseudocode for the decision-making process from Exercise 11a.

12. a. A supervisor in a manufacturing company wants to produce a report showing which employees have increased their production this year over last year so that she can issue them a certificate of commendation. She wants to have a report with three columns: last name, first name, and either the word "UP" or blanks printed under the column heading PRODUCTION. "UP" is printed when this year's production is a greater number than last year's production. Input exists as follows:

```
PRODUCTION FILE DESCRIPTION
File name: PRODUCTION
FIELD DESCRIPTION          POSITIONS    DATA TYPE    DECIMALS
Last Name                  1-20         Character
First Name                 21-30        Character
Last Year's Production     31-34        Numeric      0
This Year's Production     35-38        Numeric      0
```

   Create the decision table that shows the logic for issuing the commendations, then create the print layout chart, hierarchy chart, and flowchart for this program.

   b. Write the pseudocode for the same problem.

   c. A supervisor in the same manufacturing company wants to produce a report from the PRODUCTION input file showing bonuses she is planning to give based on this year's production. She wants to have a report with three columns: last name, first name, and bonus. The bonuses will be distributed as follows.

If this year's production is:

- ◻ 1,000 units or fewer, the bonus is $25
- ◻ 1,001 to 3,000 units, the bonus is $50
- ◻ 3,001 to 6,000 units, the bonus is $100
- ◻ 6,001 units and up, the bonus is $200

Create the print layout chart, hierarchy chart, and either the flowchart or pseudocode for this program.

d. Modify Exercise 12c to reflect the following new facts, and have the program execute as efficiently as possible:

- ◻ Only employees whose production this year is higher than last year will receive bonuses. This is true for approximately 30% of the employees.

- ◻ Sixty percent of employees produce over 6,000 units per year, 20% produce 3,001 to 6,000, 15% produce 1,001 to 3,000 units, and only 5% produce fewer than 1,001.

5

6

LOOPING

> **After studying Chapter 6, you should be able to:**
> ♦ Understand the advantages of looping
> ♦ Control a `while` loop using a loop control variable
> ♦ Increment a counter to control a loop
> ♦ Loop with a variable sentinel value
> ♦ Control a loop by decrementing a loop control variable
> ♦ Avoid common loop mistakes
> ♦ Use a `for` loop
> ♦ Use a `do until` loop
> ♦ Recognize the characteristics shared by all loops
> ♦ Nest loops
> ♦ Use a loop to accumulate totals

UNDERSTANDING THE ADVANTAGES OF LOOPING

If making decisions is what makes computers seem intelligent, it's looping that makes computer programming worthwhile. When you use a loop within a computer program, you can write one set of instructions that operates on multiple, separate sets of data. Consider the following set of tasks required for each employee in a typical payroll program:

- Determine regular pay

- Determine overtime pay, if any

- Determine federal withholding tax based on gross wages and number of dependents

- Determine state tax based on gross wages, number of dependents, and state of residence

- Determine insurance deduction based on insurance code

- Determine Social Security deduction based on gross

- Subtract federal tax, state tax, Social Security, and insurance from gross

In reality, this list is too short—companies deduct stock option plans, charitable contributions, union dues, and other items from checks in addition to the items mentioned in this list. Also, they might pay bonuses and commissions and provide sick days and vacation days that must be taken into account and handled appropriately. As you can see, payroll programs are complicated.

The advantage of having a computer perform payroll calculations is that all of the deduction instructions need to be written *only once* and can be repeated over and over again using a **loop**, (the structure that repeats actions while some condition continues).

USING A WHILE LOOP WITH A LOOP CONTROL VARIABLE

Recall the loop, or do-while structure that you learned about in Chapter 2. (See Figure 6-1.) In Chapter 3 you learned that almost every program has a **main loop**, or a basic set of instructions that are repeated for every record. The main loop is a typical loop—within it, you write one set of instructions that executes repeatedly while records continue to be read from an input file. Several housekeeping tasks execute at the start of most programs and a few clean-up tasks execute at the end. However, most of a program's tasks are located in a main loop; these tasks repeat over and over for many (sometimes hundreds, thousands, or millions) records.

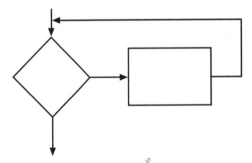

Figure 6-1   The while loop

In addition to this main loop, loops also appear within subroutines. They are used any time you need to perform a task several times and don't want to write identical or similar instructions over and over. Suppose for example, as part of a much larger program, you want to print a warning message on the computer screen when the user has made a potentially dangerous menu selection (say, "Delete all files"). To get the user's attention, you want to print the message four times. You can write this program segment as shown in Figure 6-2, but using a loop as shown in Figure 6-3 is much more efficient.

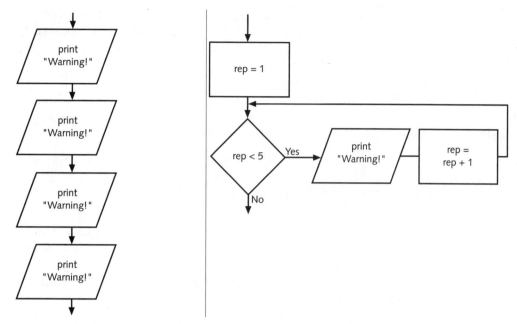

Figure 6-2: Printing four warning messages in sequence

Figure 6-3: Printing four warning messages in a loop

The flowchart segment in Figure 6–3 shows three steps that must occur in every loop:

1. You must initialize a variable that will control the loop. The variable in this case is named **rep**.

2. You must compare the variable to some value that stops the loop. In this case you compare **rep** to the value 5.

3. Within the loop, you must alter the variable. In this case, you alter **rep** by adding one to it.

On each pass through the loop, the value in the **rep** variable determines whether the loop will continue. Therefore variables like **rep** are known as **loop control variables**. Any variable that determines whether a loop will continue is a loop control variable. To stop a loop, you compare the loop control value to a **sentinel value** (also known as a limit, or ending value), in this case the value 5. The decision that controls every loop is always based on a Boolean comparison. You can use any of the six comparison operators that you learned about in Chapter 5 to control a loop.

Just as with a selection, the Boolean comparison that controls a `while` loop must compare same-type values: numeric values are compared to other numeric values and character values to other character values.

The statements that execute within a loop are known as the **loop body**. The body of the loop might contain any number of statements, including subroutine calls, decisions, and other loops. Once your program enters the body of a structured loop, the entire loop body must execute. Your program can leave a structured loop only at the comparison that tests the loop control variable.

USING A COUNTER TO CONTROL LOOPING

Suppose you own a factory and have decided to place a label on every product you manufacture. The label contains the words "Made for you personally by" followed by the first name of one of your employees. For one week's production, you need 100 personalized labels for each employee.

Assume you already have a personnel file that can be used for input. This file has more information than you'll need for this program: an employee last name, first name, Social Security number, address, date hired, and salary. The important feature of the file is that it does contain each employee's name stored in a separate record. The input file description appears in Figure 6-4.

```
File Name: EMPLOYEES
FIELD DESCRIPTION          POSITIONS      DATA TYPE       DECIMALS
Employee Last Name         1–20           Character
Employee First Name        21–35          Character
Social Security Number     36–44          Numeric         0
Address                    45–60          Character
Date Hired                 61–68          Numeric         0
Hourly Salary              69–72          Numeric         2
```

Figure 6-4   Employee data file description

In the mainline of this program, you perform three subroutines: a housekeeping subroutine (`housekeep()`), a main loop (`mainLoop()`), and a finish routine (`finishUp()`). See Figure 6-5.

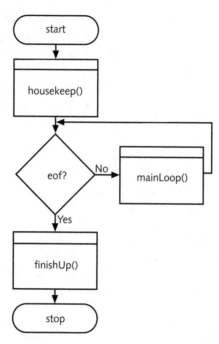

Figure 6-5   Mainline logic for label program

The first task for the label program involves naming the fields on the input record so you can refer to them within the program. As a programmer, you can choose any variable names you like, for example: `inLastName`, `inFirstName`, `inSSN`, `inAddress`, `inDate`, and `inSalary`.

In Chapter 4 you learned that starting all field names in the input record with the same prefix, such as `in`, is a common programming technique to help identify these fields in a large program and differentiate them from work areas and output areas that will have other names. Another benefit to using a prefix like `in` is that some language compilers also produce a dictionary of variable names when you compile your program. These dictionaries show at which lines in the program each data name is referenced. If all your input field names start with the same prefix, they will be together alphabetically in the dictionary and perhaps be easier to find and work with.

You also can set up a variable to hold the characters "Made for you personally by" and name it `labelLine`. You eventually will print this `labelLine` variable followed by the employee's first name (`inFirstName`).

You will need one more variable: a location called a counter. A **counter** is any numeric variable you use to count the number of times an event has occurred; in this example you need a counter to keep track of how many labels have been printed at any point.

Each time you read an employee record, the counter variable is set to zero. Then every time a label is printed, you add one to the counter. Adding one to a variable is called **incrementing** the variable. Before the next employee label is printed, the program checks the variable to see if it has reached 100 yet. When it has, that means 100 labels have been printed and the job is done for that employee. While the counter remains below 100, you continue to print labels. As with all variables, the programmer can choose any name for a counter; this program uses `labelCounter`. In this example, `labelCounter` is the loop control variable.

The `housekeep()` routine for the label program, shown in Figure 6-6, includes a step to open the files: the employee file and the printer. Unlike a program that produces a report, this program has no headings, so the next and last task performed in `house-keep()` is to read the first input record.

 Remember, you can give any name you like to subroutines within your programs. This program uses `housekeep()` for its first routine, but `housekeeping()`, `startUp()`, `prep()`, or any other name with the same general meaning could be used.

 If you don't know why the first record is read in the `housekeep()` module, go back and review the concept of the priming read presented in Chapter 2.

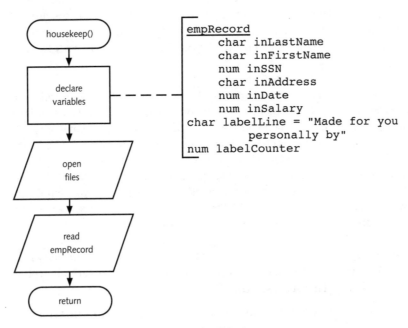

Figure 6-6   housekeep() module for label program

When housekeep( ) is done, the logical flow returns to the eof question in the main-line. If for some reason you attempt to read the first record at the end of housekeep( ) and there is no record, the answer to eof? is Yes, so then the mainLoop( ) is never entered; instead, the logic of the program flows directly to the finishUp( ) module.

Usually, however, employee records will exist and the program will enter the mainLoop( ) module. When this happens, the first employee record is sitting in mem-ory waiting to be processed. During one execution of the mainLoop( ) module, 100 labels will be printed for one employee. As the last event within mainLoop( ) module, the program reads the next employee record. Control of the program then returns to the eof question. If the new read process does not result in the eof condition, control returns to the mainLoop( ) module where 100 more labels print for a new employee.

The mainLoop( ) of this label program contains three parts:

- Set the labelCounter to 0.

- Compare the labelCounter to 100.

- While the labelCounter is less than 100, print the labelLine and the inFirstName, and add one to the labelCounter.

When the first employee record enters the mainLoop( ) module, the labelCounter is set to zero. Comparing the labelCounter to 100 results in a true condition, so the record enters the label-making loop. One label prints for the first employee, the labelCounter increases by one, and the logical flow returns to the question labelCounter < 100?. After the first label is printed, the labelCounter holds a value of only 1. It is nowhere near 100 yet, so the value of the Boolean expression is true and the loop is entered for a second time, thus printing a second label.

After the second printing labelCounter holds a value of 2. After the third printing, it holds a value of 3. Finally, after the 100th label prints, labelCounter has a value of 100. When the question labelCounter < 100? is asked, the answer will finally be no and the loop will exit.

Before leaving mainLoop( ), and after the program prints 100 labels for an employee, there is one final step: the next input record is read from the EMPLOYEES file. When mainLoop( ) is over, control returns to the eof question in the mainline of the logic. If it is not eof (if another employee record is present), the program enters mainLoop( ) again, resets labelCounter to 0, and prints 100 new labels with the next employee's name. Figure 6-7 shows the complete mainLoop( ).

6

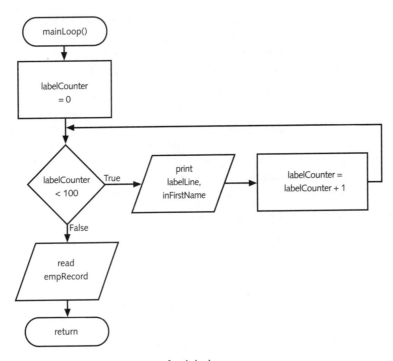

Figure 6-7 `mainLoop()` for label program

At some point while attempting to read a new record you encounter the end of the file, the `mainLoop()` is not entered again and control passes to the `finishUp()` module. In this program the `finishUp()` module simply closes the files. See Figure 6-8.

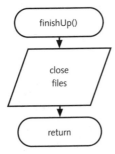

Figure 6-8 `finishUp()` module for label program

LOOPING WITH A VARIABLE SENTINEL VALUE

Sometimes you don't want to be forced to repeat every pass through a loop the same number of times. For example, instead of printing 100 labels for each employee, you might want to vary the number of labels based on how many items a worker actually produces. That way, high-achieving workers won't run out of labels and less productive workers won't have too many. Instead of printing the same number of labels for every employee, a more sophisticated program prints a different number of labels for each employee, depending on that employee's previous week's production. For example, you might decide to print enough labels to cover 110% of each employee's production rate from the previous week; this ensures that the employee will have enough labels for the week even if his or her production level improves.

For example, assume that employee production data exists on an input file called EMPPRODUCTION in the format shown in Figure 6-9.

File Name: EMPPRODUCTION			
FIELD DESCRIPTION	POSITIONS	DATA TYPE	DECIMALS
Last Name	1–20	Character	
First Name	21–35	Character	
Production Last Week	36–38	Numeric	0

Figure 6-9   Employee production file description

A real-life production file would undoubtedly have more fields in each record, but these fields supply more than enough information to produce the labels. You need the first name to print on the label, and you need the field that holds production for the last week in order to calculate the number of labels to print for each employee. This field can contain any number from 0 through 999.

To write a program that produces an appropriate number of labels for each employee, you can make some minor modifications to the original label-making program. For example, the input file variables have changed; you must declare a variable for an inLastProduction field. Additionally, you might want to create a numeric field named labelsToPrint that can hold a value equal to 110% of a worker's inLastProduction.

The major modification to the original label-making program is in the question that controls the label-producing loop. Instead of asking if labelCounter < 100, you now can ask if labelCounter < labelsToPrint. The sentinel or limit value can be a variable just as easily as it can be a constant. See Figure 6-10 for the flowchart as well as the pseudocode.

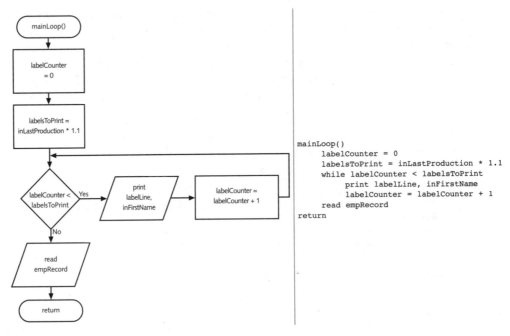

Figure 6-10   Flowchart and pseudocode for label-making mainLoop()

 Tip   The statement `labelsToPrint = inLastProduction * 1.1` calcu-lates `labelsToPrint` as 110% of `inLastProduction`. Alternatively, you can perform the calculation as `labelsToPrint = inLastProduction + .10 * inLastProduction`. The mathematical result is the same.

LOOPING BY DECREMENTING

Rather than increasing a loop control variable until it passes some sentinel value, some-times it is more convenient to reduce a loop control variable on every cycle through a loop. For example, again assume you want to print enough labels for every worker to cover 110% production. As an alternative to setting a `labelCounter` variable to 0 and increasing it after each label prints, you initially can set `labelCounter` equal to `inLastProduction * 1.1`, and subsequently reduce the `labelCounter` value every time a label prints. You continue printing labels and reducing the `labelCounter` until you have counted down to zero. Decreasing a variable by one is called **decre-menting** the variable.

For example, when you write the following you produce enough labels to equal 110% of `inLastProduction`:

```
labelCounter = inLastProduction * 1.1
while labelCounter > 0
      print labelLine, inFirstName
      labelCounter = labelCounter - 1
```

When you decrement, you can avoid declaring a special variable for the `labelsToPrint`. The `labelCounter` variable starts with a value that represents the labels to print, and works its way down to zero.

Yet another alternative would allow you to eliminate the `labelCounter` variable. You could use the `inLastProduction` variable itself to keep track of the labels. For example, the following pseudocode segment also produces a number of labels equal to 110% of each worker's `inLastProduction` value:

```
inLastProduction = inLastProduction * 1.1
while inLastProduction > 0
     print labelLine, inFirstName
     inLastProduction = inLastProduction - 1
```

In this example, `inLastProduction` is first increased by 10%. Then, while it remains above zero, there are more labels to print. However, you can't use this method if you need the value of `inLastProduction` for this record later in the loop. By decrementing the variable, you are changing its value on every cycle through the loop; when you have finished, the original value in `inLastProduction` has been lost.

 Do not think the value of `inLastProduction` is gone forever when you alter it. The original value still exists within the data file. It is the main memory location called `inLastProduction` that is being reduced.

AVOIDING COMMON LOOP MISTAKES

The two mistakes programmers make most often with loops are:

- Neglecting to initialize the loop control variable
- Neglecting to alter the loop control variable

For example, assume you remove the statement `labelCounter = 0` from the program illustrated in Figure 6-10. When `labelCounter` is compared to `labelsToPrint` at the start of the `while` loop, it is impossible to predict whether any labels will print. Because uninitialized values contain unknown, unpredictable garbage, comparing such a variable to another value is meaningless. Even if you initialize `labelCounter` to zero in the `housekeep()` module of the program, you must reset `labelCounter` to zero for each new record that is processed within the `while` loop. If you fail to reset the `labelCounter`, it just keeps increasing through the life of the program and does not accurately reflect the number of labels printed for each employee.

A different sort of error will occur if you remove the statement that adds one to the `labelCounter` from the program in Figure 6-10. This error will result in the following code:

```
while labelCounter < labelsToPrint
     print labelLine, inFirstName
```

Following this logic, if `labelCounter` is zero and `labelsToPrint` is, for example 110, then `labelCounter` will be less than `labelsToPrint` forever. Nothing in the loop changes either variable, so labels will continue to print. A loop that never stops executing is called an **infinite loop**. It is always incorrect to create a loop that cannot terminate.

When you run a computer program that uses the loop in Figure 6-10, hundreds or thousands of employee records might pass through the `mainLoop()`. If there are 100 employee records, then `labelCounter` is set to zero exactly 100 times; it must be reset to zero once for each employee in order to count each employee's labels correctly. Similarly, `labelsToPrint` is set to 1.1 times `inLastProduction`, once for each employee.

If the average employee produces 100 items during a week, then the loop within the `mainLoop()`,   the   one   controlled   by   the   statement `while labelCounter < labelsToPrint`, executes 11,000 times—110 times each for 100 employees. Again, this number of repetitions is necessary in order to print the correct number of labels.

A repetition that is *not* necessary would be to execute 11,000 separate multiplication statements to recalculate the `labelCounter`. See Figure 6-11.

```
mainLoop()
    labelCounter = 0
    while labelCounter < inLastProduction * 1.1
        print labelLine, inFirstName
        labelCounter = labelCounter + 1
    read empRecord
return
```

Figure 6-11   Inefficient pseudocode for label-making mainLoop()

Although the pseudocode shown in Figure 6-11 will produce the correct number of   labels   for   every   employee,   the   statement `while labelCounter < inLastProduction * 1.1` executes an average of 110 times for each employee. That means that the multiplication of `inLastProduction` by 1.1 occurs 110 separate times for each employee. Performing the same calculation that results in the same mathematical answer 110 times in a row is inefficient. Instead, it is superior to perform the multiplication just once for each employee and use the result 110 times, as shown in the original version of the program in Figure 6-10. In the pseudocode in Figure 6-10, you still must recalculate `labelCounter` once for each record, but not once for each label, so you have improved the program's efficiency.

The modules illustrated in Figures 6-10 and 6-11 do the same thing: print enough labels for every employee to cover 110% of production. As you become more proficient at programming, you will recognize many opportunities to perform the same tasks in alternative, more elegant, and more efficient ways.

Another common error made by beginning programmers involves initializing a variable that does not require initialization. When declaring variables for the label-making program, you might be tempted to declare num `labelCounter` = `inLastProduction` * `1.1`. It seems as though this declaration statement indicates that the value of the `labelCounter` will always be 110% of the `inLastProduction` figure. However, this approach is incorrect for two reasons. First, at the time `labelCounter` is declared, the first employee record has not yet been read into memory, so the value of `inLastProduction` is garbage; therefore the result in `labelCounter` after multiplication will also be garbage. Secondly, even if you read the first `empRecord` into memory before declaring the `labelCounter` variable, the mathematical calculation of the `labelCounter` within the `housekeep()` module would be valid for the first record only. The value of `labelCounter` must be recalculated for each employee record in the input file. Therefore, calculation of the `labelCounter` correctly belongs within the `mainLoop()` as shown in Figure 6-10.

USING THE FOR LOOP

The label-making programs discussed in this chapter each contain two loops. For example, Figures 6-12 and 6-13 show the loop within the mainline program as well as the loop within the `mainLoop()` module for the program that produces 100 labels for each employee.

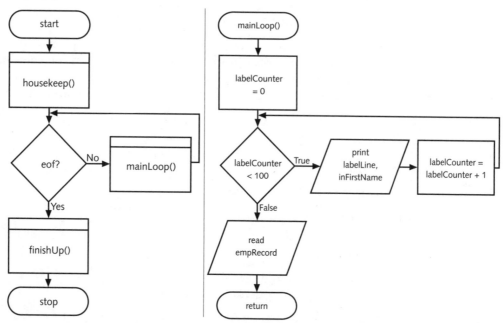

Figure 6-12: Mainline logic for label-making program

Figure 6-13: mainLoop() logic for label-making program

Entry to the `mainLoop()` in the mainline logic is controlled by the `eof` decision. Within the `mainLoop()`, label production is controlled by the `labelCounter`. When you execute the mainline logic, you cannot predict how many times the `mainLoop()` module will execute. Depending on the size of the input file, any number of records might be processed; while the program runs you don't know what the total number of records finally will be. Until you attempt to read a record and encounter the end of the file, you don't know if more records are going to become available. Because you can't determine ahead of time how many records there might be, the mainline loop in the label-making program is called an **indeterminate** or **indefinite loop**.

With some loops, you know exactly how many times they will execute. If every employee needs 100 printed labels, then the loop within the `mainLoop()` module executes exactly 100 times for each employee. This kind of loop, in which you definitely know the repetition factor, is a **definite loop**.

Every high-level computer programming language contains a **while statement** that you can use to code any loop, including indefinite loops (like the mainline loop) and definite loops (like the label-printing loop). You can write statements like the following:

```
while not eof perform mainLoop()
```

and

```
while labelCounter < 100
     print labelLine, inFirstName
     add 1 to labelCounter
```

In addition to the `while` statement, most computer languages also support a `for` statement. You can use the **for statement** or **for loop** with definite loops when you know how many times a loop will repeat. The `for` statement provides you with three actions in one compact statement. The `for` statement uses a loop control variable that it automatically:

- initializes
- evaluates
- increments

The `for` statement usually takes the form:

```
for initialValue to finalValue
     do something
```

For example, to print 100 labels you can write:

```
for labelCounter = 0 to 99
     print labelLine, inFirstName
```

This `for` statement accomplishes several tasks at once in a compact form:

- The `for` statement initializes the `labelCounter` to 0.

- The `for` statement checks the `labelCounter` against the limit value 99 and makes sure that the `labelCounter` is less than or equal to that value.

- If the evaluation is true, the `for` statement body that prints the label executes.

- After the `for` statement body executes, the `labelCounter` increases by one and the comparison to the limit value is made again.

As an alternative to using the loop for `labelCounter = 0 to 99`, you can use for `labelCounter = 1 to 100`. You can use any combination of values, as long as there are 100 whole number values between the two limits.

You never are required to use a `for` statement; the label loop executes correctly using a `while` statement with `labelCounter` as a loop control variable. However, when a loop is based on a loop control variable progressing from a known starting value to a known ending value in equal increments, the `for` loop presents you with a convenient shorthand.

The programmer needs to know neither the starting nor the ending value for the loop control variable; only the program must know those values. For example, you don't know the value of a worker's `inLastProduction` value, but when you tell the program to read a record, the program knows. To do so, you can write a `for` loop that begins for `labelCounter = 1 to inLastProduction`.

In several languages, you can provide a `for` loop with a step value. A step value is a number you use to increase a loop control variable on each pass through a loop. In most programming languages, the default loop step value is one. You specify a step value when you want each pass through the loop to change the loop control variable by a value other than one.

USING THE DO UNTIL LOOP

When you use either a `while` or a `for` loop, the body of the loop may never execute. For example, in the mainline logic in Figure 6-5, the last action in the `housekeep()` module is to read an input record. If the input file contains no records, the result of the `eof` decision is true, and the program executes the `finishUp()` module without ever entering the `mainLoop()` module.

Similarly, when you produce labels within the `mainLoop()` module shown in Figure 6-10, labels are produced `while labelCounter < labelsToPrint`. Suppose an employee record contains a zero in the `inLastProduction` field—for example, in the case of a new employee or an employee who was on vacation. In such a case, the value of `labelsToPrint` would be zero, and the label-producing body of the loop might never execute. With a `while` loop, you evaluate the loop control variable prior to executing the loop body, and the evaluation might indicate that you can't enter the loop.

When you want to ensure that a loop's body executes at least one time, you can use a do until loop. In a do until loop, the loop control variable is evaluated after the loop body executes. Therefore, the body always executes at least one time.

You first learned about the do until loop in Chapter 2. Review Chapter 2 to reinforce your understanding of the differences between a while loop and a do until loop.

Because the question that controls the loop is asked before you enter the loop body, programmers say a while loop has a pretest. Because the question that controls a do until loop occurs after the loop body executes, programmers say the do until loop contains a posttest.

For example, suppose you want to produce one label for each employee to wear as identification before you produce enough labels to cover 110% of last week's production. You can write the do until loop that appears in Figure 6-14.

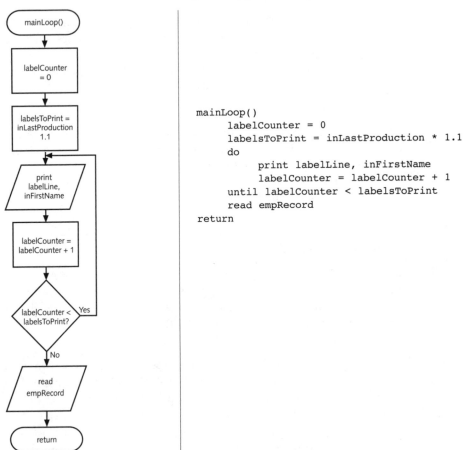

```
mainLoop()
        labelCounter = 0
        labelsToPrint = inLastProduction * 1.1
        do
                print labelLine, inFirstName
                labelCounter = labelCounter + 1
        until labelCounter < labelsToPrint
        read empRecord
return
```

Figure 6-14   do until loop for producing one extra label

Of course, you could achieve the same results by printing one label, then entering a while loop as in Figure 6-15.

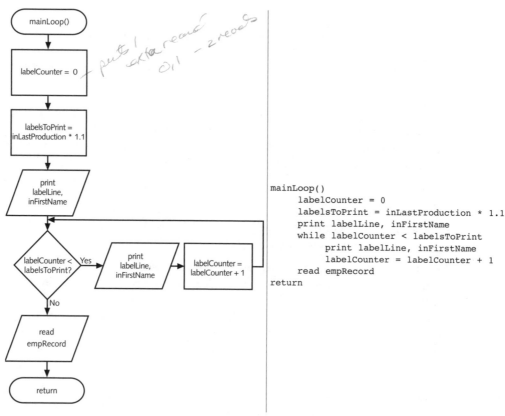

```
mainLoop()
        labelCounter = 0
        labelsToPrint = inLastProduction * 1.1
        print labelLine, inFirstName
        while labelCounter < labelsToPrint
                print labelLine, inFirstName
                labelCounter = labelCounter + 1
        read empRecord
return
```

Figure 6-15   Printing one label, then printing enough to cover production

RECOGNIZING THE CHARACTERISTICS SHARED BY ALL LOOPS

You can see from Figure 6-15 that you never are required to use a do until loop. The same results always can be achieved by performing the loop body steps once before entering a while loop. If you follow the logic of either of the loops shown in Figures 6-14 and 6-15, you will discover that when an employee has an inLastProduction value of 3, then exactly four labels print. Likewise, when an employee has an inLastProduction value of 0, then in both cases exactly one label prints. You can accomplish the same results with either type of loop; the do until loop is simply a convenience when you need a loop to execute at least one time.

In some languages, the do until loop is called a repeat until loop.

If you can express the logic you want to perform by saying "while a is true, keep doing b," you probably want to use a while loop. If what you want to accomplish seems to fit the statement, "do a until b is true," you can probably use a do until loop.

As you examine Figures 6-14 and 6-15, notice that with the do until loop the loop-controlling question is placed at the *end* of the sequence of the steps that repeat. With the while loop, the loop-controlling question is placed at the *beginning* of the steps that repeat. All structured loops share these characteristics:

- The loop-controlling question provides either entry to or exit from the repeating structure.

- The loop-controlling question provides *the only* entry to or exit from the repeating structure.

You should also notice the difference between *unstructured* loops and the structured do until and while loops. Figure 6-16 diagrams the outline of two unstructured loops. In each case, the decision labeled X breaks out of the loop prematurely. In each case, the loop control variable, (labeled LC), does not provide the only entry to or exit from the loop.

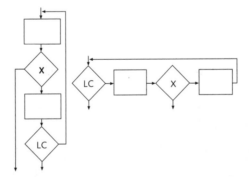

Figure 6-16   Examples of unstructured loops

NESTING LOOPS

Program logic gets more complicated when you must use loops within loops, or **nesting loops**. For example, suppose your worker records contain average *daily* production figures instead of weekly figures. But suppose you still want to print a week's worth of labels for each worker. If your company operates on a five-day work week, then within the mainLoop() of this program you must produce enough labels to cover 110% of each worker's daily label count five times. To accomplish this, you need two counters. You have declared a `labelCounter` to count labels, but now you want to produce 110% of the daily label count five times. You can declare a variable to count the days and name it `dayCounter`. Assuming you declare a variable that holds `inDailyProduction`, the `mainLoop()` logic looks like Figure 6-17.

6

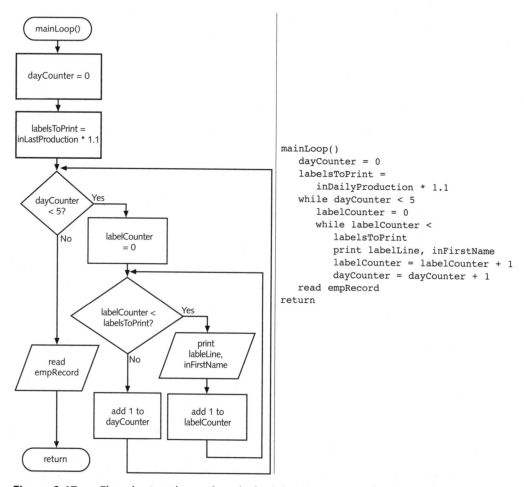

```
mainLoop()
    dayCounter = 0
    labelsToPrint =
        inDailyProduction * 1.1
    while dayCounter < 5
        labelCounter = 0
        while labelCounter <
            labelsToPrint
            print labelLine, inFirstName
            labelCounter = labelCounter + 1
            dayCounter = dayCounter + 1
        read empRecord
return
```

Figure 6-17:   Flowchart and pseudocode for labels based on five daily production counts

When you examine Figure 6-17, you see that for each new employee record, the `dayCounter` is initialized to zero and the `labelsToPrint` is set to 110% of the daily production figure. For each new day, the `labelCounter` is reset to zero. While the `dayCounter` remains under 5, you produce the daily quota of labels. When the daily quota is complete, that is, when `labelCounter` is no longer less than `labelsToPrint`, you have printed one day's worth of labels, so you add one to the dayCounter and loop back to see if dayCounter has reached 5 yet. If not, you enter the loop body and print another day's worth of labels.

In this example, if a worker's daily production is 10, the worker needs 55 labels. Because all the labels are identical, you can achieve the same results without a nested loop. You can print the necessary labels for an employee by multiplying 110% of the worker's daily average figure by five, storing the result in labelsToPrint, and executing a single loop. However, if you want the labels to indicate the day of the week, then you must use nested loops, as in Figure 6-18. Each label prints a day number (0 through 4) along with the labelLine message and the employee's first name.

```
mainLoop()
     dayCounter = 0
     labelsToPrint = inDailyProduction * 1.1
     while dayCounter < 5
          labelCounter = 0
          while labelCounter < labelsToPrint
               print "DAY: ", dayCounter, labelLine, inFirstName
               labelCounter = labelCounter + 1
          dayCounter = dayCounter + 1
     read empRecord
return
```

Figure 6-18   Required nested loops for printing labels that include a day number

 To print day numbers 1 through 5 (instead of 0 through 4), you can print dayCounter + 1 on each label.

When nesting loops, you must maintain two individual loop control variables and alter each at the appropriate time.

USING A LOOP TO ACCUMULATE TOTALS

Business reports often include totals. The supervisor who wants a list of employees who participate in the company dental plan often is as interested in *how many* such employees there are as in *who* they are. When you receive your telephone bill at the end of the month, you are usually more interested in the total than in the charges for the individual calls. Some business reports list no individual detail records, just totals. Such reports are called **summary reports**.

For example, a real estate broker might maintain a file of company real estate listings. Each record in the file contains the street address and the asking price of a property for sale. The broker wants a listing of all the properties for sale; she also wants a total value for all the company's listings. The print chart appears in Figure 6-19.

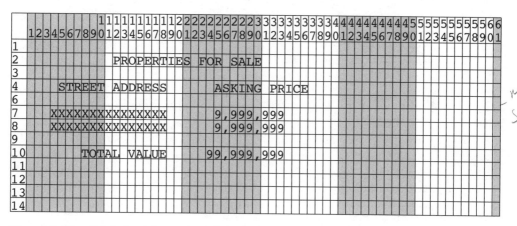

Figure 6-19   Print chart for real estate report

When you read a real estate listing record, besides printing it you must add its value to an accumulator. An **accumulator** is a variable that you use to gather or accumulate values. An accumulator is very similar to a counter. The difference lies in the value that you add to the variable; usually you add just one to a counter, whereas you add some other value to an accumulator. If the real estate broker wants to know how many listings the company holds, you count them. When she wants to know total real estate value, you accumulate it.

In order to accumulate total real estate prices, you declare a numeric variable at the beginning of the program, as shown in Figure 6-20. You must initialize the accumulator, `accumValue`, to zero. In Chapter 4, you learned that when using most programming languages declared variables do not automatically assume any particular value; the unknown value is called garbage. When you read the first real estate record, you will add its value to the accumulator. If the accumulator contains garbage, the addition will not work. Some programming languages issue an error message if you don't initialize a variable you use for accumulating; others let you accumulate, but the results are worthless because you start with garbage.

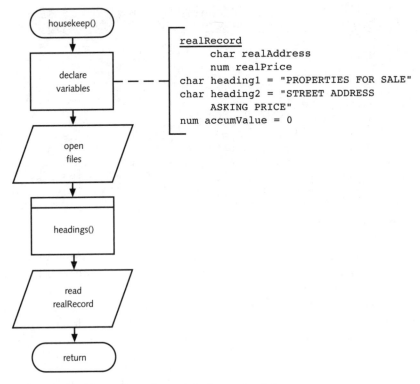

Figure 6-20   housekeep() module for real estate program

If you name the input record fields `realAddress` and `realPrice`, then the `mainLoop()` module of the real estate listing program can be written as shown in Figure 6-21. For each real estate record, you print it and add its value to the accumulator `accumValue`. Then you can read the next record.

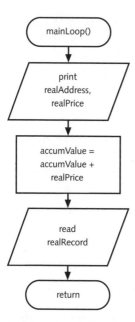

Figure 6-21   Flowchart for mainLoop() of real estate listing program

After the program reaches the end of the file, the accumulator will hold the grand total of all the real estate values. When you reach the end of the file, the `finishUp()` module executes, and it is within the `finishUp()` module that you print the accumulated value, `accumValue`. After printing the total, you can close both the input and the output files and return to the mainline where the program ends. See Figure 6-22.

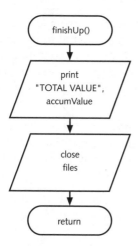

Figure 6-22   finishUp() module for real estate program

New programmers often want to reset the accumValue to zero after printing it. Although you *can* take this step without harming the execution of the program, it does not serve any useful purpose. You cannot set accumValue to zero in anticipation of having it ready for the next program. Program variables exist only for the life of the program, and even if a future program happens to contain a variable named accumValue, the variable will not necessarily occupy the same memory location. Even if you run the program a second time, the variables might occupy physical memory locations different from those they occupied during the first run. At the beginning of the program, it is the programmer's responsibility to initialize all variables that must start with a specific value. There is no benefit to changing a variable's value when it will never be used again during the current execution of the program.

CHAPTER SUMMARY

- ◘ When you use a loop within a computer program, you can write one set of instructions that operates on multiple, separate sets of data.

- ◘ Three steps must occur in every loop: You must initialize a loop control variable, compare the variable to some value that stops the loop, and alter the variable within the loop.

- ◘ A counter is a numeric variable you use to count the number of times an event has occurred. You can count occurrences by incrementing a variable.

- ◘ You can use a variable sentinel value to control a loop.

- ◘ Sometimes it is convenient to reduce or decrement a loop control variable on every cycle through a loop.

- ◘ The two mistakes programmers make most often with loops are neglecting to initialize the loop control variable, and neglecting to alter the loop control variable. Additionally, when a calculation can be performed once before entering a loop, it is inefficient to place the calculation within the loop. It is incorrect to attempt to initialize a variable by using data values that have not been read into memory yet.

- ◘ Most computer languages support a for statement or for loop that you can use with definite loops when you know how many times a loop will repeat. The for statement uses a loop control variable that it automatically initializes, evaluates, and increments.

- ◘ When you want to ensure that a loop's body executes at least one time, you can use a do until loop in which the loop control variable is evaluated after the loop body executes.

- ◘ All structured loops share these characteristics: The loop controlling question provides either entry to or exit from the repeating structure, and the loop controlling question provides *the only* entry to or exit from the repeating structure.

❑ When you must use loops within loops, you use nesting loops. When nesting loops, you must maintain two individual loop control variables and alter each at the appropriate time.

❑ Business reports often include totals. Summary reports list no detail records—only totals. An accumulator is a variable that you use to gather or accumulate values.

EXERCISES

1. Write pseudocode for the label-making program that is flowcharted in Figures 6-5 through 6-8.

2. a. Design the logic for a module that would print every number from 1 through 10 along with its square and cube. Design the print layout chart and create the flowchart for this module.

   b. Write pseudocode for the problem in Exercise 2a.

3. a. Design a program that reads credit card account records and prints payoff schedules for customers. Input records contain an account number, customer name, and balance due. For each customer, print the account number and name; then print the customer's projected balance each month for the next 10 months. Assume that there is no finance charge on this account, that the customer makes no new purchases, and that the customer pays off the balance with equal monthly payments, which are 10% of the original bill. Design the print chart, hierarchy chart, and flowchart for this program.

   b. Write pseudocode for the problem in Exercise 4a.

4. a. Design a program that reads credit card account records and prints payoff schedules for customers. Input records contain an account number, customer name, and balance due. For each customer, print the account number and name; then print the customer's payment amount and new balance each month until the card is paid off. Assume that when the balance reaches $10 or less, the customer can pay off the account. At the beginning of every month 1.5% interest is added to the balance, then the customer makes a payment equal to 5% of the current balance. Assume the customer makes no new purchases. Design the print chart, hierarchy chart, and flowchart for this program.

   b. Write pseudocode for the problem in Exercise 4a.

5. a. Assume you have a bank account that compounds interest on a yearly basis. In other words, if you deposit $100 for two years at 4% interest, at the end of one year you will have $104. At the end of two years, you will have the $104 plus 4% of that, or $108.16. Draw the logic for a program that would read in records containing a deposit amount, a term in years, and an interest rate, and for each record print the running total balance for each year of the term.

   b. Write pseudocode for the problem in Exercise 5a.

6

6. a. A school maintains class records in the following format:

```
CLASS FILE DESCRIPTION
File name: CLASS
FIELD DESCRIPTION   POSITIONS   DATA TYPE   DECIMALS  EXAMPLE
Class Code          1-6         Character             CIS111
Section No.         7-9         Numeric     0         101
Teacher             10-29       Character             Gable
Enrollment          30-31       Numeric     0         24
Room                32-35       Character             A213
```

There is one record for each class section offered in the college. Design the program that would print as many stickers as a class needs to provide one for each enrolled student, plus one for the teacher. Each sticker would leave a blank for the student's (or teacher's) name like this:

This border is preprinted, but you must design the program to print all the text you see on the sticker.

Create the hierarchy chart and flowchart for this problem.

   b. Write pseudocode for the problem in Exercise 6a.

7. a. A mail-order company often sends multiple packages per order. For each customer order, print enough mailing labels to use on each of the separate boxes that will be mailed. The mailing labels contain the customer's complete name and address along with a box number in the form "Box 9 of 9". For example, an order that requires three boxes produces three labels: "Box 1 of 3", Box 2 of 3", and "Box 3 of 3". The file description is as follows:

```
SHIPPING FILE DESCRIPTION
File name: ORDERS
FIELD DESCRIPTION   POSITIONS   DATA TYPE   DECIMALS  EXAMPLE
Title               1-3         Character             Ms
First Name          4-14        Character             Kathy
Last Name           15-25       Character             Lewis
Street              26-40       Character             847 Pine
City                41-51       Character             Aurora
State               52-53       Character             IL
Boxes               54-55       Numeric     0         3
Balance Due         56-61       Numeric     2         129.95
```

Design the print chart for the mailing label, draw the hierarchy chart, and draw the flowchart for this problem.

b. Write pseudocode for the problem in Exercise 7a.

c. Design a program that creates a report listing each customer in the order file, the number of boxes in the customer's order, and the customer's balance. At the end of the report print a total count of all boxes shipped and the grand total of all balances. Draw the print chart, hierarchy chart, and flowchart for this problem.

d. Write pseudocode for the problem in Exercise 7c.

8. a. A second-hand store is having a seven-day sale during which the price of any unsold item drops 10% each day. The inventory file includes an item number, description, and original price on day one. For example, an item that costs $10.00 on the first day costs 10% less, or $9.00, on the second day. On the third day the same item is 10% less than $9.00, or $8.10. Produce a report that shows the price of the item on each day, one through seven. Draw the print chart, hierarchy chart, and flowchart for this problem.

b. Write pseudocode for the problem in Exercise 8a.

9. a. The state of Florida maintains a census file in which each record contains the name of a county, the current population, and a number representing the rate at which population is increasing per year. The governor wants a report listing each county and the number of years it will take for the population of the county to double, assuming the present rate of growth remains constant.

```
CENSUS FILE DESCRIPTION
File name: CENSUS
FIELD DESCRIPTION   POSITIONS   DATA TYPE   DECIMALS   EXAMPLE

County Name         1-20        Character              Dade
Current
Population          21-28       Numeric     0          525000
Rate of Growth      29-30       Numeric     2          .07
```

Design the print chart for the report label, draw the hierarchy chart, and draw the flowchart for this problem.

b. Write pseudocode for the problem in Exercise 9a.

10. a. A Human Resources department wants a report that shows its employees the benefits of saving for retirement. Produce a report that shows twelve predicted retirement account values for each employee—the values if the employee saves 5, 10, or 15% of his or her annual salary for 10, 20, 30, or 40 years. The department maintains a file in which each record contains the name of an employee and the employee's current annual salary. Assume that savings grow at a rate of 8% per year. Design the print chart for the report label, draw the hierarchy chart, and draw the flowchart for this problem.

b. Write pseudocode for the problem in Exercise 10a.

11. a. Randy's Recreational Vehicles pays it salespeople once every three months. Salespeople receive one quarter of their annual base salary plus 7% of all sales made in the last three-month period. Randy creates an input file with four records for each salesperson. The first of the four records contains the salesperson's name and annual salary, while the three records that follow each contain the name of a month and the monthly sales figure. For example, the first eight records in the file might contain the following data:

Kimball	20000
April	30000
May	40000
June	60000
Johnson	15000
April	65000
May	78000
June	135500

Because the two types of records contain data in the same format, a character field followed by a numeric field, you can define one input record format containing two variables that you use with either type of record. Design the logic for the program that reads a salesperson's record, and if not at eof, reads the next three records in a loop, accumulating sales and computing commissions. For each salesperson, print the quarterly base salary, the three commission amounts, and the total salary, which is the quarterly base plus the three commission amounts. Design the print chart for the report, the hierarchy chart, and the flowchart for this problem.

b. Write pseudocode for the problem in Exercise 11a.

7

CONTROL BREAKS

After studying Chapter 7, you should be able to:

♦ Understand control break logic

♦ Perform single-level control breaks

♦ Use control data within the control break module

♦ Perform control breaks with totals

♦ Perform multiple-level control breaks

♦ Perform page breaks

UNDERSTANDING CONTROL BREAK LOGIC

A **control break** is a temporary detour in the logic of a program. In particular, programmers refer to a program as a **control break program** when a change in the value of a variable initiates special actions or causes special or unusual processing to occur. You usually write control break programs to organize output for programs that handle data records, which are organized logically in groups based on the value in a field. As you read in records, you examine the same field in each record, and when you encounter a record that contains a different value from the ones that preceded it, you perform a special action. If you have ever read a report that lists items in groups with each group followed by a subtotal, then you have read a type of **control break report**. Some other examples of control break reports produced by control break programs include:

- All employees listed in order by department number, in which a new page starts for each department

- All company clients listed in order by state of residence, with a count of clients after each state's client list

- All books for sale in a bookstore in order by category (such as reference or self-help), with a dollar total for the value of all books following each category of book

- All items sold in order by date of sale, switching ink color for each new month

Each of these reports shares two traits:

- The records used in each report are listed in order by a specific variable: department, state, category, or date.

- When that variable changes, the program takes special action: starts a new page, prints a count or total, or switches ink color.

To generate a control break report, your input records must be organized in sorted order based on the field that will cause the breaks. If you are going to write a program that prints employee records on separate pages based on their departments, then the records must be sorted in department-number order before you begin processing. As you grow more proficient in programming logic, you will learn techniques for writing programs that sort records; for now, assume that a sorting program has already been used to pre-sort your records.

 You will learn techniques for processing unsorted records in Chapter 8.

PERFORMING SINGLE-LEVEL CONTROL BREAKS

Suppose you want to print a list of employees, advancing to a new page for each department. Figure 7-1 shows the input file description, from which you can see that the employee department is a two-digit numeric field and that the file has been presorted in employee-department number order. Figure 7-2 shows the desired output—a simple list of employee names.

```
File name: EMPSBYDEPT
Sorted By: Department
FIELD DESCRIPTION    POSITIONS    DATA TYPE    DECIMALS
Department           1–2          Numeric      0
Last Name            3–14         Character
First Name           15–26        Character
```

Figure 7-1   Employee file description

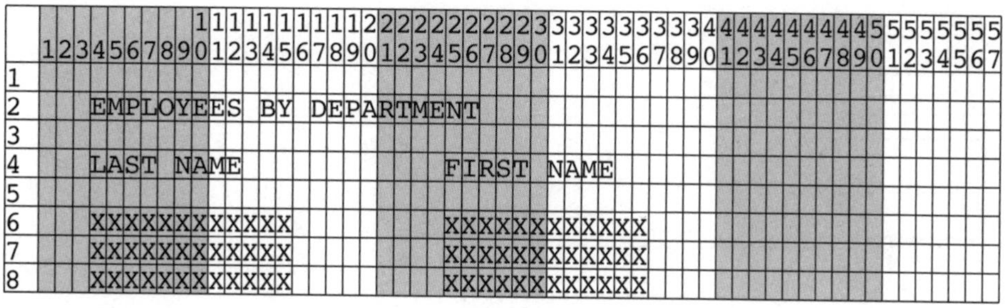

Figure 7-2   Print chart for employees listed by department

The basic logic of the program works like this: When you read each employee record from the input file, you will determine whether the employee belongs to the same department as the previous employee. If so, you simply print the employee and read another record. If there are 20 employees in a department, these steps are repeated 20 times in a row—read an employee in and print the employee out. However, eventually you will read in an employee who does not belong to the same department. At that point, before you print the employee who is in the new department, you must print headings on the top of a new page. Then you can proceed to print employees who belong to the new department.

However, there is a slight problem you must solve before you can determine whether a newly input record contains the same department number as the previously input record. When you read a record from an input file, the data that represent department, last name, and first name occupy specific physical locations in computer memory. For each new record, new data must occupy the same positions and the previous set of data is lost. For example, if you read a record containing data for Alan Andrews in Department 1, when you read the next record for Barbara Bailey in Department 2, "Barbara" replaces "Alan", "Bailey" replaces "Andrews", and 2 replaces 1. After you read in a new record, there is no way to look back at the previous record to determine whether that record had a different department number. The previous record's data has been replaced by the new record's data.

The technique you must use to "remember" the old department number is to create a special variable, called a **control break field**, to hold the previous department number. With a control break field, every time you read in a record and print it, you also can save the crucial part of the record that will signal the change or control the program break. In this case, you want to store the department number in this specially created variable. Comparing the new and old department-number values will determine when it is time to print headings at the top of a new page.

The mainline logic for the Employees by Department report is the same as the mainline logic for all the other programs you've analyzed so far. It performs a housekeeping() module, after which an eof question controls execution of a mainLoop(). At eof, a finish() module executes. See Figure 7-3.

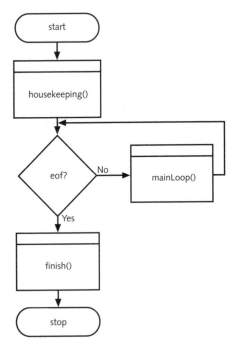

Figure 7-3   Mainline logic for Employees by Department report program

The housekeeping() module begins similarly to others you have seen. You declare variables as shown in Figure 7-4, including those you will use for the input data: empDept, empLast, and empFirst. You can also declare variables to hold the headings, and an additional variable that is named oldDept in this example. The purpose of oldDept is to serve as the control break field. Every time you read a record, you can save its department number in oldDept before you read the next record.

Note that it would be incorrect to initialize oldDept to the value of empDept when you declare oldDept. When you declare variables at the beginning of the housekeeping() module, you have not yet read in the first record, therefore empDept does not yet have any usable value. You use the value of the first empDept only after you read the first input record.

In the housekeeping() module you also open files, print headings, and read the first input record. However, before you leave housekeeping(), you can set the oldDept variable to equal the empDept value in the first input record. You will write the mainLoop() of the program to check for any change in department number; that's the signal to print headings at the top of a new page. Because you just printed headings and read in the first record, you do not want to print headings again for this record—you want to ensure that the empDept and oldDept are equal within the mainLoop().

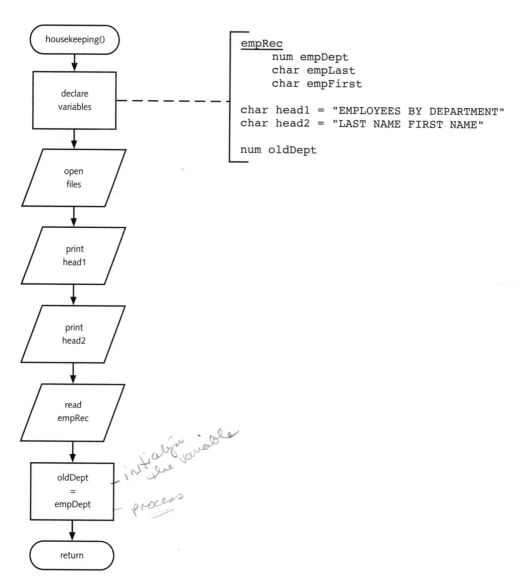

Figure 7-4   housekeeping() module for Employees by Department report program

As an alternative to the housekeeping() logic shown here, you can remove printing headings from the housekeeping() module and set the oldDept to any impossible value, for example, –1. Then in the mainLoop() the first record will force the control break and the headings will print in the newPage() control break routine.

The first task within the mainLoop() is to check whether the empDept holds the same value as oldDept. For the first record, on the first pass through the mainLoop(), the values are equal; you set them to be equal in **housekeeping()**. Therefore you proceed, printing the employee's record and reading a second record. At the end of the **mainLoop()** shown in Figure 7-5, the logical flow returns to the mainline logic shown in Figure 7-3. If it is not **eof**, the flow travels back into the **mainLoop()** module. There you compare the second record's **empDept** to **oldDept**. If the second record holds an employee from the same department, then you simply print that employee's record, and read a third record into memory. As long as each new record holds the same **empDept** value, you continue reading and printing.

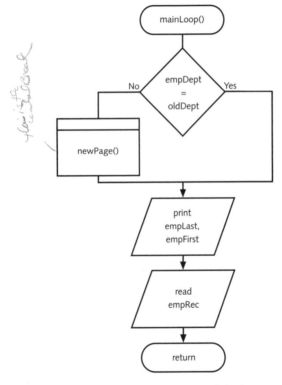

Figure 7-5   mainLoop() module for Employees by Department report program

Eventually, you will read in an employee whose **empDept** is not the same as **oldDept**. That's when the control break routine, **newPage()**, executes. The **newPage()** module must perform two tasks:

- It must print headings on top of a new page.
- It must update the control break field.

Figure 7-6 shows the **newPage()** module.

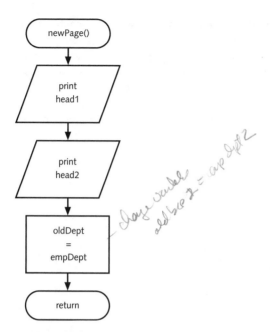

Figure 7-6   The newPage() module for Employees by Department report program

In Chapter 4 you learned that specific programming languages provide you with a means to physically advance printer paper to the top of a page. For this book, if a print chart shows a heading printing at the top of the page, then you can assume printing the heading causes the paper in the printer to advance to the top of a new page. The appropriate language-specific codes can be added when you code the program.

When you read an employee whose `empDept` is not the same as `oldDept`, you cause a break in the normal flow of the program. The new employee record must "wait" while headings print and the control break field `oldDept` acquires a new value. When the control break module ends, the waiting employee record prints on the new page. When you read the *next* employee record, the employee's `empDept` is compared to the updated `oldDept`, and if the new employee works in the same department as the one just preceding, then normal control continues with the print-and-read statements.

The `newPage()` module performs two tasks required in all control break routines:

- Performs any necessary processing for the new group—in this case, writes headings

- Updates the control break field

As an alternative to updating the control break field within the control break routine, you could set the `oldDept` equal to `empDept` just before you read each record. However, if there are 200 employees in Department 55, then you set the `oldDept` to the same value 200 times. It's more efficient to set `oldDept` to a different value only when there is a change.

The `finish()` module for the Employees by Department report program requires only that you close the files. See Figure 7-7.

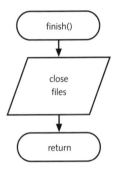

Figure 7-7   The finish() module for Employees by Department report program

USING CONTROL DATA WITHIN THE CONTROL BREAK MODULE

In the Employees by Department report program example, the control break routine printed constant headings at the top of each new page, but sometimes you need to use control data within a control break module. For example, consider the report layout shown in Figure 7-8.

		1	1	1	1	1	1	1	1	1	1	2	2	2	2	2	2	2	2	2	2	3	3	3	3	3	3	3	3	3	3	4	4	4	4	4	4	4	4	4	4	5	5	5	5	5	5	5	5

Figure 7-8   Print chart for employees listed by department identified in heading

The difference between Figure 7-2 and Figure 7-8 lies in the heading. Figure 7-8 shows variable data in the heading—the department number prints at the top of each page of employees. To create this kind of program, the one change you must make in the existing program is to modify the `newPage()` module, as shown in Figure 7-9. Instead of printing a fixed heading, you print a heading that contains two parts: a constant begin-ning ("EMPLOYEES FOR DEPARTMENT") with a variable ending (the department number for the employees who appear on the page). Notice that you use the `empDept` number that belongs to the employee record that is waiting to be printed while this con-trol break module executes. Additionally, you must ensure that the first heading on the report prints correctly. You can modify the `housekeeping()` module in Figure 7-4 so that you read the first `empRec` prior to printing the headings.

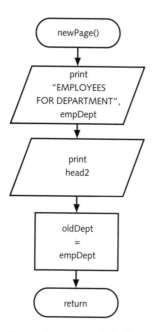

Figure 7-9   Modified newPage() module that prints department number in heading

Figure 7-10 shows a different print chart. For this report, the department number prints *following* the employee list for the department. A message that prints at the end of a page is called a **footer**. Headings usually require information about the *next* record; footers usually require information about the *previous* record.

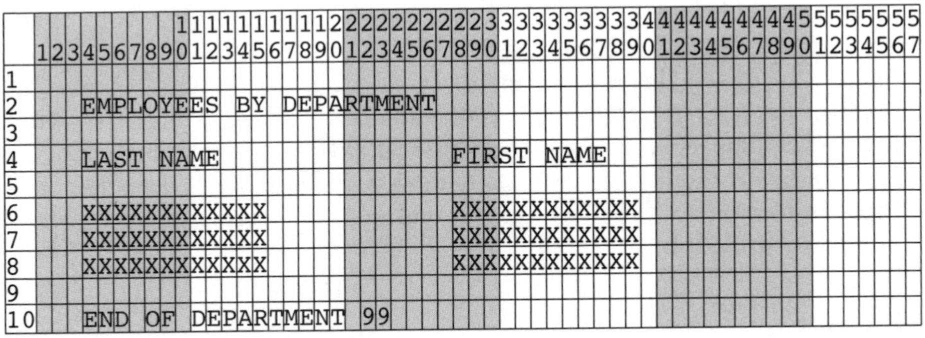

```
        1111111111222222222233333333334444444444555555 5
  1234567890123456789012345678901234567890123456789012 34567
 1
 2  EMPLOYEES BY DEPARTMENT
 3
 4  LAST NAME              FIRST NAME
 5
 6  XXXXXXXXXXXXX          XXXXXXXXXXXX
 7  XXXXXXXXXXXXX          XXXXXXXXXXXX
 8  XXXXXXXXXXXXX          XXXXXXXXXXXX
 9
10  END OF DEPARTMENT 99
```

Figure 7-10   Print chart for employees listed by department identified in footer

Figure 7-11 shows the newPage() module required to print the department number in an Employees by Department report footer. When you write a program that produces the report shown in Figure 7-10, you continuously read records with empLast, empFirst, and empDept fields. Each time an empDept does not equal the oldDept, it means that you have reached a department break and that you should perform the newPage() module. The newPage() module has three tasks:

- It must print the footer for the previous department at the bottom of the employee list.

- It must print headings on top of a new page.

- It must update the control break field.

When the newPage() module prints the footer at the bottom of the old page, you must use the oldDept number. For example, assume you have printed several employees from Department 12. When you read a record with an employee from Department 13 (or any other department), the first thing you must do is print "END OF DEPARTMENT 12". You print the correct department number by accessing the value of the oldDept. Then you can print the other headings at the top of a new page and update oldDept to the current empDept, which is 13.

Now the newPage() module performs three tasks required in all control break routines:

- It performs any necessary processing for the previous group—in this case, writes the footer.

- It performs any necessary processing for the new group—in this case, writes headings.

- It updates the control break field.

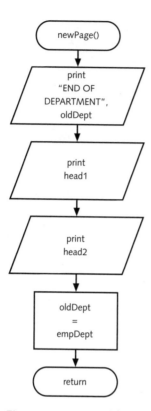

Figure 7-11   Modified newPage() module that prints department number in footer

The `finish()` module for the new program containing footers also requires an extra step. Imagine that the last five records on the input file include two employees from Department 78, Amy and Bill, and three employees from Department 85, Carol, Don, and Ellen. The logical flow proceeds as follows:

1. After the first Department 78 employee (Amy) prints, you read in the second Department 78 employee (Bill).

2. At the top of the `mainLoop()` module, Bill's department compares to `oldDept`. The departments are the same, so the second Department 78 employee (Bill) is printed. Then you read in the first Department 85 employee (Carol).

3. At the top of the `mainLoop()`, Carol's `empDept` and the `oldDept` are different, so you perform the `newPage()` module, while Carol's record waits in memory.

4. In the `newPage()` module, you print "END OF DEPARTMENT 78". Then you print headings for the top of the next page. Finally, you set `oldDept` to 85, and then return to the `mainLoop()`.

5. Back in the `mainLoop()`, you print a line of data for the first Department 85 employee (Carol), whose record waited while `newPage()` executed. Then you read in the record for the second Department 85 employee (Don).

6. At the top of `mainLoop()`, you compare Don's department number to `oldDept`. The numbers are the same, so you print Don's employee data and read in the last Department 85 employee (Ellen).

7. At the top of `mainLoop()` you determine that Ellen has the same department number, so you print Ellen's data and attempt to read from the input file where you encounter `eof`.

8. The `eof` decision in the mainline logic sends you to the `finish()` module.

You have printed the last Department 85 employee (Ellen), but the department footer for Department 85 has not printed. That's because every time you attempt to read an input record, you don't know whether there will be more records. The mainline logic checks for the `eof` condition, but if it determines that it is `eof`, the logic does not flow back into the `mainLoop()` where the `newPage()` module can execute.

To print the footer for the last department, you must print a footer one last time within the `finish()` routine. The `finish()` module in Figure 7-12 illustrates this. Taking this action is similar to printing the first heading in the `housekeeping()` module. The very first heading prints separately from all the others at the beginning; the very last footer must print separately from all the others at the end.

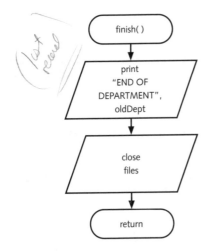

Figure 7-12   Modified finish() module for report program with footer

PERFORMING CONTROL BREAKS WITH TOTALS

Suppose you run a bookstore, and one of the files you maintain is called BOOKFILE, which has one record for every book title that you carry. Each record has fields such as `bookTitle`, `bookAuthor`, `bookCategory` (fiction, reference, self-help, and so on), `bookPublisher`, and `bookPrice`, as shown in this file description in Figure 7-13.

```
File name: BOOKFILE
Sorted by: Category
FIELD DESCRIPTION          POSITIONS      DATA TYPE       DECIMALS
Title                      1-30           Character
Author                     31-46          Character
Category                   47-56          Character
Publisher                  57-72          Character
Price                      73-77          Numeric              2
```

Figure 7-13   BOOKFILE file description

Suppose you want to print out a list of all the books that your store carries with a total number of books at the bottom of the list, as shown in Figure 7-14. You can use the logic shown in Figure 7-15. In the main loop module, named `bookListLoop()`, you print a book title, add 1 to the `grandTotal`, and read the next record. At the end of the program, in the `closeDown()` module, you print the `grandTotal` before you close the files.

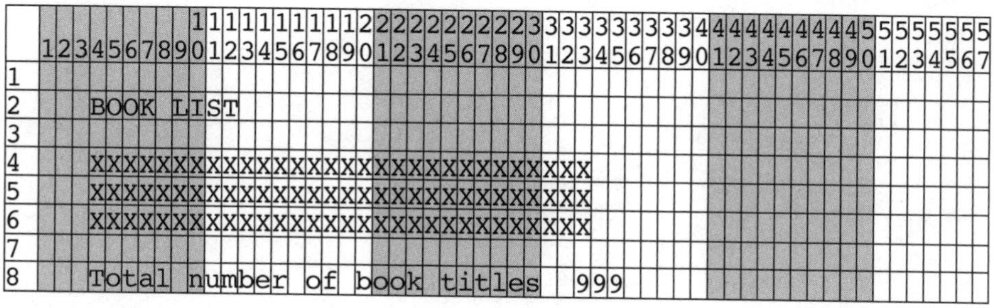

Figure 7-14   Print chart for book list

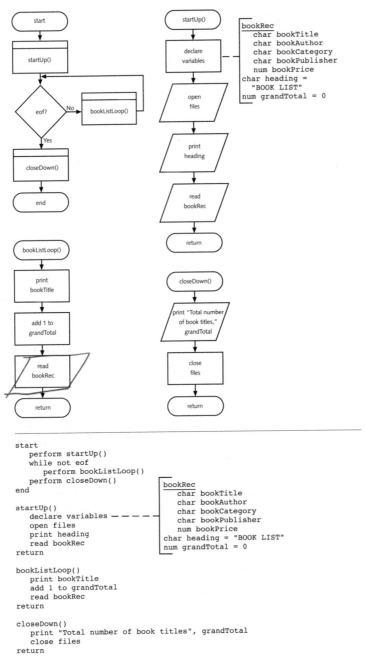

```
start
    perform startUp()
    while not eof
        perform bookListLoop()
    perform closeDown()
end

startUp()
    declare variables  — — — —
    open files
    print heading
    read bookRec
return

bookListLoop()
    print bookTitle
    add 1 to grandTotal
    read bookRec
return

closeDown()
    print "Total number of book titles", grandTotal
    close files
return
```

```
bookRec
    char bookTitle
    char bookAuthor
    char bookCategory
    char bookPublisher
    num bookPrice
char heading = "BOOK LIST"
num grandTotal = 0
```

Figure 7-15   Flowchart and pseudocode for bookstore program

As you can see from the pseudocode in Figure 7-15, the `bookListLoop()` module performs three major tasks:

1. Prints a book title.

2. Adds 1 to the `grandTotal`.

3. Reads in the next book record.

The `closeDown()` module prints the `grandTotal`. You can't print `grandTotal` any earlier in the program because the `grandTotal` value isn't complete until the last record has been read.

The logic of the preceding program is pretty straightforward. Suppose, however, that you decide you want a count for each category of book rather than just one grand total. For example, in the categories of fiction, reference, and self-help the output would consist of a list of all fiction books first, followed by a count; then all reference books followed by a count; and finally all self-help books followed by a count. The report is a control break report and the control break field is the `bookCategory`.

To produce the report with subtotals by category, you must declare two new variables: `previousCategory` and `categoryTotal`. Every time you read in a book record, you compare `bookCategory` to `previousCategory`; when there is a category change, you print the count of books for the previous category. The `categoryTotal` variable holds that count. See Figure 7-16.

7

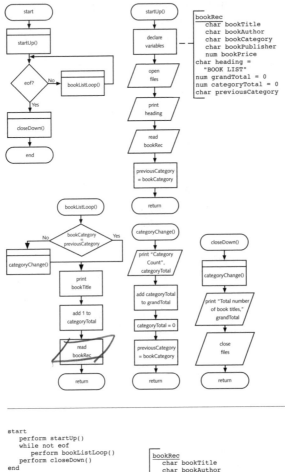

```
start
    perform startUp()
    while not eof
        perform bookListLoop()
    perform closeDown()
end

startUp()
    declare variables- - - - - - -
    open files
    print heading
    read bookRec
    previousCategory = bookCategory
return

bookListLoop()
    if bookCategory not equal to previousCategory then
        perform categoryChange()
    endif
    print bookTitle
    add 1 to categoryTotal
    read bookRec
return

categoryChange()
    print "Category count", categoryTotal
    add categoryTotal to grandTotal
    categoryTotal = 0
    previousCategory = bookCategory
return

closeDown()
    perform categoryChange()
    print "Total number of book titles", grandTotal
    close files
return
```

```
bookRec
    char bookTitle
    char bookAuthor
    char bookCategory
    char bookPublisher
    num bookPrice
char heading = "BOOK LIST"
num grandTotal = 0
num categoryTotal = 0
char previousCatergory
```

Figure 7-16   Flowchart and pseudocode for bookstore program with subtotals

Tip When you draw a flowchart, it is usually clearer to ask questions positively, as in bookCategory = previousCategory? and draw appropriate actions on the Yes or No side of the decision. In pseudocode, when action occurs only on the No side of a decision, it is usually clearer to ask negatively, as in bookCategory *not* equal to previousCategory. Figure 7-16 uses these tactics.

When you read the first record from the input file, you save the value of bookCategory in the previousCategory variable. Every time a record enters the bookListLoop() module, the program checks to see if the current record represents a new category of work by comparing bookCategory to the variable called previousCategory. When you process the first record, the categories match, so the book title prints, the categoryTotal increases by one, and you read the next record. If this next record's bookCategory value matches the previousCategory value, processing continues as usual with printing a line and adding 1 to the categoryTotal.

At some point the bookCategory for an input record does not match the previousCategory. At that point, you perform the categoryChange() module. Within the categoryChange() module, you print the count of the previous category of books. Then you add the categoryTotal to the grandTotal. Adding a total to a higher-level total is called **rolling up the totals**.

You could write the bookListLoop() so that as you process each book, you add one to the categoryTotal and add one to the grandTotal. Then there would be no need to roll totals up in the categoryChange() module. If there are 120 fiction books, you add 1 to categoryTotal 120 times; you also would add 1 to grandTotal 120 times. This technique would yield correct results, but you can eliminate executing 119 addition instructions by waiting until you have accumulated all 120 category counts before adding the total figure to grandTotal.

This control break report containing totals performs four of the five tasks required in all control break routines that include totals:

- It performs any necessary processing for the previous group—in this case it prints the categoryTotal.

- It rolls up the current level totals to the next higher level—in this case it adds categoryTotal to grandTotal.

- It resets the current level's totals to zero—in this case the categoryTotal is set to zero.

- It performs any necessary processing for the new group—in this case there is none.

- It updates the control break field—in this case previousCategory.

The closeDown() routine for this type of program is more complicated than it might first appear. It seems as though you should print the grandTotal, close the files, and

7

return to the mainline logic. However, when you read the last record, the mainline `eof` decision sends the logical flow to the `closeDown()` routine. You have not printed the last `categoryTotal`, nor have you added the count for the last category into the `grandTotal`. You must take care of both these tasks before printing the `grandTotal`. You can perform these two tasks as separate steps in `closeDown()`, but it is often simplest just to remember to perform the control break routine `categoryChange()` one last time. The `categoryChange()` module already executes after every previous category completes—that is, every time you encounter a new category during the execution of the program. You also can execute this module after the final category completes, at end of file. Encountering the end of the file is really just another form of break; it signals that the last category has finally completed. The `categoryChange()` module prints the category total and rolls the totals up to the `grandTotal` level.

When you call the `categoryChange()` module from within `closeDown()` it performs a few tasks you don't need, like setting the value of `previousCategory`. You have to weigh the convenience of calling the already-written `categoryChange()` module and executing a few unneeded statements, as opposed to taking the time to write a new module that would execute only the statements that are absolutely necessary.

It is very important to note that this control break program works whether there are three categories of books or 300. Note further that it does not matter what the categories of books are. For example, the program never asks `bookCategory = "fiction"`?. Instead, the control of the program breaks when the category field *changes* and it is in no way dependent on *what* that change is.

PERFORMING MULTIPLE-LEVEL CONTROL BREAKS

Let's say your bookstore from the last example is so successful that you have a chain of them across the country. Every time a sale is made you create a record with the fields `bookTitle`, `bookPrice`, `bookCity`, and `bookState`. You would like a report that prints a summary of books sold in each city and each state, similar to the one shown in Figure 7-17. A report such as this one that does not include any information about individual records, but instead includes group totals, is a **summary report**.

This program contains a **multiple-level control break**, that is, the normal flow of control (reading records and counting book sales) breaks away to print totals in response to more than just one change in condition. In this report a control break occurs in response to either of two conditions—when the contents of the `bookCity` variable changes as well as when the contents of the `bookState` variable changes.

Just as the file you use to create a single-level control break report must be presorted, so must the input file you use to create a multiple-level control break report. The input file that you use for the book sales report must be sorted by `bookCity` *within* `bookState`.

That is, all of one state's records, for example all records from IA, come first; then all the records from another state, such as IL, follow. Within any one state, all of one city's records come first, then all of the next city's records follow. For example, the input file that produces the report shown in Figure 7-17 contains 200 records for book sales in Ames, IA, followed by 814 records for book sales in Des Moines, IA. The basic processing entails reading a book sale record, adding one to a counter, and reading the next book sale record. At the end of any city's records, you print a total for that city; at the end of a state's records, you print a total for that state.

BOOK SALES BY CITY AND STATE	
Ames	200
Des Moines	814
Iowa City	291
Total for IA	1305
Chicago	1093
Crystal Lake	564
McHenry	213
Springfield	365
Total for IL	2235
Springfield	289
Worcester	100
Total for MA	389
Grand Total	3929

Figure 7-17   Sample run of Book Sales by City and State report

The `housekeeping()` routine of the Book Sales by City and State report program looks similar to the `housekeeping()` routine in the last control break program. You declare variables, open files, and read the first record. This time, however, there are multiple fields to save and compare to the old fields. Here you declare two special variables, `prevCity` and `prevState`, as shown in Figure 7-18. In addition, the Book Sales report shows three kinds of totals, so you declare three special variables, `cityCounter`, `stateCounter`, and `grandTotal`, which are all set to zero.

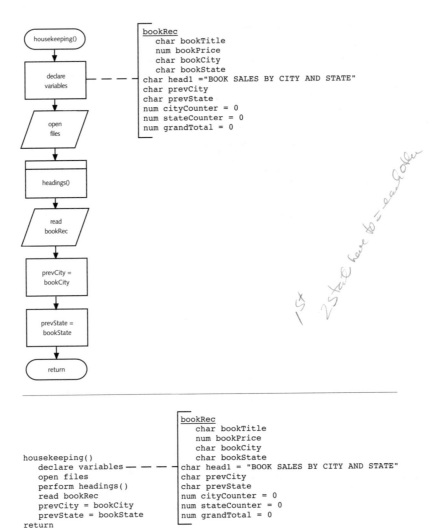

Figure 7-18   Flowchart and pseudocode for housekeeping() module for Book Sales by City and State report program

This program prints both `bookState` and `bookCity` totals, so you need two control break modules, `cityBreak()` and `stateBreak()`. Every time there is a change in the `bookCity` field, the `cityBreak()` routine performs these standard control break tasks:

- It performs any necessary processing for the previous group—prints totals for the previous city.

- It rolls up the current level totals to the next higher level—adds the city count to the state count.

- It resets the current level's totals to zero—sets the city count to zero.

- It performs any necessary processing for the new group—in this case there is none.

- It updates the control break field—sets `prevCity` to `bookCity`.

Within the `stateBreak()` module, you must perform one new type of task, as well as the control break tasks you are familiar with. The new task is the first task: within the `stateBreak()` module you must first perform a `cityBreak()` automatically (because if there is a change in the state, there must also be a change in the city). The `stateBreak()` module does the following:

- It processes the lower-level break, in this case `cityBreak()`.

- It performs any necessary processing for the previous group—prints totals for the previous state.

- It rolls up the current level totals to the next higher level—adds the state count to the grand total.

- It resets the current level's totals to zero—sets the state count to zero.

- It performs any necessary processing for the new group—in this case there is none.

- It updates the control break field—sets `prevState` to `bookState`.

The `mainLoop()` of this multiple-level control break program checks for any change in two different variables: `bookCity` and `bookState`. When the `bookCity` changes, a city total is printed, and when the `bookState` changes, a state total is printed. As you can see from the sample report in Figure 7-17, all city totals for each state print before the state total for the same state, so it might seem logical to check for a change in `bookCity` before checking for a change in `bookState`. However, the opposite is true. For the totals to be correct, you must check for any `bookState` change first. You do so because when a `bookCity` changes, the `bookState` also *might* be changing, but when the `bookState` changes, it means the `bookCity` *must* be changing.

Consider the sample input records shown in Figure 7-19, which are sorted by `bookCity` within `bookState`:

TITLE	PRICE	CITY	STATE
A Brief History of Time	20.00	Iowa City	IA
The Scarlet Letter	15.99	Chicago	IL
Math Magic	4.95	Chicago	IL
She's Come Undone	12.00	Springfield	IL
The Joy of Cooking	2.50	Springfield	IL
Walden	9.95	Springfield	MA
A Bridge Too Far	3.50	Springfield	MA

Figure 7-19 Sample data for Book Sales by City and State report

When you get to the point in the program where you read the first Illinois record (*The Scarlet Letter*), "Iowa City" is the value stored in the field `prevCity` and "IA" is the value stored in `prevState`. Since the values in the `bookCity` and `bookState` variables on the new record are both different from the `prevCity` and `prevState` fields, both a city and state total will print. However, consider the problem when you read the first record for Springfield, MA (*Walden*). At this point in the program `prevState` is "IL", but `prevCity` is the same as the current `bookCity`; both contain "Springfield." If you check for a change in `bookCity`, you won't find one at all, and no city total will print even though Springfield, MA is definitely a different city from Springfield, IL.

Because cities in different states can have the same name, writing your control break program to check for a change in city first, causes your program to not recognize that you are working with a new city. Instead, you should always check for the major-level break first. If the records are sorted by `bookCity` within `bookState`, then a change in `bookState` causes a **major-level break** and a change in `bookCity` causes a **minor-level break**. When the `bookState` value "MA", is not equal to the `prevState` value "IL", you force a `cityBreak()`, printing a city total for Springfield, IL before a state total for IL and before continuing with the Springfield, MA record. You check for a change in `bookState` first, and if there is one, you perform a `cityBreak()`. In other words, if there is a change in `bookState`, there is an implied change in `bookCity`, even if the cities happen to have the same name.

 If you need totals to print by `bookCity` within a field defined as `bookCounty` within `bookState`, you could say you have minor-, intermediate-, and major-level breaks.

Figure 7-20 shows the `mainLoop()` for the Book Sales by City and State Report program. You check for a change in the `bookState` value. If there is no change, you check for a change in the `bookCity` value. If there is no change there either, you add 1 to the counter for the city and read the next record. When there is a change in the `bookCity` value, you print the city total and add the city total to the state total. When there is a change in the **bookState** value, you perform the break routine for the last city in the state, then you print the state total and add it to the grand total.

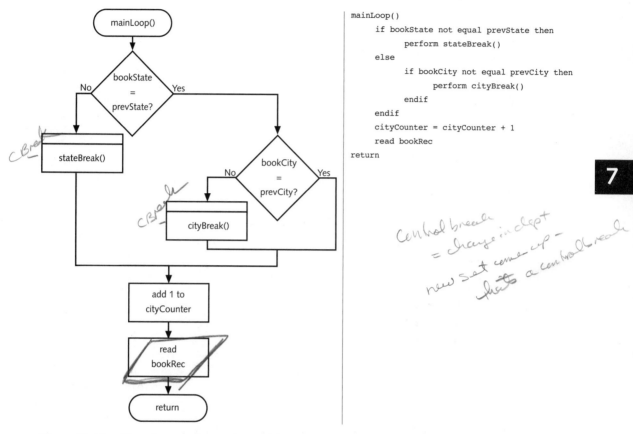

```
mainLoop()
        if bookState not equal prevState then
                perform stateBreak()
        else
                if bookCity not equal prevCity then
                        perform cityBreak()
                endif
        endif
        cityCounter = cityCounter + 1
        read bookRec
return
```

Figure 7-20   Flowchart and pseudocode for mainLoop() for Book Sales by City and State report

Figures 7-21 and 7-22 show the **stateBreak()** and **cityBreak()** modules. The two modules are very similar; the **stateBreak()** routine contains just one extra type of task. When there is a change in **bookState**, you perform the **cityBreak()** automatically before you perform any of the other necessary steps to change states.

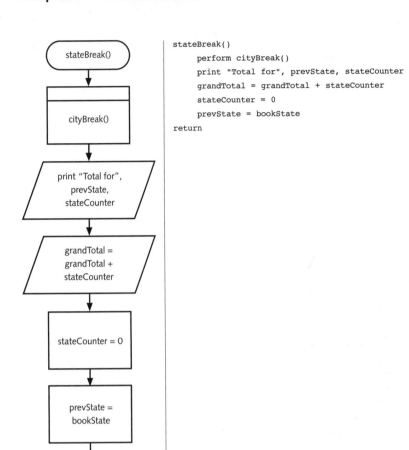

```
stateBreak()
    perform cityBreak()
    print "Total for", prevState, stateCounter
    grandTotal = grandTotal + stateCounter
    stateCounter = 0
    prevState = bookState
return
```

Figure 7-21   Flowchart and pseudocode for stateBreak() module

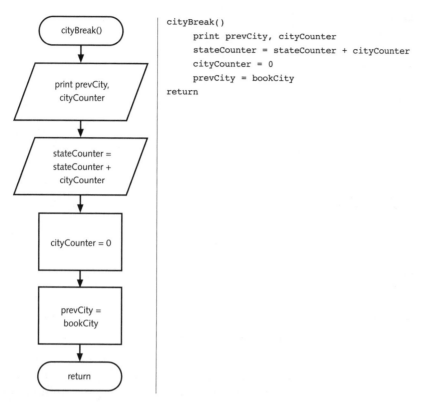

```
cityBreak()
     print prevCity, cityCounter
     stateCounter = stateCounter + cityCounter
     cityCounter = 0
     prevCity = bookCity
return
```

Figure 7-22   Flowchart and pseudocode for cityBreak() module

The sample report for the book sales by city and state shows that you print the grand total for all book sales, so within the `closeDown()` module, you must print the `grandTotal` variable. Before you can do so, however, you must perform both the `cityBreak()` and the `stateBreak()` modules one last time. You can accomplish this by performing `stateBreak()` because the first step within `stateBreak()` is to perform `cityBreak()`.

Consider the sample data shown in Figure 7-19. While you continue to read records for books sold in Springfield, MA, you continue to add to the `cityCounter` for that city. At the moment you attempt to read one more record past the end of the file, you do not know whether there will be more records; therefore, you have not yet printed either the `cityCounter` for Springfield or the `stateCounter` for MA. In the `closeDown()` module you perform `stateBreak()`, which immediately performs `cityBreak()`. Within `cityBreak()`, the count for Springfield prints and rolls up to the `stateCounter`. Then, after the logic transfers back to the `stateBreak()` module, the total for MA prints and rolls up to the `grandTotal`. Finally, you can print the `grandTotal`, as shown in Figure 7-23.

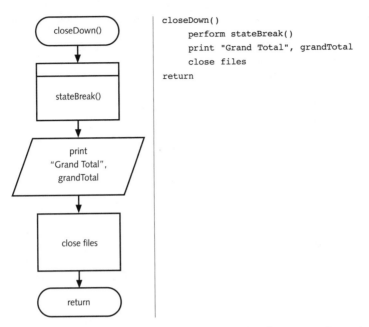

```
closeDown()
    perform stateBreak()
    print "Grand Total", grandTotal
    close files
return
```

Figure 7-23   Flowchart and pseudocode for closeDown() module

Every time you write a program, where you need control break routines, you should check whether you need to complete each of the following tasks within the modules:

- Performing the lower-level break, if any
- Performing any control break processing for the previous group
- Rolling up the current level totals to the next higher level
- Resetting the current level's totals to zero
- Performing any control break processing for the new group
- Updating the control break field

PERFORMING PAGE BREAKS

Many business programs use a control break to start a new page when a printed page fills up with output. In other words, you might want to start a new page based on the number of lines already printed rather than on the contents of an input field, such as department number. The logic in these programs involves counting the lines printed, pausing to print headings when the counter reaches some predetermined value, and then going on. This common business task is just another example of providing a break in the usual flow of control.

Some programmers may prefer to reserve the term *control break* for situations in which the break is based on the contents of one of the fields in an input record, rather than on the contents of a work field such as a line counter.

Let's say you have a file called CUSTOMERFILE that contains 1,000 customers with two character fields that you have decided to call `custLast` and `custFirst`. You want to print a list of these customers, 60 detail lines to a page. The mainline logic of the program is familiar. The only new feature is a variable called a line counter. You will use a **line–counter** variable to keep track of the number of printed lines so that you can break to a new page after printing 60 lines. See Figure 7-24.

```
start
    perform getReady()
    while not eof
            perform produceReport()
    perform cleanup()
end
```

Figure 7-24   Mainline logic of customer report program

When creating a printed report, you need to clarify whether the user wants a specific number of *total* lines per page, including headings, or a specific number of *detail* lines per page following the headings.

Within the **getReady()** module (Figure 7-25), you declare the variables, open the files, print the headings, and read the first record. Within the **produceReport()** module (Figure 7-26), you compare the `lineCounter` to 60. When you process the first record, the `lineCounter` is zero, so you print the record, add one to the `lineCounter`, and read the next record.

```
getReady()
    open files
    print head1
    print head2
    read custRec
return
```

Figure 7-25   getReady() module for customer report

```
produceReport()
    if lineCounter = 60 then
        perform startNewPage()
    endif
    print custLast, custFirst
    add 1 to lineCounter
    read custRec
return
```

Figure 7-26   produceReport() module for customer report program

7

On every cycle through the produceReport() module, you check the line counter to see if it is 60 yet. When the first record is written, lineCounter is 1. You read the second record, and if there is a second record (that is, if it is not eof), you return to the top of the produceReport() module. In that module you compare lineCounter to 60, print another line, and add 1 to lineCounter, making it equal to 2.

After 60 records read and write, lineCounter holds a value of 60. When you read the sixty-first record (and if it is not eof), you enter the produceReport() module for the 61st time. The answer to the question lineCounter = 60? is yes, and you break to perform the startNewPage() module. The startNewPage() module is a control break routine.

The startNewPage() module must print the headings that appear at the top of a new page, and it must also set the lineCounter back to zero. If you neglect to reset the lineCounter, its value will increase with each successive record and never be equal to 60 again. When resetting the lineCounter for a new page, you force execution of the startNewPage() module after 60 more records (120 total) print.

```
startNewPage()
    print head1
    print head2
    lineCounter = 0
return
```

Figure 7-27 startNewPage() module for customer report

The startNewPage() module is simpler than many control break modules because no record counters or accumulators are being maintained. In fact, the startNewPage() module must perform only two of the tasks you have seen required by control break routines.

- It does not perform the lower-level break, because there is none.

- It does not perform any control break processing for the previous group, because there is none.

- It does not roll up the current level totals to the next higher level, because there are no totals.

- It does not reset the current level's totals to zero, because there are no totals (other than the lineCounter, which is the control break field).

- It does perform control break processing for the new group by writing headings at the top of the new page.

- It does update the control break field—the line counter.

You might want to employ one little trick that you can use to remove the statements that write the headings from the getReady() module. If you initialize lineCounter to 60 when defining the variables at the beginning of the program, on the first pass through mainLoop() you can "fool" the computer into printing the first set of headings automatically. When you initialize the lineCounter to 60, you can remove the statements print head1 and print head2 from the getReady() module. With this change, when you enter the produceReport() module for the first time, lineCounter already is set to 60 and the startNewPage() module prints the headings and resets the lineCounter to zero before processing the first record from the input file.

As within control break report programs that break based on the contents of one of a record's fields, in any program that starts new pages based on a line count, you always must update the line-counting variable which causes the unusual action. Using page breaks or control breaks (or both) within reports adds a new degree of organization to your printed output and makes it easier for the user to interpret and use.

7

CHAPTER SUMMARY

❏ A control break is a temporary detour in the logic of a program; programmers refer to a program as a control break program when a change in the value of a variable initiates special actions or causes special or unusual processing to occur. To generate a control break report, your input records must be organized in sorted order based on the field that will cause the breaks.

❏ You use a control break field to hold data from a previous record. You decide when to perform a control break routine by comparing the value in the control break field to the corresponding value in the current record. At minimum, the simplest control break routines perform necessary processing for the new group and update the control break field.

❏ Sometimes you need to use control data within a control break module, such as in a heading that requires information about the next record or in a footer that requires information about the previous record. The very first heading prints separately from all the others at the beginning; the very last footer must print separately from all the others at the end.

❏ A control break report that contains and prints totals for the previous group, rolls up the current level totals to the next higher level, resets the current level's totals to zero, performs any other needed control break processing, and updates the control break field.

❏ In a program containing a multiple-level control break, the normal flow of control breaks away for special processing in response to more than just one change in condition. You should always test for a major-level break before a minor-level break, and include a call to the minor break routine within the major break module.

❑ Every time you write a program in which you need control break routines, you should check whether you need to perform each of the following tasks within the routines: Any lower-level break, any control break processing for the previous group, rolling up the current level totals to the next higher level, resetting the current level's totals to zero, any control break processing for the new group, and updating the control break field.

❑ To perform page breaks, you count the lines printed and pause to print headings when the counter reaches some predetermined value.

EXERCISES

1. What fields would you want to use as the control break fields to produce a report that lists all inventory items in a grocery store? (For example, you might choose to group items by grocery store department.) Design the print chart for the report.

2. What fields would you want to use as the control break fields to produce a report that lists all the people you know? (For example, you might choose to group friends by city of residence.) Design the print chart for the report.

3. Write the pseudocode for the employees listed by department program that is flowcharted in Figures 7-3 through 7-7 earlier in this chapter.

4. A used-car dealer keeps track of sales in the following format:

AUTO SALES FILE DESCRIPTION
File name: AUTO
Sorted by: Salesperson

FIELD DESCRIPTION	POSITIONS	DATA TYPE	DECIMALS	EXAMPLE
Salesperson	1–20	Character		Miller
Make of Car	21–30	Character		Ford
Vehicle Type	31–40	Character		Sedan
Sale Price	41–45	Numeric	0	12500

By the end of the week, a salesperson may have sold no cars, one car, or many cars. Create the logic of a program that would print one line for each salesperson with that salesperson's total sales for the week and commission earned, which is 4% of the total sales. Create the print chart, hierarchy chart, and either the flowchart or the pseudocode.

5. A community college maintains student records in the following format:

STUDENT FILE DESCRIPTION
File name: STUDENTS
Sorted by: Hour of first class

FIELD DESCRIPTION	POSITIONS	DATA TYPE	DECIMALS	EXAMPLE
Student Name	1–20	Character		Danielle Erickson
City	21–30	Character		Woodstock
Hour of First Class	31–32	Numeric	0	08
Phone Number	33–42	Numeric	0	8154379823

The records have been sorted by hour of the day. The hour of first class is a two-digit number based on a 24-hour clock (that is, a 1 p.m. first class is recorded as 13).

Create a report that students can use to organize carpools. The report lists the names and phone numbers of students from the city of Huntley. Note that some students come from cities other than Huntley; these students should not be listed on the report.

Start a new page for each hour of the day so that all students starting classes at the same hour are listed on the same page. Include the hour that each page represents in the heading for that page.

Design the print chart and hierarchy chart, and then create the flowchart or pseudocode for this program.

6. The Stanton Insurance Agency needs a report summarizing the counts of life, health, and other types of insurance policies it sells. Input records contain policy number, name of insured, policy value, and type of policy and have been sorted in alphabetical order by type of policy. At the end of the report, display a count of all the policies. Design the print chart and hierarchy chart, and then create the flowchart or pseudocode for this program.

7. If a university is organized into colleges (such as Liberal Arts), divisions (such as Languages), and departments (such as French), what would constitute the major, intermediate, and minor control breaks in a report that prints all classes offered by the university?

8. A zoo keeps track of the expense of feeding the animals it houses. Each record holds one animal's ID number, name, species (elephant, rhinoceros, tiger, lion, and so on), zoo residence (pachyderm house, large cat house, and so on), and weekly food budget. The records take the following form:

ANIMAL FEED RECORDS
File name: ANIMFOOD
Sorted by: Species within house

FIELD DESCRIPTION	POSITIONS	DATA TYPE	DECIMALS	EXAMPLE
Animal ID	1—4	Numeric	0	4116
Animal Name	5—29	Character		Elmo
Species	30—45	Character		Elephant
House	46—55	Character		Pachyderm
Weekly Food	56—59	Numeric	0	75
Budget in Dollars				

Design a report that lists each animal's ID, name, and budgeted food amount. At the end of each species group, print a total budget for the species. At the end of each house (for example, the species lion, tiger, and leopard are all in the large cat house), print the house total. At the end of the report, print the grand total. Draw the hierarchy chart and create the flowchart or pseudocode for this problem.

9. A soft-drink manufacturer produces several flavors of drink—for example, cola, orange, and lemon. Additionally, each flavor has several versions such as regular, diet, and caffeine-free. The manufacturer operates factories in several states. Assume you have input records that list version, flavor, yearly production in gallons and state. (For example: Regular Cola 5000 Kansas.) The records have been sorted in alphabetical order by version within flavor within state. Design the report that lists each version and flavor, with minor total production figures for each flavor and major total production figures for each state. Create the hierarchy chart and flowchart or pseudocode for this program.

10. An art shop owner maintains records for each item in the shop, including the title of the work, the artist who made the item, the medium (for example, watercolor, oil, or clay), and the monetary value. The records are sorted by artist within medium. Design a report that lists all items in the store with a minor total value following each artist's work, and a major total value following each medium. Allow only 40 detail lines per page. Create the hierarchy chart and flowchart or pseudocode for this program.

CHAPTER
8

ARRAYS

After studying Chapter 8, you should be able to:
- Understand how arrays are used
- Understand how arrays occupy computer memory
- Manipulate an array to replace using nested decisions
- Declare and initialize an array
- Understand the difference between run-time and compile-time arrays
- Load array values from a file
- Search an array for an exact match
- Use parallel arrays
- Force subscripts to remain within array bounds
- Improve search efficiency by using an early exit
- Search an array for a range match

UNDERSTANDING ARRAYS

An **array** is a series or list of variables in computer memory, all of which have the same name but are differentiated with special numbers called **subscripts**. Whenever you require multiple storage locations for objects, you are using a real-life counterpart of a programming array. For example, if you store important papers in a series of file folders and label each folder with a consecutive letter of the alphabet, then you are using the equivalent of an array. If you store mementos in a series of stacked shoeboxes, each labeled with a year, or if you sort mail into slots, each labeled with a name, then you are also using a real-life equivalent of a programming array.

When you look down the left side of a tax table to find your income level before looking to the right to find your income tax obligation, you are using an array. Similarly, if you look down the left side of a train schedule to find your station before looking to the right to find the train's arrival time, you also are using an array.

Each of these real-life arrays helps you organize real-life objects. You *could* store all your papers or mementos in one huge cardboard box, or find your tax rate or train's arrival time if both were printed randomly in one large book. However, using an organized storage and display system makes your life easier in each case. Using a programming array will accomplish the same results for your data.

Some programmers refer to an array as a *table* or a *matrix*.

How Arrays Occupy Computer Memory

When you declare an array, you declare a programming structure that contains multiple variables. Each variable within an array has the same name and the same data type and each separate array variable is one **element** of the array. Each array element occupies an area in memory next to, or contiguous to, the others as shown in Figure 8-1. You indicate the number of elements an array will hold—the **size of the array**—when you declare the array along with your other variables.

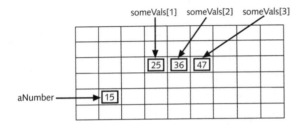

Figure 8-1   Appearance of a three-element array in computer memory

Every array element has the same group name, but also has a unique subscript indicating how far away the individual element is from the first element. Therefore any array's subscripts are always a sequence of integers such as 1 through 5 or 1 through 10. Depending on the syntax rules of the programming language you use, you place the subscript within either parentheses or square brackets following the group name; when writing pseudocode or drawing a flowchart, you can use either form of notation. This text will use square brackets to hold array element subscripts so that you don't mistake array names for method names. For example, Figure 8-1 shows how a single variable and an array are stored in computer memory. The single variable named **aNumber** holds the value 15. The array named **someVals** contains three elements, so the elements are **someVals[1]**, **someVals[2]**, and **someVals[3]**. The value stored in **someVals[1]** is 25; **someVals[2]** holds 36 and **someVals[3]** holds 47.

In general, older programming languages such as COBOL and RPG use parentheses to hold their array subscripts. Newer languages such as C#, C++, and Java use square brackets.

In some languages (for example, Java, C#, and C++) the first array element's subscript is 0; in others (for example, Visual Basic, COBOL, and RPG) it is 1. In Pascal you can identify the starting number as any value you like. In all languages, however, the subscripts must be integers (whole numbers) and sequential.

You are never required to use arrays within your programs, but learning to use arrays correctly can make many programming tasks far more efficient and professional. When you understand how to use arrays, you will be able to provide elegant solutions to problems that otherwise would require tedious programming steps.

When you describe people or events as "elegant," you mean they possess a refined gracefulness. Similarly, programmers use the term "elegant" to describe programs that are well designed and easy to understand and maintain.

MANIPULATING AN ARRAY TO REPLACE USING NESTED DECISIONS

Consider a program that keeps statistics for a recycling drive competition at a high school. The school is holding a competition between the freshman, sophomore, junior, and senior classes to see which class can collect the greatest number of aluminum cans. Each time a student brings in some cans, a clerk adds a record to a file in the following format, shown in Figure 8-2.

```
File name: STURECORDS
FIELD DESCRIPTION      POSITIONS      DATA TYPE      DECIMALS
Student class          1              Numeric        0
Cans collected         2—4            Numeric        0
```

Figure 8-2   File description for recycling records

For example, if a junior brings in 25 cans, one record is created with a 3 (for junior) in the class field and a 25 in the cans collected field. If a freshman brings in 10 cans, a record with 1 and 10 is created. If a second junior then brings in 20 more cans, the third record will contain a 3 and a 20.

At the end of the recycling competition after all the records have been collected, the file might contain hundreds of records, each holding a one-digit number representing a class and up to a three-digit number representing cans. You want to write a program that summarizes the total of the cans brought in by each class. The print chart for this report appears in Figure 8-3.

| | | | | | | | | | 1 | 1 | 1 | 1 | 1 | 1 | 1 | 1 | 1 | 2 | 2 | 2 | 2 | 2 | 2 | 2 | 2 | 2 | 3 | 3 | 3 | 3 | 3 | 3 | 3 | 3 | 3 | 4 | 4 | 4 | 4 | 4 | 4 | 4 | 4 | 4 | 5 | 5 | 5 | 5 | 5 | 5 | 5 | 5 |
| 1 | 2 | 3 | 4 | 5 | 6 | 7 | 8 | 9 | 0 | 1 | 2 | 3 | 4 | 5 | 6 | 7 | 8 | 9 | 0 | 1 | 2 | 3 | 4 | 5 | 6 | 7 | 8 | 9 | 0 | 1 | 2 | 3 | 4 | 5 | 6 | 7 | 8 | 9 | 0 | 1 | 2 | 3 | 4 | 5 | 6 | 7 | 8 | 9 | 0 | 1 | 2 | 3 | 4 | 5 | 6 | 7 |

1
2 Can Competition Report
3
4 Class Cans
5 1 99999
6 2 99999
7 3 99999
8 4 99999

Figure 8-3 Print chart for can-recycling report

If all the records were sorted in order by the student's class, this report could be a control break report. You would simply read each record for the first (freshman) class, accumulating the number of collected cans in a variable. When you read the first record from a different class, you would print out the total for the previous class, reset the total to zero, and update the control break field before continuing.

 You learned about control break logic in Chapter 7.

Assume, however, that the records have not been sorted. Without using an array, could you write the program that would accumulate the four class can-recycling totals? Of course you could. The program would have the same mainline logic as the other programs you have seen, as flowcharted in Figure 8-4.

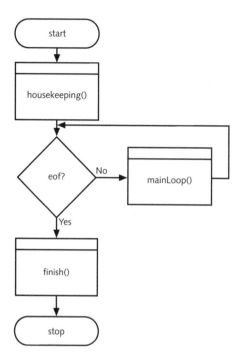

Figure 8-4 Flowchart for mainline logic of recycling program

 Later in this chapter you will see how to write the can-recycling program much more efficiently using arrays.

In the `housekeeping()` module (Figure 8-5), you declare variables including `stuClass` and `stuCans`. Then you open the files and read the first record into memory. The headings *could* print in `housekeeping()`, or, because no other printing takes place in this program until the `finish()` module, you can choose to wait and print the headings there.

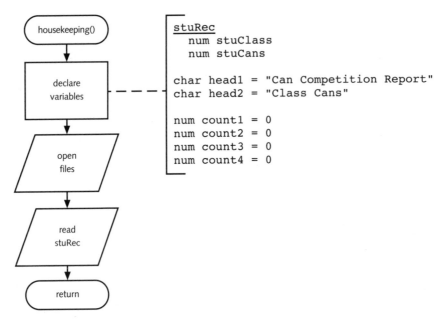

Figure 8-5   housekeeping() module for recycling program

You can use four variables, `count1`, `count2`, `count3`, and `count4`, to keep running counts of collected-can totals for the four different classes. All four of these counter variables need to be initialized to zero. You can tell by looking at the planned output that you need two heading lines, so `head1` is defined as "Can Competition Report" and `head2` as "Class Cans".

Eventually, four lines will be printed, each with a class number and a count of cans for that class. These lines cannot be printed until the `finish()` module, however, because you won't have a complete count of each class's cans until all input records have been read.

The logic within the `mainLoop()` module of the program requires adding a record's `stuCans` value to `count1`, `count2`, `count3`, or `count4`, depending on the `stuClass`. After one student's `stuCans` value has been added to one of the four accumulators you read the next record, and if it is not `eof`, you repeat the decision-making and accumulating process. When all records have been read you proceed to the `finish()` module, where you print the four summary lines with the four class counts. See Figures 8-6 and 8-7.

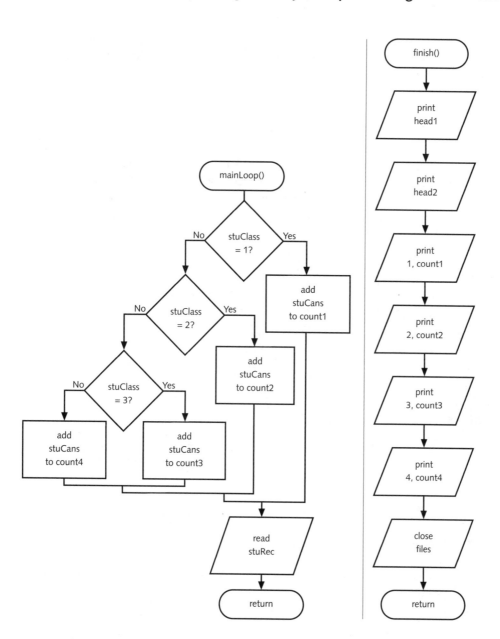

Figure 8-6   mainLoop() module for
recycling program

Figure 8-7   finish() module for
recycling program

The recycling program works just fine and there is absolutely nothing wrong with it logically. But what if the recycling drive is held at an elementary school with eight classes, in a school district with 12 grade levels, or in a company with 30 departments?

With any of these scenarios, the basic logic of the program would remain the same; however, you would need to declare many additional accumulator variables. You also would need many additional decisions within the `mainLoop()` module and many additional print statements within the `finish()` module in order to complete the processing.

Using an array provides an alternative approach to this programming problem, which greatly reduces the number of statements you need. When you declare an array, you provide a group name for a number of associated variables in memory. For example, the four can-collection count accumulators can be redefined as a single array named `count`. The individual elements become `count[1]`, `count[2]`, `count[3]`, and `count[4]` as shown in the new `housekeeping()` module in Figure 8-8.

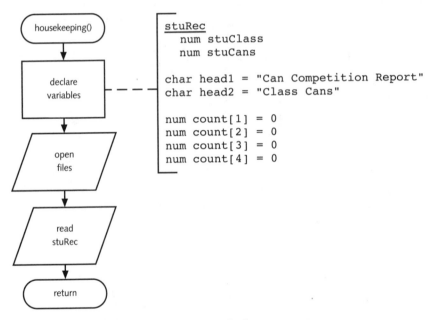

Figure 8-8   Modified housekeeping() declaring count array

With the change to `housekeeping()` shown in Figure 8-8, the `mainLoop()` changes to the version shown in Figure 8-9.

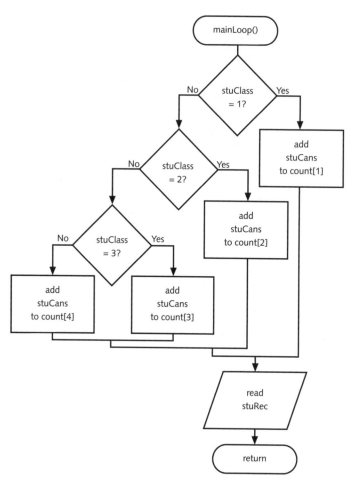

Figure 8-9   Modified mainLoop() using count array

Figure 8-9 shows that when the **stuClass** is 1, the **stuCans** are added to **count[1]**; when the **stuClass** is 4, the **stuCans** are added to **count[4]**. In other words, the value in **stuCans** is added to one of the elements of a **count** array instead of to a single variable named **count1**, **count2**, **count3**, or **count4**. Is this a big improvement over the original? Of course, it isn't. You still have not taken advantage of the benefits of using the array in this program.

The true benefit of using an array lies in your ability to use a variable as a subscript to the array rather than using a constant such as 1 or 4. Notice in the **mainLoop()** in Figure 8-9 that within each decision, the value you are comparing to **stuClass** and the constant you are using as a subscript in the resulting "Yes" process are always identical. That is, when the **stuClass** is 1, the subscript used to add **stuCans** to the **count** array is 1; when the **stuClass** is 2, the subscript used for the **count** array is 2; and so on. Therefore, why not just use `stuClass` as a subscript? You can rewrite the `mainLoop()` as shown in Figure 8-10.

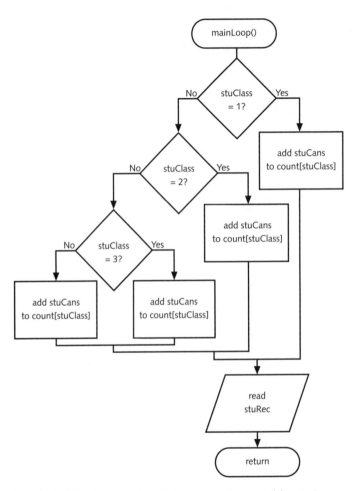

Figure 8-10 Modified mainLoop() using variable stuCans as a subscript

Of course, this flowchart segment looks no more efficient than the one in Figure 8-9. However, notice that in Figure 8-10 the process boxes after each decision are exactly the same. Each box contains `add stuCans to count[stuClass]`. If you are always going to take the same action no matter what the answer to a question is, why ask the question? Instead, you can write the `mainLoop()` module as shown in Figure 8-11.

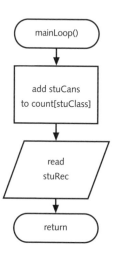

Figure 8-11   Modified mainLoop() eliminating decisions

The two steps in Figure 8-11 represent the *entire* `mainLoop()` module! When `stuClass` is 2, `stuCans` is added to `count[2]`; when `stuClass` is 4, `stuCans` is added to `count[4]`, and so on. *Now* you have a big improvement to the original `mainLoop()` from Figure 8-9. What's more, this `mainLoop()` does not change whether there are 8, 30, or any other number of classes and `count` array elements, as long as the classes are numbered sequentially. To use more than four accumulators, you would declare additional `count` elements in the `housekeeping()` module, but the `mainLoop()` logic would remain the same as it is in Figure 8-11.

The `finish()` module also can be improved. Instead of four separate print statements, you can use a variable to control a printing loop, as shown in Figure 8-12. Because the `finish()` module follows the `eof` condition, all input records have been used and `stuClass` is not currently holding any needed information. In `finish()` you can set `stuClass` to 1, then write `stuClass` and `count[stuClass]`. Then add 1 to `stuClass` and use the same set of instructions again. You can use `stuClass` as a loop control variable to print the four individual `count` values. The improvement in this `finish()` module over the one shown in Figure 8-7 is not as dramatic as the improvement in the `mainLoop()`; but in a program with more `count` elements, the only change to the `finish()` module would be in the constant value you use to control the loop. Twelve or 30 `count` values can print as easily as four if they are stored in an array.

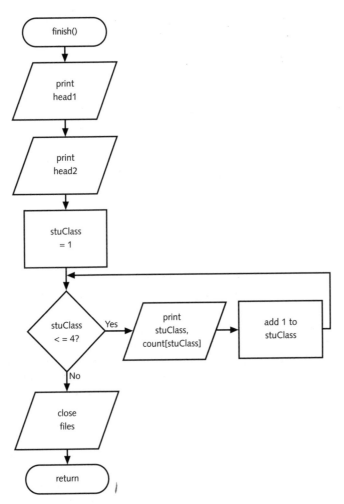

Figure 8-12   Modified `finish()` module that uses an array

Within the `finish()` module in Figure 8-12, the `stuClass` variable is handy to use as a subscript, but any variable could have been used as long as it was:

- Numeric with no decimal places

- Initialized to 1

- Incremented by 1 each time the logic passes through the loop

In other words, nothing is linking `stuClass` to the `count` array per se; within the `finish()` module you simply can use the `stuClass` variable as a subscript to indicate each successive element within the `count` array.

The can-recycling program *worked* when the `mainLoop()` contained a long series of decisions, but it is easier to write when you employ arrays. Additionally, the program is more efficient, easier for other programmers to understand, and easier to maintain. Arrays are never mandatory, but often they can drastically cut down on your programming time and make a program easier to understand.

ARRAY DECLARATION AND INITIALIZATION

In the can-recycling program, the four `count` array elements were declared and initialized to 0s in the `housekeeping()` module. The `count` values need to start at 0 so they can be added to during the course of the program. Originally (see Figure 8-8) you provided initialization in the `housekeeping()` module as:

```
num count[1] = 0
num count[2] = 0
num count[3] = 0
num count[4] = 0
```

Separately declaring and initializing each `count` element is acceptable only if there are a small number of `count`s. If the can-recycling program were updated to keep track of recycling in a company with 30 departments, you would have to initialize 30 separate fields. It would be too tedious to write 30 separate declaration statements.

Programming languages do not require the programmer to name each of the 30 `count`s: `count[1]`, `count[2]`, and so on. Instead, you can make a declaration such as one of those in Figure 8-13.

Declaration	Programming Language
DIM COUNT(30)	BASIC, Visual Basic
int count[30];	C#, C++
int count = new int[30];	Java
COUNT OCCURS 30 TIMES PICTURE 9999.	COBOL
array count [1..30] of integer;	Pascal

Figure 8-13 Declaring a 30-element array named count in several common languages

 C, C++, Pascal, and Java programmers typically use lowercase variable names. COBOL, and BASIC programmers often use all uppercase. Visual Basic programmers are likely to begin with an uppercase letter.

 The terms `int` and `integer` in the code samples within Figure 8-13 both indicate that the `count` array will hold whole-number values. The value 9999 in the COBOL example indicates that each `count` will be a four-digit integer. These terms are more specific than the `num` identifier this book uses to declare all numeric variables.

All the declarations in Figure 8-13 have two things in common: They name the `count` array and indicate that there will be 30 separate numeric elements. For flowcharting or pseudocode purposes, a statement such as `num count[30]` will indicate the same thing.

Declaring a numeric array does not necessarily set its individual elements to zero (although it does in some programming languages like BASIC and Java). Most programming languages allow the equivalent of `num count[30] all set to 0`; you should use a statement like this to initialize an array in your flowcharts or pseudocode.

Alternatively, to start all array elements with the same initial value, you can use an initialization loop within the `housekeeping()` module. An **initialization loop** is a loop structure that provides initial values for every element in any array. To create an initialization loop, you must use a numeric field as a subscript. For example, if you declare a field named `sub`, and initialize `sub` to 1, then you can use a loop like the one shown in the `housekeeping()` module in Figure 8-14 to set all the array elements to zero.

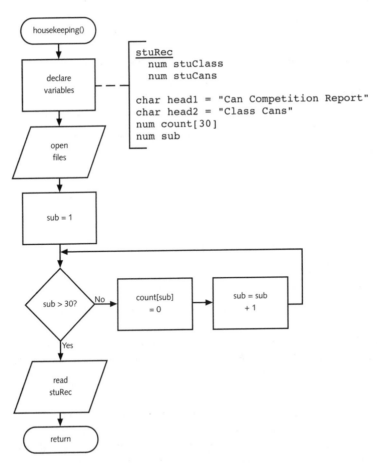

Figure 8-14   A housekeeping() module demonstrating one method of initializing array elements

RUN-TIME AND COMPILE-TIME ARRAYS

The array that you used to accumulate class counts in the can-recycling program is a **run-time array** or **execution-time array**, because the values that you want to use, the final can counts, are created during an actual run, or execution, of the program. In other words, if the freshman class is going to collect 1,000 cans, you don't know that fact at the beginning of the program. Instead, that value is accumulated during the execution of the program and not known until the end.

Some arrays are not run-time, but rather **compile-time arrays**. Recall from Chapter 1 that compiling is the act of translating a high-level language into machine code (1s and 0s). A compile-time array is one whose final desired values are fixed at the beginning of the program.

For example, let's say you own an apartment building with five floors and you have records for all your tenants with the information shown in Figure 8-15. The combination of each tenant's floor number and apartment letter provides you with a specific apartment—for example, apartment 3B.

```
File name: TENANTS
FIELD DESCRIPTION        POSITIONS        DATA TYPE        DECIMALS
Tenant name              1–40             Character
Floor number             41               Numeric          0
Apartment letter         42               Character
```

Figure 8-15   Tenant file description

Every month you print a rent bill for each tenant. Your rent charges are based on the floor of the building as shown in Figure 8-16.

```
Floor          Rent in $
1              350
2              400
3              475
4              600
5              1000 (the penthouse!)
```

Figure 8-16   Rents by floor

To create a computer program that prints each tenant's name and rent due, you could use five decisions concerning the floor number. However, it is more efficient to use a compile-time array to hold the five rent figures. The array is a compile-time array because you set its values once at the beginning of the program and they never change.

Remember that another name for an array is a *table*. If you can use paper and pencil to list the rents in a table format, using an array might be an appropriate programming option.

The mainline logic for this program is shown in Figure 8-17. The housekeeping module is named **prep()**. When you declare variables within the **prep()** module, you create an array for the five rent figures and set num **rent[1]** = 350, num **rent[2]** = 400, and so on. The rent amounts are **hard-coded** into the array; that is, they are explicitly assigned to the array elements. The **prep()** module is shown in Figure 8-18.

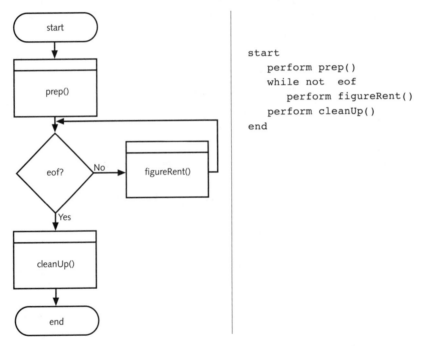

```
start
    perform prep()
    while not  eof
        perform figureRent()
    perform cleanUp()
end
```

Figure 8-17   Flowchart and pseudocode for mainline logic of rent program

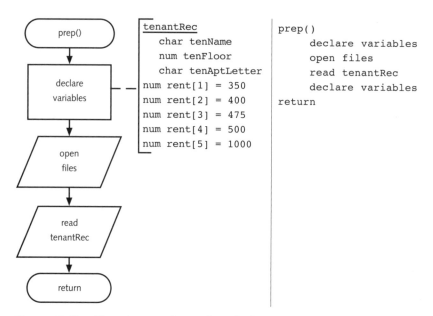

Figure 8-18   Flowchart and pseudocode for prep() module of rent program

 As an alternative to defining `rent[1]`, `rent[2]`, and so on as in Figure 8-18, most programming languages allow a more concise version that takes the general form `num rent[5] = 350, 400, 475, 600, 1000`. When you use this form of array initialization, the first value you list is assigned to the first array element and the subsequent values are assigned in order. Most programming languages allow you to assign fewer values than there are array elements declared, but none allow you to assign more values.

At the end of the `prep()` module, you read a first record into memory. When it enters `figureRent()` (the main loop), you can print three items: "Dear", `tenName`, and ", Here is your monthly rent bill" (the quote begins with a comma that follows the recipient's name). Then you must print the rent amount. Instead of making a series of selections such as `if tenFloor = 1 then print rent[1]` and `if tenFloor = 2 then print rent[2]`, you want to take advantage of the `rent` array. The solution is to create a `figureRent()` module that looks like Figure 8-19. You use the `tenFloor` variable as a subscript to access the correct `rent` array element. When deciding what variable to use as a subscript with an array, ask yourself, "Of all the values available in the array, what does the correct selection depend on?" When printing a `rent` value, the rent you use depends on the floor on which the tenant lives, so the correct action is `print rent[tenFloor]`.

 Every programming language provides ways to space your output for easy reading. For example, a common technique to separate "Dear" from the tenant's name is to include a space after the *r* in *Dear*, as in
`print "Dear ", tenName`.

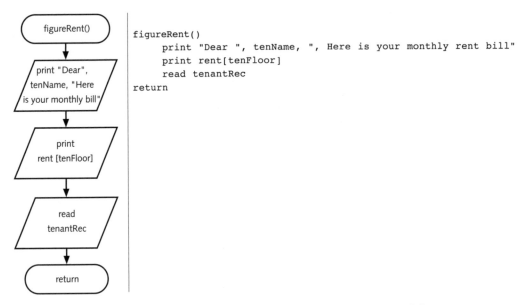

```
figureRent()
    print "Dear ", tenName, ", Here is your monthly rent bill"
    print rent[tenFloor]
    read tenantRec
return
```

Figure 8-19   Flowchart and pseudocode for the figureRent() module of the rent program

The `cleanup()` module for this program is very simple—just close the files. See Figure 8-20.

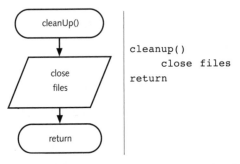

```
cleanup()
    close files
return
```

Figure 8-20   The cleanup() module for the rent program

Without a `rent` array, the `figureRent()` module would have to contain four decisions and five different resulting actions. With the `rent` array there are no decisions. Each tenant's rent is simply based on the `rent` element that corresponds to the `tenFloor` because the floor number indicates the positional value of the corresponding rent. Arrays can really lighten the load.

LOADING AN ARRAY FROM A FILE

Writing the rent program from the last section requires that you set values for five `rent` array elements within the `prep()` module. If you write the rent program for a skyscraper, you might have to initialize 100 array elements. Additionally, when the building management changes the rent amounts, you must alter the array element values within the program to reflect the new rent charges. If the rent values change frequently, it is inconvenient to have hard-coded values in your program. Instead, you can write your program so that it loads the array rent amounts from a file.

A file that contains all the rent amounts can be updated by apartment building management as frequently as needed. Suppose you receive a file named RENTFILE that always contains the current rent values. You can write the rent program so that it accepts all records from this input file within the **prep()** module. Figure 8-21 shows how this is accomplished.

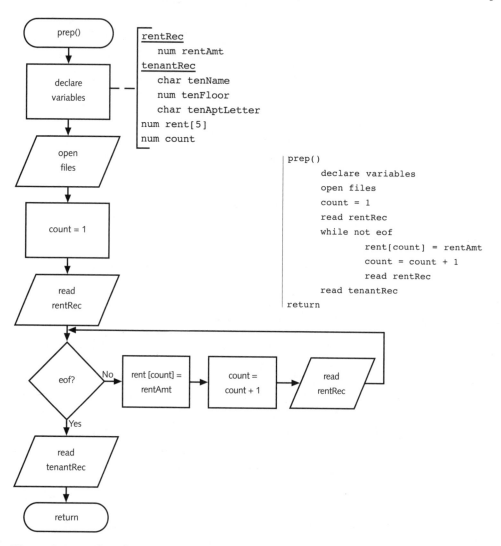

Figure 8-21   Flowchart and pseudocode for prep() module that reads rents from an input file

In the `prep()` module in Figure 8-21, you set the variable `count`, to one and read a `rentRec` record from the `RENTFILE`. Each record in the `RENTFILE` contains just one field—a numeric `rentAmt` value. For this program, assume that the rent records in the `RENTFILE` are stored in order by floor. When you read in the first `rentAmt` you store it in the first element of the `rent` array. You increase the `count` to 2, read the second record, and assuming it's not `eof`, you store the second rent in the second element of the `rent` array. After the `RENTFILE` is exhausted you begin to read the file containing the `tenantRec` records, and then the program proceeds as usual.

When you use this method, reading the rents from an input file instead of hard-coding them into the program, clerical employees can update the `rentRec` values in the `RENTFILE`. Your program takes care of loading the rents into the program array from the most recent copy of the `RENTFILE`, assuring that each rent is always accurate and up-to-date.

Another way to organize the `RENTFILE` would be to include two fields within each record-for example, `rentFloor` and `rentAmt`. Then the records would not have to be read into your program in floor number order. Instead, you could use the `rentFloor` variable as a subscript to indicate which position in the array to use to store the `rentAmt`.

You might question how the program knows which file's `eof` condition is tested when a program uses two or more input files. In some programming languages, the `eof` condition is tested on the file most recently read. In many programming languages you would have to provide more specific information along with the `eof` question, perhaps `rentRec eof?` or `tenantRec eof?`.

SEARCHING FOR AN EXACT MATCH IN AN ARRAY

In both the can-recycling program and the rent program that you've seen in this chapter, the fields that the arrays depend on conveniently hold small whole numbers. The classes in the high school are 1 through 4 and the floors of the building are 1 through 5. Unfortunately, real life doesn't always happen in small integers. Sometimes you don't have a variable that conveniently holds an array position; sometimes you have to search through an array to find a value you need.

Consider a mail-order business in which orders come in with a customer name, address, item number ordered, and quantity ordered, as shown in Figure 8-22.

File name: CUSTREC			
FIELD DESCRIPTION	POSITIONS	DATA TYPE	DECIMALS
Customer name	1–20	Character	
Address	21–40	Character	
Item number	41–43	Numeric	0
Quantity	44–45	Numeric	0

Figure 8-22   Mail-order customer file description

The item numbers are three-digit numbers, but perhaps they are not consecutive 001 through 999. Instead, over the years items have been deleted and new items have been added. For example, there might no longer be an item with number 005 or 129. Sometimes there might be a hundred-number gap or more between items.

For example, let's say that this season you are down to the items shown in Figure 8-23.

```
ITEM NUMBER
006
008
107
405
457
688
```

Figure 8-23   Available items in mail-order company

8

When a customer orders an item you want to determine whether the customer has ordered a valid item number. You could use a series of six decisions to determine whether the ordered item is valid, but a superior approach is to create an array that holds the list of valid item numbers. Then you can search through the array for an exact match to the ordered item. If you search through the entire array without finding a match for the item the customer ordered, you can print an error message, for example "No such item."

Suppose you create an array with the six elements shown in Figure 8-24. If a customer orders item 107, a clerical worker can tell whether it is valid by looking down the list and verifying that 107 is a member of the list. In a similar fashion, you can use a loop to test each `validItem` against the ordered item number.

```
num validItem[1] = 006
num validItem[2] = 008
num validItem[3] = 107
num validItem[4] = 405
num validItem[5] = 457
num validItem[6] = 688
```

Figure 8-24   Array of valid item numbers

The technique for verifying that an item number exists involves setting a subscript to 1 and setting a flag variable to indicate that you have not yet determined whether the customer's order is valid. A **flag** is a variable that you set to indicate a true or false state. Typically, a variable is called a flag when its only purpose is to tell you whether some event has occurred. For example, you can set a character variable named `foundIt` to "N", indicating "No". Then you compare the customer's ordered item number to the first item in the array. If the customer-ordered item matches the first item in the array, you can set the flag variable to "Y", or any other value that is not "N". If the items do not match, you increase the subscript and continue to look down the list of numbers stored in the array. If you check all six valid item numbers and the customer item matches none of them, then the flag variable **foundIt** still holds the value "N". If the flag variable is "N" after you have looked through the entire list, you can issue an error message indicating that no match was ever found. Assuming you declare the customer item as **custItemNo** and the subscript as **x**, then Figure 8-25 shows a flowchart segment and the pseudocode that accomplishes the item verification.

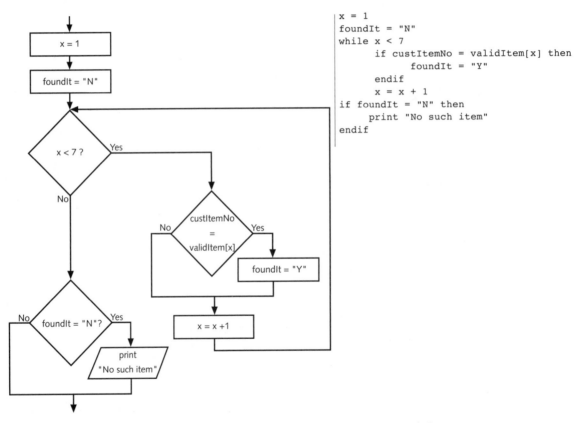

```
x = 1
foundIt = "N"
while x < 7
          if custItemNo = validItem[x] then
                    foundIt = "Y"
          endif
          x = x + 1
if foundIt = "N" then
     print "No such item"
endif
```

Figure 8-25 Flowchart and pseudocode segments for finding an exact match for a customer item number

USING PARALLEL ARRAYS

In a mail-order company when you read in a customer's order, you usually want to accomplish more than to simply verify that the item exists. You want to determine the price of the ordered item, multiply that price by quantity ordered, and print a bill. Suppose you have prices for six available items as shown in Figure 8-26.

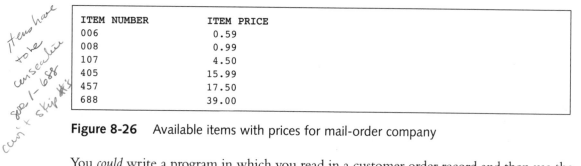

ITEM NUMBER	ITEM PRICE
006	0.59
008	0.99
107	4.50
405	15.99
457	17.50
688	39.00

Figure 8-26   Available items with prices for mail-order company

You *could* write a program in which you read in a customer order record and then use the customer's item number as a subscript to pull a price from an array. To use this method, you would need an array with at least 688 elements. If a customer orders item 405, the price is found at `validItem[custItemNo]`, which is `validItem[405]`, or the 405th element of the array. Such an array would need 688 elements, but because you sell only six items, you would waste 682 of the memory positions. Instead of reserving a large quantity of memory that remains unused, you can set up this program to use two arrays.

Consider the mainline logic in Figure 8-27 and the `ready()` routine in Figure 8-28. Two arrays are set up within the `ready()` module. One contains six elements named `validItem`; all six elements are valid item numbers. The other array also has six elements named `validItemPrice`; all six elements are prices. Each price in this `validItemPrice` array is conveniently in the same position as the corresponding item number in the other `validItem` array. Two corresponding arrays such as these are **parallel arrays** because each element in one array is associated with the element in the same relative position in the other array.

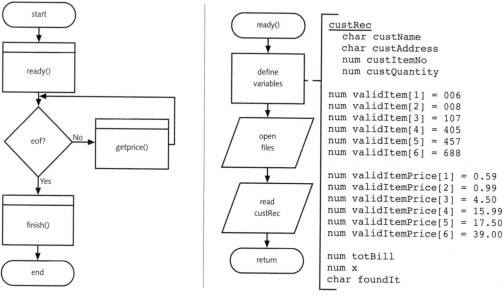

Figure 8-27   Mainline logic for price program

Figure 8-28   ready() module for price program

You can write the `getPrice()` module as shown in Figure 8-29. The general procedure is to read each item number, look through each of the `validItem` values separately, and when a match for the `custItemNo` on the input record is found, pull the corresponding parallel price out of the list of `validItemPrice`s.

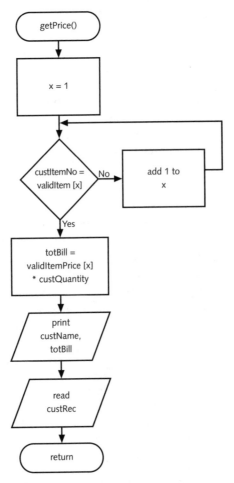

Figure 8-29   The getPrice() module for price program

You must create a variable to use as a subscript for the arrays. If you name the subscript `x`, then you can start by setting `x` equal to 1. Then if `custItemNo` is the same as `validItem[x]`, you can use the corresponding price from the other table, `validItemPrice[x]`, to calculate the customer's bill.

Some programmers object to using a cryptic variable name such as x because it is not descriptive. These programmers would prefer a name like priceIndex. Others approve of short names like x when the variable is used only in a limited area of a program, as it is used here, to step through an array. There are many style issues like this on which programmers disagree. As a programmer it is your responsibility to find out what conventions are used among your peers in your organization.

Within the getPrice() module, if custItemNo is *not* the same as validItem[x], then add 1 to x. Because x now holds the value 2, next you compare the customer's requested item number to validItem[2]. The value of x keeps increasing, and eventually a match between custItemNo and some validItem[x] should be found.

Once you find a match for the custItemNo in the validItem array, you know that the price of that item is in the same position in the other array, validItemPrice. When validItem[x] is the correct item, validItemPrice[x] must be the correct price.

Suppose that a customer orders item 457 and walk through the flowchart yourself to see if you come up with the correct price.

REMAINING WITHIN ARRAY BOUNDS

The getPrice() module in Figure 8-29 is not perfect. The logic makes one dangerous assumption: that every customer will order a valid item number. If a customer is looking at an old catalog and orders item 007, the program will never find a match. The value of x will just continue to increase until it reaches a value higher than the number of elements in the array. At that point one of two things will happen. When you use a subscript value that is higher than the number of elements in an array, some programming languages will stop execution of the program and issue an error message. Other programming languages will not issue an error message but will continue to search through computer memory beyond the end of the array. Either way, the program doesn't end elegantly. When you use a subscript that is not within the range of acceptable subscripts, your subscript is said to be **out of bounds**. Ordering a wrong item number is a frequent error; a good program should be able to handle the mistake and not allow the subscript to go out of bounds.

You can improve the price-finding program by adding a flag variable and a test to the getPrice() module. You can set the flag when you find a valid item in the validItem array, and after searching the array, check whether the flag has been altered. See Figure 8-30.

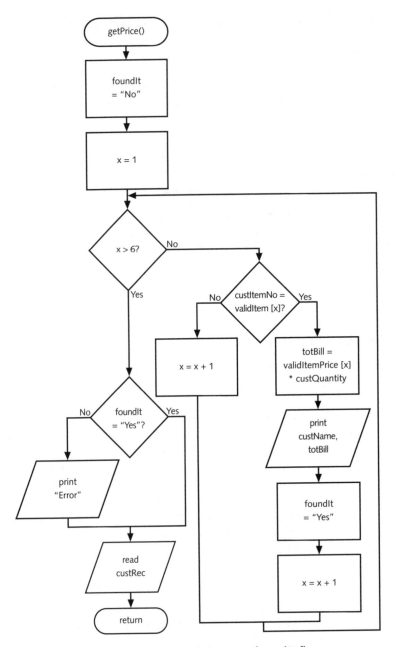

Figure 8-30   The getPrice() module using foundIt flag

In the `ready()` module, you can declare a variable named `foundIt` that acts as a flag. When you enter the `getPrice()` module you can set `foundIt` equal to "No". Then after setting `x` to 1, check to see if `x` is greater than 6 yet. If it is not, compare the `custItemNo` to `validItem[x]`. If they are equal, you know the position of the item's price and you can use the price to print the customer's bill and set the `foundIt` flag to "Yes". If the `custItemNo` is not equal to `validItem[x]`, you increase `x` by 1 and continue to search through the array. When `x` is 7, you shouldn't look through the array any more; you've gone through all six legitimate items and you've reached the end. If `foundIt` doesn't have a "Yes" in it at this point, it means you never found a match for the ordered item number; you never took the Yes path leading from the `custItemNo = validItem[x]?` question. If `foundIt` does not have "Yes" stored in it, you should print an error message; the customer has ordered a nonexistent item.

IMPROVING SEARCH EFFICIENCY USING AN EARLY EXIT

The mail-order program is still a little inefficient. The problem is that if lots of customers order item 006 or 008, their price is found on the first or second pass through the loop. The program continues searching through the item array, however, until `x` exceeds the value 6. To stop the search once the item has been found and `foundIt` is set to "Yes", force `x` to 7 immediately. Then, when the program loops back to check whether `x` is greater than 6 yet, the loop will be exited and the program won't bother checking any of the higher item numbers. Leaving a loop as soon as a match is found is called an **early exit**; it improves the program's efficiency. The larger the array, the more beneficial it becomes to exit the searching loop as soon as you find what you're looking for.

Figure 8-31 shows the final version of the `getPrice()` module. You search the `validItem` array, element by element. If an item number is not matched in a given location, the subscript is increased and the next location is checked. As soon as an item number is located in the array, you print a line, turn on the flag, and force the subscript to a high number (seven) so the program will not check the item number array any further.

8

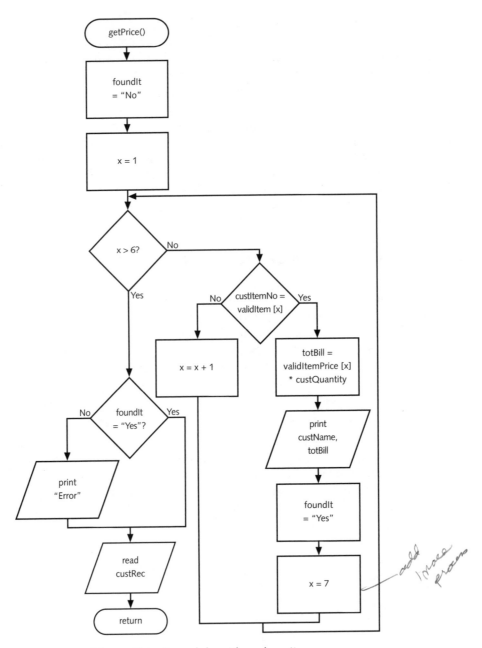

Figure 8-31   The getPrice() module with early exit

SEARCHING AN ARRAY FOR A RANGE MATCH

Customer item numbers need to match numbers in a table exactly in order to determine the correct price of an item. Sometimes, however, programmers want to work with ranges of values in arrays. A **range of values** is any set of contiguous values, for example 1 though 5.

Recall the customer file description from earlier in this chapter, shown again in Figure 8-32.

File name: CUSTREC			
FIELD DESCRIPTION	POSITIONS	DATA TYPE	DECIMALS
Customer name	1—20	Character	
Address	21—40	Character	
Item number	41—43	Numeric	0
Quantity	44—45	Numeric	0

Figure 8-32   Customer file description

Suppose the company decides to offer quantity discounts as shown in Figure 8-33.

Number of items ordered	Discount %
1—9	0
10—24	10
25—48	15
49 or more	25

Figure 8-33   Discounts on orders by quantity

You want to be able to read in a record and determine a discount percentage based on the value in the quantity field. One ill-advised approach might be to set up an array with as many elements as any customer might ever order and store the appropriate discount for each possible number, as shown in Figure 8-34.

```
num discount[1] = 0
num discount[2] = 0
  .
  .
num discount[9] = 0
num discount[10] = 10
  .
  .
num discount[48] = 15
num discount[49] = 25
num discount[50] = 25
  .
  .
```

Figure 8-34   Usable—but inefficient—discount array

This approach has three drawbacks:

- It requires a very large array that uses a lot of memory.
- You must store the same value repeatedly. For example, each of the first nine elements receives the same value, zero.
- Where do you stop adding array elements? Is a customer order quantity of 75 items enough? What if a customer orders 100 or 1000 items? No matter how many elements you place in the array, there's always a chance that a customer will order more.

A better approach is to create just four discount array elements, one for each of the possible discount rates, as shown in Figure 8-35.

```
num discount[1] = 0
num discount[2] = 10
num discount[3] = 15
num discount[4] = 25
```

Figure 8-35   Superior discount array

With the new four-element `discount` array, you need a parallel array to search through to find the appropriate level for the discount. At first, beginning programmers might consider creating an array named `discountRange` and testing whether the quantity ordered equals one of the four stored values. For example:

```
num discountRange[1] = 1 through 9
num discountRange[2] = 10 through 24
num discountRange[3] = 25 through 48
num discountRange[4] = 49 and higher
```

However, you cannot create an array like the one above. Each element in any array is simply a single variable. A variable like `payRate` can hold 6 or 12, but it can't hold every value 6 *through* 12. Similarly, the `discountRange[1]` variable can hold a 1, 2, 9, or any other single value, but it can't hold 1 *through* 9; there is no such numeric value.

One solution is to create an array that holds only the low-end value of each range, as Figure 8-36 shows.

```
num discountRange[1] = 1
num discountRange[2] = 10
num discountRange[3] = 25
num discountRange[4] = 49
```

Figure 8-36   discountRange array using low end of each discount range

Now the process is to compare each `custQuantity` value with the *last* range limit (`discountRange[4]`). If the `custQuantity` is at least that value, 49, the customer gets the highest discount rate (`discount[4]`). If the `custQuantity` is not at least

discountRange[4], then you check to see if it is at least discountRange[3], or 25.
If so, the customer receives discount[3], and so on. If you declare a variable named
rate to hold the correct discount rate, and another variable named sub to use as a subscript, then you can use the determineDiscount() module shown in Figure 8-37.
This determineDiscount() module uses a loop to find the appropriate discount rate
for an order, then calculates and prints a customer bill.

An alternative approach is to store the high end of every range in an array.
Then you start with the *lowest* element and check for values *less than or
equal to* each array element value.

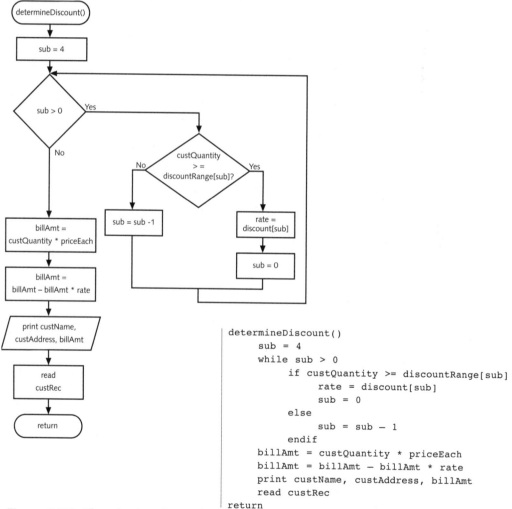

```
determineDiscount()
      sub = 4
      while sub > 0
            if custQuantity >= discountRange[sub]
                  rate = discount[sub]
                  sub = 0
            else
                  sub = sub − 1
            endif
      billAmt = custQuantity * priceEach
      billAmt = billAmt − billAmt * rate
      print custName, custAddress, billAmt
      read custRec
return
```

Figure 8-37 Flowchart and pseudocode for discount determination

When using an array to store range limits, you use a loop to make a series of comparisons that would otherwise require many separate decisions. Your program is written using fewer instructions than would be required if you did not use an array, and modifications to your program will be easier to make in the future.

CHAPTER SUMMARY

- An array is a series or list of variables in computer memory, all of which have the same name but are differentiated with special numbers called subscripts.

- When you declare an array, you declare a programming structure that contains multiple elements, each of which has the same name and the same data type. Each array element has a unique integer subscript indicating how far away the individual element is from the first element.

- You often can use a variable as a subscript to an array, replacing multiple nested decisions.

- You can declare and initialize all of the elements in an array using a single statement that provides a type, a name, and a quantity of elements for the array. You also can initialize array values within an initialization loop.

- An array whose values are determined during the execution of a program is a run-time array, or execution-time array. An array whose final desired values are fixed at the beginning of the program is a compile-time array.

- You can load an array from a file. This step is often performed in a program's housekeeping module.

- Searching through an array to find a value you need involves initializing a subscript, using a loop to test each array element, and setting a flag when a match is found.

- In parallel arrays, each element in one array is associated with the element in the same relative position in the other array.

- Your programs should assure that subscript values do not go out of bounds, that is, take on a value out of the range of legal subscripts.

- When you need to compare a value to a range of values in an array, you can store either the low- or high-end value of each range for comparison.

EXERCISES

1. The city of Cary is holding a special census. The census takers collect one record for each citizen as follows:

```
CENSUS FILE DESCRIPTION
File name: CENSUS
Not sorted
FIELD DESCRIPTION       POSITIONS       DATA TYPE       DECIMALS
Age                     1–3             Numeric         0
Gender                  4               Character
Marital status          5               Character
Voting district         6–7             Numeric         0
```

   The voting district field contains a number from 1 through 22.

   Design the report, draw the hierarchy chart, and draw the logic of the program that would produce a count of the number of citizens residing in each of the 22 voting districts.

2. a. The Midville Park District maintains records containing information about players on its soccer teams. Each record contains a player's first name, last name, and team number. The teams are:

```
Soccer Teams
Team number         Team name
1                   Goal Getters
2                   The Force
3                   Top Guns
4                   Shooting Stars
5                   Midfield Monsters
```

   Design the print chart, hierarchy chart, and flowchart or pseudocode for a report that lists all players along with their team numbers and team names.

   b. Create the logic for a program that produces a count of the number of players registered for each team listed in Exercise 2a.

3. a. An elementary school contains 30 classrooms numbered 1 through 30. Each classroom can contain any number of students up to 35. Each student takes an achievement test at the end of the school year and receives a score from 0 through 100. One record is created for each student in the school; each record contains a student ID, classroom number, and grade. Design the print chart, hierarchy chart, and logic for a program that lists the total points scored for each of the 30 classrooms.

   b. Modify Exercise 3a so that each classroom's average of the test scores prints rather than each classroom total.

   c. The school in Exercises 3a and 3b maintains a file containing the teacher's name for each classroom. Each record in this file contains a room number 1 through 30, and the last name of the teacher. Modify Exercise 3b so that the correct teacher's name appears on the list with his or her class's average.

8

4. A fast-food restaurant sells the following products:

```
Fast-Food Items
Product          Price
Cheeseburger     2.49
Pepsi            1.00
Chips             .59
```

Create a flowchart or pseudocode for a program that reads in a record containing a customer number and item name, then prints either the correct price or the message "Sorry, we do not carry that" as output.

5. Each week, the home office for a fast-food restaurant franchise distributes a file containing new prices for the items it carries. The file contains the item name and current price. Create a flowchart or pseudocode for a program that loads the current values into arrays. Then the program reads in a customer record containing a customer number and item name, and prints either the correct price or the message "Sorry, we do not carry that" as output.

6. The city of Redgranite is holding a special census. The census takers collect one record for each citizen as follows:

```
CENSUS FILE DESCRIPTION
File name: CENSUS
Not sorted
```

FIELD DESCRIPTION	POSITIONS	DATA TYPE	DECIMALS
Age	1–3	Numeric	0
Gender	4	Character	
Marital status	5	Character	
Voting district	6–7	Numeric	0

Design the report, draw the hierarchy chart, and draw the logic of the program that produces a count of the number of citizens residing in each of the following age groups: under 18, 18 through 30, 31 through 45, 46 through 64, and 65 and older.

7. a. A company desires a breakdown of payroll by department. Input records are as follows:

```
PAYROLL FILE DESCRIPTION
File name: PAY
```

FIELD DESCRIPTION	POSITIONS	DATA TYPE	DECIMALS	EXAMPLE
Employee last name	1–20	Character		Dykeman
First name	21–30	Character		Ellen
Department	31	Numeric	0	3
Hourly salary	32–36	Numeric	2	12.50
Hours worked	37–38	Numeric	0	40

Input records are organized in alphabetical order by employee, *not* in department number order.

The output is a list of the seven departments in the company (numbered 1 through 7) and the total gross payroll (rate times hours) for each department. Create the print layout chart, hierarchy chart, and flowchart or pseudocode for this program.

b. Modify Exercise 7a so that the report lists department names as well as numbers. The names are:

Department names and numbers

Department number	Department name
1	Personnel
2	Marketing
3	Manufacturing
4	Computer Services
5	Sales
6	Accounting
7	Shipping

c. Modify the report created in Exercise 7b so that it prints a line of information for each employee before printing the department summary at the end of the report. Each detail line must contain the employee's name, department number, department name, hourly wage, hours worked, gross pay, and withholding tax.

Withholding taxes are based on the following percentages of gross pay:

Withholding Taxes

Weekly salary	Withholding %
0.00–200.00	10
200.01–350.00	14
350.01–500.00	18
500.01–up	22

8. The Perfect Party Catering Company keeps records concerning the events it caters as follows:

EVENT RECORDS
File name: CATER

FIELD DESCRIPTION	POSITIONS	DATA TYPE	DECIMALS	EXAMPLES
Event number	1–5	Numeric	0	15621
Host name	6–25	Character		Profeta
Month	26–27	Numeric	0	10
Day	28–29	Numeric	0	15
Year	30–33	Numeric	0	2003
Meal selection	34	Numeric	0	4
Number of guests	35–40	Numeric	0	150

Additionally, a meal file contains the meal selection codes (such as 4), name of entree (such as "Roast beef"), and current price per guest (such as 19.50).

Design the print chart for a report that lists each event number, host name, date, meal, guests, gross total price for the party, and price for the party after discount. Print the month *name*—for example, "October"—rather than "10". Print the meal selection—for example, "Roast beef"—rather than "4". The gross total price for the party is the price per guest for the meal, times the number of guests. The final price includes a discount based on the following table:

Discounts for Large Parties

Number of guests	Discount
1–25	$0
26–50	$75
51–100	$125
101–250	$200
251 and over	$300

Create the hierarchy chart and either the flowchart or pseudocode for this problem.

9. *Daily Life Magazine* wants an analysis of the demographic characteristics of its readers. The Marketing department has collected reader survey records in the following format:

```
MAGAZINE READER FILE DESCRIPTION
File name: MAGREADERS
Not sorted
```

FIELD DESCRIPTION	POSITIONS	DATA TYPE	DECIMALS	EXAMPLE
Age	1–3	Numeric	0	38
Gender	4	Character		F
Marital status	5	Character		M
Annual income	6–11	Numeric	0	45000

a. Create the logic for the program that would produce a count of readers by age groups as follows: under 20, 20–29, 30–39, 40–49, and 50 and older.

b. Create the logic for the program that would produce a count of readers by gender within age group—that is, under 20 females, under 20 males, and so on.

c. Create the logic for the program that would produce a count of readers by income groups as follows: under $20,000, $20,000–$24,999, $25,000–$34,999, $35,000–$49,000, and $50,000 and up.

10. Glen Ross Vacation Property Sales employs seven salespeople as follows:

```
Salespeople
ID Number        Name
103              Darwin
104              Kravitz
201              Shulstad
319              Fortune
367              Wickert
388              Miller
435              Vick
```

When a salesperson makes a sale, a record is created including the date, time, and dollar amount of the sale as follows: The time is expressed in hours and minutes, based on a 24-hour clock. The sale amount is expressed in whole dollars.

```
SALE Records
File name: SALES
```

FIELD DESCRIPTION	POSITIONS	DATA TYPE	DECIMALS	EXAMPLES
Salesperson	1–3	Numeric	0	319
Month	4–5	Numeric	0	02
Day	6–7	Numeric	0	21
Year	8–11	Numeric	0	2003
Time	12–15	Numeric	0	1315
Sale amount	16–22	Numeric	0	95900

Salespeople earn a commission that differs for each sale based on the following rate schedule:

```
Commission rates
Sale amount             Rate
$0–50,000               .04
$51,000–$125,000        .05
$126,000–$200,000       .06
$201,000 and up         .07
```

Design the print chart, hierarchy chart, and either the flowchart or pseudocode that produces each of the following reports:

a. A report listing each salesperson number, name, total sales, and total commissions.

b. A report listing each month of the year as both a number and a word (for example, "01 January"), and the total sales for the month for all salespeople.

c. A report listing total sales as well as total commissions earned by all salespeople for each of the following time frames based on hour of the day: 00–05, 06–12, 13–18, and 19–23.

ADVANCED ARRAY
MANIPULATION

After studying Chapter 9, you should be able to:

♦ Describe the need for sorting data

♦ Swap two values in computer memory

♦ Use a bubble sort

♦ Use a variable for the array size in a bubble sort

♦ Avoid making unnecessary comparisons in a bubble sort

♦ Avoid making unnecessary passes through the list in a bubble sort

♦ Use an insertion sort

♦ Use a selection sort

♦ Use indexed files

♦ Use a linked list

♦ Use multidimensional arrays

UNDERSTANDING THE NEED FOR SORTING RECORDS

When you store data records, they exist in some sort of sequential order. Examples of records in **sequential order** include employee records stored in numeric order by Social Security number or department number, or in alphabetic order by last name or department name. Even if the records are stored in a random order—for example, the order in which a data-entry clerk felt like entering them—they still are in *some* order, although probably not the order desired for processing or viewing. When this is the case, the data need to be **sorted**, or placed in order, based on the contents of one or more fields. When you sort data, you can sort either in **ascending order**, arranging records from lowest to highest value within a field, or **descending order**, arranging records from highest to lowest value. Here are some examples of occasions when you would need to sort records:

- A college stores students' records in ascending order by student ID number, but the registrar wants to view the data in descending order by credit hours earned so he can contact students who are close to graduation.

- A department store maintains customer records in ascending order by customer number, but at the end of a billing period, the credit manager wants to contact customers whose balances are 90 or more days overdue. The manager wants to list these overdue customers in descending order by the amount owed so the customers maintaining the biggest debt can be contacted first.

- A sales manager keeps records for her salespeople in alphabetical order by last name, but needs to list the annual sales figure for each salesperson so that she can determine the median annual sale amount. The **median** value in a list is the middle value; it is not the same as the arithmetic average, or **mean**.

Sorting is usually reserved for a relatively small number of data items. If thousands of customer records are stored and they frequently need to be accessed in order based on different fields (alphabetical order by customer name one day, zip code order the next), the records would probably not be sorted at all, but would be indexed or linked. The end of this chapter covers indexing and linking.

When computers sort data, they always use numeric values. This is clear when you sort records by fields such as customer number or balance due. However, even alphabetic sorts are numeric because everything that is stored in a computer is stored as a number using a series of 0s and 1s. In every popular computer coding scheme, "B" is numerically one greater than "A" and "y" is numerically one less than "z". Unfortunately, whether "A" is represented by a number that is greater or smaller than the number representing "a" depends on your system. Therefore, to obtain the most useful and accurate list of alphabetically sorted records, you should be consistent in the use of capitalization.

Because "A" is always less than "B", alphabetic sorts are always considered ascending sorts.

The most popular coding schemes include ASCII, Unicode, and EBCDIC. Each is a code in which a number represents every computer character.

It's possible that as a professional programmer you will never have to write a program that sorts records, because organizations can purchase pre-written or "canned" sorting programs. However, it is beneficial to understand the sorting process so that you can write a special purpose sort when needed. Understanding sorting also improves your array-manipulating skills.

UNDERSTANDING HOW TO SWAP TWO VALUES

Many sorting techniques have been developed. A concept that is central to most sorting techniques involves swapping two values. When you swap the values stored in two variables, you set the first variable equal to the value of the second, and the second variable equal to the value of the first. However, there is a trick to reversing any two values. Assume you have declared two variables as follows:

```
num score1 = 90
num score2 = 85
```

If you first assign score1 to score2, both score1 and score2 hold 90, and the value 85 is lost. Similarly, if you first assign score2 to score1, both variables hold 85, and the 90 is lost.

The solution lies in creating a temporary variable to hold one of the scores, then you can accomplish the swap as shown in Figure 9-1. First, the value in score2, 85, is assigned to a temporary holding variable, named temp. Then the score1 value, 90, is assigned to score2. At this point, both score1 and score2 hold 90. Then the 85 in temp is assigned to score1. Therefore, after the swap process, score1 holds 85 and score2 holds 90.

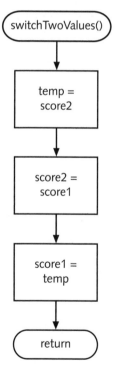

9

Figure 9-1   A module that swaps two values

In Figure 9-1 you can accomplish identical results by assigning `score1` to `temp`, assigning `score2` to `score1`, and finally assigning `temp` to `score2`.

USING A BUBBLE SORT

One of the simplest sorting techniques to understand is a bubble sort. You can use a **bubble sort** to arrange records in either ascending or descending order. In a bubble sort, items in a list compare with each other in pairs, and when an item is out of order, it swaps with the item below it. With an ascending bubble sort, after each adjacent pair of items in a list is compared once, the largest item in the list will have "bubbled" to the bottom. After many passes through the list, the smallest items rise to the top like bubbles in a carbonated drink.

Assume that five student test scores are stored in a file and you want to sort them in ascending order for printing. To begin, you can define three subroutines in the mainline logic as shown in Figure 9-2: `housekeeping()`, `sortScores()`, and `finishUp()`.

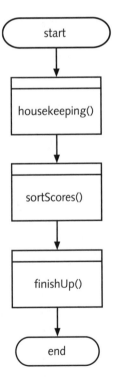

Figure 9-2   Mainline logic for score-sorting program

The housekeeping() module of this program defines a variable name for each individual score in the input file and sets up an array of five elements in which to store the five scores. The entire file is then read into memory, one score at a time, and each score is stored in one element of the array. See Figure 9-3.

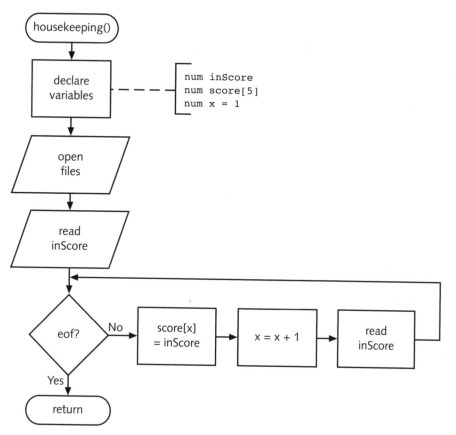

Figure 9-3   housekeeping() module for score-sorting program

When the program logic enters the sortScores() module, five scores have been placed in the array. For example, assume they are:

```
score[1] = 90
score[2] = 85
score[3] = 65
score[4] = 95
score[5] = 75
```

To begin sorting this list of scores, you compare the first two scores. If they are out of order, you reverse their positions, or swap their values. That is, if score[1] is more than score[2], then score[1] will assume the value 85 and score[2] will take on the value 90. After this swap, the scores will be in slightly better order than they were originally.

You could reverse the values of score[1] and score[2] using the following code:

```
temp = score[2]
score[2] = score[1]
score[1] = temp
```

However, this code segment's usefulness is limited in use because it switches only elements 1 and 2 of the **score** array. A more universal **switchValues()** module is shown in Figure 9-4. This module switches *any* two adjacent elements in the **score** array when the variable **x** represents the position of the first of the two elements and the value **x + 1** represents the subsequent position.

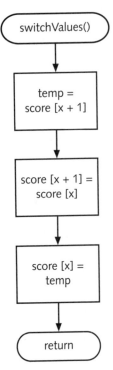

Figure 9-4   The switchValues() module that swaps any two adjacent values in an array

For an ascending sort, you need to perform the **switchValues()** module whenever any given element x of the **score** array has a value greater than the next element, x + 1, of the **score** array. For any x, if the xth element is not greater than the element at position x + 1, the switch should not take place. See Figure 9-5.

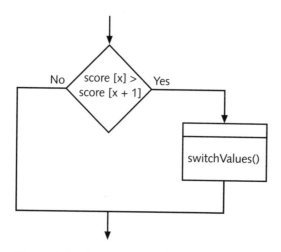

Figure 9-5   Decision showing when to call switchValues() module

For a descending sort, write the decision so that you perform the switch when `score[x]` is *less than* `score[x + 1]`.

9

You must execute the decision `score[x] > score[x + 1]?` four times—when x is 1, 2, 3, and 4. You should not attempt to make the decision when x is 5, because then you would compare `score[5]` to `score[5 + 1]`, and there is no valid `score[6]` in the array. Therefore Figure 9-6 shows the correct loop, which continues to make array element swaps while x is less than 5.

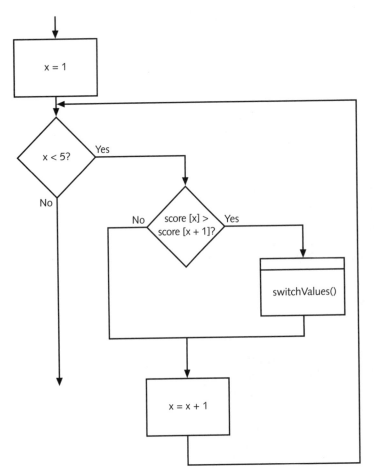

Figure 9-6 Loop that compares entire list of five scores

If you have these original scores:

```
score[1] = 90
score[2] = 85
score[3] = 65
score[4] = 95
score[5] = 75
```

then the logic proceeds like this:

1. Set **x** to 1.

2. **x** is less than 5, so enter the loop.

3. Compare **score[x]**, 90, to **score[x + 1]**, 85. The two scores are out of order, so they are switched.

The list is now:

```
score[1] = 85
score[2] = 90
score[3] = 65
score[4] = 95
score[5] = 75
```

4. After the swap, add 1 to x so x is 2.

5. x is less than 5, so enter the loop a second time.

6. Compare score[x], 90, to score[x + 1], 65. These two values are out of order, so swap them.

Now the result is:

```
score[1] = 85
score[2] = 65
score[3] = 90
score[4] = 95
score[5] = 75
```

7. Add 1 to x so x is now 3.

8. x is less than 5, so enter the loop.

9. Compare score[x], 90, to score[x + 1], 95. These values are in order, so no switch is made.

10. Add 1 to x, making it 4.

11. x is less than 5, so enter the loop.

12. score[x], 95, is larger than score[x + 1], 75, so switch them.

Now the list is as follows:

```
score[1] = 85
score[2] = 65
score[3] = 90
score[4] = 75
score[5] = 95
```

13. Add 1 to x.

14. x is 5, so do not enter the loop again.

9

When **x** reaches 5, every element in the list has been compared with the one adjacent to it. The highest score, a 95, has "sunk" to the bottom of the list. However, the scores still are not in order. They are in slightly better ascending order than they were to begin with, because the largest value is at the bottom of the list, but they are still out of order. You need to repeat the entire procedure illustrated in Figure 9-6 so that 85 and 65 (the current **score[1]** and **score[2]** values) can switch places, and 90 and 75 (the current **score[3]** and **score[4]** values) can switch places. Then the scores will be 65, 85, 75, 90, 95. You will have to perform the procedure to go through the list yet again to swap the 85 and 75.

As a matter of fact, if the scores had started out in the worst possible order (95, 90, 85, 75, 65), the process shown in Figure 9-6 would have to take place four times. In other words, you would have to pass through the list of values four times making appropriate swaps before the numbers would appear in perfect ascending order. You need to place the loop in Figure 9-6 within another loop that executes four times.

Figure 9-7 shows the complete logic for the **sortScores()** module. The **sortScores()** module uses a loop control variable named **y** to cycle through the list of scores four times. With an array of five elements, it takes four comparisons to get through the array once, and it takes four sets of those comparisons to get the entire array in sorted order.

When you sort the elements in an array, the general rule is that whatever the number of elements in the array, the greatest number of pair comparisons you need to make during each loop is *one less* than the number of elements in the array. Additionally you need to process the loop *one less* number of times than the number of elements in the array. For example, if you want to sort a 10-element array, you make nine pair comparisons on each of nine rotations through the loop, executing a total of 81 score comparison statements.

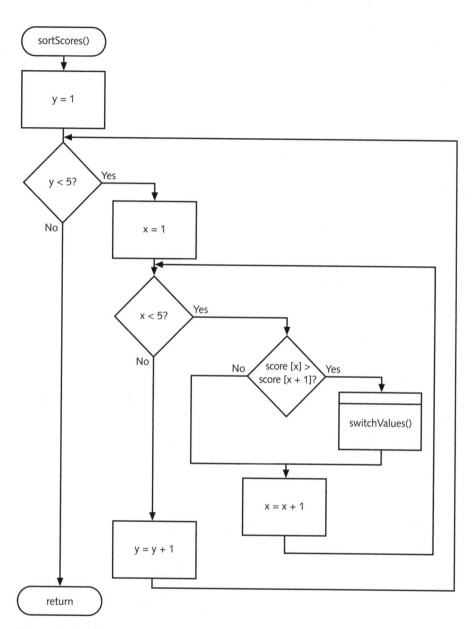

Figure 9-7   The sortScores() module

 In many cases you do not want to sort a single data item such as a score. Instead, for example, you might want to sort data records that contain fields such as ID number, name, and score, placing the records in score order. The sorting procedure remains basically the same, but you need to store entire records in an array. Then you make your comparisons based on a single field, but you make your swaps using entire records.

REFINING THE BUBBLE SORT BY USING A VARIABLE FOR THE ARRAY SIZE

Keeping in mind that when performing a bubble sort you need to perform one less pair comparison than you have elements, you can add a refinement that makes the sorting logic easier to understand. When performing a bubble sort on an array, you compare two separate loop control variables with a value that equals the number of elements in the list. If the number of elements in the array is stored in a variable named `numberOfEls`, the general logic for a bubble sort is shown in Figure 9–8.

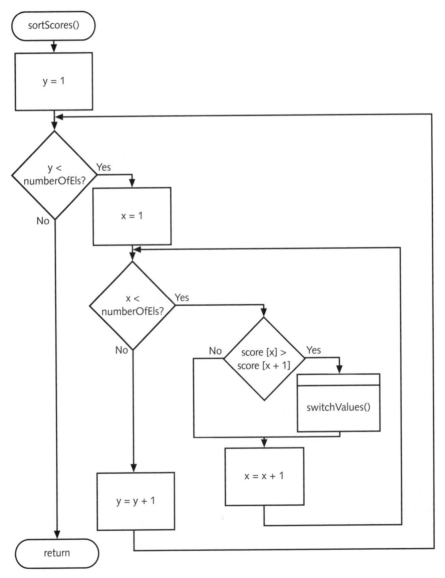

Figure 9-8   Generic bubble sort routine logic using a variable for the number of elements

To use the logic shown in Figure 9-8, you must declare `numberOfEls` along with the other variables in the `housekeeping()` module. There you can set the value of `numberOfEls` to 5 , because you know there are five elements in the array to be sorted. Besides being useful for sorting, the `numberOfEls` variable also will be useful in any module that prints the scores, sums them, or performs any other activity with the list. For example, the `finishUp()` module in Figure 9-9 uses the `numberOfEls` variable to control the print loop. The advantage to using a `numberOfEls` variable instead of a constant such as 5 in your program is that if you modify the program array to accommodate more or fewer scores in the future, you can simply change the value in `numberOfEls` once where it is defined. Then you do not need to alter every instance of a constant number throughout the program; the `numberOfEls` variable automatically holds the correct value.

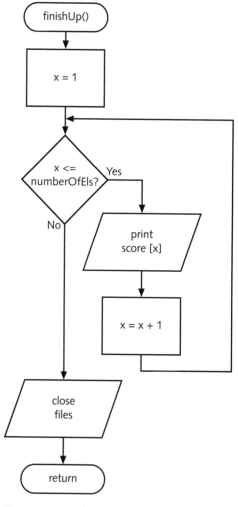

9

Figure 9-9   The finishUp() module of score-sorting program

Sometimes you don't want to initialize the `numberOfEls` variable at the start of the program. You might not know how many array elements there are—for example, sometimes there are only three or four scores to sort. In other words, what if the size of the list to be sorted varies? Rather than initializing `numberOfEls` to a final value, you can count the input scores, then give `numberOfEls` its value after you know how many scores exist.

When you read each `inScore` during `housekeeping()`, you can increase `x` by one. Figure 9-10 shows a `housekeeping()` module that uses this approach. In this example, the `score` array is created to hold 100 elements, a number larger than you anticipate you will need. The variable `x` is initialized to zero. After you read one `inScore` value, `x` is increased to one and the first `inScore` is stored in the first array location. After a second score is read, `x` is increased to two, the second score is stored in the second array location and so on. After you reach `eof`, `x` indicates the number of elements in the array so you can set `numberOfEls` to `x`. With this approach, it doesn't matter if there are not enough `inScore` values to fill the array. You simply make one less pair comparison than the number of the value held in `numberOfEls` instead of always making a larger fixed number of pair comparisons.

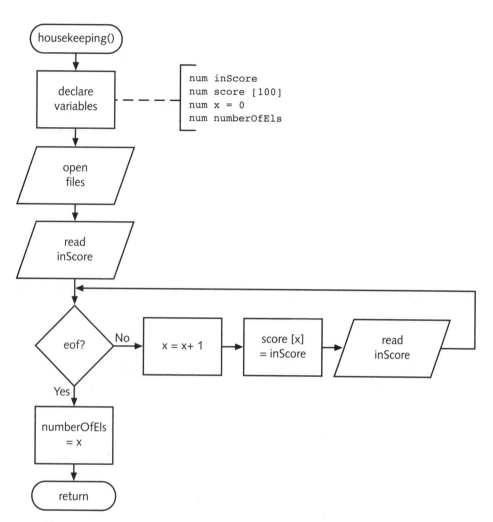

Figure 9-10   housekeeping() module for variable size array

When you count the input records and use the **numberOfEls** variable, it does not matter if there are not enough scores to fill the array. However, it does matter if there are more scores than the array can hold. Every array must have a finite size and it is an error to try to store data past the end of the array. When you don't know how many elements will be stored in an array, you must overestimate the number of elements you declare. If the number of scores in the **score** array can be 100 or fewer, then you can declare the **score** array to have a size of 100, and you can use 100 elements or fewer. Figure 9-11 shows the pseudocode that provides one possibility for an additional improvement to the **housekeeping()** module in Figure 9-10. If you use the logic in Figure 9-11, you read **inScore** values until **eof**, but if the array subscript **x** exceeds 100, you display a warning message and do not attempt to store any additional **inScore** values in the **score** array.

```
housekeeping()
    declare variables - - - - - - - - -┌num inScore
    open files                          │num score[100]
    read inScore                        │num x = 0
    while not eof                       │num y
        if x > 100 then                 │num numberOfEls
            print "Warning! Too many scores"
        else
            score[x] = inScore
            x = x + 1
            read inScore
        endif
    numberOfEls = x
return
```

Figure 9-11   Pseudocode for housekeeping() that prevents overextending the array

REFINING THE BUBBLE SORT BY REDUCING UNNECESSARY COMPARISONS

You can make additional improvements to the bubble sort created in the last sections. As illustrated in Figure 9-8, when performing the sorting module for a bubble sort you pass through a list, making comparisons and swapping values if two values are out of order. If you are performing an ascending sort, then after you have made one pass through the list, the largest value is guaranteed to be in its correct final position at the bottom of the list. Similarly, the second-largest element is guaranteed to be in its correct second-to-last position after the second pass through the list and so on. If you continue to compare every element pair in the list on every pass through the list, you are comparing elements that are already guaranteed to be in their final correct position.

On each pass through the array, you can afford to stop your pair comparisons one element sooner. In other words, after the first pass through the list, there is no longer a need to check the bottom element; after the second pass, there is no need to check the two bottom elements. You can accomplish this by setting a new variable, pairsToCompare, to the value of numberOfEls − 1. On the first pass through the list, every pair of elements is compared, so pairsToCompare *should* equal numberOfEls − 1. In other words, with five array elements to sort, there are four pairs to compare. For each subsequent pass through the list, pairsToCompare should be reduced by 1, because after the first pass there's no need to check the bottom element any more. See Figure 9-12.

```
sortScores()
    pairsToCompare = numberOfEls - 1
    y = 1
    while y < numberOfEls
        x = 1
        while x <= pairsToCompare
            if score[x] > score[x + 1] then
                switchValues()
            endif
            x = x + 1
        y = y + 1
        pairsToCompare = pairsToCompare - 1
return
```

Figure 9-12   Pseudocode for sortScores() module using pairsToCompare variable

REFINING THE BUBBLE SORT BY ELIMINATING UNNECESSARY PASSES THROUGH THE LIST

A final improvement that could be made to the bubble sort in Figure 9-12 is one that reduces the number of passes through the array. If array elements are so badly out of order that they are in reverse order, then it takes as many passes through the list as one less than the value in **numberOfEls** to complete all the comparisons and swaps needed to get the list in order. However, when the array elements are nearly in order to start, all the elements might be correctly arranged after only a few passes through the list. All subsequent passes result in no swaps. For example, assume the original scores are as follows:

```
score[1] = 65
score[2] = 75
score[3] = 85
score[4] = 90
score[5] = 95
```

The bubble sort module in Figure 9-12 would pass through the array four times, making four sets of pair comparisons. It would always find that each **score[x]** is *not* greater than the corresponding **score[x + 1]**, so no switches would ever be made. The scores would end up in the proper order, but they *were* in the proper order in the first place, therefore a lot of time is wasted.

A possible remedy is to add a flag that you set to one value on any pass through the list when elements must be swapped, and that remains holding a different value when all elements are already in the correct order. For example, you can create a variable named **switchOccurred** and set it to "No" at the start of each pass through the list. You can change its value to "Yes" each time the **switchValues()** subroutine is performed (that is, each time a switch is necessary).

If you ever "make it through" the entire list of pairs without making a switch, the switchOccurred flag will *not* have been set to "Yes", meaning that no switch has occurred and that the array elements must already be in the correct order. This *might* be on the first or second pass through. If the array elements are already in the correct order at that point, there is no need to make more passes through the list. However, when a list starts out in the worst possible order, a switch needs to be made *every time through the list*. You can stop making passes through the list when switchOccurred is "No" after a complete trip through the array.

Figure 9-13 illustrates a sort that uses a switchOccurred flag. At the beginning of the sortScores() module, initialize switchOccurred to "Yes" before entering the comparison loop the first time. Then immediately set switchOccurred to "No". When a switch occurs—that is, when the switchValues() module executes—set switchOccurred to "Yes".

```
sortScores()
    pairsToCompare = numberOfEls - 1
    switchOccurred = "Yes"
    while switchOccurred = "Yes"
        x = 1
        switchOccurred = "No"
        while x <= pairsToCompare
            if score[x] > score[x + 1] then
                switchValues()
                switchOccurred = "Yes"
            endif
            x = x + 1
        pairsToCompare = pairsToCompare - 1
    return
```

Figure 9-13   Bubble sort with switchOccurred flag

With the addition of the flag in Figure 9-13, you no longer need the variable y, which was keeping track of the number of passes through the list. Instead, you just keep going through the list until you can make a complete pass without any switches. For a list that starts out in perfect order, you go through the loop only once. For a list that starts out in the *worst* possible order, you will make a switch with every pair each time through the loop until pairsToCompare has been reduced to 0. In this case, on the last pass through the loop x is set to 1, switchOccurred is set to "No", x is no longer less than or equal to pairsToCompare, and the loop is exited.

USING AN INSERTION SORT

The bubble sort works well and is relatively easy for novice array users to understand and manipulate, but even with all the improvements you added to the original bubble sort in the last lesson, it is actually one of the least efficient sorting methods available. An **insertion sort** provides an alternative method for sorting data and it usually requires fewer comparison operations.

As with the bubble sort, when using an insertion sort you also look at each pair of elements in an array. When you find an element that is smaller than the one before it, this element is "out of order." As soon as you locate such an element, search the array backward from that point to see where an element smaller than the out-of-order element is located. At that point, you open a new position for the out-of-order element by moving each subsequent element down one position. Then you insert the out-of-order element into the newly opened position.

For example, consider these scores:

```
score[1] = 65
score[2] = 80
score[3] = 95
score[4] = 75
score[5] = 90
```

Using an insertion sort, you compare score[1], 65, and score[2], 80, determine that they are in order, and leave them alone. Then you compare score[2], 80, and score[3], 95, and also leave them alone. When you compare score[3], 95, and score[4], 75, you determine that the 75 is "out of order." Next, you look backward from the score[4] of 75. The value of score[3] is not smaller than score[4], nor is score[2]; but since score[1] is smaller than score[4], score[4] should follow score[1]. So you store score[4] in a temporary variable, then move score[2], [3], and [4] "down" the list to higher subscripted positions. You move score[3], 95, to the score[4] position. Then move score[2], 80, to the score[3] position. Finally, assign the value of the temporary variable, 75, to the score[2] position. The results:

```
score[1] = 65
score[2] = 75
score[3] = 80
score[4] = 95
score[5] = 90
```

You then continue down the list, comparing each pair of variables. A complete insertion sort module is shown in Figure 9-14.

```
insertionSort()
    y = 1
    while y < numberOfEls
        x = 1
        while x < numberOfEls
            if score[x + 1] < score[x] then
                temp = score[x + 1]
                pos = x
                while score[pos] > temp AND pos > 0
                    score[pos + 1] = score[pos]
                    pos = pos - 1
                score[pos + 1] = temp
            endif
            x = x + 1
        y = y + 1
return
```

Figure 9-14   Sample insertion sort module

The logic for the insertion sort is slightly more complicated than that for the bubble sort, but the insertion sort is more efficient because for the average out-of-order list, it takes fewer "switches" to put the list in order.

USING A SELECTION SORT

A selection sort provides another sorting option. In an **ascending selection sort**, the first element in the array is assumed to be the smallest. Its value is stored in a variable—for example, smallest—and its position in the array, 1, is stored in another variable—for example, position. Then every subsequent element in the array is tested. If one with a smaller value than smallest is found, smallest is set to the new value and position is set to that element's position. After the entire array has been searched, smallest will hold the smallest value and position will hold its position.

The element originally in position[1] is then switched with the smallest value, so at the end of the first pass through the array the lowest value ends up in the first position, and the value that was in the first position is where the smallest value used to be.

For example, assume you have the following list of scores:

```
score[1] = 95
score[2] = 80
score[3] = 75
score[4] = 65
score[5] = 90
```

First, you place 95 in smallest. Then check score[2]; it's less than 95, so place 2 in position and 80 in smallest. Then test score[3]. It's smaller than smallest, so place 3 in position and 75 in smallest. Then test score[4]. Since it is smaller than smallest, place 4 in position and 65 in smallest. Finally, check score[5]; it *isn't* smaller than smallest.

So at the end of the first pass through the list, position is 4 and smallest is 65. You move the value 95 to score[position], or score[4], and the value of smallest, 65, to score[1]. The list becomes:

```
score[1] = 65
score[2] = 80
score[3] = 75
score[4] = 95
score[5] = 90
```

Now that the smallest value is in the first position, you repeat the whole procedure starting with position[2]. After you have passed through the list numberOfEls - 1 times, all elements will be in the correct order. Walk through the logic shown in Figure 9-15.

9

```
selectionSort()
    position = 1
    while position < numberOfEls
        x = position
        smallest = score[x]
        y = x + 1
        while y <= numberOfEls
            if score[y] < smallest then
                x = y
                smallest = score[y]
            endif
            y = y + 1
        score[x] = score[position]
        score[position] = smallest
        position = position + 1
return
```

Figure 9-15   Sample selection sort module

Like the insertion sort, the selection sort almost always requires fewer switches than the bubble sort, but the variables might be a little harder to keep track of because the logic is a little more complex. Thoroughly understanding at least one of these sort techniques provides you with a valuable tool for arranging data and increases your understanding of the capabilities of arrays.

USING INDEXED FILES

Sorting a list of five scores does not require significant computer resources. However, many data files contain thousands of records and each record might contain dozens of data fields. Sorting large numbers of data records requires considerable time and computer memory. When a large data file needs to be processed in ascending or descending order based on some field, it is usually more efficient to store and access records based on their logical order rather than to sort and access them in their physical order. When records are stored, they are stored in some physical order. For example, if you write the names of 10 friends, each one on an index card, the stack of cards has a **physical order**. You can arrange the cards alphabetically by the friends' last names, chronologically by age of the friendship, or randomly by throwing the cards in the air and picking them up as you find them. Whichever way you do it, the records still follow each other in *some* order. In addition to their current physical order, you can think of the cards as having a **logical order** based on any criteria you choose—from the tallest friend to the shortest, from the one who lives farthest away to the closest, and so on. Sorting the cards in a new physical order takes time; using the cards in their logical order without physically rearranging them is often more efficient.

A common method of accessing records in logical order is to use an index. Using an index involves identifying a key field for each record. A record's **key field** is the field whose contents make the record unique from all other records in a file. For example, multiple employees can have the same last name, first name, salary, or street address, but each employee possesses a unique Social Security number, so a Social Security number field makes a good key field for a personnel file. Similarly, a product number makes a good key field on an inventory file.

When you **index** records, you store a list of key fields paired with the storage address for the corresponding data record. When you use an index, you can store records on a **random-access storage device**, such as a disk. Each record can be placed in any physical location on the disk, and you can use the index as you would use the index in the back of a book. If you pick up a 600-page American history text because you need some facts about Betsy Ross, you do not want to start on page one and work your way through the text. Instead, you turn to the index, discover Betsy Ross is located on page 418, and go directly to that page.

As pages in a book have numbers, computer locations have **addresses**. In Chapter 1 you learned that every variable has a numeric address in computer memory; likewise, every data record on a disk has a numeric address where it is stored. You can store records in any physical order on the disk, but the index can find the records in order based on their addresses. For example, you might store employees on a disk in the order in which they are hired. However, you often need to process the employees in Social Security number order. When adding each new employee to such a file, you can physically place the employee anywhere there is room available on the disk. Her Social Security number is inserted in proper order in the index, along with the physical address where her record is located.

You do not need to determine a record's exact physical address in order to use it. A computer's operating system takes care of locating available storage for your records.

You can picture an index based on Social Security numbers by looking at Figure 9-16.

Social Security Number	Location
111-22-3456	6400
222-44-7654	4800
333-55-1234	2400
444-88-9812	5200

Figure 9-16 Sample index

When you want to access the data for employee 333-55-1234, you tell your computer to look through the Social Security numbers in the index, find a match, then proceed to the memory location specified. Similarly, when you want to process records in order based on Social Security number, you tell your system to retrieve records at the locations in the index in sequence. Thus, even though employee 111-22-3456 may have been hired last and the record is stored at the highest physical address on the disk, if the employee record has the lowest Social Security number it will be accessed first during any ordered processing.

When a record is removed from an indexed file, it does not have to be physically removed. It can simply be deleted from the index and thus will not be part of any further processing.

USING LINKED LISTS

Another way to access records in a desired order, even though they might not be physically stored in that order, is to create a linked list. In its simplest form, creating a **linked list** involves creating one extra field in every record of stored data. This extra field holds the physical address of the next logical record. For example, a record that holds a customer's ID, name, and phone number might contain the fields:

```
custId
custName
custPhoneNum
custNextCust
```

Every time you use a record, you access the next record based on the address held in the `custNextCust` field.

Every time you add a new record to a linked list, you look through the list searching for the correct logical location for the new record. For example, assume that customer records are stored at the addresses shown in Figure 9-17 and that they are linked in customer number order.

Address of Record	custId	custName	custPhoneNum	custNextCust
0000	111	Baker	234-5676	7200
7200	222	Vincent	456-2345	4400
4400	333	Silvers	543-0912	6000
6000	444	Donovan	329-8744	eof

Figure 9-17   Linked customer list

You can see from Figure 9-17 that each customer's record contains a custNextCust field that stores the address of the next customer who follows in customer ID number order. The next customer's address might be physically distant and the addresses are not in sequential order, but each customer links to the next customer who follows by ID value.

If a new customer with number 245 and the name Newberg is acquired, the computer operating system would find an available storage location for her, perhaps 8400. Then the procedure would be:

1. Compare the new customer's ID, 245, with the first record's ID, 111. The value 245 is higher, so you save the current address 0000 in a variable you can name saveAddress. Examine the next customer record that physically exists at the custNextCust address, 7200.

2. Compare 245 with 222. The value 245 is higher, so save the current address, 7200, in saveAddress and examine the next customer record at address 4400.

3. Compare 245 with 333. The value 245 is lower, so that means customer 245 should logically precede customer 333. Set the custNextCust field in Newberg's record (customer 245) to 4400, which is the address of customer 333. Also set the custNextCust field of the record located at saveAddress (7200, Vincent, customer 222) to the new address, 8400. The updated list appears in Figure 9-18.

Address of Record	custId	custName	custPhoneNum	custNextCust
0000	111	Baker	234-5676	7200
7200	222	Vincent	456-2345	8400
8400	245	Newberg	222-9876	4400
4400	333	Silvers	543-0912	6000
6000	444	Donovan	329-8744	eof

Figure 9-18   Updated customer list

As with indexing, when removing records from a linked list, the records do not need to be physically deleted. If you need to remove customer 333 from the preceding list, all you need to do is change Newberg's `custNextCust` field to Donovan's address: 6000. Silvers' record would then be bypassed during any further processing.

More sophisticated linked lists store *two* additional fields with each record. One field stores the address of the next record and the other field stores the address of the *previous* record so that the list can be accessed either forward or backward.

USING MULTIDIMENSIONAL ARRAYS

An array that represents a single list of values is a **single-dimensional array** or **one-dimensional array**. For example, an array that holds five rent figures that apply to five floors of a building can be displayed in a single column as in Figure 9-19.

```
rent[1] = 350
rent[2] = 400
rent[3] = 475
rent[4] = 600
rent[5] = 1000
```

Figure 9-19   A single-dimensional `rent` array

You used the single-dimensional `rent` array in Chapter 8.

The location of any `rent` value in Figure 9-19 depends on only a single variable—the floor of the building. Sometimes, however, locating a value in an array depends on more than one variable. If you must represent values in a table or grid that contains rows and columns instead of a single list, then you might want to use a **multidimensional array**, specifically, a **two-dimensional array**.

Assume that the floor is not the only factor determining rent in your building, but that another variable, `numberOfBedrooms`, also needs to be taken into account. The rent schedule might be the one shown in Figure 9-20.

Floor	1-bedroom apartment	2-bedroom apartment	3-bedroom apartment
1	350	390	435
2	400	440	480
3	475	530	575
4	600	650	700
5	1000	1075	1150

Figure 9-20   Rent schedule based on floor and number of bedrooms

Each element in a two-dimensional array requires two subscripts to reference it—one subscript to determine the row and a second to determine the column. Thus the 15 separate `rent` values for a two-dimensional array based on the rent table in Figure 9-20 would be those shown in Figure 9-21.

```
rent[1][1] =   350
rent[1][2] =   390
rent[1][3] =   435
rent[2][1] =   400
rent[2][2] =   440
rent[2][3] =   480
    .
    .
    .
rent[5][3] = 1150
```

Figure 9-21   `rent` array values based on floor and number of bedrooms

If you store tenant records that contain two fields named `floor` and `numberOfBedrooms`, then the appropriate rent can be printed out with the statement: `print rent[floor][numberOfBedrooms]`. The first subscript represents the two-dimensional `rent` array row; the second subscript represents the `rent` array column.

Some languages access two-dimensional array elements with commas separating the subscript values; for example, the second-floor, three-bedroom rate might be written `rent[2,3]`. In every language, you provide a subscript for the row first and for the column second.

Just as within a one-dimensional array, each element in a multidimensional array must be the same data type.

Two-dimensional arrays are never actually *required*. The same 15 categories of rent information could be stored in three separate single-dimensional arrays of five elements each, as shown in Figure 9-22.

```
rentOne[1] = 350      rentTwo[1] = 390      rentThree[1] = 435
rentOne[2] = 400      rentTwo[2] = 440      rentThree[2] = 480
rentOne[3] = 475      rentTwo[3] = 530      rentThree[3] = 575
rentOne[4] = 600      rentTwo[4] = 650      rentThree[4] = 700
rentOne[5] = 1000     rentTwo[5] = 1075     rentThree[5] = 1150
```

Figure 9-22   Three separate one-dimensional arrays

If you use the three separate arrays in Figure 9-22, then you can determine rent with the logic in Figure 9-23.

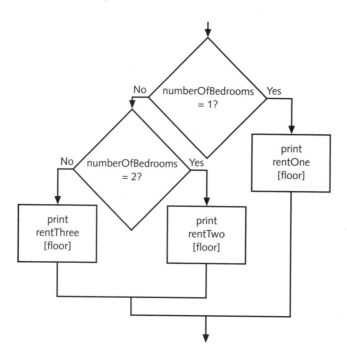

Figure 9-23   Determining rent with three one-dimensional arrays

Of course, don't forget that even one-dimensional arrays are never *required* to be able to solve a problem. You could also make 15 separate decisions to determine the rent. See Figure 9-24.

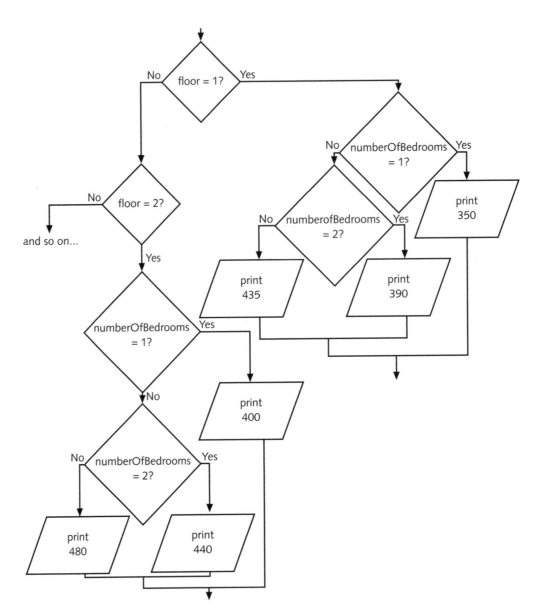

Figure 9-24   Determining rent with no array

Using three single-dimensional arrays as in Figure 9-23 makes the rent-determining process easier than using no array, as in Figure 9-24. However, if you use a two-dimensional array, as in Figure 9-25, the rent-determining process is as simple as it can be.

Some languages allow **three-dimensional arrays** in which you access values using three subscripts. For example, rent might not only be determined by the two factors, `floor` and `numberOfBedrooms`. There might also be 12 different buildings. The third dimension of a three-dimensional array to hold all these different rents would be a variable such as `buildingNumber`.

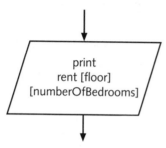

print
rent [floor]
[numberOfBedrooms]

Figure 9-25   Determining rent with a two-dimensional array

Some languages allow even more dimensions. It's usually hard for people to keep track of more than three dimensions, but if five variable factors determine rent—for example, floor number, number of bedrooms, building number, city number, and state number— you might want to try to use a five-dimensional array.

9

CHAPTER SUMMARY

◻ When the sequential order of data records is not the order desired for processing or viewing, the data need to be sorted in ascending or descending order based on the contents of one or more fields.

◻ You can swap two values by creating a temporary variable to hold one of the values. Then you can assign the second value to the temporary variable, assign the first value to the second, and assign the temporary value to the first variable.

◻ In a bubble sort, items in a list compare in pairs, and when an item is out of order, it swaps with the item below it. With an ascending bubble sort, after each adjacent pair of items in a list is compared once, the largest item in the list will have "bubbled" to the bottom. When you sort the elements in an array, the greatest number of pair comparisons you need to make during each loop is *one less* than the number of elements in the array. Additionally you need to process the loop *one less* number of times than the number of elements in the array.

◻ When performing a bubble sort on an array, you compare two separate loop control variables with a value that equals the number of elements in the list. The advantage to using a variable instead of a constant to hold the number of elements is that if you modify the program array to accommodate more or fewer scores in the future, you can simply change the value in the variable once where it is defined. Additionally, if you don't know how many elements will be sorted, you can count them and store the value in the variable.

❑ On each pass through an array that is being sorted using a bubble sort, you can afford to stop your pair comparisons one element sooner.

❑ To avoid making unnecessary passes through a list while performing a bubble sort, you can add a flag that you test on every pass through the list to determine when all elements are already in the correct order.

❑ When using an insertion sort you also look at each pair of elements in an array. When you find an element that is out of order, search the array backward from that point, find an element smaller than the out-of-order element, move each subsequent element down one position, and insert the out-of-order element into the list at the newly opened position.

❑ In an ascending selection sort, the first element in the array is assumed to be the smallest. Its value and position are stored. Then every subsequent element in the array is tested, and if one has a smaller value, the new value and position are sorted. After searching the entire array, the original first value is then switched with the smallest value. Then you repeat the process with each subsequent list value.

❑ You can use an index to access data records in a logical order that differs from their physical order. Using an index involves identifying a key field for each record.

❑ Creating a linked list involves creating an extra field within every record to hold the physical address of the next logical record.

❑ You use a multidimensional array when locating a value in an array depends on more than one variable.

EXERCISES

1. Write pseudocode that reflects the logic of the score-sorting program that is flowcharted in Figures 9-1 through 9-9.

2. Professor Zak allows students to drop the two lowest scores on the ten 100-point quizzes she gives during the semester. Develop the logic for a program that reads in student records that contain ID number, last name, first name, and 10 quiz scores. The output lists student ID, name, and total points on the eight highest quizzes.

3. The Hinner College Foundation holds an annual fundraiser for which the foundation director maintains records that each contains a donor name and contribution amount. Assume that there are never more than 300 donors. Develop the logic for a program that sorts the donation amounts in descending order. Output lists the highest five donation amounts.

4. A greeting-card store maintains customer records with data fields for first name, last name, address, and annual purchases in dollars. At the end of the year, the store manager invites the 100 customers with the highest annual purchases to an exclusive sale event. Develop the flowchart or pseudocode for this problem.

5. a. The Village of Ringwood has taken a special census. Every census record contains a household ID number, size, and income. Ringwood has exactly 75 households. Village statisticians are interested in the median household size and the median household income. Develop the logic for a program that determines these figures.

   b. The village of Marengo has also taken a special census and collected records similar to those of Ringwood. The exact number of household records has not yet been determined, but you know that there are fewer than 1,000 households in Marengo. Determine the same statistics as in Exercise 5a.

6. Develop the flowchart that corresponds to the pseudocode for the insertion sort shown in Figure 9-14.

7. Develop the flowchart that corresponds to the pseudocode for the selection sort shown in Figure 9-15.

8. Create the flowchart or pseudocode that reads in a file of 10 employee salaries and prints them out from lowest to highest. Use an insertion sort.

9. Create the flowchart or pseudocode that reads in a file of 10 employee salaries and prints them out from highest to lowest. Use a selection sort.

10. The MidAmerica Bus Company charges passengers fares based on the number of travel zones they cross. Additionally, discounts are provided for multiple passengers traveling together. Ticket fares are shown in the following table.

ZONES CROSSED

PASSENGERS	1	2	3	4
1	7.50	10.00	12.00	12.75
2	14.00	18.50	22.00	23.00
3	20.00	21.00	32.00	33.00
4	25.00	27.50	36.00	37.00

Develop the logic for a program that reads in records containing number of passengers and zones crossed. The output is the ticket charge.

11. a.   In golf, par is a number that represents a standard number of strokes a player will need to complete a hole. Instead of using an absolute score, players can compare their scores on a hole to the par figure and determine whether they are above or below par. Families can play nine holes of miniature golf at the Family Fun Miniature Golf Park. So that family members can compete fairly, the course provides a different par for each hole based on the player's age. The par figures are shown in the following table.

HOLES

AGE	1	2	3	4	5	6	7	8	9
4 and under	8	8	9	7	5	7	8	5	8
5–7	7	7	8	6	5	6	7	5	6
8–11	6	5	6	5	4	5	5	4	5
12–15	5	4	4	4	3	4	3	3	4
16 and over	4	3	3	3	2	3	2	3	3

Develop the logic for a program that reads in records containing a player's name, age, and nine-hole scores. For each player, print a page that contains the player's name and score on each of the nine holes with one of the phrases "Over par", "Par", or "Under par" next to each score.

b.   Modify the program in Exercise 11a so that at the end of each golfer's report the golfer's total score displays. Include the figure indicating how many strokes over or under par the player is for the entire course.

10

USING MENUS
AND VALIDATING INPUT

After studying Chapter 10, you should be able to:

♦ Understand the need for interactive, menu-driven programs

♦ Create a program that uses a single-level menu

♦ Code modules as black boxes

♦ Improve menu programs

♦ Use a case structure to manage a menu

♦ Create a program that uses a multilevel menu

♦ Validate input

♦ Understand types of data validation

USING INTERACTIVE PROGRAMS

You can divide computer programs into two broad categories based on how they get their data. Programs for which all the data are gathered prior to running use **batch processing**. Programs that depend on user input while they are running use **interactive processing**.

Many computer programs use batch processing with sequential files of data records that have been collected for processing. All standard billing, inventory, payroll, and similar programs work this way, and all the program logic you have developed while working through this text also works like this. Records used for batch processing are gathered over a period of time—hours, days, or even months. Programs that use batch processing typically read an input record, process it according to coded instructions, output the result, and then read another record. Batch processing gets its name because the data records are not processed at the time they are created; instead, they are "saved" and processed in a batch. For example, you do not receive a credit-card bill immediately after every purchase, when the record is created. All purchases during a one-month period are gathered and processed at the end of that billing period.

Many computer programs cannot be run in batches. They must run interactively—that is, they must interact with a user while they are running. Ticket reservation programs for airlines and theaters must select tickets while you are interacting with them, not at the end of the month. A computerized library catalog system must respond to library patrons' requests immediately, not at the end of every week. Interactive computer programs are often called **real-time applications**, because they run while a transaction is taking place, not at some later time. You also can refer to interactive processing as **online processing**, because the user's data or requests are gathered during the execution of the program. A batch processing system can be **off-line**; that is, you can collect data such as time cards or purchase information well ahead of the actual computer processing of the paychecks or bills.

A **menu** program is a common type of interactive program in which the user sees a number of options on the screen and can select any one of them. For example, an educational program that drills you on elementary arithmetic skills might display three options as shown in Figure 10-1.

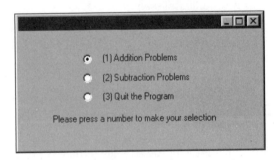

Figure 10-1 Arithmetic drill menu

The final option, *Quit the Program*, is very important; without it, there would be no elegant way for the program to terminate. A menu without a *Quit* option is very frustrating to the user.

Some menu programs require the user to enter a number to choose a menu option. For example, the user enters a *2* to perform a subtraction drill from the menu shown in Figure 10-1. Other menu programs require the user to enter a letter of the alphabet—for example, *S* for a subtraction drill. Still other programs allow the user to use a pointing device such as a mouse to point to a choice on the screen. The most sophisticated programs allow users to employ the selection method that is most convenient at the time.

Many organizations provide a menu to callers to handle routing of telephone calls.

USING A SINGLE-LEVEL MENU

Suppose you want to write a program that displays a menu like the one shown in Figure 10-1. The program drills a student's arithmetic skills—if the student chooses the first option, five addition problems display, and if the student chooses the second option, five subtraction problems display. This program uses a **single-level menu**; that is, the user makes a selection from only one menu before using the program for its ultimate purpose—arithmetic practice. With more complicated programs, a user's choice from an initial menu often leads to other menus where the user must make several selections before reaching the desired destination.

Suppose you want to write a program that requires the user to enter a digit to make a menu choice. The mainline logic for an interactive menu program is not substantially different from any of the other sequential file programs you've seen so far in this book. You can create `startUp()`, `looping()`, and `cleanUp()` modules, as shown in Figure 10-2.

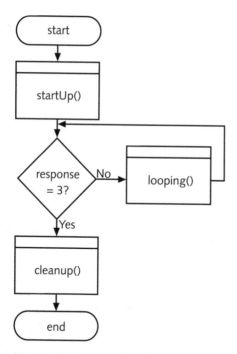

10

Figure 10-2   Mainline logic for arithmetic drill menu program

The only difference between the mainline logic in Figure 10-2 and that of other programs you have worked with lies in the main loop control question. When a program's input data come from a data file, asking whether the input file is at the end-of-file (**eof**) condition is appropriate. An interactive, menu-driven program is not controlled by an end-of-file condition, but by a user's menu response. The mainline logic, then, is more appropriately controlled by the user's response. For example, Figure 10-2 shows the mainline logic containing the question **response = 3?**

The **startUp()** module in the arithmetic drill program defines variables and opens files. The name of one of the variables is **response**; this is the numeric variable that will hold the user's menu choice. The **startUp()** module also displays the menu for the first time so that the user can make a choice. See Figure 10-3.

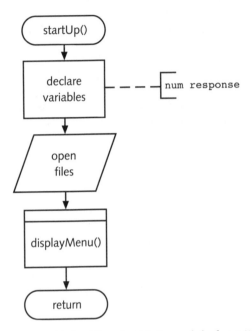

Figure 10-3   The startUp() module for arithmetic drill program

You can include the set of instructions that display the user menu directly in the **startUp** module, or you can place the instructions in their own module; for example, you can use a **displayMenu()** module like the one shown in Figure 10-4. The **displayMenu()** module writes four menu lines on the screen, and then a **read response** statement reads in the user's numeric choice from the keyboard.

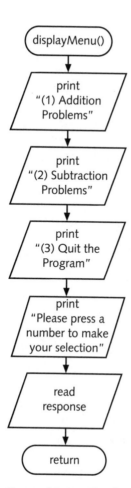

Figure 10-4   The displayMenu() module of arithmetic drill program

When the logic of the program leaves startUp(), the user has entered a value for response. In the mainline logic (Figure 10-2), if the response is not *3* (for the *Quit the Program* option), then the program enters the looping() module. The looping() routine performs one of two subroutines, addition() or subtraction(), based on the decision made about the user's input. Following the performance of the chosen arithmetic drill, the program calls the displayMenu() module again, and the user has the opportunity to select the same arithmetic drill, a different one, or the *Quit the Program* option. See Figure 10-5.

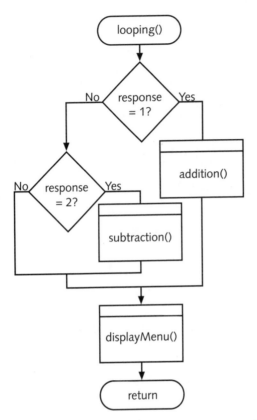

Figure 10-5   The looping() module for arithmetic drill program

When the **looping()** module ends, control passes to the main program. If the user has entered a value of *3* to select the *Quit the Program* option during a **displayMenu()** routine, the outcome of the question **response = 3?** sends the program to the **cleanUp()** module. That module simply closes the files, as shown in Figure 10-6.

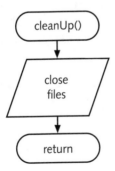

Figure 10-6   The cleanUp() module for arithmetic drill program

CODING MODULES AS BLACK BOXES

Any steps you want can occur within the `addition()` and `subtraction()` modules. The contents of these modules do not affect the main structure of the program in any way. You can write an `addition()` module that requires the user to solve simple addition problems like `3 + 4`, or you can write an `addition()` module that requires the user to solve more difficult, multidigit problems like `9267 + 3488`. As you will recall from Chapter 2, part of the advantage of modular, structured programs lies in your ability to break programs into routines that can be assigned to any number of programmers and then be pieced back together at each routine's single entry or exit point. Thus, any number of different `addition()` or `subtraction()` modules can be used within the arithmetic drill program.

Programmers often refer to modules such as `addition()` and `subtraction()` as existing within a **black box** meaning that the module statements are "invisible" to the rest of the program. You probably own many real-life objects that are black boxes to you—a television or a stereo, for example. You might not know how these devices work internally, and if someone substitutes new internal mechanisms in your devices, you might not know or care so long as the devices continue to work properly. Similarly, many different `addition()` or `subtraction()` modules can function within the arithmetic drill menu program.

Because many versions of a module can substitute for one another, programmers frequently don't bother with module details at all when they first develop a program. They concentrate on the mainline logic and understanding what the called modules will do, not how they will do it. When programmers develop systems containing many modules, they often code "empty" black box procedures, called **stubs**. Later they can code the details in the stub routines.

Figure 10-7 shows a possible `addition()` module. The module displays five problems one at a time, waits for the user's response, and displays a message indicating whether the user is correct.

 You can write a `subtraction()` module using a format that is almost identical to the `addition()` module. The only necessary change is the computation operation used in the actual problems.

The `addition()` module shown in Figure 10-7 is repetitious; a basic set of statements repeats five times, changing only the actual problem values that the user should add. A more elegant solution involves storing the problem values in arrays and using a loop. For example, if you declare two arrays as shown in Figure 10-8, then the loop in Figure 10-9 displays and checks five problems. The power of using an array allows you to alter a subscript in order to display five separate addition problems.

10

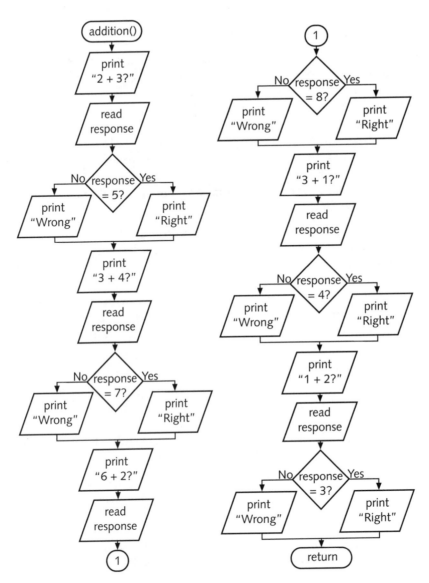

Figure 10-7   The addition() module version 1

```
num probValFirst[1] = 2
num probValFirst[2] = 3
num probValFirst[3] = 6
num probValFirst[4] = 3
num probValFirst[5] = 1

num probValSecond[1] = 3
num probValSecond[2] = 4
num probValSecond[3] = 2
num probValSecond[4] = 1
num probValSecond[5] = 2
```

Figure 10-8   Arrays for addition problems

10

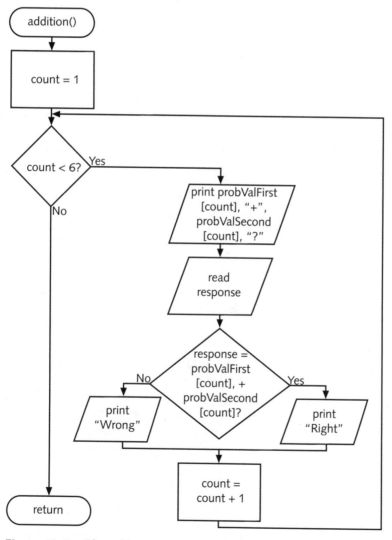

Figure 10-9   The addition() module version 2, using arrays

To use the `addition()` module shown in Figure 10-9, you have to declare the numeric variable `count`.

The `addition()` module in Figure 10-9 is more compact and efficient than the module shown in Figure 10-7. However, a student will not want to use the `addition()` module more than two or three times. Every time a user executes the program, the same five addition problems display. Once students have solved all the addition problems, they probably will be able to provide memorized answers without practicing arithmetic skills at all. Fortunately, most programming languages provide you with built-in modules or **functions**, which are subroutines that automatically provide a mathematical value such as a square root, absolute value, or random number. The random number generating functions usually take a form similar to `random(x)`, where `x` is a value you provide for the maximum random number you want. Different computer systems use different formulas for generating a random number; for example, many use part of the current clock time when the random number function is called. However, a programming language's built-in functions can operate as black boxes just as your program modules do, so you need not know exactly how the functions do their jobs. You can use the random number generating function without knowing how it determines the specific random number. Figure 10-10 shows an `addition()` module in which two random numbers, each 10 or less, are generated for each of five arithmetic problems. Using this technique, you do not have to store values in an array, and users encounter different addition problems every time they use the program.

Popular spreadsheet programs also contain functions. As in programming, they are built-in modules that return requested values such as square root or absolute value. Most spreadsheets also contain dozens of specialized functions to support financial applications such as computing the future value of an investment and calculating a loan payment.

To use the logic shown in Figure 10-10, you also must remember to declare `first` and `second` as numeric variables.

You can make many additional improvements to any of the `addition()` modules shown in Figures 10-7, 10-9, and 10-10. For example, you might want to give the user several chances to calculate the correct answer, or you might want to vary the messages displayed. However you change the `addition()` or `subtraction()` modules in the future, the main structure of the menu program does not have to change; modularization has made your program easily modifiable to meet changing needs.

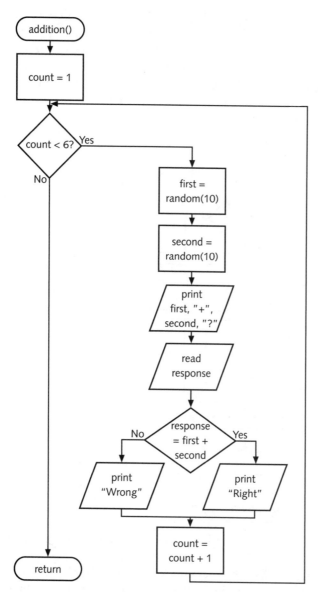

Figure 10-10   The addition() module version 3, using random values

MAKING IMPROVEMENTS TO A MENU PROGRAM

When the menu displays at the end of the looping() module of the arithmetic drill program, if the user selects anything *other than 3*, the looping() module is entered again. Note that if the user chooses *4* or *9,* or any other invalid menu item, the menu simply reappears. Unfortunately, the repeated display of the menu can confuse the user. Perhaps the user is familiar with another program in which option *9* has always meant *Quit*. When using the arithmetic drill program the user who does not read the menu carefully might press *9*, get the menu back, press *9*, and get the menu back again. The programmer can assist the user by displaying a message when the selected **response** is not one of the allowable menu options, as shown in Figure 10-11.

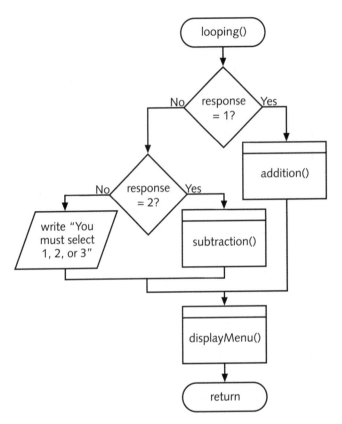

Figure 10-11   Adding error message to looping() module for arithmetic drill program

In programming there is a saying that no program is ever really completed. You always can continue to make improvements. For example, the **looping()** module in Figure 10-11 shows that a helpful message ("You must select 1, 2, or 3") appears when the user selects an inappropriate option. However, if users do not understand the message, or simply do not stop to read the message, they might keep entering invalid data. As a user-friendly improvement to your program, you can add a counter that keeps track of a user's invalid responses. You can decide that after, say, three invalid entries, you will issue a stronger message, such as "Please see the system administrator for help." Figure 10-12 shows this logic. Of course, you must remember to declare `errorCount` in your variable list in the `startUp()` module, and initialize it to zero. Then each time the user chooses an invalid response and you display the message "You must select 1, 2, or 3", you can add 1 to the `errorCount`. When the `errorCount` exceeds 2, you display the stronger message.

You can make an additional improvement to the `looping()` module in Figure 10-12. Suppose the user starts the program and enters a 5. The value of `response` is not 1, 2, or 3, so you add 1 to `errorCount`, display the message "You must select 1, 2, or 3", and display the menu. Suppose the user enters a 5 again. Once again the response is not 1, 2, or 3, so you add 1 to `errorCount`, which is now 2, display the message "You must select 1, 2, or 3", and display the menu. If the user enters a 5 again, the `errorCount` exceeds 2 and the user gets the message "Please see the system administrator for help." Assume the user gets help and figures out that he or she must type 1, 2, or 3. The user then might successfully use the program for several more minutes. However, the next time the user makes a selection error, the `errorCount` will increase to 4 and the stronger "system administrator" message will appear immediately, even though this is only the user's first "new" mistake. If you want to give the user three more chances before the stronger message displays again, then you should reset the `errorCount` to zero every time the user makes a valid choice. This technique will allow the user to make three bad selections after any good selection before the stronger message appears. See Figure 10-13.

10

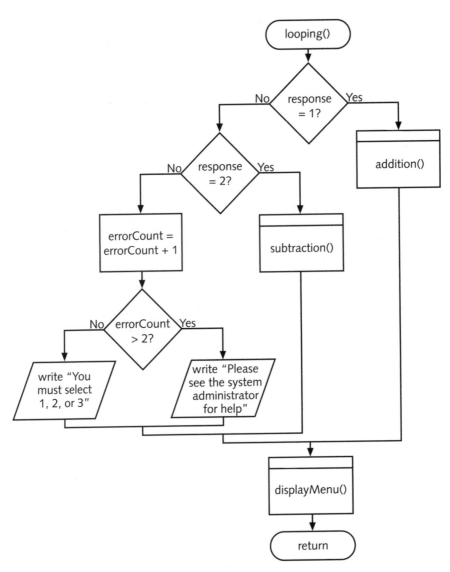

Figure 10-12   The looping() module with a stronger error message

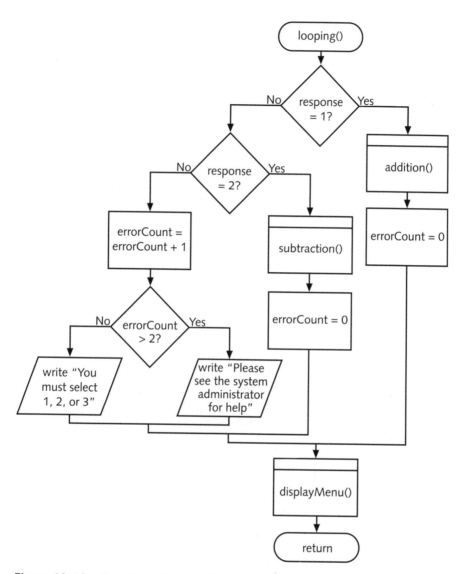

Figure 10-13   Resetting the errorCount to zero after any valid selection

USING THE CASE STRUCTURE TO MANAGE A MENU

The arithmetic drill program contains just three valid user options: numeric entries that represent Addition, Subtraction, or Quit. Many menus include more than three options, but the main logic of such programs is not substantially different from that in programs with only three. You just include more decisions that lead to additional subroutines. For example, Figure 10-14 shows the main logic for a menu program with four optional arithmetic drills.

In Chapter 2 you learned about the case structure. You can use the case structure to make decisions when you need to test a single variable against several possible values. The case structure is particularly convenient to use in menu-driven programs, because you decide from among several courses of action based on the value in the user's response variable. The case structure often is a more convenient way to express a series of individual decisions.

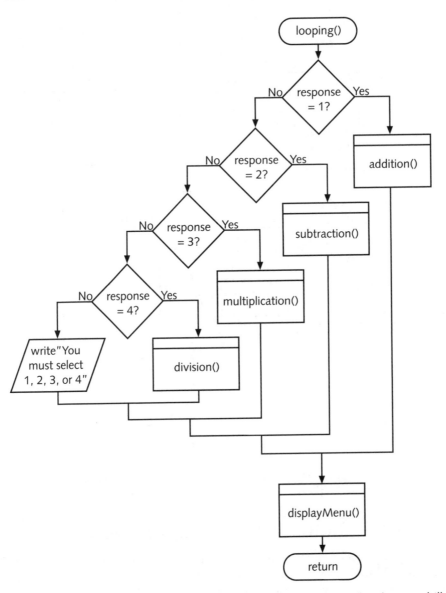

Figure 10-14   Main logic of menu program with four optional arithmetic drills

As you learned in Chapter 2, the syntax of case structures in most programming languages allows you to make a series of comparisons, and if none are true, an *Other* or *Default* option executes. Using a default option is a great convenience in a menu-driven program, because a user usually can enter many more invalid responses than valid ones. Figure 10-15 shows the logic of a four-option arithmetic drill program that uses the case structure.

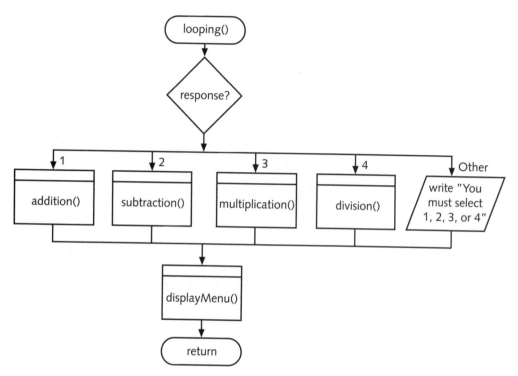

Figure 10-15   Menu program using the case structure

All menu-driven programs should be **user–friendly**, meaning that they should make it easy for the user to make desired choices. Instead of requiring a user to type numbers to select an arithmetic drill, you can improve the menu program by allowing the user the additional option of typing the first letter of the desired option, for example *A* for addition. To enable the menu program to accept alphabetic characters as a variable named **response**, you must make sure you declare **response** as a character variable in the **startUp( )** module. Numeric variables can hold only numbers, but character variables can hold alphabetic characters (such as *A)* as well as numbers.

Programmers often overlook the fact that computers recognize uppercase letters as being different from their lowercase counterparts. Thus a response of *A* is different from a response of *a*. A good menu-driven program probably would allow any of three responses for the first option of *(1) Addition—1, A,* or *a*. Figure 10-16 shows the case structure that performs the menu option selection when the user can enter a variety of responses for each menu choice.

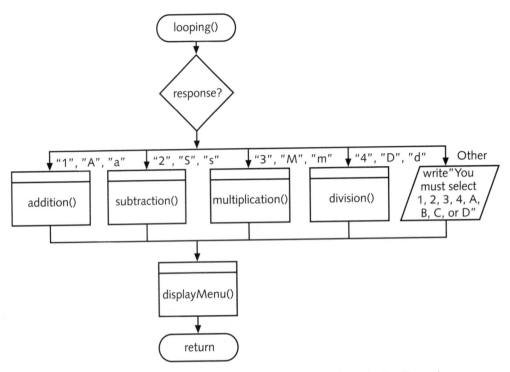

Figure 10-16   Menu program using the case structure with multiple allowed responses

USING MULTILEVEL MENUS

Sometimes a program requires more options than can easily fit in one menu. When you need to present the user with a large number of options, you invite several potential problems:

- Not all the options will appear on the screen, and the user might not realize that additional options are available.

- The screen is too crowded to be visually pleasing when you try to force all the options to fit on the screen.

- Users become confused and frustrated when you present them with too many choices.

When you have many menu options to present, using a multilevel menu might be more effective than using a single-level menu. With a **multilevel menu**, the selection of a menu option leads to another menu where the user can make further, more refined selections.

For example, an arithmetic drill program might contain three difficulty levels for each type of problem. After the user sees a menu like the one shown in Figure 10-17, he or she can choose to quit the program. You refer to a menu that controls whether or not the program will continue as the **main menu** of a program. Alternatively, the user can choose to continue the program, selecting an Addition, Subtraction, Multiplication, or Division arithmetic drill. No matter which drill the user chooses you can display a second menu like the one shown in Figure 10-18. A second-level menu is a **submenu**.

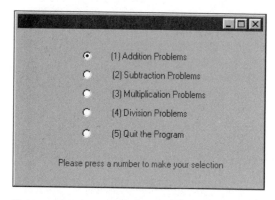

Figure 10-17   First or main menu for arithmetic drill program

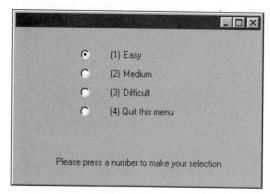

Figure 10-18   Second or submenu for arithmetic drill program

The mainline logic of this multilevel menu program calls a `startUp()` module in which the first menu presents options for the four types of arithmetic problems—*Addition, Subtraction, Multiplication,* and *Division.* When the user makes a selection—for example, *Addition*—the mainline logic determines that `response` is not *5*, so the `looping()` module executes. Figures 10-19, 10-20, and 10-21 show pseudocode for the mainline logic, `startUp()` module, and `displayMenu()` module, respectively.

```
start
    perform startUp()
    while response not equal to 5
        perform looping()
    perform cleanUp()
end
```

Figure 10-19　Pseudocode for mainline logic for multilevel menu program

```
startUp()
    declare variables --------| num response
    open files                | num difficultyResponse
    perform displayMenu()
return
```

Figure 10-20　Pseudocode for startUp() module for multilevel menu program

```
displayMenu()
    print "(1) Addition"
    print "(2) Subtraction"
    print "(3) Multiplication"
    print "(4) Division"
    print "(5) Quit"
    print "Please press a number to make your selection."
    read response
return
```

Figure 10-21　Pseudocode for displayMenu() module for multilevel menu program

Unless the user chooses to quit the program by entering a 5 for **response** in the **startUp()** module, the **looping()** module executes. The **looping()** module uses a case structure to select one of five actions. Either the user has entered the correct **response** to select addition, subtraction, multiplication, or division problems, or the user has selected an invalid option. If the user selects an invalid option, an error message "Sorry. Invalid entry." appears. Whether or not the user selects an entry that performs one of the four arithmetic drill modules, the final step in the **looping()** module displays the menu again and waits for the next **response**. Back in the mainline logic, the new **response** value is tested, and if the user has entered anything other than 5, the **looping()** routine will execute again. Figure 10-22 shows the pseudocode for **looping()**.

```
looping()
    based on response
            case 1
                    perform addition()
            case 2
                    perform subtraction()
            case 3
                    perform multiplication()
            case 4
                    perform division()
            default
                    print "Sorry. Invalid entry."
    perform displayMenu()
return
```

Figure 10-22   Pseudocode for looping() module for multilevel menu program

If the user selects a valid option, then the `looping()` module executes one of the four arithmetic drill modules. For example, if the user selects *1* for *Addition Problems*, then the `addition()` module executes.

Within the `addition()` module, the first task is to allow the user to select a problem difficulty level from a submenu like the one shown in Figure 10-18. Figure 10-23 shows the pseudocode for the `addition()` module. Within the `addition()` module, you call another module to display the difficulty level. Shown in Figure 10-24, this module allows the user to choose easy, medium, or difficult addition problems. If the user selects to quit this menu by entering a *4*, then the user will leave the `addition()` module and return to the main menu, either to choose a different type of arithmetic problem, choose addition again, or quit the program. In the `displayDifficultyMenu()` module, if the user makes a selection other than *4*, the case structure in the `addition()` module determines one of four actions: either one of three addition problem modules executes or the user is informed that the choice is invalid. In any case, the last action of the `addition()` module is to display the difficulty level menu again. As long as users choose options other than *4*, they can continue to select addition problem drills at any of the three difficulty levels.

10

```
addition()
    perform displayDifficultyMenu()
    while difficultyResponse is not equal to 4
            based on difficultyResponse
                case 1
                        perform easyAddProblems()
                case 2
                        perform mediumAddProblems()
                case 3
                        perform difficultAddProblems()
                default
                        print "Sorry. Invalid selection."
            perform displayDifficultyMenu()
    return
```

Figure 10-23   Pseudocode for addition() module for multilevel menu program

```
displayDifficultyMenu()
    print "(1) Easy"
    print "(2) Medium"
    print "(3) Difficult"
    print "(4) Quit this menu"
    print "Please press a number to make your selection."
    read difficultyResponse
return
```

Figure 10-24   Pseudocode for `displayDifficultyMenu()` module for multilevel menu program

The `subtraction()`, `multiplication()`, and `division()` modules can contain code similar to that in the `addition()` module. That is, each module can cause a sub-menu of difficulty levels to display. The actual arithmetic problems do not execute until the user reaches the `easyAddProblems()` module or one of its counterparts.

Many programs have multiple menu levels. For example, you might want the `easyAddProblems()` module to display a new menu asking the user for the number of problems to attempt. Figure 10-25 shows a possible menu.

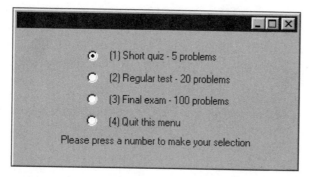

Figure 10-25   Third menu for arithmetic drill program

You would not need to learn any new techniques to create as many levels of menus as the application warrants. The module that controls each new level can:

1. Display a menu.

2. Accept a response.

3. While the user does not select the *quit* option for the specific menu level, perform another module based on the selection (or inform the user of an error).

4. Display the menu and accept a response again.

10

VALIDATING INPUT

Menu programs rely on a user's input to select one of several paths of action. Other types of programs also require user data entry. Whether they are using a menu or supplying information to a program, you cannot count on users to enter valid data. Users will make incorrect choices because they don't understand the valid choices or simply because they make typographical errors. Therefore, the programs you write will be improved if you employ **defensive programming**, which means trying to prepare for all possible errors before they occur. Incorrect user entries are by far the most common source of computer errors.

Validating data is also called *editing* data.

You can circumvent potential problems caused by a user's invalid data entries by validating the user's input. **Validating input** involves checking the user's responses to ensure they fall within acceptable bounds. Validating input does not eliminate all program errors. For example, if a user can choose option *1* or option *2* from a menu, validating the input means you check to make sure the user response is *1* or *2*. If the user enters a *3*, you can issue an error message. However, if the user enters a *2* when she really wants a *1*, there is no way you can validate the response. Similarly, if a user must enter his birth date, you can validate that the month falls between 1 and 12; you usually cannot verify that the user has typed his true birth date.

 Programmers employ the acronym GIGO to mean "garbage in, garbage out." It means that if your input is incorrect, your output is worthless.

The correct action to take when you find invalid data depends on the application. Within an interactive program, you might require the user to reenter the data. If your program uses a data file, you might print a message so someone can correct the invalid data. Alternatively, you can force the invalid data to a default value. **Forcing** a field to a value means you override incorrect data by setting the field to a specific value. For example, you might decide that if a month value does not fall between 1 and 12, you will force the field to 0 or 99. This will indicate to those who use the data that no valid value exists.

New programmers often make the following two kinds of mistakes when validating data:

- They use incorrect logic to check for valid responses when there is more than one possible correct entry.

- They fail to account for the user making multiple invalid entries.

For example, assume a user is required to respond with a *Y* or *N* to a yes-or-no question. The pseudocode in Figure 10-26 appears to check for valid responses.

```
print "Do you want to continue? Enter Y or N."
read userAnswer
if userAnswer not equal to "Y" OR userAnswer not equal to "N" then
        print "Invalid response. Please type Y or N"
        read userAnswer
endif
```

Figure 10-26 Invalid method for validating user response

The logic shown in Figure 10-26 intends to make sure that the user enters a *Y* or an *N*. However, if you use the logic shown in Figure 10-26, every user will see the "Invalid response" error message no matter what the user types. Remember when you use OR logic that only one of the two expressions used in each half of the OR expression must be true for the whole expression to be true. For example, if the user types a *B*, then the userAnswer is not equal to *Y*. Therefore, userAnswer **not equal to "Y"** is true and the "Invalid response" message displays. However, if the user types an *N*, the userAnswer also is not equal to *Y*. Again, the condition in the if statement is true and the

"Invalid response" message prints even though the response is actually valid. Similarly, if the user types a *Y*, userAnswer not equal to "Y" is false, but userAnswer not equal to "N" is true, so again "Invalid response" prints. Every character that exists is either not *Y* or not *N*, even "Y" and "N". The correct logic prints the "Invalid response" message when the userAnswer is not *Y* *and it is also not N.* See Figure 10-27.

 You first learned about OR decision logic in Chapter 5.

```
print "Do you want to continue? Enter Y or N."
read userAnswer
if userAnswer not equal to "Y" AND userAnswer not equal to "N" then
     print "Invalid response. Please type Y or N"
     read userAnswer
endif
```

Figure 10-27   Improved method for validating user response

If you use the logic shown in Figure 10-27, when the user types an invalid response you will correctly display the error message and get a new userAnswer. However, you have not made allowance for the user typing an invalid response a second time. Instead of using a decision statement to check for a valid response, you can use a loop to continue to issue error messages and get new input so long as the user continues to make invalid selections. Figure 10-28 shows the logic for the best method to validate user input.

```
print "Do you want to continue? Enter Y or N."
read userAnswer
while userAnswer not equal to "Y" AND userAnswer not equal to "N"
     print "Invalid response. Please type Y or N"
     read userAnswer
```

Figure 10-28   Best method for validating user response

UNDERSTANDING TYPES OF DATA VALIDATION

The data you use within computer programs are varied. It stands to reason that validating data requires a variety of methods. In the last section you learned to check for an exact match of a user response to the character "Y" or "N". In addition, some of the techniques you want to master include validating:

- Data type

- Range

- Reasonableness and consistency of data

- Presence of data

Validating a Data Type

Some programming languages allow you to check data to make sure they are the correct type. Although this technique varies from language to language, you can often make a statement like the one shown in Figure 10-29. In this program segment the phrase `"not numeric"` is used to check whether the entered data fall within the category of numeric data.

```
print "Enter salary."
read employeeSalary
while employeeSalary not numeric
        print "Salary not numeric. Please reenter."
        read employeeSalary
```

Figure 10-29   Method for checking data for correct type

 Some languages require you to check data against the actual machine codes (such as ASCII or EBCDIC) used to store the data to determine if the data are the appropriate type.

Validating a Data Range

Sometimes a user response or other data must fall within a range of values. For example, when the user enters a month, you typically require it to fall between 1 and 12 inclusive. The method you use to check for a valid range is similar to one you use to check for an exact match; you continue to prompt for and receive responses while the user's response is out of range. See Figure 10-30.

```
print "Enter month."
read userAnswer
while userAnswer < 1 OR userAnswer > 12
        print "Invalid response. Please enter month 1 through 12."
        read userAnswer
```

Figure 10-30   Method for validating user response within range

Validating Reasonableness and Consistency of Data

Data items can be the correct type and within range, but still be incorrect. You have experienced this phenomenon yourself if anyone has ever misspelled your name or over-billed you. The data might have been the correct type—that is, alphabetic letters were used in your name—but the name itself was incorrect. There are many data items that you cannot check for reasonableness; it is just as reasonable that your name is Catherine as it is that your name is Katherine or Kathryn.

However, there are many data items that you can check for reasonableness. If you make a purchase on May 3, 2004, then the payment cannot possibly be due prior to that date. Perhaps within your organization, if you work in Department 12, you cannot possibly make more than $20.00 per hour. If your zip code is 90201, your state of residence cannot be New York. If your pet's breed is stored as "Great Dane", then its species cannot be "bird." Each of these examples involves comparing two data fields for reasonableness and consistency. You should consider making as many such comparisons as possible when writing your own programs.

Validating Presence of Data

Sometimes data are missing from a file, either on purpose or by accident. A job applicant might fail to submit an entry for the `salaryAtPreviousJob` field or a client has no entry for the `emailAddress` field. A data-entry clerk might accidentally skip a field when typing records. Many programming languages allow you to check for missing data with a statement similar to `if emailAddress is blank perform noEmailModule()`. You can place any instructions you like within the `noEmailModule()`, including forcing the field to a default value or issuing an error message.

Good defensive programs try to foresee all possible inconsistencies and errors. The more accurate your data, the more useful information you will produce as output from your programs.

10

CHAPTER SUMMARY

❑ Programs for which all the data are gathered prior to running use batch processing. Programs that depend on user input while they are running use interactive, real-time, online processing. A menu program is a common type of interactive program in which the user sees a number of options on the screen and can select any one of them.

❑ When you create a single-level menu, the user makes a selection from only one menu before using the program for its ultimate purpose. The user's response controls the mainline logic of a menu program.

❑ When you code a module as a black box, the module statements are invisible to the rest of the program. Many versions of a module can substitute for one another. When programmers develop systems containing many modules, they often code "empty" black box procedures, called stubs; later they can code the details in the stub routines. Additionally, most programming languages provide you with built-in black box functions.

❑ A programmer can improve a menu program and assist the user by displaying a message when the selected response is not one of the allowable menu options. Another user-friendly improvement to a program adds a counter that keeps track of a user's invalid responses and issues a stronger message after a specific number of invalid responses.

❑ You can use the case structure to make decisions when you need to test a single variable against several possible values. The case structure is particularly convenient to use in menu-driven programs because you decide from among several courses of action based on the value in the user's response variable.

❑ When a program requires more options than can easily fit in one menu, you can use a multilevel menu. With a multilevel menu, the selection of an option from a main menu leads to a submenu where the user can make further, more refined selections. With multilevel menus, the module that controls each new level can display a menu, accept a response, and while the user does not select the *quit* option for that menu level, perform another module based on the selection (or inform the user of an error). Finally, the module for each menu level displays the menu and accepts a response again.

❑ You can circumvent potential problems caused by a user's invalid data entries by validating the user's input. Validating input involves checking the user's responses to ensure they fall within acceptable bounds and taking one of several possible actions. Common mistakes when validating data include using incorrect logic and failing to account for the user making multiple invalid entries.

❑ Some of the techniques you want to master include: validating data type, range, reasonableness and consistency of data, and presence of data.

EXERCISES

1. a. Draw the logic for a flowchart or write the pseudocode for a program that gives you the following options for a trivia quiz:

   (1) Movies

   (2) Television

   (3) Sports

   (4) Quit

   When the user selects an option, display a question that falls under the category. After the user responds, display whether the answer was correct.

   b. Modify the program in Exercise 1a so that when the user selects a trivia quiz topic option, you display five questions in the category instead of just one.

2. Draw the logic for the flowchart or write the pseudocode for a program that presents you with the following options for a banking machine:

   (1) Deposit

   (2) Withdrawal

   (3) Quit

   After you select an option, the program asks you for the amount of money to deposit or withdraw, then displays your balance and allows you to make another selection. When the user selects *Quit*, display the final balance.

3. Draw the logic for the flowchart or write the pseudocode for a program that gives you the following options:

(1) Hot dog	1.50
(2) Fries	1.00
(3) Lemonade	.75
(4) End order	

   You should be allowed to keep ordering from the menu until you press *4* for *End order*, at which point you should see a total amount due for your entire order.

4. Draw the logic for the flowchart or write the pseudocode for a program that gives you the following options when registering for college classes:

(1) English 101	3
(2) Math 260	5
(3) History 100	3
(4) Sociology 151	4
(5) Quit	

   You should be allowed to select as many classes as you want before you choose the *Quit* option, but you should *not* be allowed to register for the same class

10

twice. The program accumulates the hours for which you have registered and displays your tuition bill at $50 per credit hour.

5. Suggest two subsequent levels of menus for each of the first two options in this main menu:

   (1) Print records from file

   (2) Delete records from file

   (3) Quit

6. Draw the flowchart or write the pseudocode for a program that displays the rules for a sport or a game. The user can select from a menu like the following:

   (1) Sports

   (2) Games

   (3) Quit

   If the user chooses *1* for *Sports*, then display options for four different sports of your choice (for example, soccer or basketball).

   If the user chooses *2* for *Games*, display options for:

   (1) Card games

   (2) Board games

   (3) Quit

   Display options for at least two card games (for example, Hearts) and two board games (for example, Monopoly) of your choice. Then display a one- or two-sentence summary of the game rules.

7. Draw the menus, then draw the flowchart or write the pseudocode for a program that displays United States travel and tourism facts. The main menu should allow the user to choose a region of the country. The next level should allow the user to select a state in that region. The final level should allow the user to select a city, at which point the user can view facts such as the city's population and average temperature. Write the complete module for only one region, one state, and one city.

8. Design the menus, then draw the flowchart or write the pseudocode for an interactive program for a florist. The first screen asks the user to choose indoor plants, outdoor plants, nonplant items, or quit. When the user chooses indoor or outdoor plants, list at least three appropriate plants of your choice. When the user chooses a plant, display its correct price. If the user chooses the nonplant option, offer a choice of gardening tools, gift items, or quit. Depending on the user selection, display at least three gardening tools or gift items. When the user chooses one, display its price.

9. Design the menus, and then draw the flowchart or write the pseudocode for an interactive program for a company's customer database. Store the customers' ID numbers in a 20-element array; store their balances due in a parallel 20-element array. The menu options include, add customers to the database, find a customer in

the database, print the database, and quit. If the user chooses to add customers, allow the user to enter a customer ID and balance to the current list, but do not let the list exceed 20 customers. If the user chooses to print, then print all existing IDs and balances; if there are none, issue a message. If the user chooses to find a customer, issue a message if there are none, otherwise provide a second menu with three options—find by number, find by balance, or quit. Assume there will be only one customer with any ID number but there might be several customers with the same balance.

10. Design the logic for a program that creates job applicant records including all input data, plus starting salary. The program asks a user for his or her first name, middle initial, last name, birth date (month, day, and year), current age, date of application (month, day, and year), and job title for which they are applying. Available jobs and starting salaries appear in the following table:

Job title	Salary
Clerk I	26,000
Clerk II	30,000
Administrative assistant	37,500
Technical writer	39,000
Programmer I	42,500
Programmer II	50,000

Perform as many validation checks as you can think of to make sure that complete and accurate records are created.

10

11

SEQUENTIAL FILE MERGING, MATCHING, AND UPDATING

After studying Chapter 11, you should be able to:

- ◆ Understand sequential files and the need for merging them
- ◆ Create the mainline and `housekeeping()` logic for a merge program
- ◆ Create the `mainLoop()` and `finishUp()` modules for a merge program
- ◆ Modify the `housekeeping()` module to check for eof
- ◆ Understand master and transaction file processing
- ◆ Match files to update master file fields
- ◆ Allow multiple transactions for a single master file record
- ◆ Update records in sequential files

UNDERSTANDING SEQUENTIAL DATA FILES AND THE NEED FOR MERGING FILES

A **sequential file** is a file where records are stored one after another in some order. One option is to store records in a sequential file in the order in which the records are created. For example, if you maintain records of your friends, you might store them in order based on how long you have known them where your best friend from kindergarten is record 1 and the friend you just made last week is record 30.

Often, however, the order of the records in a sequential file is based on the contents of one or more fields in each record. Perhaps it is most useful for you to store your friends sequentially in alphabetical order by last name, or maybe in order by birthday.

Other examples of sequential files include:

- A file of employees stored in order by Social Security number
- A file of parts for a manufacturing company stored in order by part number
- A file of customers for a business stored in alphabetical order by last name

Recall from Chapter 9 that the field on which you sort records is the key field.

Businesses often need to merge two or more sequential files. **Merging files** involves combining two or more files while maintaining the sequential order. For example:

- You have a file of current employees in Social Security number order and a file of newly hired employees, also in Social Security number order. You need to merge these two files into one combined file before running this week's payroll program.

- You have a file of parts manufactured in the Northside factory in part number order and a file of parts manufactured in the Southside factory, also in part number order. You need to merge these two files into one combined file creating a master list of available parts.

- You have a list of last year's customers in alphabetical order and a list of this year's customers in alphabetical order. You want to create a mailing list of all customers in order by last name.

Before you can merge files, two closely related conditions must be met:

- Each file used in the merge must be sorted in order based on some field.

- Each file used in the merge must be sorted in the same order (ascending or descending) on the same field as the others.

Suppose your business has two locations, one on the East Coast and one on the West Coast, and each location maintains a customer file in alphabetical order by customer name. Each file contains fields for name and customer balance. You can call the fields in the East Coast file eastName and eastBalance and the fields in the West Coast file westName and westBalance. You want to merge the two files creating one master file containing records for all customers. Figure 11-1 shows some sample data for the files; you want to create a merged file like the one shown in Figure 11-2.

```
East Coast File                West Coast File
eastName     eastBalance       westName      westBalance
Able         100.00            Chen          200.00
Brown         50.00            Edgar         125.00
Dougherty     25.00            Fell           75.00
Hanson       300.00            Grand         100.00
Ingram       400.00
Johnson       30.00
```

Figure 11-1   Sample data for two customer files

mergedName	mergedBalance
Able	100.00
Brown	50.00
Chen	200.00
Dougherty	25.00
Edgar	125.00
Fell	75.00
Grand	100.00
Hanson	300.00
Ingram	400.00
Johnson	30.00

Figure 11-2   Merged customer file

CREATING THE MAINLINE AND HOUSEKEEPING() LOGIC FOR A MERGE PROGRAM

The mainline logic for a program that merges two files is the same main logic you've used before in other programs: a housekeeping() module, a mainLoop() module that repeats until the end of the program, and a finishUp() module. Most programs you have written repeat the mainLoop() module until the eof condition occurs. In a program that merges files, there are two input files, so checking for eof on one of them is insufficient. Instead, the mainline logic will check a flag variable that you create with a name such as bothAtEof. You will set the bothAtEof flag to "Y" after you have encountered eof on both input files. Figure 11-3 shows the mainline logic.

 You first used flag variables in Chapter 8.

11

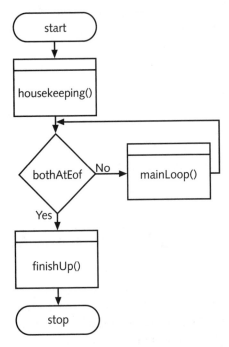

Figure 11-3 Flowchart for mainline logic of merge program

When you declare variables within the `housekeeping()` module, you must declare the `bothAtEof` flag and initialize it to any value other than "Y". In addition, you need to define two input files, one for the file from the East Coast office and one for the file from the West Coast. Figure 11-4 shows that the files are called `eastFile` and `westFile`. Their variable fields are `eastName`, `eastBalance`, `westName`, and `westBalance`, respectively.

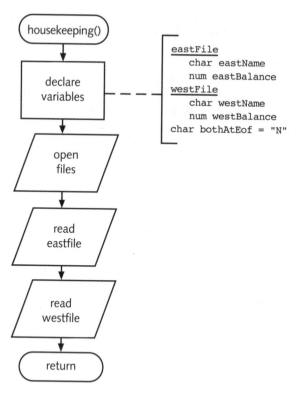

Figure 11-4   Flowchart for housekeeping() module in merge program, version 1

The output from this program is a merged file containing all records from the two input files. Logically, writing to a file and writing a printed report are very similar—each involves sending data to an output device. The major difference is that when you write a data file, typically you do not include headings or other formatting for people to read like you do when creating a printed report. A **data file** contains data only for another computer program to read.

 In many organizations, both data files and printed report files are sent to disk storage devices when they are created. Later, as time becomes available on the organization's busy printers, the report disk files are transferred to paper.

 You will modify this `housekeeping()` module later in this chapter after you learn about handling the `eof` condition in this program.

Typically, you read the first file input record into memory at the end of a `housekeep-ing()` module. In this file merging program with two input files, you will read one record from *each* input file into memory at the end of the `housekeeping()` module.

11

CREATING THE mainLoop() AND finishUp() MODULES FOR A MERGE PROGRAM

When you begin the `mainLoop()` module, two records—one from `eastFile` and one from `westFile`—are sitting in the memory of the computer. One of these records needs to be written to the new output file first. Which one? If you want the list in alphabetical order, write the one that has the lower alphabetical value in the name field first. Therefore, the `mainLoop()` module begins as shown in Figure 11-5.

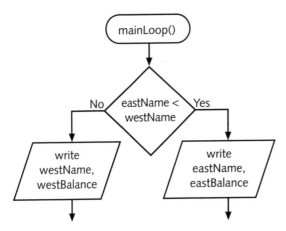

Figure 11-5   Beginning of the mainLoop() module

Using the sample data from Figure 11-1, you can see that the record containing "Able" should be written to the output file while Chen's record waits in memory because the `eastName` "Able," is alphabetically lower than the `westName` "Chen".

Should Chen's record be written to the output file next? Not necessarily. It depends on the next `eastName` following Able's record on the `eastFile`. You need to read that `eastFile` record into memory and compare it to "Chen". Since in this case the next record on the `eastFile` contains the name "Brown," this `eastFile` record is written.

Is it Chen's turn to be written now? You really don't know until you read another record from the `eastFile` and compare. Since this record contains the name "Dougherty", it is indeed time to write Chen's record. After Chen's record is written to output, should you now write Dougherty's record? You don't know until you read the next record from the `westFile` whether that record should be placed before or after Dougherty's record.

Therefore, the `mainLoop()` proceeds like this: compare two records, write the record with the lower alphabetical name, and read another record from the *same* input file. See Figure 11-6.

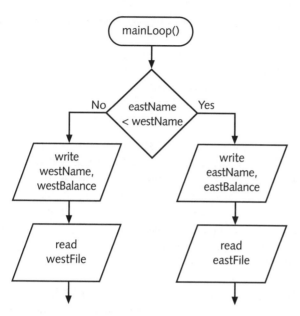

Figure 11-6 Continuation of mainLoop() module for merge program

Recall the names from the two original files (Figure 11-7) and walk through the processing steps.

1. Compare "Able" and "Chen". Write Able's record. Read Brown's record.

2. Compare "Brown" and "Chen". Write Brown's record. Read Dougherty's record.

3. Compare "Dougherty" and "Chen". Write Chen's record. Read Edgar's record.

4. Compare "Dougherty" and "Edgar". Write Dougherty's record. Read Hanson's record.

5. Compare "Hanson" and "Edgar". Write Edgar's record. Read Fell's record.

6. Compare "Hanson" and "Fell". Write Fell's record. Read Grand's record.

7. Compare "Hanson" and "Grand". Write Grand's record. Read from the `westFile`, encountering `eof`.

eastName	westName
Able	Chen
Brown	Edgar
Dougherty	Fell
Hanson	Grand
Ingram	
Johnson	

Figure 11-7   Names from two files to merge

What happens now? Is the program over? It shouldn't be, because records for Hanson, Ingram, and Johnson all need to be included on the new output file and none of them are written yet. You need to find a way to write the Hanson record as well as read and write all the remaining `eastFile` records. And you can't just write statements to read and write from the `eastFile`; sometimes when you run this program, records on the `eastFile` will finish first alphabetically, and in that case you need to continue reading from the `westFile`.

An elegant solution to this problem involves setting the field on which the merge is based to a "high" value when the end of the file is encountered. A **high value** is one that is greater than any possible value in a field. Programmers often use all 9s in a numeric field and all Zs in a character field to indicate a high value. Every time you read from the `westFile` you can check for `eof`, and when it occurs, set the `westName` to "ZZZZZ". Similarly, when reading the `eastFile`, set `eastName` to "ZZZZZ" when `eof` occurs. When both `eastName` and `westName` are "ZZZZZ", then you set the `bothAtEof` variable to "Y". Figure 11-8 shows the complete `mainLoop()` logic.

You might choose to completely fill the `eastName` and `westName` fields with Zs instead of using only five. Although it is unlikely that a person will have the last name ZZZZZ, you should be careful to make sure that the value you choose for a high value is actually a higher value than any legitimate value.

Several programming languages contain a name you can use for a value that occurs when every bit in a byte is an "on" bit creating a value that is even higher than all Zs or all 9s. For example, in COBOL this value is called HIGH-VALUES and in RPG it is called HIVAL.

Using the sample data in Figure 11-7, when `westFile` is read and `eof` is encountered, `westName` gets set to "ZZZZZ". Now when you enter the `mainLoop()` again, `eastName` and `westName` are compared and `eastName` is still "Hanson". The `eastName` (Hanson) is lower than the `westName` (ZZZZZ), so the data for `eastName`'s record writes to the output file, and another `eastFile` record (Ingram) is read.

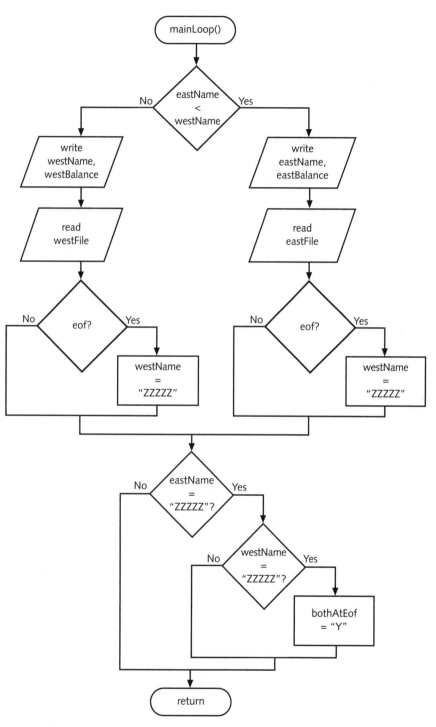

Figure 11-8   The mainLoop() module for merge program completed

The complete run of the file merging program now executes the first six steps as listed previously and then proceeds as shown in Figure 11–8 and as follows:

7. Compare "Hanson" and "Grand". Write Grand's record. Read from the `westFile`, encountering `eof` and setting `westName` to "ZZZZZ".

8. Compare "Hanson" and "ZZZZZ". Write Hanson's record. Read Ingram's record.

9. Compare "Ingram" and "ZZZZZ". Write Ingram's record. Read Johnson's record.

10. Compare "Johnson" and "ZZZZZ". Write Johnson's record. Read from the `eastFile`, encountering `eof` and setting `eastName` to "ZZZZZ".

11. Now that both names are "ZZZZZ", set the flag `bothAtEof` equal to "Y".

When the `bothAtEof` flag variable equals "Y", the mainline logic then proceeds to the `finishUp()` module. Figure 11-9 shows `finishUp()`.

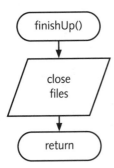

Figure 11-9 The finishUp() module for merge program

 Notice that if two names are equal during the merge process, for example when there is a "Hanson" record in each file, then both Hansons will be included in the final file. When the `eastName` and `westName` match, the `eastName` is not lower than the `westName`, so you write the `westFile` "Hanson" record. After you read the next `westFile` record, `eastName` will be lower than the next `westName`, and the `eastFile` "Hanson" record will be output.

MODIFYING THE HOUSEKEEPING() MODULE TO CHECK FOR EOF

Recall that in the housekeeping() module for this merge program you read one record from each of the two input files. Although it is unlikely that you will reach the end of file after attempting to read the first record on a file, it is good practice to check for eof every time you read. In the housekeeping() module you read from one of the input files. Whether you encounter eof or not, you then read from the other input file. If both files are at eof—that is, if both key fields are previously set to "ZZZZZ"—you can set the bothAtEof flag to "Y". Then, if bothAtEof is "Y", meaning that there are no records to merge, the mainline logic will immediately send the program to the finishUp() module. Figure 11-10 shows the modified housekeeping() module.

11

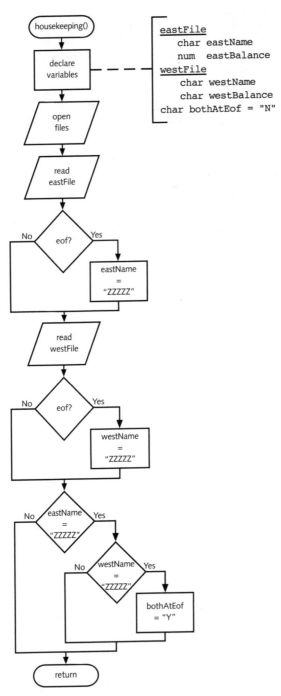

Figure 11-10   Modified housekeeping() module for merge program

MASTER AND TRANSACTION FILE PROCESSING

When two related sequential files seem "equal", in that they hold the same *type* of information—for example, when one holds customers from the East Coast and one holds customers from the West Coast—you often need to merge the files to use as a single unit. Some related sequential files, however, are unequal and you do not want to merge them. For example, you might have a file containing records for all your customers sorted on a key field that holds a customer ID number and contains additional customer data such as name, address, and balance due. You might have another file that contains data for every purchase a customer makes. Such a file would also be sorted by customer number and contain purchase information such as a dollar amount. Although both files contain a customer ID number, the file with the customer names and addresses is an example of a master file. You use a **master file** to hold relatively permanent data about your customers. The file with the customer purchases is a **transaction file** that holds more temporary data. You may maintain certain customers' names and addresses for years, but the transaction file will contain new data daily, weekly, or monthly depending on your organization's billing cycle. Often, you periodically use a transaction file to find a **matching record** in a master file, so you can **update the master file** by making changes to the values in its fields. For example, the file containing transaction purchase data might be used to update each master file record's balance due field. At other times, you might match a transaction file's records to its master file counterpart creating an entity that draws information from both files—an invoice for example.

Here are a few other examples of files that have a master-transaction relationship:

- A library maintains a master file of all patrons and a transaction file with information about each book or other items checked out.

- A college maintains a master file of all students and a transaction file for each course registration.

- A telephone company maintains a master file for every telephone line (number) and a transaction file with information about every call.

When you update a master file, you can take two approaches:

- You can actually change the information on the master file. When you use this approach, the information that existed on the master file prior to the transaction processing is lost.

- You can create a copy of the master file, making the changes on the new version. Then you can store the previous version of the master file for a period of time in case there are questions or discrepancies regarding the update process. The saved version of a master file is the **parent file**; the updated version is the **child file**.

 When a child file is updated, it becomes a parent, and its parent becomes a grandparent. Individual organizations create policy concerning the number of generations of backup files they will save before discarding them.

11

MATCHING FILES TO UPDATE FIELDS IN MASTER FILE RECORDS

The logic you use to perform a match between master and transaction file records is similar to the logic you use to perform a merge. As with a merge, you must begin with both files sorted in the same order on the same field.

Assume you have a master file with the fields shown in Figure 11-11.

File name: CUSTOMERS			
FIELD NAME	POSITIONS	DATA TYPE	DECIMALS
custNumber	1–3	numeric	0
custName	4–23	character	
custAddress	24–43	character	
custPhone	44–53	numeric	0
custTotalSales	54–60	numeric	2

Figure 11-11   Master customer file description

The `custTotalSales` field holds the total dollar amount of all purchases the customer has ever made. At the end of each week you want to update this field with any new sale transaction that occurred during the week. Assume a transaction file contains one record for every transaction that has occurred and that each record holds the customer number, the transaction date, and the amount of the transaction. The fields in the transaction file are shown in Figure 11-12.

File name: TRANSACTIONS			
FIELD NAME	POSITIONS	DATA TYPE	DECIMALS
transNumber	1–3	numeric	0
transDate	4–11	numeric	0
transAmount	12–17	numeric	2

Figure 11-12   Transaction file description

You want to create a new master file on which almost all information is the same as on the original file, but the `custTotalSales` field increases to reflect the most recent transaction. The process involves going through the old master file one record at a time and determining whether there is a new transaction for that customer. If there is no transaction for a customer, the new customer record will contain exactly the same information as the old customer record. If however, there is a transaction for a customer, the `transAmount` adds to the `custTotalSales` field before you write the updated master file record to output.

The mainline logic (Figure 11-13) and `housekeeping()` (Figure 11-14) module for this matching program look similar to their counterparts in a file merging program. Two records are read, one from the master file and one from the transaction file. When you encounter **eof** for either file, store a high value (999) in the customer number field. Using the **readCust( )** and **readTrans( )** modules moves the reading of files and checking for **eof** off into their individual modules, as shown in Figure 11-15.

```
start
     perform housekeeping()
     while bothAtEof = "N"
             perform mainLoop()
     perform finishUp()
end
```

Figure 11-13   Mainline logic for file matching program

```
housekeeping()                                    custRec
     declare variables — — — — — — —                 num CustNumber
     open files                                       char custName
     perform readCust()                               char custAddress
     perform readTrans()                              num custPhone
     if custNumber = 999 then                         num custTotalSales
             if transNumber = 999 then             transRec
                     bothAtEof = "Y"                  num transNumber
             endif                                    num transDate
     endif                                            num transAmount
return                                            char bothAtEof = "N"
```

Figure 11-14   The housekeeping() module for file match program

In the file-merging program, you placed "ZZZZZ" in the customer name field at end of file because character fields were being compared. In this example, because you are using numeric fields (customer numbers) you can store 999 at the end of the file. The value 999 is the highest possible numeric value for a three-digit number in the customer number field.

```
readTrans()                          readCust()
   read transRec                        read custRec
   if eof then                          if eof then
       transNumber = 999                    custNumber = 999
   endif                                endif
return                               return
```

Figure 11-15   The readTrans and readCust modules for match program

In the file-merging program, your first action in the **mainLoop( )** was to determine which file held the record with the lower value; then you wrote that file to output. In a matching program you need to determine more than whether one file's key field is

11

larger than another's; it's also important to know if they are *equal*. In this example, you want to update the master file record's `custTotalSales` field only if the transaction contains an exact match for the customer number. Therefore, in the `mainLoop()` module you compare the `custNumber` and the `transNumber`. Three possibilities exist:

- The `transNumber` equals the `custNumber`.
- The `transNumber` is higher than the `custNumber`.
- The `transNumber` is lower than the `custNumber`.

When you compare records from the two input files, if the `custNumber` and the `transNumber` are equal, you add the `transAmount` to the `custTotalSales`, and then write the updated master record to the output file. Then you read in both a new master record and a new transaction record.

 The logic used here assumes there can be only one transaction per customer. Later in this chapter you will develop the logic for a program in which the customer can have multiple transactions.

If the `transNumber` is higher than the `custNumber`, this means there wasn't a sale for that customer. That's all right; not every customer makes a transaction every period. If the `transNumber` is higher than the `custNumber` when you compare records, then you simply write the original customer record to output with exactly the same information it contained when input; then you get the next customer record to see if this customer made the transaction.

Finally, when you compare records from the master and transaction files, if the `transNumber` is lower than the `custNumber` on the master file, you are trying to record a transaction for which no master record exists. That means there must be an error, because a transaction should always have a master record. You can handle this error in a variety of ways; here you will write an error message to an output device before reading the next transaction record. A human operator can then read the message and take appropriate action.

Whether the `transNumber` was higher than, lower than, or equal to the `custNumber`, at the bottom of the `mainLoop()` module you check whether both `custNumber` and `transNumber` are 999; when they are, you set the `bothAtEof` flag to "Y".

Figure 11-16 shows some sample data you can use to walk through the logic for this program.

```
Master File                          Transaction File
custNumber     custTotalSales        transNumber      transAmount
100            1000.00               100              400.00
102              50.00               105              700.00
103             500.00               108              100.00
105              75.00               110              400.00
106            5000.00
109            4000.00
110             500.00
```

Figure 11-16   Sample data for matching program

The program proceeds as follows:

1. Read customer 100 from the master file and customer 100 from the transaction file. Customer numbers are equal, so 400.00 from the transaction file is added to 1000.00 in the master file, and a new master file record is written out with a 1400.00 total sales figure. Then read a new record from each file.

2. The customer number on the master file is 102 and the customer number on the transaction file is 105, so there are no transactions today for customer 102. Write out the master record exactly the way it came in and read a new master record.

3. Now the master customer number is 103 and the transaction customer number is still 105. This means customer 103 has no transactions, so you write out the master record as is and read a new one.

4. Now the master customer number is 105 and the transaction number is 105. The new total sales figure is 775.00 and a new master record is written out. Read one record from each file.

5. Now the master number is 106 and the transaction number is 108. Write out customer record 106 as is and read another master.

6. Now the master number is 109 and the transaction number is 108. An error has occurred. The transaction record indicates that you made a sale to customer 108, but there is no master record for customer number 108. Either there is an error in the transaction customer number, or the transaction is correct but you have failed to create a master record. Either way, write an error message so that a clerk is notified and can handle the problem. Then get a new transaction record.

7. Now the master number is 109 and the transaction number is 110. Write out master record 109 with no changes and read a new one.

8. Now the master number is 110 and the transaction number is 110. Add the 400.00 transaction to the previous 500.00 figure and write out a new record with a 900.00 value in the **custTotalSales** field. Read one record from each file.

9. Since both files are finished, end the job.

11

Figure 11-17 shows the pseudocode for the logic just described. The result is a new master file in which some records contain exactly the same data they contained going in, but others (for which a transaction has occurred) have been updated with a new total sales figure.

```
mainLoop()
    if custNumber = transNumber then
           custTotalSales = custTotalSales + transAmount
           write custRec
           perform readCust()
           perform readTrans()
    else
           if transNumber > custNumber then
                  write custRec
                  perform readCust()
           else
                  write "An Error has occurred in transaction", transNumber
                  perform readTrans()
           endif
    endif
    if custNumber = 999
           if transNumber = 999
                  bothAtEof = "Y"
           endif
     endif
 return
```

Figure 11-17   Pseudocode for mainLoop() logic for file matching program

ALLOWING MULTIPLE TRANSACTIONS FOR A SINGLE MASTER FILE RECORD

In the last example, the logic provided for, at most, one transaction record per master customer record. You would use very similar logic if you wanted to allow multiple transactions for a single customer. Figure 11-18 shows the new logic. A small but important difference exists between logic that allows multiple transactions and logic that allows only a single transaction per master file record. If a customer can have multiple transactions, whenever a transaction matches a customer you add the transaction amount to the master total sales field. *Then* you read only from the transaction file. The next transaction might also pertain to the same master customer. Only when a transaction number is greater than a master file customer number do you write the customer master record.

```
mainLoop()
     if custNumber = transNumber then
          custTotalSales = custTotalSales + transAmount
          perform readTrans()
     else
          if transNumber > custNumber then
               write custRec
               perform readCust()
          else
               write "An Error has occurred in transaction ", transNumber
               perform readTrans()
          endif
     endif
     if custNumber = 999
          if transNumber = 999
               bothAtEof = "Y"
          end if
     endif
return
```

Figure 11-18   The mainLoop() logic allowing multiple transactions for each master file record

UPDATING RECORDS IN SEQUENTIAL FILES

11

In the example in the last section, you needed to update a field in some of the records in a master file with new data. A more sophisticated update program allows you to make changes to data in a record and update a master file by adding new records or eliminating the ones you no longer want.

Assume you have a master employee file as shown on the left side of Figure 11-19. Sometimes a new employee is hired and must be added to this file, or an employee quits and must be removed from the file. Sometimes you need to change an employee record by recording a raise in salary for example, or a change of department.

For this kind of program it's common to have a transaction file in which each record contains all the same fields as the master file, with one exception. The transaction file has one extra field to indicate whether this transaction is meant to be an addition, a deletion, or a change—for example, a one-letter code of "A", "D", or "C". Figure 11-19 shows the master and transaction file layouts.

```
File name: EMPREC              File name: TRANSREC
FIELD NAME         POSITIONS   FIELD NAME         POSITIONS
empNum             1-3         transNum           1-3
empName            4-23        transName          4-23
empSalary          24-28       transSalary        24-28
empDept            29-30       transDept          29-30
                               transCode          31
```

Figure 11-19   Master and transaction files for update program

An **addition record** on the transaction file would contain data in the fields `transNum`, `transName`, `transSalary`, and `transDept`; an addition record represents a new employee, and data for all the fields must be entered for the first time. In addition, such a record contains an "A" in the `transCode` field.

A **deletion record** really needs data in only two fields—a "D" in `transCode` and a number in `transNum`. If a `transNum` matches an `empNum` on a master record, then you have identified a record you want to delete. You do not need data indicating the salary, department, or anything else for a record you are deleting.

A **change record** contains a "C" code and needs data only in the fields that are going to be changed. In other words, if an employee's salary is not changing the `transSalary` field will be blank; but if the employee is transferring to Department 28, then the department field of the transaction record would hold a 28.

The mainline logic for an update program is the same as that for the merging and matching programs shown in Figure 11-13. Within the `housekeeping()` module you declare the variables, open the files, and read the first record from each file. You can use the `readEmp()` and `readTrans()` modules to set the key fields `empNum` and `transNum` to high values at `eof`. See Figures 11-20 and 11-21.

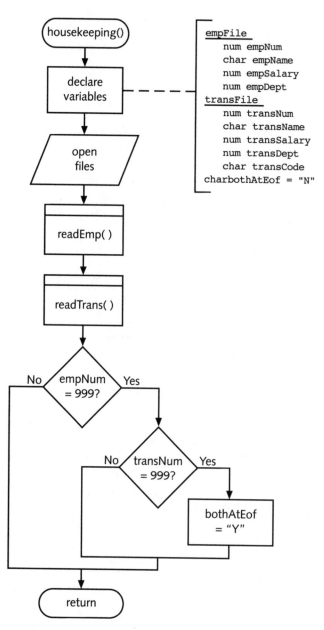

11

Figure 11-20 The housekeeping() module for update program

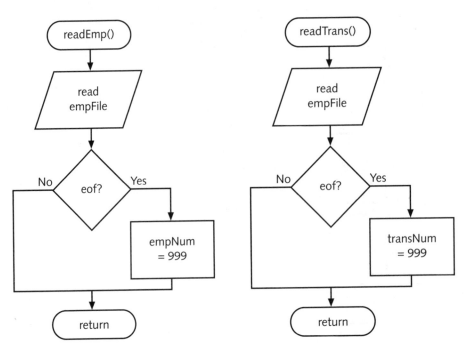

Figure 11-21   The readEmp() and readTrans() modules

The `mainLoop()` module of the update program begins like the `mainLoop()` in the matching program. You need to know whether the `empNum` on the master file and the `transNum` on the transaction file are equal, or if one or the other is higher. To keep the `mainLoop()` simple, you can create modules for each of these three scenarios: `theyAreEqual()`, `empIsLargerThanTrans()`, and `transIsLargerThanEmp()`. (Of course, you might choose shorter module names.) At the end of the `mainLoop()` module you can set the `bothAtEof` flag variable to "Y" if both files have completed. Figure 11-22 shows the `mainLoop()` module.

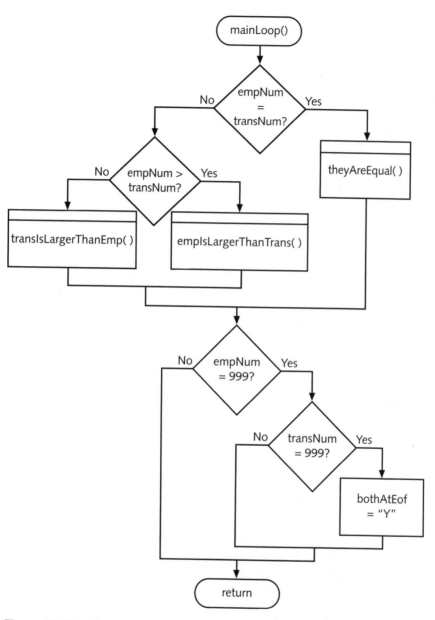

Figure 11-22   The mainLoop() of update program

You perform the `theyAreEqual()` module only if a record on the master file and a record on the transaction file contain the same employee number. This should be the situation when a change is made to a record (for example, a change in salary) or when a record is to be deleted. If the master file and the transaction file records are equal, but the `transCode` on the transaction record is an "A", then an error has occurred. You should not be attempting to add a full employee record when the employee already exists in the master file.

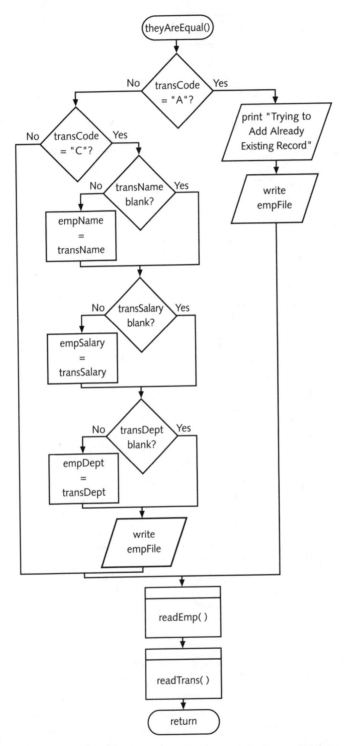

Figure 11-23   The theyAreEqual() module for update program

As shown in Figure 11-23, within the `theyAreEqual()` module you check the `transCode` and perform one of three actions:

- If the code is an "A", print an error message. But what is the error? (Is the code wrong? Was this meant to be a change or a deletion of an existing employee? Is the employee number wrong—was this meant to be the addition of some new employee?) Because you're not completely sure, you can only print out an error message to let an employee know that an error has occurred; then the employee can handle the error. You should also write the existing master record to output exactly the same way it came in without making any changes.

- If the code is a "C", you need to make changes. You must check each field on the transaction record. If any field is blank, the data on the new master record should come from the old master record. If, however, a field on the transaction record contains data, these data are intended to constitute a change and the corresponding field on the new master record should be created from the transaction record. For each changed field then, you replace the contents of the old field on the master file with the new value in the corresponding field on the transaction file and then write the master file record.

- If the code is not an "A" or a "C", it must be a "D" and the record should be deleted. How do you delete a record from a new master file? Just don't write it out to the new master file!

Various programming languages have different ways of checking a field to determine if it is blank. In some languages, you compare the field to a space character, as in `transName = " "`. In other languages you can use a predefined language-specific constant like `blank`, as in `transName = blank`.

To keep the illustration simple here, you can assume that all the transaction records have been checked by a previous program and all `transCode` values are "A", "C", or "D". If this were not the case, you can simply add one more decision to the `theyAreEqual()` module. If the `transCode` is not "C", instead of assuming it is "D", ask if it is "D". If so, delete the record; if not, it must be something other than "A", "C", or "D", so write an error message.

Finally, at the end of the `theyAreEqual()` module, after the master file record and the transaction file record have matched and the appropriate action has been taken, you read one new record from each of the two input files.

Suppose within the `mainLoop()` the master file record and the transaction file record do *not* match. If the master file record has a higher number than the transaction file record, then you execute the `empIsLargerThanTrans()` module as shown in Figure 11-24. This means you have read a transaction record for which there is no master record.

11

If the transaction record contains code "A", that's fine because an addition transaction shouldn't have a master record. The transaction record data simply become the new master record and each of its fields is written to the new output file.

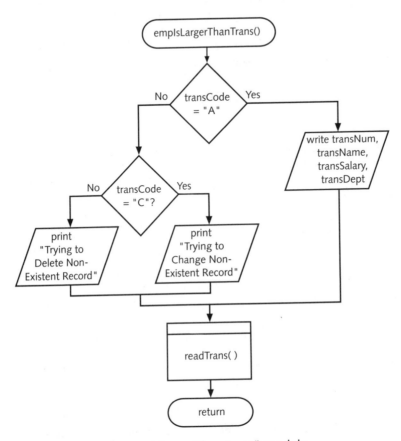

Figure 11-24   The empIsLargerThanTrans() module

However, if the transaction code is "C" or "D" an error has occurred. Either you are attempting to make a change to a nonexistent record or you are attempting to delete a nonexistent record. Either way, a mistake has been made. You must print an error message.

At the end of the `empIsLargerThanTrans()` routine, you should not read another master file record. After all, there could be several more transactions that represent new additions to the master file. You want to keep reading transactions until a transaction matches or is greater than a master record. Therefore only a transaction record should be read.

The last possibility in the `mainLoop()` module is that a master file record is smaller than the transaction file record in memory. If there is no transaction for a given master file record, then the `transIsLargerThanEmp()` module is entered. This just means that the master file record has no changes or deletions, so you simply write the new master record out exactly like the old master record and read another master record. See Figure 11-25.

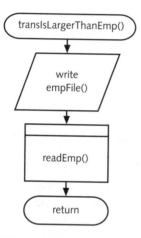

Figure 11-25 The transIsLargerThanEmp() module

At some point, one of the files will reach eof. If the transaction file reaches the end first, transNum is set to 999 in the readTrans() routine. Each time the mainLoop() module is entered after transNum is set to 999, the empNum will be lower than transNum and the transIsLargerThanEmp() routine will execute. That module writes out records from the master file without alteration and this is exactly what you want to happen. There obviously were no transactions for these final records on the master file, because all the records in the transaction file were used to apply to earlier master file records.

On the other hand, if the master file reaches its end first, empNum is set to 999 in the readEmp() module. Now each time the program enters the mainLoop(), the transNum will be lower than the empNum. The empIsLargerThanTrans() module will execute for all remaining transaction records. In turn, each remaining transaction will be compared to the possible code values. If any remaining transaction records are additions, they will write to the new master as new records. However, if the remaining transaction records represent changes or deletions, a mistake has been made because there are no corresponding master file records.

Whichever file reaches the end first, the other continues to be read from and processed. When that file reaches eof, the bothAtEof flag will finally be set to "Y". Then you can perform the finishUp() module, as shown in Figure 11-26.

11

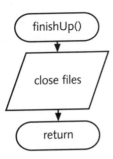

Figure 11-26   The finishUp() module for update program

Merging files, matching files, and updating a master file from a transaction file require a significant number of steps, because as you read each new input record you must account for many possible scenarios. Planning the logic for programs like these takes a fair amount of time, but by planning the logic carefully you can create programs that perform valuable work for years to come. Separating the various outcomes into manageable modules keeps the program organized and allows you to develop the logic one step at a time.

CHAPTER SUMMARY

❐ A sequential file is a file whose records are stored one after another in some order. The field on which you sort records is the key field. Merging files involves combining two or more files while maintaining the sequential order. Each file used in a merge must be sorted in the same order on the same field as the others.

❐ The mainline logic for a program that merges two files contains a **housekeeping()** module, a **mainLoop()** module that repeats until the end of the program, and a **finishUp()** module. The mainline logic will check a flag variable that you declare in the **housekeeping()** module and turn on when both input files are finished.

❐ When beginning the **mainLoop()** module of a merge program, you compare records from each file to be merged. You write the appropriate record from one of the files to output and read a record from the same file. When you encounter the end of file on one of the two input files set the field on which the merge is based to a high value.

❐ In the **housekeeping()** module of a merge program, you read from two input files, check for the end of each file, and set a flag if both input files are at **eof**.

❐ You use a master file to hold relatively permanent data and a transaction file to hold more temporary data that correspond to records in the master file. When you update a master file you can take two approaches: you can actually change the information on the master file or you can create a copy of the master file, making the changes on the new version.

❏ The logic you use to perform a match between master and transaction file records involves comparing the files to determine whether there is a transaction for each master record; when there is, you update the master record. When a master record has no transaction, you write the master record as is; when a transaction record has no corresponding master, you have an error.

❏ Using the logic that allows multiple transactions per master file record, whenever a transaction matches a master file record, you process the transaction, then you read only from the transaction file. Only when a transaction file key field is greater than a master file key field do you write the master record.

❏ A sophisticated update program allows you to make changes to data in a record and update a master file by adding new records or eliminating records you no longer want. For this kind of program it's common to have a transaction file in which each record contains all the same fields as the master file, with an additional code that indicates the type of transaction.

EXERCISES

1. The Springwater Township School district has two high schools—Jefferson and Audubon. Each school maintains a student file with fields containing student ID, last name, first name, and address. Each file is in student ID number order. Write the flowchart or pseudocode for the program that merges the two files into one file containing a list of all students in the district, maintaining student ID number order.

2. a. The Redgranite Library keeps a file of all books borrowed every month. Each file is in Library of Congress number order and contains additional fields for author and title. Write the flowchart or pseudocode for the program that merges the files for January and February to create a list of all books borrowed in the two-month period.

   b. Modify the program from Exercise 2a so that if there is more than one record for a book number, you print the book information only once.

   c. Modify the program from Exercise 2b so that if there is more than one record for a book number, you not only print the book information only once, but also print a count of the total number of times the book was borrowed.

3. a. Hearthside Realtors keeps a file for each salesperson in the office. Each file contains the salesperson's transactions for the year in descending sale price order. Two salespeople, Diane and Mark, have formed a partnership. Write the flowchart or pseudocode that produces a merged list of their transactions.

   b. Modify the program in Exercise 3a so that the appropriate salesperson's name appears following each transaction.

11

4. Dartmoor Medical Associates maintains two patient files—one for the Lakewood office and one for the Hanover office. Each record contains the name, address, city, state, and zip code of a patient with the file maintained in zip code order. Write the flowchart or pseudocode that merges the two files to produce one master name and address file that Dartmoor can use for addressing its monthly *Healthy Lifestyles* newsletter mailing in zip code order.

5. a. The Timely Talent Temporary Help Agency maintains an employee master file that contains employee ID number, last name, first name, address, and hourly rate for each of the temporary employees it sends out on assignments. The file has been sorted in employee ID number order.

   Each week, a transaction file is created with a job number, address, customer name, employee ID, and hours worked for every job filled by Timely Talent workers. The transaction file is also sorted in employee ID order.

   Write the flowchart or pseudocode for the program that matches the master and transaction file records and print one line for each transaction indicating job number, employee ID number, hours worked, hourly rate, and gross pay. Assume each temporary worker works at most one job per week; print one line for each worker who has worked that week.

   b. Modify Exercise 5a so that any individual temporary worker can work any number of separate jobs in a week. Print one line for each job that week.

   c. Modify Exercise 5b so that although any worker can work any number of jobs in a week, you accumulate the worker's total pay for all jobs and print one line per worker.

6. a. Claypool College maintains a student master file that contains student ID number, last name, first name, address, total credit hours completed, and cumulative grade point average for each of the students who attend the college. The file has been sorted in student ID number order.

   Each semester a transaction file is created with the student's ID, the number of credits completed during the new semester, and the grade point average for the new semester. The transaction file is also sorted in student ID order.

   Write the flowchart or pseudocode for a program that matches the master and transaction file records and updates the total credit hours completed and the cumulative grade point average on a new master record. Calculate the new grade new point average as follows:

   ◻ Multiply the credits on the master file times the grade point average on the master file, giving old honor points

   ◻ Multiply the credits on the transaction file times the grade point average on the transaction file, giving transaction honor points

   ◻ Add the two honor point values, giving total honor points

◻ Add master and transaction credit hours, giving total credit hours

◻ Divide total honor points by total credit hours, giving the new grade point average

7. You run a talent agency that books bands for social functions. You maintain a master file in which the records are stored in order by band code. The records have the following format:

TALENT FILE DESCRIPTION
File name: BANDS

FIELD DESCRIPTION	POSITIONS	DATA TYPE	DECIMALS	EXAMPLE
Band Code	1–3	numeric	0	176
Band Name	4–33	character		The Polka Pals
Contact Person	34–53	character		Jay Sakowicz
Phone	54–63	numeric	0	8154556012
Musical Style	64–71	character		Polka
Hourly Rate	72–76	numeric	2	07500

Once a month you make changes to the file using transaction records with the same format as the master records, plus one additional field that holds a transaction code. The transaction code is "A" if you are adding a new band to the file, "C" if you are changing some of the data in an existing record, and "D" if you are deleting a band from the file.

An addition transaction record contains a band code, an "A" in the transaction code field, and the new band's data. During processing, an error can occur if you attempt to add a band code that already exists on the file. This is not allowed, and an error message is printed.

A change transaction record contains a band code, a "C" in the transaction code field, and data for only those fields that are changing. For example, a band that is raising its hourly rate from $75 to $100 would contain empty fields for the band name, contact person information, and style of music, but the hourly rate field would contain the new rate. During processing, an error can occur if you attempt to change data for a band number that doesn't exist on the master file; print an error message.

A deletion transaction record contains a band code, a "D" in the transaction code field, and no other data. During processing, an error can occur if you attempt to delete a band number that doesn't exist on the master file; print an error message.

Two forms of output are created. One is the new updated master file with all changes, additions, and deletions. The other is a printed report of errors that occurred during processing. Rather than just a list of error messages, each line of the printed output should list the appropriate band code along with the corresponding message.

Design the print chart for the error report along with the hierarchy chart, and either a flowchart or pseudocode for the program.

11

8. Cozy Cottage Realty maintains a master file in which records are stored in order by listing number in the following format:

REALTY FILE DESCRIPTION
File name: HOUSES

FIELD DESCRIPTION	POSITIONS	DATA TYPE	DECIMALS	EXAMPLE
Listing Number	1–6	numeric	0	200319
Address	7–35	character		348 Alpine Road
List Price	36–43	numeric	0	139900
Bedrooms	44	numeric	0	3
Baths	45–46	numeric	1	1.5

Every day the realty company makes changes to the file using transaction records with the same format as the master records, plus one additional field that holds a transaction code. The transaction code is "A" to add a new listing, "C" to change some of the data in an existing record, and "D" to delete a listing that is sold or no longer on the market.

An addition transaction record contains a listing number, an "A" in the transaction code field, and the new house listing's data. During processing, an error can occur if you attempt to add a listing number that already exists on the file. This is not allowed and an error message is printed.

A change transaction record contains a listing number, a "C" in the transaction code field, and data for only those fields that are changing. For example, a listing that is dropping in price from $139,900 to $133,000 would contain empty fields for the address, bedrooms, and baths, but the price field would contain the new list price. During processing an error can occur if you attempt to change data for a listing number that doesn't exist on the master file; print an error message.

A deletion transaction record contains a listing code number, a "D" in the transaction code field, and no other data. During processing, an error can occur if you attempt to delete a listing number that doesn't exist on the master file; print an error message.

Two forms of output are created. One is the new updated master file with all changes, additions, and deletions. The other is a printed report of errors that occurred during processing. Rather than just a list of error messages, each line of the printed output should list the appropriate house listing number along with the corresponding message.

Design the print chart for the error report along with the hierarchy chart and either a flowchart or pseudocode for the program.

12

ADVANCED MODULARIZATION TECHNIQUES AND OBJECT-ORIENTED PROGRAMMING

After studying Chapter 12, you should be able to:

♦ Understand the principles of modularization and abstraction

♦ Pass variables to modules

♦ Return a value from a module

♦ Use an IPO chart

♦ Understand the advantages of encapsulation

♦ Understand the principles of object-oriented programming

♦ Define classes

♦ Instantiate and use objects

♦ Understand inheritance

♦ Understand polymorphism

♦ Understand the advantages of object-oriented programming

UNDERSTANDING THE PRINCIPLES OF MODULARIZATION AND ABSTRACTION IN PROCEDURAL PROGRAMS

Throughout most of computer programming history, which now totals about 50 years, the majority of programs were written procedurally. A **procedural program** consists of a series of steps or procedures that take place one after the other. The programmer determines the exact conditions under which a procedure takes place, how often it takes place, and when the program stops. The logic for every program you have developed so far using this book has been procedural.

 You first learned the term *procedural program* in Chapter 4.

It is possible to write procedural programs as one long series of steps. However, by now you should appreciate the benefits of **modularization**, or breaking programs into reasonable

units called modules, subroutines, functions, or methods. The following are benefits of modularization:

- Provides **abstraction**; in other words, it makes it easier to see the "big picture"
- Allows multiple programmers to work on a problem, each contributing one or more modules that later can be combined into a whole program
- Allows you to reuse your work; you can call the same module from multiple locations within a program
- Allows you to identify structures more easily

 You first learned the term *modular* in Chapter 2; you learned about *abstraction* in Chapter 3.

As beneficial as using modules is, the modules and subroutines you have used throughout this book also have two major drawbacks:

- Although the modules you have used allow multiple programmers to work on a problem, each programmer must know the *names* of *all* the variables used in other modules within the program.
- Although the modules you have used enable you to reuse your work by allowing you to call them from multiple locations within a program, you can't use the modules in different programs unless the new programs use the *same variable names*.

These two limitations stem from the same fact: the variables you have used throughout this book have been global variables. A **global variable** is one that is available to every module in a program. That is, every module has access to the variable, can use its value, and can change its value. When you declare a variable named `grandTotal` in a program's `housekeeping()` module, add to it in a `mainLoop()` module, and print it in a `finish()` module, then `grandTotal` is a global variable within that program.

With many older computer programming languages all variables are global variables. Newer, more modularized languages allow you to use local variables as well. A **local variable** is one whose name and value are known only to its own module. A local variable is declared within a module and ceases to exist when the module ends.

 Languages that use only global variables are most likely to call their modules subroutines. Languages that allow local variables and the passing of values are more likely to call their modules procedures, methods, or functions.

 Many languages refer to a local variable as *going out of scope* at the end of its module. In other words, the program "loses sight of" the variable.

When you declare local variables within modules, you do so in a `declare variables` step. Usually this is the first step within a module, but some languages allow you to declare variables at any point within a module. Sometimes you declare a local variable because the value is needed only within one module. For example, consider a very simple program that asks a student just one arithmetic question. For simplicity, this example won't loop; it provides a single user with a single question. A program such as this one could be contained in a single main module, but you can divide it into three separate modules as shown in Figure 12-1. The program contains three steps: `housekeeping()`, `askQuestion()`, and `finish()`.

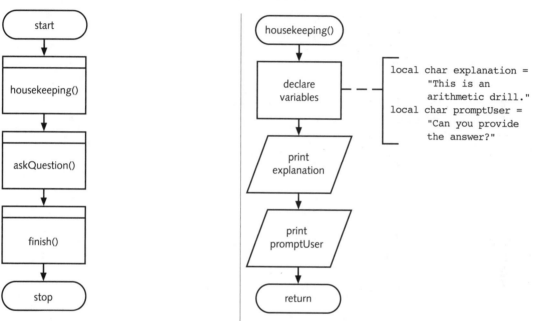

Figure 12-1   Mainline logic for a program that uses local variables

Figure 12-2   housekeeping() module for a program that uses local variables

Figure 12-2 shows the `housekeeping()` module in which directions are displayed on the screen. Within `housekeeping()` you can declare variables named `explanation` and `promptUser` that hold the directions. The `explanation` and `promptUser` variables can be local to the `housekeeping()` module because the `askQuestion()` and `finish()` modules never need access to these variables—these modules do not need to use the variables or alter them in any way.

> Programming languages that use local variables do not require you to modify the variable declaration with the term *local*, as shown in Figure 12-2. The term *local* is used in Figure 12-2 just for emphasis.

Within the `askQuestion()` module you display an arithmetic problem, accept an answer, determine whether the answer is correct, and write a message. The `askQuestion()` module does not need to know about the `explanation` and `promptUser` variables, but the `askQuestion()` module does need a `userAnswer` variable in which to store the user's answer to the arithmetic problem. Within the `askQuestion()` module you declare the `userAnswer` variable, use it to hold the user's answer, and then use it again to determine whether the user's answer is correct. By the time you reach the end of the `askQuestion()` module, the `userAnswer` variable has served its purpose; there is no reason for either the `housekeeping()` module or the `finish()` module to have access to it. Figure 12-3 shows the `userAnswer` variable being declared locally within the `askQuestion()` module.

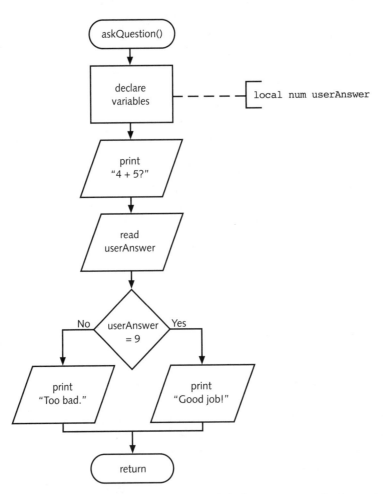

Figure 12-3 The askQuestion() module for a program that uses local variables

This arithmetic drill program employs a principle known as **encapsulation**, also known as **information hiding** or **data hiding** which means that the data or variables you use are completely contained within, and accessible only to the module in which they are declared. In other words, the data and variables are "hidden from" the other program modules. Using encapsulation provides you with two advantages:

- Because each module needs to use only the variable names declared within the module, multiple programmers can create the individual modules without knowing the data names used by the other modules.

- Because the variable names in each module are hidden from all other modules, programmers can even use the same variable names as those used in other modules and no conflict will arise.

Consider the `housekeeping()` module for the arithmetic drill program shown in Figure 12-2. Programmers who work on this module can give the local variables any name they want. For example, a programmer *could* decide to call the `promptUser` variable `userAnswer` as shown in Figure 12-4. In a program that employs local variables, giving the `housekeeping()` module's variable this name would have no effect on the usefulness of the identically named variable defined in the `askQuestion()` module. The two `userAnswer` variables are completely separate variables with unique memory addresses. One holds the character prompt "Can you provide the answer?" and the other holds a numeric user answer. Changing the value of `userAnswer` in one module, which is what happens when the user enters an arithmetic problem answer in the `askQuestion()` module, has no effect whatsoever on the separate `userAnswer` variable in the other module. A large program might contain dozens of modules and each module might contain dozens of variable names. As programs grow in size and complexity it is a great convenience for a programmer who is working on one module not to have to worry about conflicting with all the other variable names used in the program.

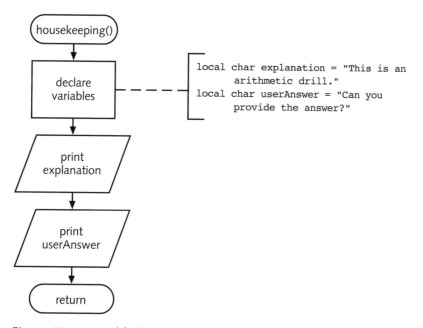

Figure 12-4   Modified housekeeping() module with userAnswer variable

12

PASSING VARIABLES TO MODULES

It may be convenient for a programmer to use local variables without worrying about naming conflicts, but using local variables produces a problem. By definition, a local variable is accessible to one module only and sometimes more than one module needs access to the same variable value. Consider the arithmetic drill program. Instead of a single arithmetic problem, it is more reasonable to expect such a program to ask the user a series of problems and keep score. Figure 12-5 shows a revised askQuestion() module that accesses an array to provide a series of five questions for the arithmetic drill. The module compares the user's answer to the correct answer that is stored in the corresponding position in a parallel array and adds 1 to a correctCount variable when the answer is correct.

Suppose you want to print the count of correct answers, the percentage of correct answers, and one of five messages based on the user's performance. There are enough steps involved in the process of displaying the final statistics that you want to place these steps in their own module, named finalStatistics(). But if you want to modularize the process that prints the final statistics, you must access the correctCount value from within the finalStatistics() module. If correctCount is declared locally within askQuestion(), the finalStatistics() module does not have access to it. On the other hand, if correctCount is declared locally in the finalStatistics() module, then the askQuestion() module cannot add to it. If you attempt to solve the dilemma by declaring a local correctCount variable in *each* module, they are not the same variable, and adding to the correctCount variable in one module does not alter the value of the unique correctCount variable in the other module. If you decide not to use local variables but declare correctCount as a global variable, the program will work, but you will have avoided using the principle of encapsulation and will have lost the advantages it provides.

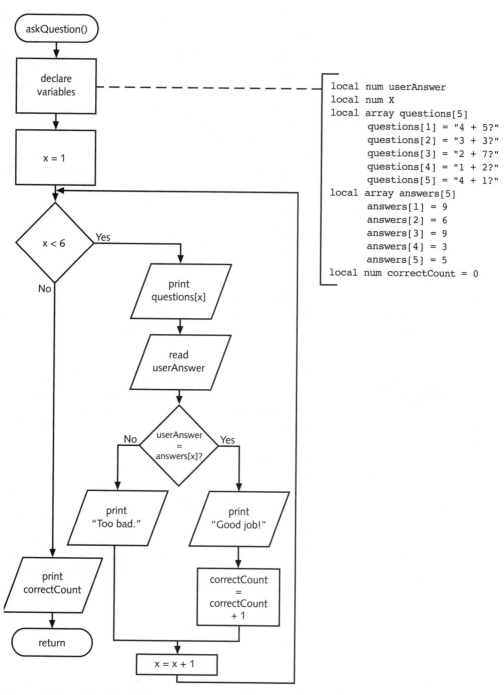

Figure 12-5 Modified askQuestion() module that provides five problems and keeps score

12

The solution to using a locally declared variable within another module lies in passing the local variable from one module to the other. **Passing a variable** means that you are sending a copy of data in one module of a program to another module for use. Exactly how you accomplish this differs slightly among languages, but it usually involves including the variable name within parentheses in the call to the module that needs to receive a copy of the value. Figure 12-6 shows how you can modify the askQuestion() module to pass a copy of the correctCount value to the finalStatistics() module. Then, in the finalStatistics() module you declare a name for the passed value within parentheses in the **module header** or introductory title statement; Figure 12-7 shows how the finalStatistics() module receives the value as part of its module's header. The passed variable named within the module header often is called a **parameter** or an **argument**.

In Figure 12-7 the finalStatistics() module declares a numeric variable named numRight in its header statement. Declaring a variable within the parentheses of the module header indicates that this variable is not a regular variable that is declared locally within the module, but is a special variable that receives its value from the outside. In Figure 12-7 numRight receives its value when the askQuestion() module in Figure 12-6 calls the finalStatistics() module. The askQuestion() module passes the value of correctCount to finalStatistics(); then within the finalStatistics() module, numRight takes on the value of correctCount and the percentage of correct answers is calculated using numRight.

Passing a copy of a value to a module sometimes is called *passing by value*. Some languages allow you to pass the actual memory address of a variable to a module; this is called *passing by reference*. When you pass by reference you lose some of the advantages of information hiding because the module has access to the address of the passed variable, not just a copy of the value of the passed variable. However, program performance improves because the computer doesn't have to make a copy of the value, thereby saving time.

Within the finalStatistics() module of the arithmetic drill program, you *could* choose to name the passed local value correctCount instead of numRight. Whether the variable name that holds the count in finalStatistics() is the same as the corresponding value in the askQuestion() module is irrelevant. The correctCount and numRight variables represent two unique memory locations, no matter what name you decide to give the variable that holds the count of right answers within the finalStatistics() module.

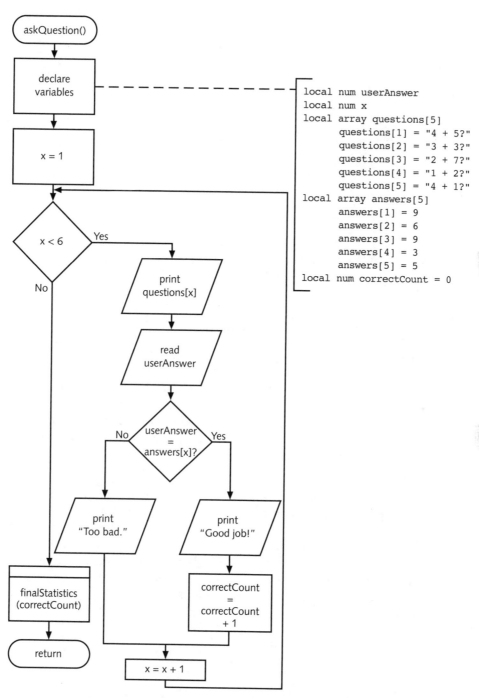

Figure 12-6   Modified askQuestion() module that passes correctCount() to finalStatistics()

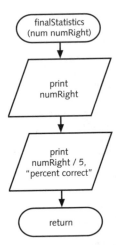

Figure 12-7   The finalStatistics() module that receives the correctCount() value
and calls it numRight()

RETURNING A VALUE FROM A MODULE

Suppose you decide to organize the arithmetic drill program so that the
`finalStatistics()` module computes the user's correct percentage, but the
`askQuestion()` module handles the printing of the final statistics. In this case, you pass
`correctCount` to the `finalStatistics()` module as before, but the
`finalStatistics()` module must **return the value** of the calculated correct percentage back to the `askQuestion()` module. Just as you can pass a value into a module, you can pass back, or return a value to a calling module. Usually, this is accomplished
within the return statement of the called module as shown in Figure 12-8.

Notice that within the `askQuestion()` module you call the `finalStatistics()`
module and pass in the `correctCount` value. Then you assign the return value of the
`finalStatistics()` module to the variable named `correctPercent`. The
`correctPercent` variable is declared locally within the `askQuestion()` module. This
step indicates that the value returned by the `finalStatistics()` module will be the
value assigned to the `correctPercent` variable. Then you can use the
`correctPercent` variable within the remainder of the `askQuestion()` module.

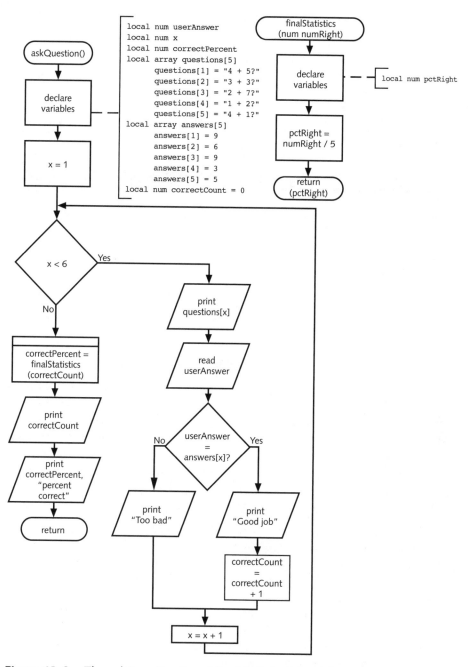

Figure 12-8 The askQuestion() and finalStatistics() modules with a value passed into and out of the finalStatistics() module

12

USING AN IPO CHART

When designing modules to use within larger programs, some programmers find it helpful to use an **IPO chart**, which identifies and categorizes each item needed within the module as pertaining to input, processing, or output. For example, when you design the `finalStatistics()` module in the arithmetic drill program you can start by placing each of the module's components in one of the three processing categories, as shown in Figure 12-9.

Input	Processing	Output
correct count	divide correct count by total number of problems producing percentage correct	percentage correct

Figure 12-9   IPO chart for finalStatistics() module

The IPO chart in Figure 12-9 provides you with an overview of the processing steps involved in the `finalStatistics()` module. Like a flowchart or pseudocode, an IPO chart is just another tool to help you plan the logic of your programs.

UNDERSTANDING THE ADVANTAGES OF ENCAPSULATION

When writing a module that receives a variable you can give the variable any name you like. This feature is especially beneficial if you consider that a well-written module may be used in dozens of programs, each supporting its own unique variable names. To beginning programmers, using only global variables seems like a far simpler option than declaring local variables and being required to pass them from one module to another. If a variable holds a count of correct responses, why not create a single variable, call it `correctCount`, and let every module in the program have access to the data stored there?

As an example of why this is a limiting idea, consider this: The `finalStatistics()` module of the arithmetic drill program might be useful in other programs within the organization—maybe the company creates drills in subjects other than arithmetic, but all drills require final statistics. If it is well written, the `finalStatistics()` module can be used by other programs in the company for years to come. If the variables that `finalStatistics()` uses are not declared to be local, then every programmer working on every application within the organization will have to know the names of those variables to avoid conflict. If `correctCount` is global, then all programmers who use the module must be aware of the name and the purpose of the variable and avoid using it in any other context.

If the `finalStatistics()` module is so useful that you sell it to other companies, and if `correctCount` is global, all programmers in the *world* will need to know its name and will have to avoid using it for any other purpose in their programs. The name `correctCount` represents just one variable. Multiply the limitations on global variable name usage by all the variable names used in the programs all over the world, and you can see that using global variable names correctly will soon become impossible. The logistics would be similar to providing a unique first name to every person at birth; you could do it, but you would end up using awkward, cryptic names.

Even if you could provide unique variable names for every program, there are other benefits to using local variables that are passed to modules. Passing values to a module helps facilitate encapsulation. A programmer can write a program (or module) and use procedures developed by others without knowing the details of those procedures. For example, you do not need to understand how a telephone connects you to the person you want to talk to; you need only to understand the **interface** or outside connection to the procedure; that is, you need to know only what number to enter into a telephone to get a specific result. Using a procedure requires only that you know what information to send to the procedure. You don't need to know—maybe you don't even care— how the procedure uses the data you send, so long as the results are what you want.

When procedures use local variables, the procedures become miniprograms that are relatively autonomous. Routines that contain their own sets of instructions and their own variables are not dependent on the program that calls them. The details within a routine are hidden and contained or encapsulated, which helps to make the routine reusable.

Many real-world examples of encapsulation exist. When you build a house, you don't invent plumbing and heating systems. You incorporate systems that have already been designed. You don't need to know all the fine details of how the systems work; they are self-contained units you attach to your house. This certainly reduces the time and effort it takes to build a house. Assuming the plumbing and electrical systems you choose are already in use in other houses, choosing existing systems also improves your house's **reliability**. Not only is it unnecessary to know how your furnace works, but if you replace one model with another, you don't care if its internal operations are different. Whether heat is created from electricity, natural gas, or a hamster on a wheel, only the result—a warm house—is important to you.

Similarly, software that is reusable saves time and money and is more reliable. If the `finalStatistics()` module has been tested previously you can be confident that it will work correctly when you use it within a different program. If another programmer creates a new and improved `finalStatistics()` module you don't care how it works so long as it correctly calculates and prints using the data you send to it.

The concept of passing variables to modules allows programmers to create variable names locally in a module without changing the value of similarly named variables in other modules. The ability to pass values to modules makes programming much more flexible because independently created modules can exchange information efficiently. However, there are limitations to the ways procedural programs use modules. Any program that uses a module must not reuse its name for any other module within the same program. You also must know exactly what type of data to pass to a module, and if you have use for a similar module that works on a different type of data or a different number of data items, you must create a new module with a different name. These limitations are eliminated in programs that are object-oriented.

12

AN OVERVIEW OF OBJECT-ORIENTED PROGRAMMING

Object-oriented programming is a style of programming that focuses on an application's data and the methods you need to manipulate that data. Object-oriented programming uses all of the concepts you are familiar with from modular procedural programming, such as variables, modules, and passing values to modules. Modules in object-oriented programs continue to use sequence, selection, and looping structures and make use of arrays. However, object-oriented programming adds several new concepts to programming and involves a different way of thinking. There's even a considerable amount of new vocabulary involved. First you will read about object-oriented programming concepts in general; then you will learn the specific terminology.

 Most object-oriented programming languages use the term *method* in place of module, subroutine, or procedure.

With object-oriented programming:

- You analyze the objects you are working with and the tasks that need to be performed with, and on those objects.

- You pass messages to objects, requesting the objects to take action.

- The same message works differently (and appropriately) when applied to different objects.

- A module or procedure can work appropriately with different types of data it receives, without the need to write separate modules.

- Objects can share or inherit traits of objects that have already been created, reducing the time it takes to create new objects.

- Encapsulation and information hiding are more complete than with the modules used in procedural programs.

But what, first of all, is an object? The real world is full of objects. Consider a door. A door needs to be opened and closed. You open a door with an easy-to-use interface known as a doorknob. Object-oriented programmers would say you are "passing a message" to the door when you "tell" it to open by turning its knob. The same message (turning a knob) has a different result when applied to your radio than when applied to a door. The procedure you use to open something—call it the "open" procedure—works differently on a door to a room than it does on a desk drawer, a bank account, a computer file, or your eyes, but you can call all of these procedures "open."

With object-oriented programming you focus on the objects that will be manipulated by the program—for example, a customer invoice, a loan application, or a menu from which the user will select an option. You define the methods each of the objects will use; you also define the information that must be passed to those methods.

With object-oriented programming you can create multiple methods with the same name, which will act differently and appropriately when used with different types of objects. For example, you can use a method named `print()` to print a customer invoice, loan application, or envelope. Because you use the same method name, `print()`, to describe the different actions needed to print these diverse objects, you can write statements in object-oriented programming languages that are more like English; you can use the same method name to describe the same type of action no matter what type of object is being acted upon. Using the method name `print()` is easier than remembering `printInvoice()`, `printLoanApplication()`, and so on. Object-oriented languages understand verbs in context, just as people do.

Another important concept in object-oriented programming is **inheritance**, which is the process of acquiring the traits of one's predecessors. In the real world, a new door with a stained-glass window inherits most of its traits from a standard door. It has the same purpose, it opens and closes in the same way, and it has the same knob and hinges. The door with the stained-glass window simply has one additional trait—its window. Even if you have never seen a door with a stained-glass window, when you encounter one you know what it is and how to use it because you understand the characteristics of all doors. With object-oriented programming, once you have created an object, you can develop new objects that possess all the traits of the original object plus any new traits you desire. If you develop a `customerBill` object, there is no need to develop an `overdueCustomerBill` object from scratch. You can create the new object to contain all the characteristics of the already developed object and simply add necessary new characteristics. This not only reduces the work involved in creating new objects, but also makes them easier to understand because they possess most of the characteristics of already developed objects.

Real-world objects often employ encapsulation or information hiding. When using a door you usually are unconcerned with the latch or hinge construction features, and you don't have access to the interior workings of the knob or what might be written on the inside of the door panel. You care only about the functionality and the interface. Similarly, the detailed workings of objects you create within object-oriented programs can be hidden from outside programs and modules if you want them to be. When the details are hidden, programmers can focus on the functionality and the interface, as people do with real-life objects.

In summary, in order to understand object-oriented programming you must consider four concepts that are integral components of all object-oriented programming languages:

- classes
- objects
- inheritance
- polymorphism

12

DEFINING CLASSES

A **class** is a category of things. An **object** is a specific item that belongs to a class; an object is an **instance** of a class. A class defines the characteristics of its objects and the methods that can be applied to its objects.

For example, Dish is a class. When you know an object is a Dish, you know it can be held in your hand and you can eat from it. myDilbertMugWithTheChipInTheHandle is an object and an instance of the Dish class. Because you can say "My coffee mug **is a** Dish.", this is called an **is-a relationship**. Each button on the toolbar of a word processing program is an instance of a Button class. In a program used to manage a hotel, `pentHouse` and `bridalSuite` are instances of HotelRoom.

In object-oriented languages like C++ and Java, most class names are written with the initial letter and each new word in uppercase, such as *Dish* or *HotelRoom*. Specific objects' names usually are written in lowercase or using camel casing.

A class contains three parts:

- Every class has a name.

- Most classes contain data, although this is not required.

- Most classes contain methods, although this is not required.

For example, you can create a class named `Employee`. Data members of the `Employee` class include fields like `idNum`, `lastName`, `hourlyWage`, and `weeklySalary`. You have worked with very similar constructs throughout this book; the name and data of a class constitute what procedural programming languages call a record. When working with classes, you call the data fields **attributes**.

The methods of a class include all actions you want to perform with the class; these are what you call modules or subroutines in procedural programming. Appropriate methods for the `Employee` class include `setEmployeeData()`, `calculateWeeklyPay()`, and `showEmployeeData()`. The job of `setEmployeeData()` is to give values to an `Employee`'s data fields, the purpose of `calculateWeeklyPay()` is to multiply the `Employee`'s `hourlyWage` by 40, and the purpose of `showEmployeeData()` is to print the values in the `Employee`'s data fields. In other words, the `Employee` class methods are simply what you would have created as modules in a procedural program that uses employee records. The major difference is that with object-oriented languages, you think of the class name, data, and methods as a single encapsulated unit.

Programmers often use a class diagram to illustrate class features. A **class diagram** contains a rectangle divided into three sections as shown in Figure 12-10. The top section contains the name of the class, the middle section contains the names of the attributes, and the bottom section contains the methods. The generic class diagram shows two attributes and three methods, but for a given class there might be any number of either, including none. Figure 12-11 shows the class diagram for the Employee class.

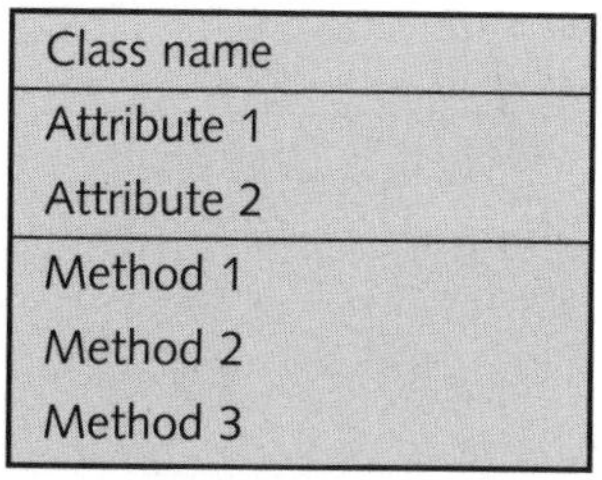

Class name
Attribute 1
Attribute 2
Method 1
Method 2
Method 3

Figure 12-10   Generic class diagram

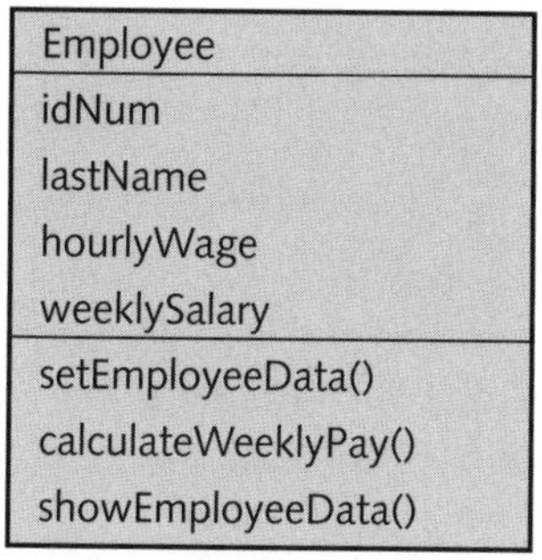

Employee
idNum
lastName
hourlyWage
weeklySalary
setEmployeeData()
calculateWeeklyPay()
showEmployeeData()

Figure 12-11   Employee class diagram

Figures 12-10 and 12-11 show that a class diagram is intended to be only an overview of class attributes and methods. A class diagram plays a role similar to that played by the hierarchy charts you have used to describe procedural programs; a class diagram shows *what* data and method the class will use, not the details of the methods nor *when* they will be used. It is a design tool that helps you see the big picture in terms of class requirements. Later, when you write the code that actually creates the class, you include data types and method implementation details. For example, Figure 12-12 shows the pseudocode you can use to show the details for the **Employee** class.

12

```
class Employee
    num idNum
    char lastName
    num hourlyWage
    num weeklySalary

setEmployeeData(num id, char last, num rate)
    idNum = id
    lastName = last
    if rate <= 25.00 then
        hourlyWage = rate
    else hourlyWage = 25.00
    endif
return
calculateWeeklyPay()
    weeklySalary = hourlyWage * 40
return
showEmployeeData()
    print idNum, lastName, weeklySalary
return
```

Figure 12-12   Employee class

In addition to the data fields required, Figure 12-12 shows the complete methods for the **Employee** class. Notice that the header for the **setEmployeeData()** method indicates that this method will require three arguments—a numeric ID number, a character name, and a numeric pay rate. These values that are passed in from the outside are then assigned to the field names within the **Employee** class. This is the commonly used method of assigning values to class fields. Usually you do not want any outside programs or methods to alter your class's data fields unless you have control over the process, so you force other programs and methods to use a procedure such as **setEmployeeData()**. For example, if the only way a program can set the fields of the **Employee** class shown in Figure 12-12 is by using the **setEmployeeData()** method, then you guarantee that the **hourlyWage** field will never hold a value greater than 25.00. Object-oriented programmers usually specify that their data fields will have **private** access—that is, the data cannot be accessed by any method that is not part of the class. The methods themselves, like **setEmployeeData()**, support **public access**—which means that other programs and methods may use these methods that control access to the private data.

INSTANTIATING AND USING OBJECTS

When you write an object-oriented program, you create objects that are members of a class in the same way you create variables in procedural programs. Instead of declaring a numeric variable named **money** with a statement that includes the type and identifying name such as **num money**, you **instantiate**, or create a class object with a statement that includes the type of object and an identifying name, such as **Employee mySecretary**.

When you declare **money** as a numeric variable, you automatically gain many capabilities—for example, you can perform math with the value in the **money** variable and you can compare its value to other numeric variables. Similarly, when you declare **mySecretary** as an **Employee** type object, you also automatically gain many capabilities. You can use any of an **Employee's** methods (**setEmployeeData()**, **calculateWeeklyPay()**, and **showEmployeeData()**) with the **mySecretary** object. The usual syntax is to provide an object name, a dot (period), and a method name. For example, you can write a program such as the one shown in pseudocode in Figure 12-13.

```
start
     declare variables-------------Employee mySecretary
     mySecretary.setEmployeeData(123, "Tyler", 12.50)
     mySecretary.calculateWeeklyPay()
     mySecretary.showEmployeeData()
end
```

Figure 12-13   Program that uses an Employee object

In the program in Figure 12-13, the focus is on the object—the **Employee** named **mySecretary**—and the methods you can use with that object. This is the essence of object-oriented programming.

UNDERSTANDING INHERITANCE

12

The concept of class is useful because of its reusability; you can create new classes that are descendents of existing classes. The **descendent classes** (or **child classes**) can inherit all of the attributes of the **original class** (or **parent class**), or the descendent class can override those attributes that are inappropriate. In geometry, a **Cube** is a descendent of a **Square**. A **Cube** has all the attributes of a **Square** plus one more: depth. A **Cube**, however, has a different method of calculating total area (or volume, not surface area) than a **Square** has. In programming, if you have previously created a **Square** class and you need a **Cube** class, it makes sense to inherit existing features from the **Square** class, adding only the new feature (depth) that a **Cube** requires and modifying the method that calculates volume.

 Some programmers call a parent class a *base class* or *superclass*. You can refer to a child class as a *derived class* or *subclass*.

As another example, to accommodate part-time workers in your personnel programs, you might want to create a child class from the **Employee** class. Part-time workers need an ID, name, and hourly wage just as regular employees do, but the regular **Employee** pay calculation assumes a 40-hour work week. You might want to create a **PartTimeEmployee**

class that inherits all the data fields contained in an `Employee`, but adds a new one—`hoursWorked`. In addition, you want to create a new modified `setEmployeeData()` method that includes assigning a value to `hoursWorked`, and a new `calculateWeeklySalary()` method that operates correctly for `PartTimeEmployee` objects. This new method multiplies `hourlyWage` by `hoursWorked` instead of by 40. The `showEmployeeData()` module that already exists within the `Employee` class works appropriately for both the `Employee` and the `PartTimeEmployee` classes, so there is no need to include a new version of this module within the `PartTimeEmployee` class; `PartTimeEmployee` objects can simply use their parent's existing method. When you create a child class, you can show its relationship to the parent with a class diagram like the one for `PartTimeEmployee` in Figure 12-14. The complete `PartTimeEmployee` class appears in Figure 12-15.

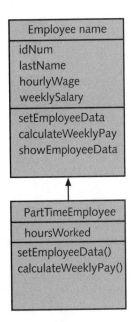

Figure 12-14 PartTimeEmployee class diagram

```
class PartTimeEmployee descends from Employee
num hoursWorked

setEmployeeData(num id, char last, num rate, num hours)
    Employee's setEmployeeData (id, last, rate)
    hoursWorked = hours
return
calculateWeeklyPay()
    weeklySalary = hourlyWage * hours
return
```

Figure 12-15 The PartTimeEmployee class

The `PartTimeEmployee` class shown in Figure 12-15 contains five data fields—all the fields that an `Employee` contains plus one new one, `hoursWorked`. The `PartTimeEmployee` class also contains three methods. The methods `setEmployeeData()` and `calculateWeeklyPay()` have been rewritten for the `PartTimeEmployee` child class. These methods **override** (take precedence over) the parent class method when a `PartTimeEmployee` object uses them. Notice that the `setEmployeeData()` method in the `PartTimeEmployee` class requires an extra argument that the `Employee` class version does not. The `PartTimeEmployee` class uses three of the four arguments it receives to pass on to its parent where the `idNum`, `lastName`, and `hourlyWage` fields can be set.

The `PartTimeEmployee` class also contains the `showEmployeeData()` method, which it inherits unchanged from its parent. When you write a program such as the one shown in Figure 12-16, different `setEmployeeData()` and `calculateWeeklyPay()` methods containing different statements are called for the two objects, but the same `showEmployeeData()` method is called in each case.

```
start
        declare variables--------[Employee mySecretary
                                 [PartTimeEmployee myDriver
        mySecretary.setEmployeeData(123, "Tyler", 12.50)
        myDriver.setEmployeeData(345, "Greene", 8.50, 15)
        mySecretary.calculateWeeklyPay()
        myDriver.calculateWeeklyPay()
        mySecretary.showEmployeeData()
        myDriver.showEmployeeData()
end
```

Figure 12-16 Program that uses Employee and PartTimeEmployee objects

A good way to determine if a class is a parent or a child is to use the "is-a" test. A child "is an" example of its parent. For example, a `PartTimeEmployee` "is an" `Employee`. However, it is not necessarily true that an `Employee` "is a" `PartTimeEmployee`.

When you create a class that is meant only to be a parent class and not to have objects of its own, you create an abstract class. For example, suppose you create an `Employee` class and two child classes, `PartTimeEmployee` and `FullTimeEmployee`. If your intention is that every object belongs to one of the two child classes and that there are no "plain" `Employee` objects, then `Employee` is an abstract class.

12

UNDERSTANDING POLYMORPHISM

Methods or functions need to operate differently depending on the context. Object-oriented programs use the feature **polymorphism** to allow the same operation to be carried out differently depending on the context; this is never allowed in nonobject-oriented languages.

With the `Employee` and `PartTimeEmployee` classes you need a different `calculateWeeklyPay()` method depending on the type of object you use. Without polymorphism, you must write a different module with a unique name for each method, because two methods with the same name cannot coexist in a program. Just as your blender can produce juice whether you insert a fruit or a vegetable, with polymorphism a `calculateWeeklyPay()` method produces a correct result whether it operates on an `Employee` or a `PartTimeEmployee`. Similarly, you may want a `computeGradePointAverage()` method to operate differently for a Pass-Fail course than it does for a graded one, or you might want a word processing program to produce different results when you press Delete with one word in a document highlighted than when you press Delete with a filename highlighted.

When you write a polymorphic method in an object-oriented programming language you must write each version of the method, and that can entail a lot of work. The benefit of polymorphism does not seem obvious while you are writing the methods, but the benefits are realized when you can use the methods in all sorts of applications. When you can use a single, simple, easy-to-understand method name such as `showData()` with all sorts of objects, such as `Employees`, `PartTimeEmployees`, `InventoryItems`, and `BankTransactions`, then your objects behave more like their real-world counterparts and your programs are easier to understand.

An object-oriented concept closely related to polymorphism is method overloading. **Method overloading** occurs when different methods exist with the same name but different argument lists. Just as your blender can produce juice whether you insert two vegetables or three, overloading a method allows the same method to accept different types and numbers of arguments to manipulate. For example, you can create two `multiply()` methods, one that accepts two arguments and one that accepts three. You must create both versions of the method, but when using it you remember only one name: `multiply()`. As with polymorphism, the method acts appropriately based on the context.

 When two objects of different classes can use the same method name you are using polymorphism. When you create a child class that contains a method with the same name as a method in the parent class, you are overriding the parent's method. When a single object can use methods with the same name but different argument lists, you are using method overloading.

Figure 12-17 shows an `Inventory` class that contains several versions of a `changeData()` method. When an `Inventory` item uses the `changeData()` method the computer will determine which of the three available methods to call based on the arguments used with the method.

```
class Inventory
   num stockNum
   char itemDescription
   num price

setInvData(num id, char desc, num pr)
   stockNum = id
   itemDescription = desc
   price = pr
return

changeData(char desc)
   itemDescription = desc
return
changeData(num pr)
   price = pr
return

changeData(char desc, num pr)
   itemDescription = desc
   price = pr
return

showInvData()
   print stockNum, itemDescription, price
return
```

Figure 12-17   Inventory class

When you execute the program shown in Figure 12-18 each of the three `changeData()` methods will be called one time, depending on the argument used. When you read the program it should seem clear in each instance whether the programmer intends to change the price, description, or both. The method name `changeData()` is clear, appropriate, and easy to remember, no matter which type of data needs the change. Using `changeData()` with appropriate arguments is superior to being required to remember to use multiple method names such as `changeDescription()`, `changePrice()`, and `changeDescriptionAndPrice()`.

12

```
start
    declare variables --------------- [Inventory wheelCover
    wheelCover.setInvData(3772, "Chrome cover", 49.95)
    wheelCover.changeData(39.95)
    wheelCover.changeData("Deluxe chrome cover")
    wheelCover.changeData(89.95, "Super deluxe chrome cover")
    wheelCover.showInvData()
return
```

Figure 12-18   Program that uses all three versions of changeData()

THE ADVANTAGES OF OBJECT-ORIENTED PROGRAMMING

Using the features of object-oriented programming languages provides you with many benefits as you develop your programs. When using objects in programs you save development time because each object automatically includes appropriate, reliable methods. When using inheritance you can develop new classes more quickly by extending classes that already exist and work; you need to concentrate only on new features the new class adds. When using preexisting objects you need to concentrate only on the interface to those objects, not on the internal instructions that make them work. By using method overloading and polymorphism you can use reasonable, easy-to-remember names for methods and concentrate on their purpose rather than on memorizing different method names.

CHAPTER SUMMARY

◻ A procedural program consists of a series of steps or procedures that take place one after the other. Breaking programs into reasonable units called modules, subroutines, functions, or methods provides abstraction, allows multiple programmers to work on a problem, allows you to reuse your work, and allows you to identify structures more easily. By using local rather than global variables, you can take advantage of encapsulation, creating modules without knowing the data names used by other programmers.

◻ When multiple modules need access to the same variable value, you can pass a variable to the module. The passed variable is called a parameter or an argument and usually is named within the module header.

◻ Just as you can pass a value into a module, you can pass back or return a value to a calling module.

◻ When designing modules to use within larger programs, some programmers find it helpful to use an IPO chart, which identifies and categorizes each item needed within the module as pertaining to input, processing, or output.

◻ The concept of passing variables to modules allows programmers to create variable names locally in a module without changing the value of similarly named variables in other modules. Passing values to a module helps facilitate encapsulation; you need only to understand the interface to the procedure. Additionally, passing variables helps to make modules reusable and improves their reliability.

❑ Object-oriented programming is a style of programming that focuses on an application's data and the methods you need to manipulate that data. With object-oriented programming you create classes and objects. You pass messages to objects; the same message works differently (and appropriately) when applied to different objects. Additionally, objects can share or inherit traits of objects that have already been created reducing the time it takes to create new objects. Encapsulation and information hiding are more complete than with the modules used in procedural programs.

❑ A class is a category of items and an object is a specific item that belongs to a class; an object is an instance of a class. A class defines the characteristics of its objects and the methods that can be applied to its objects. A class contains a name and most classes contain data and methods; you can use a class diagram to illustrate these components. Object-oriented programmers usually specify that their data fields will have private access and that their methods have public access.

❑ When writing an object-oriented program you instantiate objects that are members of a class using a type and an identifying name. You can use a class's methods with an object; the usual syntax is to provide an object name, a dot (period), and a method name.

❑ You can create classes that are descendents of existing classes. The descendent classes (or child classes) can inherit all of the attributes of the original class (or parent class), or the descendent class can override those attributes that are inappropriate. A child class method with the same name overrides the parent's method.

12

❑ Object-oriented programs use polymorphism to allow the same operation to be carried out differently depending on the context. Method overloading occurs when different methods exist with the same name but different argument lists.

❑ When using objects in programs you save development time. While using preexisting objects you need to concentrate only on the interface to those objects, not on the internal instructions that make them work.

EXERCISES

1. Create an IPO chart for each of the following modules:

   a. the module that produces your paycheck

   b. the module that calculates your semester tuition bill

   c. the module that calculates your monthly car payment

2. a. Plan the logic for a program that contains two modules. The first module asks for your employee ID number. Pass the ID number to a second module that prints a message indicating whether the ID number is valid or invalid. A valid employee ID number falls between 100 and 799 inclusive.

   b. Plan the logic for a program that contains two modules. The first module asks for your employee ID number. Pass the ID number to a second module that returns a code to the first module that indicates whether the ID number is valid or invalid. A valid employee ID number falls between 100 and 799 inclusive. The first module prints an appropriate message.

3. a. Plan the logic for an insurance company's premium-determining program that contains three modules. The first module prompts the user for the type of policy needed—health or auto. Pass the user's response to the second module where the premium is set—$250 for a health policy or $175 for an auto policy. Pass the premium amount to the last module for printing.

   b. Modify Exercise 3a so that the second module calls one of two additional modules—one that determines the health premium or one that determines the auto premium. The health insurance module asks users whether they smoke; the premium is $250 for smokers and $190 for nonsmokers. The auto insurance module asks users to enter the number of traffic tickets they have received in the last three years. The premium is $175 for those with three or more tickets, $140 for those with one or two tickets, and $95 for those with no tickets. Each of these two modules returns the premium amount to the second module, which sends the premium amount to the printing module.

4. Identify three objects that might belong to each of the following classes:

   a. Automobile

   b. NovelAuthor

   c. CollegeCourse

5. Identify three different classes that might contain each of these objects:

   a. Ludwig von Beethoven

   b. My pet cat named Socks

   c. Apartment 14 at 101 Main Street

6. Design a class named CustomerRecord that holds a customer number, name, and address. Include methods to set the values for each data field and print the values for each data field. Create the class diagram and write the pseudocode that defines the class.

7. Design a class named House that holds the street address, price, number of bedrooms, and number of baths in a House. Include methods to set the values for each data field. In the set methods do not allow the price, bedrooms, or baths to be negative. Include a method that displays all the values for a House. Create the class diagram and write the pseudocode that defines the class.

8. Design a class named Loan that holds an account number, name of account holder, amount borrowed, term, and interest rate. Include methods to set values for each data field. In the set methods do not allow the amount borrowed to be negative or over $100,000, the term to be over 30 years, or the interest rate to be over 17%. Also include a method that prints all the loan information. Create the class diagram and write the pseudocode that defines the class.

9. a. Design a class named Book that holds a stock number, author, title, price, and number of pages for a book. Include methods to set and print the values for each data field. Create the class diagram and write the pseudocode that defines the class.

   b. Design a class named TextBook that is a child class of Book. Include a new data field for the grade level of the book. Override the Book class methods that set and print the data so that you accommodate the new grade-level field. Create the class diagram and write the pseudocode that defines the class.

10. a. Design a class named Player that holds a player number and name for a sports team participant. Include methods to set the values for each data field and print the values for each data field. Create the class diagram and write the pseudocode that defines the class.

    b. Design two classes named BaseballPlayer and BasketballPlayer that are child classes of Player. Include a new data field in each class for the player's position. Include an additional field in the BaseballPlayer class for batting average. Include a new field in the BasketballPlayer class for free-throw percentage. Override the Player class methods that set and print the data so that you accommodate the new fields. Create the class diagram, then write the pseudocode that defines the class.

12

13

PROGRAMMING GRAPHICAL USER INTERFACES

After studying Chapter 13, you should be able to:

♦ Understand the principles of event-driven programming

♦ Describe the actions that GUI components can initiate

♦ Design graphical user interfaces

♦ Modify the attributes of GUI components

♦ List the steps to building an event-driven application

♦ Understand throwing exceptions

UNDERSTANDING EVENT-DRIVEN PROGRAMMING

From the 1950s, when people began to use computers to help them perform many jobs, right through the 1960s and 1970s, almost all interaction between humans and computers was based on the command line. The **command line** is the location on your computer screen at which you type entries to communicate with the computer's operating system. An **operating system** is the software that you use to run a computer and manage its resources. Interacting with a computer operating system was difficult because the user had to know the exact syntax (that is, the correct sequence of words and symbols that form the operating system's command set) to use when typing commands, and had to spell and type those commands accurately.

Fortunately for today's computer users, operating system software is available that allows them to use a mouse or other pointing device to select pictures or **icons** on the screen. This type of environment is a **graphical user interface**, or **GUI**. Computer users can expect to see a standard interface in the GUI programs they use. Rather than memorizing difficult commands that must be typed at a command line, GUI users can select options from menus and click on buttons to make their preferences known to a program. Users can select objects that look like their real-world counterparts and get the expected results. For example, users may select an icon that looks like a pencil when they want to write a memo, or they may drag an icon shaped like a folder to another icon that resembles a recycling bin when they want to delete a file.

GUI programs are called **event-based** or **event-driven** because actions occur based on user-initiated events such as clicking a mouse button. When you program with event-driven languages, the emphasis is on the objects that the user can manipulate, such as buttons and menus, and on the events that the user can initiate with those objects, such as clicking or double-clicking. The programmer writes instructions that correspond to each type of event.

Event-driven programs require unique considerations for the programmer. The program logic you have developed so far for most of this book is procedural; each step occurs in the order the programmer determines. In a procedural program, if you issue a prompt and a statement to read the user's response, you have no control over how much time the user takes to enter a response, but you do control the sequence of events—the processing goes no further until the input is completed. In contrast, with event-driven programs, the user might initiate any number of events in any order. For example, if you use a word processing program, you have dozens of choices at your disposal at any moment. You can type words, select text with the mouse, click a button to change text to bold or to italics, choose a menu item, and so on. With each word processing document you create, you choose options in any order that seems appropriate at the time. The word processing program must be ready to respond to any event you initiate.

Within an event-driven program, a component from which an event is generated is the **source** of the event. A button that a user can click is an example of a source; a text field that one can use to enter text is another source. An object that is "interested in" an event you want to respond to is a **listener**. It "listens for" events so it knows when to respond. Not all objects can receive all events—you probably have used programs in which clicking on many areas of the screen has no effect at all. If you want an object, such as a button, to be a listener for an event such as a mouse click, you must write the appropriate program statements.

Although event-based programming is relatively new, the instructions that programmers write to correspond to events are still simply sequences, selections, and loops. Event-driven programs still declare variables, use arrays, and contain all the attributes of their procedural-program ancestors. An event-based program may contain components with labels like "Sort Records," "Merge Files," or "Total Transactions." The programming logic you use when writing code for each of these processes is the same logic you have learned throughout this book. Writing event-driven programs simply involves thinking of possible events as the modules that constitute the program.

 In object-oriented languages, the procedural modules that depend on user-initiated events are often called *scripts*.

User-Initiated Actions and GUI Components

To understand GUI programming, you need to have a clear picture of the possible events a user can initiate. These include the events listed in Figure 13-1.

Event	Description
key press	pressing a key on the keyboard
mouse point	placing the mouse pointer over an area on the screen
mouse click or left mouse click	pressing the left mouse button
right mouse click	pressing the right mouse button
mouse double-click	pressing the left mouse button two times in rapid sequence
mouse drag	holding the left mouse button down while moving the mouse over the desk surface

Figure 13-1   Common user-initiated events

You also need to be able to picture common GUI components. Some are listed in Figure 13-2. Figure 13-3 shows a screen that contains several common GUI components.

GUI components	Description
Label	A rectangular area that displays text
Text field	A rectangular area into which the user can type a line of text
Button	A rectangular object you can click; usually it appears to press inward like a push button
Check box	A label positioned beside a square; you can click the square to display or remove a check mark—allows the user to turn an option on or off
Check box group	A group of check box objects in which the options are mutually exclusive; when the user selects any one check box, the others are turned off—often round rather than square and called a set of radio buttons or option buttons
List box	When the user clicks a list arrow, a menu of options appears; when the user selects an option from the list, the selected item replaces the original item in the display—all other items are unselected (with some list boxes, the user can make multiple selections)
Toolbar	A strip of icons that activate menu items

13

Figure 13-2   Common GUI components

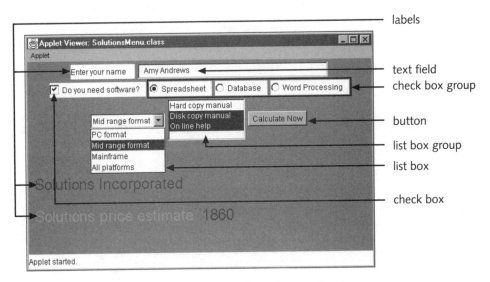

Figure 13-3   Illustration of common GUI components

When you program in a language that supports event-driven logic, you do not create the GUI components you need from scratch. Instead, you call prewritten routines or methods that draw the GUI components on the screen for you. The components themselves are preexisting objects complete with names, attributes, and methods. In some programming languages you write statements that call the methods that create the GUI objects; in others you can drag GUI objects onto your screen from a toolbar. Either way, you do not worry about the details of constructing the components. Instead, you concentrate on the actions that you want to take place when a user initiates an event from one of the components. Thus GUI components are excellent examples of the best principles of object-oriented programming—they represent objects with attributes and methods that operate like black boxes, making them easy for you to use.

GUI components are often referred to as *widgets*, which is short for *windows gadgets*.

When you use already-created GUI components, you are instantiating objects that belong to a prewritten class. For example, you might use a `Button` class. Depending on the programming language you use, the `Button` class might contain attributes such as `color` and `label` and methods such as `setLabel()`, in which you define the words that appear on the `Button`'s surface, and `doubleClick()`, in which you define the actions that will take place when a user double-clicks the `Button` object. To create a `Button` object, you write a statement similar to `Button myProgramButton`, in which `Button` represents the type and `myProgramButton` represents the object you create.

DESIGNING GRAPHICAL USER INTERFACES

You should consider several general design principles when creating a program that will use a GUI:

- The interface should be natural and predictable.
- The interface should be attractive, easy to read, and nondistracting.
- To some extent, it's helpful if the user can customize your applications.
- The program should be forgiving.
- The GUI is only a means to an end.

The Interface Should Be Natural and Predictable

The GUI program interface should represent objects like their real-world counterparts. In other words, it makes sense to use an icon that looks like a recycling bin when you want to allow a user to delete files. Using a recycling bin icon is "natural" in that people use one in real life when they want to discard real-life items. Using a recycling bin is also predictable, because a number of other programs employ the recycling bin icon. Some icons may be natural, but if they are not predictable as well, then they are not as effective. An icon that depicts a recycling truck is just as "natural" as far as corresponding to the real world, but because other programs do not use a truck icon for this purpose, it is not as predictable.

Graphical user interfaces should also be predictable in their layout. For example, with most GUI programs you use a menu bar at the top of the screen, and the first menu item is almost always *File*. If you design a program interface in which the menu runs vertically down the right side of the screen, or in which *File* is the last menu option instead of the first, you will confuse the people who use your program. Either they will make mistakes when using it, or they may give up using it entirely. It doesn't matter if you can prove that your layout plan is more efficient than the standard one—if you do not use a predictable layout, your program will meet rejection from users in the marketplace.

The Interface Should Be Attractive, Easy to Read, and Nondistracting

If your interface is attractive, people are more likely to use it. If it is easy to read, they are less likely to make mistakes and more likely to want to use it. And if the interface is easy to read, it will more likely be considered attractive. When it comes to GUI design, fancy fonts and weird color combinations are the signs of amateur designers. In addition, you should make sure that unavailable screen options are either sufficiently dimmed or removed, so the user does not waste time clicking on components that aren't functional.

13

Dimming a component is also called *graying* the component.

Screen designs should not be distracting. When there are too many components on a screen, users can't find what they're looking for. When a text field or button is no longer needed, it should be removed from the interface. You also want to avoid distracting users with overly creative design elements. When users click a button to open a file, they might be amused the first time a file name dances across the screen or the speakers play a tune. But after one or two experiences with your creative additions, users find that intruding design elements simply hamper the actual work of the program.

GUI programmers sometimes refer to screen space as *real estate*. Just as a plot of real estate becomes unattractive when it supports no open space, your screen becomes unattractive when you fill the limited space with too many components.

To Some Extent, It's Helpful If The User Can Customize Your Applications

Every user works in his or her own way. If you are designing an application that will use numerous menus and toolbars, it's helpful if users can position the components in the order that's easiest for them to work with. Users appreciate being able to change features like color schemes. Allowing a user to change the background color in your application may seem frivolous to you, but to users who are color-blind, it might make the difference in whether they use your application at all.

The Program Should Be Forgiving

Perhaps you have had the inconvenience of accessing a voice mail system in which you selected several sequential options only to find yourself at a dead end with no recourse but to hang up and redial the number. Good program design avoids equivalent problems. You should always provide an escape route to accommodate users who have made bad choices or changed their minds. By providing a Back button or functional Escape key, you provide more functionality to your users.

The GUI Is Only a Means to an End

The most important principle of GUI design is to remember always that any GUI is only an interface. Using a mouse to click on items and drag them around is not the point of any business programs except those that train people how to use a mouse. Instead, the point of a graphical interface is to help people be more productive. To that end, the design should help the user see what options are available, allow the use of components in the ordinary way, and not force the user to concentrate on how to interact with your application. The real work of any GUI program is done after the user clicks a button or makes a list box selection. Then actual program tasks take place.

MODIFYING THE ATTRIBUTES OF GUI COMPONENTS

When you design a program with premade or preprogrammed graphical components, you will want to change their appearance to customize them for the current application. Each programming language provides its own means of changing components' appearances, but all involve changing the values stored in the components' attribute fields. Some common changes include setting the following items:

- the size of the component
- the color of the component
- the screen location of the component
- the font for any text contained in or on the component
- the component to be visible or invisible
- the component to be dimmed or undimmed, sometimes called enabled or disabled

You must learn the exact names of the methods and what type of arguments you are allowed to use in each programming language you learn, but all languages that support creating event-driven applications allow you to set components' attributes.

THE STEPS TO DEVELOPING AN EVENT-DRIVEN APPLICATION

In Chapter 1, you first learned the steps to developing a computer program. They are:

1. Understand the problem.
2. Plan the logic.
3. Code the program.
4. Translate the program into machine language.
5. Test the program.
6. Put the program into production.

Developing an event-driven application is more complicated than developing a standard procedural program. You can include three new steps between understanding the problem and developing the logic. The complete list of development steps for an event-driven application is as follows:

1. Understand the problem.
2. Create storyboards.
3. Define the objects.
4. Define the connections between the screens the user will see.

13

5. Plan the logic.

6. Code the program.

7. Translate the program into machine language.

8. Test the program.

9. Put the program into production.

The three new steps involve elements of object-oriented, GUI design—creating storyboards, defining objects, and defining the connections between user screens. As with procedural programming, you cannot write an event-driven program unless you first understand the problem.

Understanding the Problem

Suppose you want to create a simple, interactive program that determines premiums for prospective insurance customers. The users should be able to use a graphical interface to select a policy type—health or auto. Next the users answer pertinent questions, such as how old they are, whether they smoke, and what their driving records are like. Although most insurance premium amounts would be based on more characteristics than these, assume that policy rates are determined using the factors shown in Figure 13-4. The final output of the program is a second screen that shows the semiannual premium amount for the chosen policy.

Health policy premiums	Auto policy premiums
base rate: $500	base rate: $750
add $100 if over age 50	add $400 if more than 2 tickets
add $250 if smoker	subtract $200 if over age 50

Figure 13-4   Insurance premiums based on customer characteristics

Creating Storyboards

A **storyboard** represents a picture or sketch of a screen the user will see when running a program. Filmmakers have long used storyboards to illustrate key moments in the plots they are developing; similarly, GUI storyboards represent "snapshot" views of the screens the user will encounter during the run of a program. If the user could view up to four screens during the insurance premium program, then you would draw four storyboard cells or frames.

Figure 13-5 shows two storyboard sketches for the insurance program. They represent the introductory screen at which the user selects a premium type and answers questions, and the final screen that displays the semiannual premium.

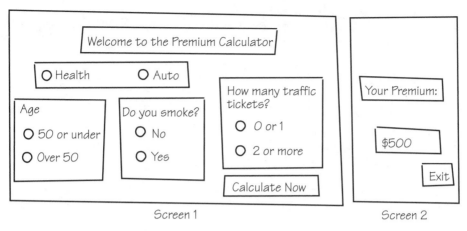

Figure 13-5   Storyboard for insurance program

Defining the Objects in an Object Dictionary

An event-driven program may contain dozens, or even hundreds, of objects. To keep track of them, programmers often use an object dictionary. An **object dictionary** is a list of the objects used in a program, including which screens they are used on and whether any code, or script, is associated with them.

Figure 13-6 shows an object dictionary for the insurance premium program. The type and name of each object to be placed on a screen is listed in the left column. The second column shows the screen number on which the object appears. The next column names any variables that are affected by an action on the object. The right column indicates whether any code or script is associated with the object. For example, the label named `welcomeLabel` appears on the first screen. It has no associated actions—it does not call any methods nor change any variables; it is just a label. The `calculateButton`, however, does cause execution of a method named `calcRoutine()`. This method calculates the semiannual premium amount and stores it in the `premiumAmount` variable. Depending on the programming language you use, you might need to name `calcRoutine()` something similar to `calculateButton.click()` to identify it as the module that executes when the user clicks the `calculateButton`.

Some organizations also include the disk location where an object is stored as part of the object dictionary.

Object name	Screen number	Variables affected	Script?
Label welcomeLabel	1	none	none
Choice healthOrAuto	1	policyType	none
Choice age	1	ageOfInsured	none
Choice smoker	1	insuredIsSmoker	none
Choice tickets	1	numTickets	none
Button calculateButton	1	premiumAmount	calcRoutine()
Label yourPremium	2	none	none
Text field premAmtField	2	none	none
Button exitButton	2	none	exitRoutine()

Figure 13-6   Object dictionary for insurance premium program

Defining the Connections Between the User Screens

The insurance premium program is a small one, but with larger programs you may need to draw the connections between the screens to show how they interact. Figure 13-7 shows an **interactivity diagram** for the screens used in the insurance premium program. The figure shows that the first screen calls the second screen and the program ends.

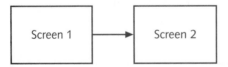

Figure 13-7   Diagram of interaction for insurance premium program

Figure 13-8 shows how a diagram might look for a more complicated program in which the user has several options available at screens 1, 2, and 3. Notice how each screen may lead to different screens depending on the options the user selects at any one screen.

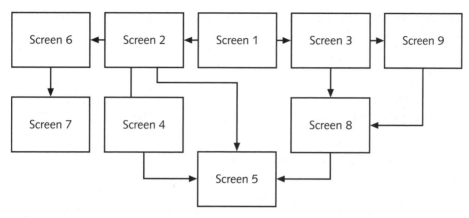

Figure 13-8 Diagram of interaction for a hypothetical complicated program

Planning the Logic

In an event-driven program, you design the screens, define the objects, and define how the screens will connect. Then you can plan the logic for each of the modules (or methods or scripts) that the program will use. For example, based on the program requirements shown in Figure 13-4, you can write the pseudocode for the `calcRoutine()` of the insurance premium program, as shown in Figure 13-9. The `calcRoutine()` does not execute until the user clicks the `calculateButton`. At that point, the user's choices are used to calculate the premium amount.

```
calcRoutine()
     if policyType = "H" then
           premiumAmount = 500
           if ageOfInsured > 50 then
               premiumAmount = premiumAmount + 100
           endif
           if insuredIsSmoker = "Y" then
               premiumAmount = premiumAmount + 250
           endif
     else
           premiumAmount = 750
           if numTickets > 2 then
               premiumAmount = premiumAmount + 400
           endif
           if ageOfInsured > 50 then
               premiumAmount = premiumAmount - 200
           endif
     endif
return
```

13

Figure 13-9 Pseudocode for calcRoutine()

The pseudocode in Figure 13-9 should look very familiar to you—it uses decision-making logic you have used since the early chapters of this book. The basic structures of sequence, selection, and looping will continue to serve you well whether you are programming in a procedural or event-driven environment.

OBJECT-ORIENTED ERROR HANDLING: THROWING EXCEPTIONS

A great deal of the effort that goes into writing programs involves checking data items to make sure they are valid and reasonable. A great advantage to using GUI data-entry objects is that you can control much of what a user enters by limiting the user's options. For example, if the only insurance policy types a user can select are *Health* or *Auto*, then you can eliminate checking for a valid policy type within your interactive program. However, there are many occasions on which you must allow the user to enter data. Data-entry operators who create the files used in business computer applications spend their entire working day entering facts and figures that your applications use; operators can and do make typing errors. When programs depend on the data that average, nontypist users enter interactively, the chance of error is even more likely. In Chapter 10, you learned some useful techniques to check for valid and reasonable input data. Object-oriented, event-driven programs employ a more specific group of methods called **exception handling methods**. The methods check for and manage errors. The generic name used for errors in object-oriented languages is **exceptions**, because, presumably, errors are not usual occurrences; they are the "exceptions" to the rule.

Programmers had to deal with error conditions long before object-oriented methods were conceived. Probably the most often used error-handling method was to terminate the program, or at least the module in which the offending statement occurred. For example, Figure 13-10 shows a segment of pseudocode that causes the insurance premium `calcRoutine()` module to end if the `policyType` is invalid; in the second line of code the module ends abruptly when the `policyType` is not "A" or "H". Not only is this method of handling an error unforgiving, it isn't even structured. Recall that a structured module should have one entry and one exit point. The module in Figure 13-10 contains two exit points at the two `return` statements.

```
calcRoutine()
      if policyType not = "H" and policyType not = "A" then
            return
      else
            if policyType = "H" then
                    premiumAmount = 500
                    if ageOfInsured > 50 then
                            premiumAmount = premiumAmount + 100
                    endif
                    if insuredIsSmoker = "Y" then
                            premiumAmount = premiumAmount + 250
                    endif
            else
                    premiumAmount = 750
                    if numTickets > 2 then
                            premiumAmount = premiumAmount + 400
                    endif
                    if ageOfInsured > 50 then
                            premiumAmount = premiumAmount - 200
                    endif
            endif
      endif
return
```

Figure 13-10   Unforgiving, unstructured method of error handling

In the example in Figure 13-10, if the `policyType` is an invalid value, the module in which the code appears is terminated. If the program that contains this module is a spreadsheet or a game, the user may be annoyed that the program has stopped working and that an early exit has been made. If the program that contains this module determines whether an emergency room patient is covered for a surgical procedure, the results may be far more serious.

13

Rather than ending a program prematurely just because it encounters a piece of invalid data, a more elegant solution involves looping until the data item becomes valid, as shown in the example in Figure 13-11. The flag variable `errorFlag` is set to 1 at the beginning of the module, so that the `while` loop statements will execute at least once. You set the `errorFlag` to 0, and then check the `policyType` so you can perform the correct policy calculations. If the `policyType` is neither "H" nor "A", you prompt the user to reenter the policy type, and then set the `errorFlag` to 0 so that the loop repeats.

You first used a loop to ensure valid data in Chapter 10.

```
calcRoutine()
      errorFlag = 1
      while errorFlag = 1
            errorFlag = 0
            if policyType = "H" then
                  premiumAmount = 500
                  if ageOfInsured > 50 then
                        premiumAmount = premiumAmount + 100
                  endif
                  if insuredIsSmoker = "Y" then
                        premiumAmount = premiumAmount + 250
                  endif
            else
                  if policyType = "A" then
                        premiumAmount = 750
                        if numTickets > 2 then
                              premiumAmount = premiumAmount + 400
                        endif
                        if ageOfInsured > 50 then
                              premiumAmount = premiumAmount - 200
                        endif
                  else
                        print "Invalid policy type. Please reenter"
                        read policyType
                        errorFlag = 1
                  endif
            endif
return
```

Figure 13-11   Using a loop to handle interactive errors

There are at least two drawbacks to using the error-handling logic shown in Figure 13-11. First, one of the principles of modular and object-oriented programming is reusability. The purpose of the calcRoutine() module is to calculate premiums based on user data. The program you are working on now may allow the user to reenter policy data any number of times, but other programs in the insurance system may need to limit the number of chances the user gets to enter correct data or may allow no second chance at all. A flexible calcRoutine() will simply calculate the premium amount without deciding what to do about data errors. The calcRoutine() will be most flexible if it can detect an error and then notify the calling program or module that an error has occurred. Each program or module that uses the calcRoutine() module then can determine how to handle the mistake.

The other drawback to forcing the user to reenter data is that the technique works only with interactive programs. Program errors can occur as a result of many factors other than invalid data entry by a user sitting at a terminal. For example, a disk drive might not be ready, a file might not exist on the disk, or stored data items might be invalid. You cannot continue to reprompt a disk file for valid data; if stored data is invalid, it remains invalid. Object-oriented exception handling techniques overcome the limitations of simply repeating a request.

In object-oriented terminology, an exception is an object that you **throw**, or pass, from the module where a problem occurs to another module that will **catch**, or receive, the exception and handle the problem. The exception object can be any data type—a numeric or character data item or a programmer-created object such as a record complete with its own data fields and methods. For example, Figure 13-12 shows a `calcRoutine()` module that throws an `errorFlag` only if the `policyType` is neither "H" nor "A". If the `policyType` is "H" or "A", the premium is calculated and the module ends naturally.

```
calcRoutine()
      errorFlag = 1
      if policyType = "H" then
             premiumAmount = 500
             if ageOfInsured > 50 then
                    premiumAmount = premiumAmount + 100
             endif
             if insuredIsSmoker = "Y" then
                    premiumAmount = premiumAmount + 250
             endif
      else
             if policyType = "A" then
                    premiumAmount = 750
                    if numTickets > 2 then
                           premiumAmount = premiumAmount + 400
                    endif
                    if ageOfInsured > 50 then
                           premiumAmount = premiumAmount - 200
                    endif
             else
                    throw errorFlag
             endif
      endif
 return
```

Figure 13-12   Throwing an exception

The module in Figure 13-12 can be used within the program segment shown in Figure 13-13. In this program segment a variable named `thrownCode` is set to 1. This ensures that the `while` loop will execute at least once. Then the `calcRoutine()` (Figure 13-12) executes. If the `calcRoutine()` throws the `errorFlag` that has a value of 1, then the program segment in Figure 13-13 will bypass all statements following the method call (`perform  calcRoutine()`) and proceed directly to the `catch` statement. This means that the statement `thrownCode = 0` will be skipped. In the `catch` statement, the program will catch the thrown value and store it in the `thrownCode` variable. The two statements `print "Reenter the policy type"` and `read policyType` constitute the **catch block**, or group of statements that execute when a value is caught. The catch block statements execute if and only if a value has been caught and stored in the `thrownCode` variable. Then, because the statement that sets `thrownCode` to 0 was bypassed, `thrownCode` is still 1, so the `while` loop executes again and the `calcRoutine()` is attempted again. If the `calcRoutine()` is successful (that is, if the `policyType` is a valid one), then nothing is thrown from the `calcRoutine()` and the `catch` block in Figure 13-13 never executes. If the `calcRoutine()` is successful, it does not throw anything, so the logic proceeds to the statement following `perform calcRoutine()`, which is the statement that sets `thrownCode` to 0, stopping the loop from executing again. In this case, the `catch` block is bypassed, and the program proceeds to any statements that follow the program segment.

```
thrownCode = 1
while thrownCode = 1
      perform calcRoutine()
      thrownCode = 0
      catch (num thrownCode)
              print "Reenter the policy type"
              read policyType
```

Figure 13-13   Program segment using calcRoutine()

 You declare `thrownCode` as a numeric variable in the `catch` block in much the same way as you declare a passed variable in a method header—by providing the variable with a type and a name. When the `calcRoutine()` throws its `errorFlag` variable, its value becomes known as `thrownCode` within the `catch` block. You could provide the thrown variable with any legal identifier within the `catch` block.

The program segment in Figure 13-13 is difficult to follow if you are new to exception handling techniques. You can see the flexibility of using thrown exceptions when you consider the program segments in Figures 13-14 and 13-15. The program segment in Figure 13-14 also uses the `calcRoutine()`, but does not allow the user to reenter the `policyType`. If the `calcRoutine()` throws a value, the block of code following the `catch` in Figure 13-14 executes. This program prints a message that includes the error code. This logic would be even more useful if several error code values were possible. The user could analyze the code and take appropriate action.

```
perform calcRoutine()
catch (num thrownCode)
      print "Error #", thrownCode, "has occurred"
```

Figure 13-14   A program segment using calcRoutine in which the catch block uses thrownCode

The program segment in Figure 13-15 simply assumes the premium amount is zero for invalid policy types. When the `catch` block in Figure 13-15 executes, the program doesn't use the value that is thrown. The fact that a value *is* thrown is all that is required to cause the `catch` block to execute; the value does not have to be used in any way.

```
perform calcRoutine()
catch (num thrownCode)
      premiumAmount = 0
```

Figure 13-15   A program segment using calcRoutine in which the catch block does not use thrownCode

The general principle of exception handling in object-oriented programming is that a module that uses data should be able to detect errors, but not be required to handle them. The handling should be left to the application that uses the object, so that each application can use each module appropriately.

CHAPTER SUMMARY

◻ Interacting with a computer operating system from the command line is difficult; it is easier to use an event-driven graphical user interface (GUI) where users manipulate objects such as buttons and menus. Within an event-driven program, a component from which an event is generated is the source of the event. An object that is "interested in" an event you want to respond to is a listener.

◻ The possible events a user can initiate include a key press, mouse point, click, right-click, double-click, and drag. Common GUI components include labels, text fields, buttons, check boxes, check box groups, lists, and toolbars. GUI components are excellent examples of the best principles of object-oriented programming—they represent objects with attributes and methods that operate like black boxes.

◻ When you create a program that will use a GUI, the interface should be natural, predictable, attractive, easy to read, and nondistracting. It's helpful if the user can customize your applications. The program should be forgiving, and you should not forget that the GUI is only a means to an end.

◻ You can modify the attributes of GUI components. For example, you can set the size, color, screen location, font, visibility, and enabled status of the component.

◻ Developing an event-driven application is more complicated than developing a standard procedural program. You must understand the problem, create storyboards, define the objects, define the connections between the screens the user will see, plan the logic, code the program, translate the program into machine language, test the program, and put the program into production.

13

❑ Traditional error-handling methods have limitations. Object-oriented error-handling involves throwing exceptions. An exception is an object that you throw from the module where a problem occurs to another module that will catch it and handle the problem. The general principle of exception handling in object-oriented programming is that a module that uses data should be able to detect errors, but not be required to handle them. The handling should be left to the application that uses the object, so that each application can use each module appropriately.

EXERCISES

1. Take a critical look at three GUI applications with which you are familiar—for example, a spreadsheet, a word processing program, and a game. Describe how well each conforms to the GUI design guidelines listed in this chapter.

2. Select one element of poor GUI design in a program with which you are familiar. Describe how you would improve the design.

3. Select a GUI program that you have never used before. Describe how it conforms to the GUI design guidelines listed in this chapter.

4. Design the storyboards, interactivity diagram, object dictionary, and any necessary scripts for an interactive program for customers of Sunflower Floral Designs. Allow customers the option of choosing a floral arrangement ($25 base price), cut flowers ($15 base price), or a corsage ($10 base price). Let the customer choose roses, daisies, chrysanthemums, or irises as the dominant flower. If the customer chooses roses, add $5 to the base price. After the customer clicks an "Order Now" button, display the price of the order.

5. Design the storyboards, interactivity diagram, object dictionary, and any necessary scripts for an interactive program for customers of Toby's Travels. Allow customers the option of at least five trip destination options and four means of transportation, each with a unique price. After the customer clicks the "Plan Trip Now" button, display the price of the trip.

6. a. Design a method that calculates the cost of a painting job for College Student Painters. Variables include whether the job is location "I" for interior, which carries a base price of $100, or "E" for exterior, which carries a base price of $200. College Student Painters charges an additional $5 per square foot over the base price. The method should throw an exception if the location code is invalid.

   b. Write a module that calls the module designed in Exercise 6a. If the module throws an exception, force the price of the job to zero.

   c. Write a module that calls the module designed in Exercise 6a. If the module throws an exception, require the user to reenter the location code.

   d. Write a module that calls the module designed in Exercise 6a. If the module throws an exception, force the location code to "E" and the base price to $200.

7. Design the storyboards, interactivity diagram, object dictionary, and any necessary scripts for an interactive program for customers of The Mane Event Hair Salon. Allow customers the option of choosing a haircut ($15), coloring ($25), or perm ($45). After the customer clicks a "Select" button, display the price of the service.

8. a. Design a method that calculates the cost of a semester's tuition for a college student at Mid-State University. Variables include whether the student is an in-state resident ("I" for in-state, or "O" for out-of-state) and the number of credit hours for which the student is enrolling. The method should throw an exception if the residency code is invalid. Tuition is $75 per credit hour for in-state students and $125 per credit hour for out-of-state students. If a student enrolls in six hours or fewer, there is an additional $100 surcharge. Any student enrolled in 19 hours or more pays only the rate for 18 credit hours.

   b. Write a module that calls the module designed in Exercise 8a. If the module throws an exception, force the tuition to zero.

13

PROGRAM DESIGN

After studying Chapter 14, you should be able to:

♦ Understand the need for good program design

♦ Appreciate the advantages of storing program components in separate files

♦ Select superior variable and module names

♦ Design module statements

♦ Organize your program modules to reduce coupling and increase cohesion

♦ Understand the need for maintaining good programming habits

UNDERSTANDING THE NEED FOR GOOD PROGRAM DESIGN

As your programs become larger and more complicated, the need for good planning and design increases. Think of an application you use, such as a word processor or a spreadsheet. The number and variety of user options are staggering. Not only would it be impossible for a single programmer to write such an application, but without thorough planning and design, the components would never work together properly. Ideally, each program module you design needs to work well as a standalone module and as an element of larger systems. Just as a house with poor plumbing or a car with bad brakes is fatally flawed, a computer-based application can be great only if each component is designed well.

STORING PROGRAM COMPONENTS IN SEPARATE FILES

When you start to work on professional programs, you will see that many of them are quite lengthy with some containing hundreds of variables and thousands of lines of code. Programs often contain dozens of decisions and loops. Throughout this book you have learned to manage lengthy procedural programs by breaking them into modules. If you write object-oriented programs, you organize program components as a series of object classes. However, whether a program consists of a single long series of instructions, or multiple methods and classes, it is still difficult to manage all the program components.

Most modern programming languages allow you to store program components in separate files. If you write a module and store it in the same file as the program that uses it, your program files become large and hard to work with, whether you are trying to read them on a screen or on multiple printed pages. In addition, when you define a useful module or object class, you will want to use it in many programs. Of course, you can copy class and module definitions from one file to another, but this method is time consuming as well as prone to error. A better solution (if you are using a language that allows it) is to store your modules in individual files and use an instruction to include them in any program that uses them. The statement needed to access modules from separate files varies from language to language, but it usually involves using a verb such as *include*, *import*, or *copy* followed by the name of the file that contains the module.

For example, suppose your company has a standard employee record definition, part of which is shown in Figure 14-1. Files with the same format are used in many applications within the organization—personnel reports, production reports, payroll, and so on. It would be a tremendous waste of resources if every programmer rewrote this file definition in multiple applications. Instead, once a programmer writes the statements that constitute the file definition, those statements should be imported in their entirety into any program that uses a record with the same structure. For example, Figure 14-2 shows how the data fields in Figure 14-1 would be defined in the C++ programming language. If the statements in Figure 14-2 are saved in a file named Employees, then any C++ program can include the statement `#include Employees` and all the data fields are automatically defined.

The pound sign (#) is used with the include statement in C++ to notify the compiler that it is part of a special type of statement called a *pre-processor directive*.

EMPLOYEE FILE DESCRIPTION FILE NAME: EMPLOYEES		
Field description	Data type	Decimals
Employee ID	numeric	0
Last name	character	
First name	character	
Hire date	numeric	0
Hourly wage	numeric	2
Birth date	numeric	0
Termination date	numeric	0

Figure 14-1   Partial EMPLOYEES file description

```
class Employee
{
      int employeeID;
      string lastName;
      string firstName;
      long hireDate;
      double hourlyWage;
      long birthDate;
      long terminationDate;
};
```

Figure 14-2   Data fields in Figure 14-1 defined in the C++ language

 Don't be concerned with the syntax used in the file description in Figure 14-2. The words *class*, *int*, *string*, *long*, and *double* are all part of the C++ programming language and are not important to you now. Simply concentrate on how the variable names reflect the field descriptions in Figure 14-1.

Suppose you write a useful module that checks dates to guarantee their validity. For example, the two digits that represent a month can be neither less than 01 nor greater than 12, and the two digits that represent the day can contain different possible values based on the month. Any program that uses the employee file description shown in Figure 14-1 might want to call the date-validating module several times in order to validate any employee's hire date, birth date, and termination date. Not only do you want to call this module from several locations within any one program, you want to call it from many programs. For example, programs used for company ordering and billing would each contain several dates. If the date-validating module is useful and well written, you might even want to market it to other companies. By storing the module in its own file, you enable its use to be flexible. When you write a program of any length, you should consider storing each of its components in its own file.

Storing components in separate files can provide an advantage beyond ease of reuse. When you let others use your programs or modules, you often provide them with only the compiled (that is, machine-language) version of your code, not the **source code**, which is composed of readable statements. Storing your program statements in a separate, nonreadable, compiled file is an example of **implementation hiding**, or hiding the details of how the program or module works. The manner in which your code functions is hidden from the programmers who use your code. A programmer who cannot see your well-designed modules is more likely to use them simply as they were intended and refrain from making adjustments in your code, thereby introducing error. Of course, in order to work with your modules or data definitions, a programmer must know the names and types of data you are using. Typically, you provide programmers who use your definitions with written documentation of the data names and purposes.

14

Recall from Chapter 1 that when you write a program in a programming language, you must compile or interpret it into machine language before the computer can actually carry out your instructions.

Selecting Variable and Module Names

An often-overlooked element in program design is the selection of good data and module names (sometimes generically called **identifiers**). In Chapter 1 you learned that every programming language has specific rules for the construction of names—some languages limit the number of characters, some allow dashes, and so on—but there are other general guidelines:

- Use meaningful names. Creating a data field named `someData` or a module named `firstModule()` makes a program cryptic. You will forget the purpose of these identifiers within your own programs. All programmers occasionally use short, nondescriptive names such as `x` or `temp` in a quick program written to test a procedure or as an array subscript. However, in most cases data and module names should be meaningful.

Programmers refer to programs that contain meaningful names as *self-documenting*. This means that even without further documentation, the program code explains itself to readers.

- Usually, you should use pronounceable names. A variable name like `pzf` is neither pronounceable nor meaningful. A name that looks meaningful when you write it, like `preparead()` might mean "Prepare ad" to you, but is "Prep a read" to others. Look at your names critically to make sure they are pronounceable. Very standard abbreviations do not have to be pronounceable. For example, most business people would interpret `ssn` as a Social Security number.

Don't forget that not all programmers share your culture. An abbreviation that seems obvious in meaning to you might be quite cryptic to someone in a different part of the world.

- Be judicious in your use of abbreviations. You can save a few keystrokes when creating a module called `getStat()`, but is its purpose to find the state in which a city is located, output some statistics, or determine the status of some flag variables? Similarly, is a variable named `fn` meant to hold a first name, file number, or something else?

To save typing time when you develop a program, you can use a short name like efn. After the program operates correctly, you can use an editor's search and replace feature to replace your coded name with a more meaningful name like employeeFirstName.

Some newer compilers support an automatic statement completion feature that saves typing time. After the first time you use a name like employeeFirstName, you need to type only the first few letters before the compiler editor offers a list of available names from which to choose. The list is constructed from all names you have used in the file that begin with the same characters.

- Usually, avoid digits in a name. Zeroes get confused with the letter "O" and lowercase "l"s are misread as the numeral "1". Of course, use your judgment: budgetFor2004 is probably not going to be misinterpreted.

- Use the system your language allows to separate words in long, multiword variable names. For example, if the programming language you will use allows dashes or underscores, then a method name like initialize-data() or initialize_data() is easier to read than initializedata(). If you use a language that allows camel casing, then use initializeData(). If you use a language that is case sensitive, it is legal but confusing to use variable names that differ only in case, for example empName, EmpName, and Empname.

- Consider including a form of the verb *to be*, such as *is* or *are*, in names for variables that are intended to hold a status. For example, use isFinished as a flag variable that holds a "Y" or "N" to indicate whether a file is exhausted. The shorter name finished is likely to be confused with a module that executes when a program is done.

Using a form of *to be* is also a good practice when naming Boolean variables. You will learn more about Boolean variables later in this chapter.

14

When you begin to write programs, the process of determining what data variables and modules you will need and what to name them all might seem overwhelming. The design process is crucial, however. When you acquire your first professional programming assignment, the design process might very well have been completed already. Most likely, your first assignment will be to write or make modifications to one small member module of a much larger application. The more the original programmers stuck to these guidelines, the better the original design is, and the easier your job of modification will be.

DESIGNING MODULE STATEMENTS

In addition to selecting good identifiers, you can use the following tactics to contribute to the clarity of the statements within your program modules.

- Avoid confusing line breaks.
- Use temporary variables to clarify long statements.
- Use constants where appropriate.

Avoid Confusing Line Breaks

Some older programming languages require that program statements be placed in specific columns. Most modern programming languages are free form; you can arrange your lines of code any way you see fit. As in real life, with freedom comes responsibility; when you have flexibility in arranging your lines of code, you must take care to make sure your meaning is clear. With free-form code, programmers often do not provide enough line breaks, or they provide inappropriate ones.

Figure 14-3 shows an example of selection code that does not provide enough line breaks for clarity. If you have been following the examples used throughout this book, the code in Figure 14-4 looks clearer to you; it also will look clearer to most other programmers.

```
determineDiscount(Record custRec)
    declare variables --------------------------------------- local num discount
                                                              local num seniorDiscount = .10
                                                              local num childDiscount = .20
                                                              local num seniorAge = 65
                                                              local num childAge = 12

    if custAge >= seniorAge then discount = seniorDiscount else if custAge <=
childAge
    then discount = childDiscount else discount = 0 endif endif
        price = price — price * discount
return(discount)
```

Figure 14-3   The determineDiscount() module with insufficient line breaks

```
determineDiscount(Record custRec)
     declare variables ------------------------------------------- local num discount
     if custAge >= seniorAge then                                  local num seniorDiscount = .10
           discount = seniorDiscount                               local num childDiscount = .20
     else                                                          local num seniorAge = 65
           if custAge <= childAge then                             local num childAge = 12
                 discount = childDiscount
           else
                 discount = 0
           endif
     endif
     price = price - price * discount
return(discount)
```

Figure 14-4   The determineDiscount() module with appropriate line breaks

Figure 14-4 shows that more, but shorter lines usually improve your ability to understand a program's logic. Sometimes, however, long lines of code are unavoidable. For example, when you create a module that requires a long list of passed parameters in the header or a conditional test that requires a long series of ANDs or ORs, you might not have any choice other than to continue a line of code on a second line. In these cases, try to break a line so that the reader knows a continuation follows. For example, Figure 14-5 shows a module that contains both a long header parameter list and a long `if` statement. By breaking the parameter list after a comma, the reader knows that more code must follow. Similarly, by breaking the `if` after the AND, the reader knows that the `if` test is not complete and at least one more condition must be contained in the next statement.

```
calculateInsurancePremium(num custAge, char multipleCars, num ticketsIssued,
     num yearsExperience, char passedDriversEd)
        declare variables ------------------------------------- local num premium
        if custAge >= minAge AND                                local num lowRate = 225
              multipleCars = yesCode AND                        local num highRate = 375
              ticketsIssued <= minTickets AND                   local char yesCode = "Y"
              yearsExperience <= minYears AND                   local num minAge = 25
              passedDriversEd = yesCode then                    local num minTickets = 2
                    premium = lowRate                           local num minYears = 5
        else
                    premium = highRate
        endif
return(premium)
```

Figure 14-5   The calculateInsurancePremium() module with appropriate line breaks

14

Use Temporary Variables to Clarify Long Statements

When you need several mathematical operations to determine a result, consider using a series of temporary variables to hold intermediate results. For example, Figure 14-6 shows two ways to calculate a value for a real estate `salespersonCommission` variable. Each method achieves the same result—the salesperson's commission is based on the square feet multiplied by the price per square foot plus any premium for a lot with special features, such as a wooded or waterfront lot. However, the second example uses two temporary variables, `sqFootPrice` and `totalPrice`. When the computation is broken down into less complicated, individual steps it is easier to see how the total price is calculated. In calculations with even more computation steps, performing the arithmetic in stages would become increasingly helpful.

Programmers might say using temporary variables like the example in Figure 14-6 is *cheap*. When executing a lengthy arithmetic statement, even if you don't explicitly name temporary variables, the programming language compiler creates them behind the scenes, so declaring them yourself does not cost much in terms of program execution time.

```
salespersonCommission = (sqFeet * pricePerSquareFoot + lotPremium) *
    commissionRate
sqFootPrice = sqFeet * pricePerSquareFoot
totalPrice = sqFootPrice + lotPremium
salespersonCommission = totalPrice * commissionRate
```

Figure 14-6   Two ways of achieving the same salespersonCommission result

Another way to make long statements clearer is to use temporary Boolean variables. Boolean variables can hold one of two possible values—`true` or `false`. If you are using a language that supports Boolean-type variables, you can use them to shorten a multi-part decision and make it clearer. Figure 14-7 shows that if you store the results of true/false tests in well-named Boolean variables, you later can use the Boolean variables to shorten an `if` statement, which makes its purpose clear.

Both code segments in Figure 14-7 print student data when the student is an English major, has a grade point average of at least 3.25, and has completed at least 90 credit hours, but the `if` statement in the second example is easier to interpret at a glance. Each of the variables—`isEngMajor`, `isHonorStudent`, and `isSenior`—represents a `true` or `false` state. The `if` in the second code example more clearly mirrors the way people speak and the way your boss is likely to give instructions. People are more likely to say, "Print students who are English majors, honor students, and seniors" than they are to say "Print students whose major is English, whose grade point average is above the minimum, and whose credit hours indicate senior status."

You first used the term Boolean when you learned about decision-making in Chapter 5.

```
printEnglishHonorSeniors(Record stuRec)
     declare variables    -------------------------------------------------  local char engMajor = "English"
     if stuMajor = engMajor AND                                              local num honorsLimit = 3.25
         stuGradePoint >= honorsLimit AND                                    local num seniorStatus = 90
         stuCredits >= seniorStatus then
              print stuIdNum, stuFirstName, stuLastName
     endif
return

printEnglishHonorSeniors(Record stuRec)
     declare variables    -------------------------------------------------  local char engMajor = "English"
     isEngMajor = (stuMajor = engMajor?)                                     local num honorsLimit = 3.25
     isHonorStudent = (stuGradePoint >= honorsLimit?)                        local num seniorStatus = 90
     isSenior = (stuCredits >= seniorStatus?)                                local Boolean isEngMajor
     if isEngMajor AND isHonorStudent AND isSenior then                      local Boolean isHonorStudent
         print stuIdNum, stuFirstName, stuLastName                           local Boolean isSenior
     endif
return
```

Figure 14-7   Two ways of printing the same student list

Use Constants where Appropriate

Whenever possible, use named values in your programs. If your program contains a statement like `salesTax = price * taxRate` instead of `salesTax = price * .06`, you gain two benefits:

- It is easier for readers to know that the price is being multiplied by a tax rate instead of a discount, commission, or some other rate represented by .06.

- When the tax rate changes, you make one change to the value where `taxRate` is defined rather than searching through a program for every instance of .06.

For example, the program in Figure 14-7 uses constants `engMajor`, `honorsLimit`, and `seniorStatus`. If any of the selection criteria change—for example, if the school administration changes the name of the major on student records to "Literature" or changes the grade point average criteria for honors status to 3.5—then the changes to the constants are made in the declaration list and the actual program code does not have to be disturbed.

14

ORGANIZING MODULES

When you begin to design computer programs, it is difficult to decide how much to put into a module or subroutine. For example, a process that requires 40 instructions can be contained in a single module, two 20-instruction modules, 20 two-instruction modules, or any other combination. In most programming languages, any of these combinations is allowed. That is, you can write a program that will execute and produce correct results no matter how you divide the individual steps into modules. However, placing either too many or too few instructions in a single module makes a program harder to follow and reduces flexibility. When deciding how to organize your program steps into modules, you should adhere to two general rules:

- Reduce coupling.

- Increase cohesion.

REDUCING COUPLING

Coupling is a measure of the strength of the connection between two program modules; it is used to express the extent to which information is exchanged by subroutines. Coupling is either tight or loose depending on how much one module depends on information from another. **Tight coupling**, which occurs when modules excessively depend on each other, makes programs more prone to errors; there are many data paths to keep track of, many chances for bad data to pass from one module to another, and many chances for one module to alter information needed by another module. **Loose coupling** occurs when modules do not depend on others. In general, you want to reduce coupling as much as possible because connections between modules make them more difficult to write, maintain, and reuse.

Imagine four cooks wandering in and out of the kitchen and preparing a stew. If each is allowed to add seasonings at will without the knowledge of the other cooks, you could end up with a culinary disaster. Similarly, if four payroll program modules are allowed to alter your gross pay figure "at will" without the "knowledge" of the other modules, you could end up with a financial disaster. A program in which several modules have access to your gross pay figure has modules that are tightly coupled. A superior program would control access to the payroll figure by limiting its passage to modules that need it.

You can evaluate whether coupling between modules is loose or tight by looking at the intimacy between modules and the number of parameters that are passed between them.

- Tight coupling: The least intimate situation is one in which modules have access to the same globally defined variables; these modules have tight coupling. When one module changes the value stored in a variable, other modules are affected.

- Loose coupling: The most intimate way to share data is to pass a copy of needed variables from one module to another. That way, the sharing of data is always purposeful—variables must be explicitly passed to and from modules that use them. The loosest (best) subroutines and functions pass single parameters rather than many variables or entire records, if possible.

Usually, you can determine that coupling is occurring at one of several levels. **Data coupling** is the loosest type of coupling; therefore, it is the most desirable. Data coupling is also known as **simple data coupling** or **normal coupling**. Data coupling occurs when modules share a data item by passing parameters. For example, a module that determines a student's eligibility for the dean's list might receive a copy of the student's grade point average to use in making the determination.

Data-structured coupling is similar to data coupling, but an entire record is passed from one module to another. For example, consider a module that determines whether a customer applying for a loan is creditworthy. You might write a module that receives the entire customer record and uses many of its fields in order to determine whether the customer should be granted the loan. If you need many of the customer fields—such as salary, length of time on the job, savings account balance, and so on—then it makes sense to pass a customer's record to a module. Figure 14-8 shows an example of such a module.

```
checkCredit(Record custRec)
    declare variables--------------------------local char creditIsOk
    creditIsOk = yesCode                       local char yesCode = "Y"
    if custSalary < minSalary then  local num minSalary = 300.00
        creditIsOk = noCode                    local char noCode = "N"
    endif                                      local num minTime = 2
    if custTimeOnJob < minTime then local num minSavings = 20000.00
        creditIsOk = noCode
    endif
    if custSavingsBal < minSavings then
        creditIsOk = noCode
    endif
    return(creditIsOk)
```

Figure 14-8   Module that determines customer creditworthiness

In the **checkCredit()** module, an entire record (**custRec**) rather than any single data field is passed to the module. The coupling could have been made looser by writing three separate modules: one to check salary, one to check time on the job, and one to check savings balance. However, since so many fields in the customer's record are needed, in this case it is very appropriate to pass the entire record to the module.

Control coupling occurs when a main program (or other module) passes a parameter to a module, controlling the module's actions or telling it what to do. For example, Figure 14-9 shows a module that receives a user's choice and calls one of several other modules.

14

```
selectFunction(num userChoice)
      if userChoice = 1 then
                    perform addRecordToFile()
      else
            if userChoice = 2 then
                    perform deleteRecordFromFile()
            else
                  if userChoice = 3 then
                          perform printRecords()
                  else
                          perform invalidChoice()
                  endif
            endif
      endif
return
```

Figure 14-9   selectFunction() module

Of course, this kind of coupling is appropriate at times, but the implication is that any module that calls the `selectFunction()` module is aware of how `selectFunction()` works. After all, an appropriate choice had to be made and passed to `selectFunction()`. The program that uses `selectFunction()` probably prompts the user for a choice and passes that choice to `selectFunction()`. Therefore, the calling program must know how to phrase the prompt correctly in order to elicit an appropriate `userChoice`. This coupling is relatively tight. This is a problem, because if you make a change to the `selectFunction()` module—for example, by adding a new option or changing the order of the existing options—then all the programs and other modules that use `selectFunction()` will have to know about the change. If they don't, their prompts will offer incorrect choices, and they won't be sending the appropriate `userChoice` value to the module. Once you have to start keeping track of all the modules and programs that might call a module, the opportunity for errors in a system increases dramatically.

External coupling and **common coupling** occur, respectively, when two or more modules access the same global variable or record. When data can be modified by more than one module, programs become harder to write, read, and modify. That's because if you make a change in a single module, many other modules can be affected. For example, if one module increases a field that holds the year from two digits to four, then all other modules that use the year will have to be altered before they can operate correctly. For another example, if one module can increase your gross pay figure by 10% based on years of service and another module can increase your pay by 20% based on annual sales, it makes a difference which module operates first. It's possible that a third module won't work when the salary increases over a specified limit. If you avoid external or common coupling and pass variables instead, you can control how and when the modules receive the data.

Pathological coupling occurs when two or more modules change one another's data. An especially confusing case occurs when `moduleOne()` changes data in `moduleTwo()`, `moduleTwo()` changes data in `moduleThree()`, and `moduleThree()` changes data in `moduleOne()`. This makes programs extremely difficult to follow and you should avoid them at all costs.

INCREASING COHESION

Analyzing coupling lets you see how modules connect externally with other modules and programs. You also want to analyze a module's **cohesion**, which refers to how the internal statements of a module or subroutine serve to accomplish its purposes. In highly cohesive modules, all the operations are related or "go together". Such modules are usually more reliable than those that have low cohesion; they are considered stronger, and they make programs easier to write, read, and maintain.

Functional Cohesion

Functional cohesion occurs when all operations in a module contribute to the performance of only one task. Functional cohesion is the highest level of cohesion; you should strive for it in all functions you write. For example, a module that calculates gross pay appears in Figure 14-10. The module receives two parameters, **hours** and **rate**, and computes gross pay including time-and-a-half for overtime. The functional cohesion of this module is high because each of its instructions contributes to one task—computing gross pay. If you can write a sentence describing what a module does and use only two words—for example, "Compute gross", "Cube value", or "Print record"—the module is probably functionally cohesive.

```
computeGrossPay(num hours, num rate)
    declare variables----------------------------------------local num gross
    if hours <= workWeek then                                local num workWeek = 40
            gross = hours * rate
    else
            gross = (workWeek * rate) + (hours - workWeek) * (rate * 1.5)
    endif
return(gross)
```

Figure 14-10 The computeGrossPay() module

You might work in a programming environment that has a rule such as "No module will be longer than can be printed on one page" or "No module will have more than 30 lines of code". The rule-maker is trying to achieve more cohesion, but this is an arbitrary way of going about it. It's possible for a 2-line module to have low cohesion and—although less likely—a 40-line module to have high cohesion. Because good functionally

14

cohesive modules perform only one task, they tend to be short. However, the issue is not size. If it takes 20 statements to perform one task within a module, then the module is still cohesive.

Sequential Cohesion

Sequential cohesion takes place when a module performs operations that must be carried out in a specific order on the same data. Sequential cohesion is a slightly weaker type of cohesion than functional cohesion because even though the module might perform a variety of tasks, the tasks are linked because they use the same data, often transforming the data in a series of steps.

For example, Figure 14-11 shows a module that computes a customer's bill based on several factors. Assume that the `custOrder` record contains the fields `custItemNum`, `custQuantity`, `custOriginDate`, `custState`, and `custZipCode`. The customer is charged either $25 or $35 per item, depending on the item ordered. This per-item charge is multiplied by the quantity ordered. Then the customer receives a 5% discount if the order is for over 100 items and an additional 10% discount if the customer has patronized the business since 2000 or before. If the customer is an Illinois resident sales tax is added, and if the customer is not located in the immediate zip code a $10 delivery charge is added.

```
computeBalanceDue(Record custOrder)
      declare variables-------------------------------------------------local num balance
      if custItemNum = item1 then                                       local num item1 = 1001
            balance = price1                                            local num price1 = 25.00
      else                                                             local num price2 = 35.00
            balance = price2                                            local num minimumOrder = 100
      endif                                                            local num orderDiscount = .05
      balance = balance * custQuantity                                 local num loyalYear = 2000
      if custQuantity > minimumOrder then                              local num loyalDiscount = .10
            balance = balance - balance * orderDiscount                local char localState = "IL"
      endif                                                            local num taxRate = .06
      if custOriginDate <= loyalYear then                              local num localZipCode = 60014
            balance = balance - balance * loyalDiscount                local num deliveryCharge = 10.00
      endif
      if custState = localState then
            balance = balance + balance * taxRate
      endif
      if custZipCode not = localZipCode then
            balance = balance + deliveryCharge
      endif
 return(balance)
```

Figure 14-11   The computeBalanceDue() module

The steps in this module are sequentially cohesive because they occur in a specific order on the same data. Testing the ordered quantity before the length of patronage is important—the results will differ if these tests are not made in the correct order. Similarly, if delivery charges are not taxable, then the tax must be computed before a delivery charge is added to the balance. Of course, each of these calculations could be diverted into its own module; very often, you can break a sequentially cohesive module down into more functionally cohesive units. However, for practical purposes a sequentially cohesive module is an acceptable programming form. If you write a sentence describing what a module does and repeatedly use the same noun, the module is probably sequentially cohesive. For instance, if you find yourself describing a module by writing "Input the year, make sure it is a valid year, determine if it is a leap year, and print the year", the module is performing a series of actions on the year and is sequentially cohesive.

Communicational Cohesion

Communicational cohesion occurs in modules that perform tasks that share data. The tasks are not related, just the data are. If the tasks must be performed in order, the module is sequentially cohesive. If the tasks are not performed in any sequential order but just share the same data, the module is communicationally cohesive; this is considered a weaker form of cohesion than functional or sequential cohesion. For example, consider a module that produces a rating of prospective customers on their likelihood of buying your product. Assume you have a product that appeals to high-income, older, married people. Figure 14-12 shows a `determineCustomerScore()` module that adds a point to a customer's score for each factor that contributes to the likelihood the customer will buy the product.

```
determineCustomerScore(Record custRecord)
      declare variables--------------------------------local num score = 0
      if custIncome > incomeThreshold then  local num incomeThreshold = 75000
            score = score + 1               local num ageThreshold = 55
      endif                                 local char marriedCode = "M"
      if custAge >= ageThreshold then
            score = score + 1
      endif
      if custMaritalStatus = marriedCode then
            score = score + 1
      endif
return(score)
```

Figure 14-12   The determineCustomerScore() module

The `determineCustomerScore()` module in Figure 14-12 is communicationally cohesive because the steps involved share data; the value `score` is adjusted repeatedly throughout the module. Other examples of modules with communicational cohesion include modules that validate a value by performing several tests (Is the value positive?

Is it less than 100? Is it a perfect square?) and modules that perform several different operations on the same data based on an input value. For example, Figure 14-13 shows a module that takes one of several actions based on a transaction code.

```
performTransaction(num custBalance, num transactionAmount, char code)
    declare variables------------------------------------------------local char purchaseCode = "P"
    if code = purchaseCode then                                     local char returnCode = "R"
        custBalance = custBalance + transactionAmount               local char discountCode = "D"
    else                                                            local num discountRate = .10
        if code = returnCode then
            custBalance = custBalance - transactionAmount
        else
            if code = discountCode then
                    custBalance = custBalance - discountRate * custBalance
            endif
        endif
    endif
return(custBalance)
```

Figure 14-13   The performTransaction() module

Because the same data item (`custBalance`) is manipulated in different fashions, the `performTransaction()` module is communicationally cohesive. The data items are shared, but the actions on the data are different. You can obtain more cohesion by writing three functionally cohesive modules, perhaps named `applyPurchaseToBalance()`, `applyReturnToBalance()`, and `applyDiscountToBalance()`.

Temporal, Procedural, Logical, and Coincidental Cohesion

Temporal cohesion takes place when the tasks in a module are related by time. That is, the tasks are placed together because of *when* they must take place—for example, at the beginning of a program. The prime examples of temporally cohesive modules you have seen are `housekeeping()` and `finishUp()` modules.

Procedural cohesion takes place when, as with sequential cohesion, the tasks of a module are done in sequence. However, unlike sequential cohesion, the tasks in procedural cohesion do not share data. Main program modules are often procedurally cohesive; they consist of a series of steps that must be performed in sequence, but perform very different tasks, such as `housekeeping()`, `mainLoop()`, and `finishUp()`. A main module can also be called a **dispatcher module**, because it dispatches messages to a sequence of more cohesive modules. If you sense that a module you have written has only procedural cohesion (that is, it consists of a series of steps that use unrelated data), you probably want to turn it into a dispatcher module. You accomplish this by changing the module so that it calls other modules in which the diverse tasks take place. Each of the new modules can be functionally, sequentially, or communicationally cohesive.

Logical cohesion takes place when a member module performs one or more tasks depending on a decision, whether the decision is in the form of a **case** structure or a series of **if** statements. The actions performed might go together logically (that is, perform the same type of action), but they don't work on the same data. Like a module that has procedural cohesion, a module that has only logical cohesion should probably be turned into a dispatcher. If you can write a sentence describing what a module does, and you use "if" and the same verb repeatedly with different objects, the module is probably logically cohesive. For example, "If code is 1, read a record from the floppy disk drive; if code is 2, read a record from the hard drive; otherwise, read a record from the keyboard" is a sentence that describes a logically cohesive module. This module should be modified so that the code dispatches processing to one of three record-reading modules.

Coincidental cohesion, as the name implies, is based on coincidence where the operations in a module just happen to have been placed together. Obviously, this is the weakest form of cohesion and is not desirable. However, if you modify programs written by others, you might see examples of coincidental cohesion. Perhaps the program designer did not plan well, or perhaps an originally well-designed program was modified to reduce the number of modules, and now a number of unrelated statements are grouped in a single module.

Coincidental cohesion is almost an oxymoron—cohesion that is simply coincidental is really no cohesion at all.

There is a time and a place for shortcuts. If you need a result from spreadsheet data in a hurry, you can type in two values and take a sum rather than creating a formula with proper cell references. If a memo must go out in five minutes, you don't have to change fonts or add clip art with your word processor. Similarly, if you need a quick programming result, you might very well use cryptic variable names, tight coupling, and coincidental cohesion. When you create a professional application, however, you will want to keep professional guidelines in mind.

MAINTAINING GOOD PROGRAMMING HABITS

When you learn a programming language and begin to write lines of program code, it is easy to forget the principles you have learned in this text. Having some programming knowledge and a keyboard at your fingertips can lure you into typing lines of code before you think things through. But every program you write will be better if you plan before you code. If you maintain the habits of first drawing flowcharts or writing pseudocode that you have learned here, your future programming projects will go more smoothly. If you walk through your program logic on paper (called **desk-checking**) before starting to type statements in C++, COBOL, Visual Basic, or Java, your programs will run correctly sooner. If you plan ahead to create high cohesion and loose coupling, you will be rewarded with programs that are easier to get up and running along with being easier to maintain.

14

CHAPTER SUMMARY

❑ As your programs become larger and more complicated, the need for good planning and design increases.

❑ Most modern programming languages allow you to store program components in separate files and use instructions to include them in any program that uses them. Storing components in separate files can provide the advantages of easy reuse and implementation hiding.

❑ When selecting data and module names, use meaningful, pronounceable names. Be judicious in your use of abbreviations, avoid digits in a name, and visually separate words in multiword names. Consider including a form of the verb *to be*, such as *is* or *are*, in names for Boolean variables and those that are intended to hold a status.

❑ When writing program statements, you should avoid confusing line breaks, use temporary variables to clarify long statements, and use constants where appropriate.

❑ When deciding how to organize your program steps into modules, you should attempt to reduce coupling and increase cohesion.

❑ Coupling is a measure of the strength of the connection between two program modules. Tight coupling, where there is much dependence between modules, makes programs more prone to errors. Loose coupling occurs when modules do not depend on others. You can classify coupling as data, data-structured, control, external, common, or pathological.

❑ A module's cohesion is a measure of the extent to which its internal statements serve to accomplish its purposes. Highly cohesive modules are usually more reliable than those that have low cohesion. Levels of cohesion can be classified as functional, sequential, communicational, temporal, procedural, logical, and coincidental.

❑ Every program you write will be better if you plan before you code.

EXERCISES

1. Critically review at least two programs you flowcharted or wrote pseudocode for earlier in this book. Identify the places where you should choose different module and variable names.

2. Exchange flowcharts or pseudocode with another student. Suggest at least two new names for variables or modules in the student's logic.

3. A real-life example of a device that employs implementation hiding is a microwave oven—it heats food even if you do not understand how it works. Name three other devices from everyday life that demonstrate the concept of implementation hiding.

4. Critically review programs for which you have drawn flowcharts or written pseudocode earlier in this book. Identify at least one example of each of the following:

   a. tight coupling

   b. loose coupling

   c. data coupling

   d. data-structured coupling

   e. control coupling

   f. external coupling

   g. common coupling

   h. pathological coupling

5. Critically review programs for which you have drawn flowcharts or written pseudocode earlier in this book. Identify at least one example of each of the following:

   a. functional cohesion

   b. sequential cohesion

   c. communicational cohesion

   d. temporal cohesion

   e. procedural cohesion

   f. dispatcher module

   g. logical cohesion

   h. coincidental cohesion

6. Suggest improvements to the following program:

```
start
  perform module1()
  while not eof
     perform payrollReport()
  perform iLoveAerosmith()
end

module1()
  declare variables--------|payRec
  open files               |  num pId
  perform h()              |  char name
  read payRec              |  num payRate
return                     |  num phourswkd
                           |  char head1 = "PAYROLL REPORT"
                           |  num gross
                           |  num t
                           |  num count = 0
```

14

```
h()
  print head1
return

payrollReport()
  gross = phourswkd * payRate
  if gross > 400 then t = gross * .15 else t = 0 endif
  print name, gross, t
  count = count + gross
  read payRec
return

iLoveAerosmith()
  print "Total payroll in dollars is", count
  close files
return
```

7. The Tap-It Typing Service prepares term papers for students. It maintains a file of current projects including client number, topic, number of pages, and date due. The charge for a term paper is calculated as follows: The base price for any paper under 11 pages is $20. Additional pages cost .80 each. There is a $5 surcharge for papers due in May and December. Design the logic for this program using the principles outlined in this chapter.

15

SYSTEM MODELING WITH UML

> **After studying Chapter 15, you should be able to:**
> ◆ Understand the need for system modeling
> ◆ Describe the UML
> ◆ Work with use case diagrams
> ◆ Use class and object diagrams
> ◆ Use sequence and collaboration diagrams
> ◆ Use statechart diagrams
> ◆ Use activity diagrams
> ◆ Use component and deployment diagrams
> ◆ Decide which UML diagrams to use

UNDERSTANDING THE NEED FOR SYSTEM MODELING

Computer programs often stand alone to solve a user's specific problem. For example, a program might exist only to print paychecks for the current week. Most computer programs, however, are part of a larger system. Your company's payroll system, might be comprised of dozens of programs including programs that produce employee paychecks, apply raises to employee records, alter employee deduction options, and print W2 forms at the end of the tax year. Each program you write as part of a system might be related to several others. Some programs depend on input from other programs in the system or produce output to be fed into other programs. Similarly, an organization's accounting, inventory, and customer ordering systems each consist of many interrelated programs. Producing a set of programs that operates together correctly requires careful planning. **System design** is the detailed specification of how all the parts of a system will be implemented and coordinated.

 Usually, system design refers to *computer* system design, but even a noncomputerized manual system can benefit from good design techniques.

Many textbooks cover the theories and techniques of system design. If you continue to study in a Computer Information Systems program at a college or university, you probably will be required to take a semester-long course in system design. Explaining all the techniques of system design is beyond the scope of this book. However, some basic principles parallel those you have used throughout this book in designing individual programs:

- Large systems are easier to understand when you break them down into subsystems.

- Good modeling techniques are increasingly important as the size and complexity of systems increase.

- Good models promote communication among technical and nontechnical workers while assuring good business solutions.

In other words, developing a model for a single program or an entire business system requires organization and planning. In this chapter you will learn the basics of one popular design tool, the UML, that is based on these principles. UML allows you to envision systems with an object-oriented perspective, breaking a system into subsystems, focusing on the big picture, and hiding the implementation details. Additionally, UML provides a means for programmers and business people to communicate about system design. Understanding UML's principles helps you design a variety of system types and talk about systems with the people who will use them.

 In addition to modeling a system before creating it, system analysts sometimes model an existing system to get a better picture of its operation. Creating a model for an existing system is called reverse engineering.

WHAT IS UML?

UML stands for **Unified Modeling Language**. The **UML** is a standard way to specify, construct, and document systems that use object-oriented methods. (The UML is a modeling language, not a programming language. The systems you develop using the UML probably will be implemented later in object-oriented programming languages such as Java, C++, C#, or Visual Basic.) As with flowcharts, pseudocode, and hierarchy charts, the UML has its own notation that consists of a set of specialized shapes and conventions. You can use the UML's shapes to construct different kinds of software diagrams and model different kinds of systems. Just as you can use a flowchart or hierarchy chart to diagram real-life activities, organizational relationships, or computer programs, you also can use the UML for many purposes, including modeling business activities, organizational processes, or software systems.

UML was created at Rational Software by Grady Booch, Ivar Jacobson, and Jim Rumbaugh. The Object Management Group (OMG) adopted UML as a standard for software modeling in 1997. The OMG includes more than 800 software vendors, developers, and users who seek a common architectural framework for object-oriented programming. You can view or download the entire UML specification and usage guidelines from the OMG at *www.omg.org/uml/*.

 You can purchase compilers for most programming languages from a variety of manufacturers. Similarly, you can purchase a variety of tools to help you create UML diagrams, but the UML itself is vendor-independent.

When you draw a flowchart or write pseudocode, your purpose is to illustrate the individual steps in a process. When you draw a hierarchy chart you use more of a "big picture" approach. Like a hierarchy chart, you use the UML to create top-view diagrams of business processes that let you hide details and focus on functionality. This approach lets you start with a generic view of an application and introduce details and complexity later. UML diagrams are useful as you begin designing business systems, when customers who are not technically oriented must accurately communicate with the technical staff members who will create the actual systems. The UML was purposefully designed to be nontechnical so that developers, customers, and implementers (programmers) could all "speak the same language." If business and technical people can agree on what a system should do, the chances improve that the final product will be useful.

The UML provides nine different diagram types that you can use to model systems. Each of the diagram types lets you see a business process from a different angle and appeals to a different type of user. Just as an architect, interior designer, electrician, and plumber use different diagram types to describe the same building, different computer users appreciate different perspectives. For example, a business user will most value a system's use case diagrams because they illustrate who is doing what. On the other hand, programmers will find class and object diagrams more useful because they help explain details of how to build classes and objects into applications. The nine UML diagram types are:

- Use case diagrams
- Class diagrams
- Object diagrams
- Sequence diagrams
- Collaboration diagrams
- Statechart diagrams
- Activity diagrams
- Component diagrams
- Deployment diagrams

15

You can categorize UML diagrams as those that illustrate the dynamic, or changing aspects of a system and those that illustrate the static, or steady, aspects of a system. Dynamic diagrams include use case, sequence, collaboration, statechart, and activity diagrams. Static diagrams include class, object, component, and deployment diagrams.

Each of the nine UML diagram types supports multiple variations and understanding them all would require an entire textbook. This chapter presents an overview and simple examples of each type of diagram, which will provide a good foundation for the further study of UML.

USING USE CASE DIAGRAMS

The **use case** diagram shows how a business works from the perspective of those who approach it from the outside, or those who actually *use* the business. This category includes many types of users—for example employees, customers, and suppliers. Although users can also be governments, private organizations, machines, or other systems, it is easiest to think of them as people, so users are called **actors** and are represented by stick figures in use case diagrams. The actual use cases are represented by ovals.

Use cases do not necessarily represent all the functions of a system; they are the system functions or services that are visible to its actors. In other words, they represent the cases by which an actor uses and presumably benefits from the system. Determining all the cases for which users interact with systems helps you divide a system logically into functional parts.

Establishing use cases usually follows from analyzing the main events in a system. For example, from a librarian's point of view, two main events are **acquireNewBook()** and **checkOutBook()**. Figure 15-1 shows a use case diagram for these two events.

librarian

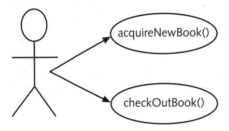

Figure 15-1   Use case diagram for librarian

> Many system developers would use standard English form in their UML diagrams, for example `check out book` instead of `checkOutBook()`. Because you are used to seeing method names in camel casing and with trailing parentheses throughout this book, this discussion of UML will continue with the same format.

In many systems there are variations in use cases. The three possible types of variations are:

- extend
- include
- generalization

An **extend** is a use case variation that shows functions beyond those found in a base case. For example, checking out a book for a new library patron who doesn't have a library card is slightly more complicated than checking out a book for an existing patron. Each variation in the sequence of actions required in a use case is a **scenario**. Each use case has at least one main scenario, but might have several more that are extensions or variations of the main one. Figure 15-2 shows how you would diagram the relationship between the use case `checkOutBook()` and the more specific scenario `checkOutBookForNewPatron()`. Extended use cases are shown in an oval with a dashed arrow pointing to the more general base case.

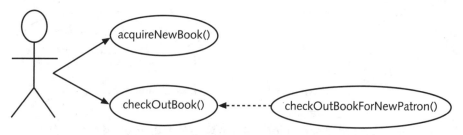

Figure 15-2   Use case diagram for librarian with scenario extension

For clarity, you can add "<<extend>>" near the line that shows a relationship extension. Such a feature, which adds to the UML vocabulary of shapes to make them more meaningful for the reader, is called a **stereotype**. Figure 15-3 includes a stereotype.

15

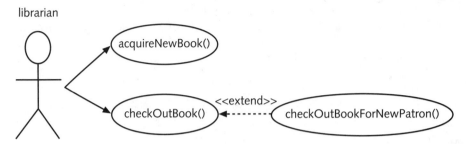

Figure 15-3   Use case diagram for librarian using stereotype

In addition to extend relationships, use case diagrams also can show include relationships. You use an **include** relationship when a case can be part of multiple use cases. This concept is very much like that of a subroutine or submodule. You show an include use case in an oval with a dashed arrow pointing to the subroutine use case. For example, `issueLibraryCard()` might be a function of `checkOutBook()` when the patron is new, but it might also be a function of `registerNewPatron()`, which occurs when a patron registers at the library but does not want to check out books yet. See Figure 15-4.

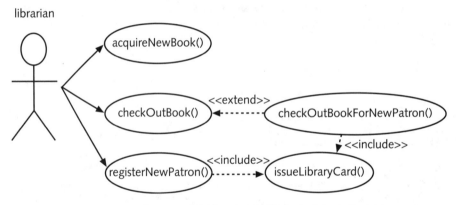

Figure 15-4   Use case diagram for librarian with include relationship

You use a **generalization** when a use case is less specific than others and you want to be able to substitute the more specific case for the general one. For example, a library has certain procedures for acquiring new materials, whether they are videos, tapes, CDs, paperbacks, or hardcover books. However, the procedures might become more specific during a particular acquisition—perhaps the librarian must procure plastic cases for circulating videos or assign locked storage locations for CDs. Figure 15-5 shows the generalization `acquireNewItem()` with two more specific situations: acquiring videos and CDs. The more specific scenarios are attached to the general scenario with open-headed dashed arrows.

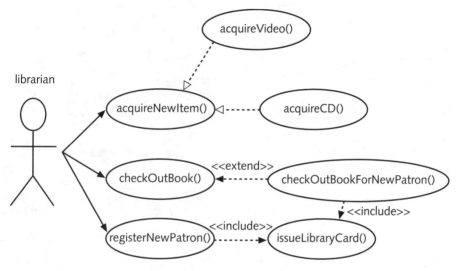

Figure 15-5   Use case diagram for librarian with generalizations

Many use case diagrams show multiple actors. For example, Figure 15-6 shows that a library clerk cannot perform as many functions as a librarian; the clerk can check out books and register new patrons but cannot acquire new materials.

15

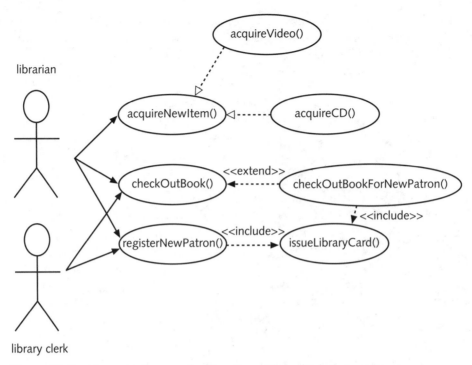

Figure 15-6   Use case diagram for librarian with multiple actors

While designing an actual library system, you could add many more use cases and actors to the use case diagram. The purpose of such a diagram is to encourage discussion between system developer and librarian. Library staff members can visualize activities they perform and correct the system developer if inaccuracies exist. The final software products developed for such a system are far more likely to satisfy users than those developed without this design step.

A use case diagram is only a tool to aid communication. No single "correct" use case diagram exists; you might correctly represent a system in several ways. For example, you might choose to emphasize the actors in the library system as shown in Figure 15-7, or to emphasize system requirements as shown in Figure 15-8. Diagrams that are too crowded are neither visually pleasing nor very useful. Therefore, the use case diagram in Figure 15-7 shows all the specific actors and their relationships, but purposely omits more specific system functions, while Figure 15-8 shows many actions that are often hidden from users but purposely omits more specific actors. For example, the activities carried out to `manageNetworkOutage()`, if done properly, should be invisible to library patrons checking out books.

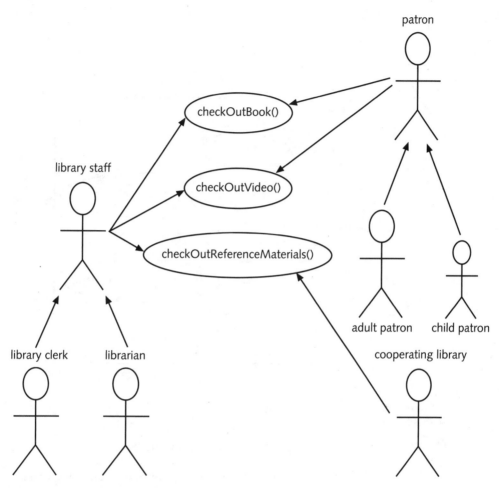

Figure 15-7   Use case diagram emphasizing actors

15

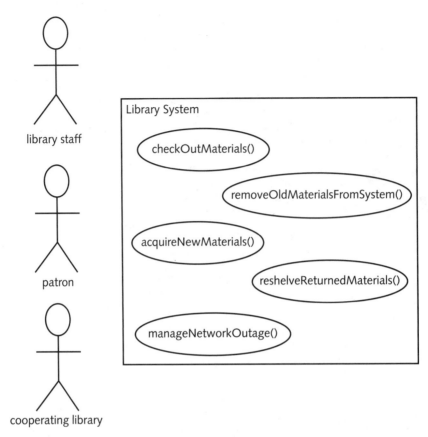

Figure 15-8   Use case diagram emphasizing system requirements

In Figure 15-8, the relationship lines between the actors and use cases have been removed because the emphasis is on the system requirements, and too many lines would make the diagram confusing. When system developers omit parts of diagrams for clarity, they refer to the missing parts as **elided**. For the sake of clarity, eliding extraneous information is perfectly acceptable. The main purpose of UML diagrams is to facilitate clear communication.

USING CLASS AND OBJECT DIAGRAMS

You use a **class diagram** to illustrate the names, attributes, and methods of a class or set of classes. Class diagrams are more useful to a system's programmers than to its users because they closely resemble code the programmers will write. A class diagram illustrating a single class contains a rectangle divided into three sections; the top section contains the name of the class, the middle section contains the names of the attributes, and the bottom section contains the names of the methods. Figure 15-9 shows the class diagram for a Book class. Each `Book` object contains an `idNum`, `title`, and `author`. Each `Book` object also contains methods to create a `Book` when it is acquired, and to retrieve or get `title` and `author` information when the `Book`'s `idNum` is supplied.

Book
idNum
title
author
create
getInfo(idNum)

Figure 15-9   Book class diagram

You first used class diagrams in Chapter 12.

In the last section you learned how to use generalizations with use case diagrams to show general and more specific use cases. With use case diagrams you drew an open-headed arrow from the more specific case to the more general one. Similarly, you can use generalizations with class diagrams to show more general (or parent) and more specific (or child) classes that inherit attributes from parents. For example, Figure 15-10 shows `Book` and `Video` classes that are more specific than the general `LibraryItem` class. All `LibraryItem` objects contain an `idNum` and `title`, but each `Book` item also contains an `author` and each `Video` item also contains a `runningTime`. In addition, `Video` items contain a `rewind()` method not found in the more general `LibraryItem` class. Child classes contain all the attributes of their parents and usually contain additional attributes not found in the parent.

You first learned about inheritance and parent and child classes in Chapter 12.

15

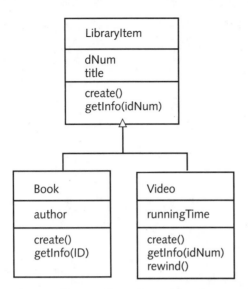

Figure 15-10   LibraryItem class diagram showing generalization

Class diagrams can include symbols that show the relationships between objects. You can show two types of relationships:

- An association relationship
- A whole-part relationship

An **association relationship** describes the connection or link between objects. You represent an association relationship between classes with a straight line. Frequently you include information about the arithmetical relationship (called **cardinality** or **multiplicity**) between the objects. For example, Figure 15-11 shows the association relationship between a `Library` and the `LibraryItems` it lends. Exactly one `Library` object exists, and it can be associated with any number of `LibraryItems` from 0 to infinity, represented by an asterisk. Figure 15-12 adds the `Patron` class to the diagram and shows how you indicate that any number of `Patrons` can be associated with the `Library`, but that each `Patron` can borrow only up to five `LibraryItems` at a time, or currently might not be borrowing any. Additionally, each `LibraryItem` can be associated with at most one `Patron`, but at any given time might not be on loan.

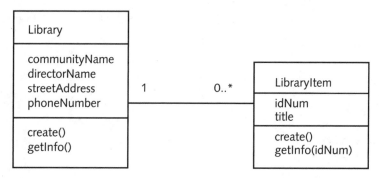

Figure 15-11   Class diagram with association relationship

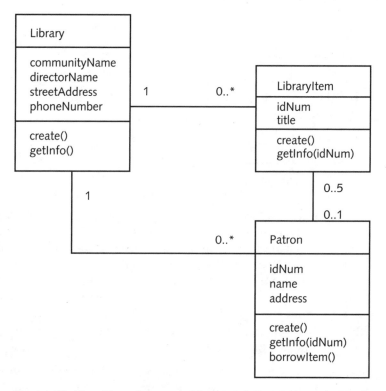

Figure 15-12   Class diagram with several association relationships

A **whole–part relationship** describes an association in which one or more classes make up the parts of a larger whole class. For example, 50 states "make up" the United States and 10 departments might "make up" a company. This type of relationship is also called an **aggregation**, and is represented by an open diamond at the "whole part" end of the line that indicates the relationship. You also can call a whole-part relationship a **has–a relationship** because the phrase describes the association between the whole and one of its parts; for example, "The company *has a* Personnel Department." Figure 15-13 shows a whole-part relationship for a `Library`.

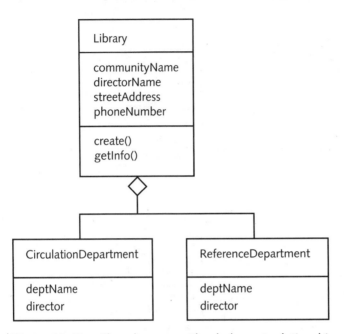

Figure 15-13   Class diagram with whole-part relationship

Object diagrams are similar to class diagrams, but they model specific instances of classes. You use an object diagram to show a snapshot of an object at one point in time so you can more easily understand its relationship to other objects. Imagine looking at the travelers in a major airport. If you try to watch them all at once you see a flurry of activity, but it is hard to understand all the tasks (buying a ticket, checking luggage, and so on) a traveler must accomplish to take a trip. However, if you concentrate on one traveler and follow his actions through the airport from arrival to takeoff, you get a clearer picture of the required activities. An object diagram serves the same purpose; you concentrate on a specific instance of a class to better understand how a class works.

Figure 15-14 contains an object diagram showing the relationship between one `Library`, `LibraryItem`, and `Patron`. Notice the similarities between Figures 15-12 and 15-14. If you need to describe the relationship between three classes you can use either model interchangeably. You simply use the model that seems clearer to you and your intended audience.

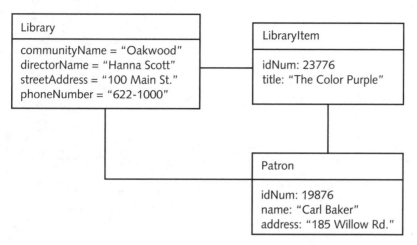

Figure 15-14   Object diagram for Library

USING SEQUENCE AND COLLABORATION DIAGRAMS

You use a **sequence diagram** to show the timing of events in a single use case. A sequence diagram makes it easier to see the order in which activities occur. The horizontal axis (**x-axis**) of a sequence diagram represents objects and the vertical axis (**y-axis**) represents time. You create a sequence diagram by placing objects that are part of an activity across the top of the diagram along the x-axis starting at the left with the object or actor that begins the action. Beneath each object on the x-axis you place a vertical dashed line that represents the period of time the object exists. Then you use horizontal arrows to show how the objects communicate with each other over time.

For example, Figure 15–15 shows a sequence diagram for a scenario that a librarian can use to create a book checkout record. The librarian begins a `create()` method with `Patron idNum` and `Book idNum` information. The `BookCheckOutRecord` object requests additional `Patron` information (such as name and address) from the `Patron` object with the correct `Patron idNum` and additional `Book` information (such as title and author) from the `Book` object with the correct `Book idNum`. When the `BookCheckOutRecord` contains all the data it needs, a completed record is returned to the librarian.

In Figures 15-15 and 15-16, `patronInfo` and `bookInfo` represent group items that contain all of a `Patron`'s and `Book`'s data. For example, `patronInfo` might contain an `idNum`, `lastName`, `firstName`, `address`, and `phoneNumber`.

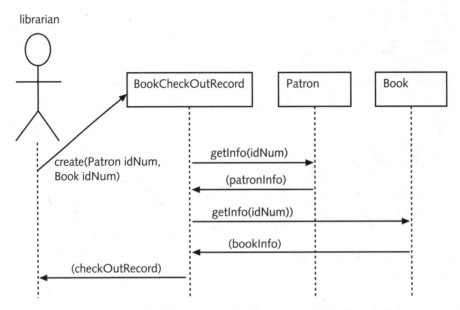

Figure 15-15   Sequence diagram for checking out a Book for a Patron

A **collaboration diagram** emphasizes the organization of objects that participate in a system. It is similar to a sequence diagram, except that it contains sequence numbers to represent the precise order in which activities occur. Figure 15–16 shows the same sequence of events as Figure 15–15, but the steps to creating a `BookCheckOutRecord` are clearly numbered. Decimal numbered steps (1.1, 1.2, and so on) represent substeps of the main steps. Checking out a library book is a fairly straightforward event, so a sequence diagram sufficiently illustrates the process. Collaboration diagrams become more useful with more complicated systems.

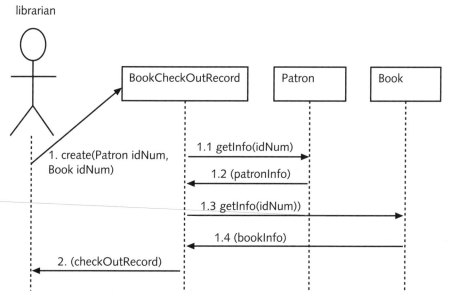

Figure 15-16   Collaboration diagram for checking out a Book for a Patron

USING STATECHART DIAGRAMS

A **statechart diagram** shows the different statuses of a class or object at different points in time. You use a statechart diagram to illustrate aspects of a system that show interesting changes in behavior over time. Conventionally, you use rounded rectangles to represent each state and labeled arrows to show the sequence in which events affect the states. A solid dot indicates the start and stop states for the class or object. Figure 15-17 contains a statechart diagram you can use to describe the states of a Book.

 So that your diagrams are clear, you should use the correct symbol in each UML diagram you create, just as you should use the correct symbol in each program flowchart. However, if you create a flowchart and use a rectangle for an input or output statement where a parallelogram is conventional, others will still understand your meaning. Similarly, with UML diagrams, the exact shape you use is not nearly as important as the sequence of events and relationships between objects.

15

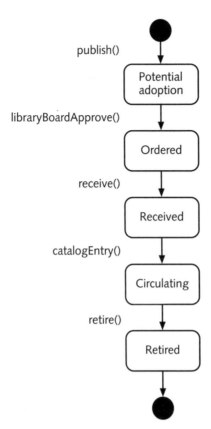

publish()

libraryBoardApprove()

receive()

catalogEntry()

retire()

Figure 15-17   Statechart diagram for Book class

USING ACTIVITY DIAGRAMS

The UML diagram that most closely resembles a conventional flowchart is an activity diagram. In an **activity diagram** you show the flow of actions of a system, including branches that occur when decisions affect the outcome. Conventionally, activity diagrams use flowchart start and stop symbols (called **lozenges**) to describe actions and solid dots to represent start and stop states. Like flowcharts, activity diagrams use diamonds to describe decisions. Unlike flowcharts, the diamonds in UML activity diagrams usually are empty; the possible outcomes are documented along the branches emerging from the decision symbol. As an example, Figure 15-18 shows a simple activity diagram with a single branch.

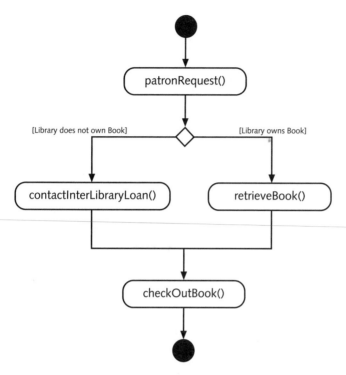

Figure 15-18   Activity diagram showing branch

Many real-life systems contain activities that are meant to occur simultaneously. For example, when you apply for a home mortgage with a bank, a bank officer might perform a credit or background check while an appraiser determines the value of the house you are buying. When both activities are complete, the loan process continues. UML activity diagrams show simultaneous activities using forks and joins. A fork is similar to a decision, but whereas the flow of control follows only one path after a decision, a **fork** defines a branch in which all paths are followed simultaneously. A **join**, as its name implies, reunites the flow of control after a fork. You indicate forks and joins with thick straight lines. Figure 15-19 shows how you might model the way an inter-library loan system processes book requests. When a request is received, simultaneous searches begin at three local libraries that are part of the library system.

15

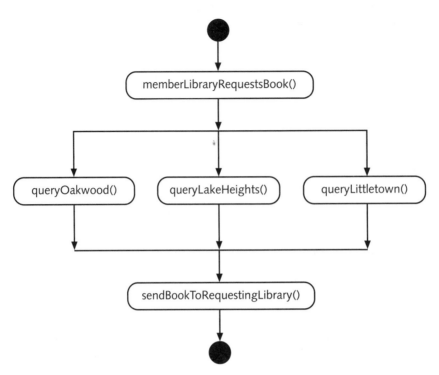

Figure 15-19   Activity diagram showing fork and join

A fork does not have to indicate strictly simultaneous activity. The actions in the branches for a fork might only be concurrent or interleaved.

USING COMPONENT AND DEPLOYMENT DIAGRAMS

Component and deployment diagrams model the physical aspects of systems. You use a **component diagram** when you want to emphasize the files, database tables, documents, and other components that a system's software uses. You use a **deployment diagram** when you want to focus on a system's hardware. You can use a variety of icons in each type of diagram, but each icon must convey meaning to the reader. Figures 15-20 and 15-21 show component and deployment diagrams that illustrate aspects of a library system. Figure 15-20 contains icons that symbolize paper and Internet requests for library items, the library database, and two tables that constitute the database. Figure 15-21 shows some commonly used icons that represent hardware components.

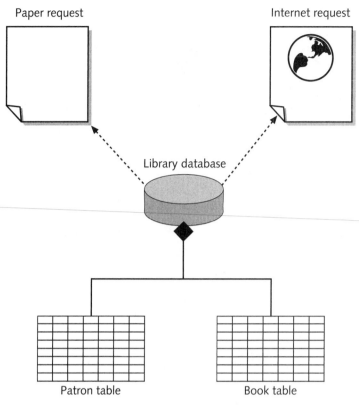

Figure 15-20   Component diagram

In Figure 15-20, notice the filled diamond connecting the two tables to the database. Just as it does in a class diagram, the diamond aggregation symbol shows the whole-part relationship of the tables to the database. You use an open diamond when a part might belong to several wholes (Door and Wall objects belong to many House objects), but you use a filled diamond when a part can belong to only one whole at a time (the Patron table can belong only to the Library database). You can use most UML symbols in multiple types of diagrams.

15

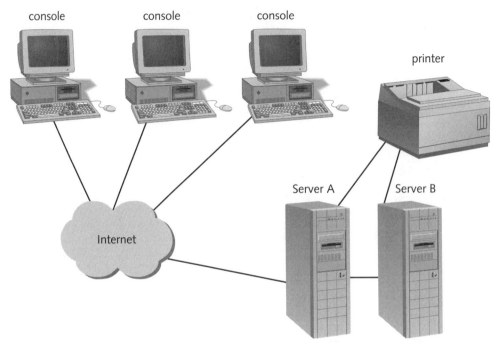

Figure 15-21   Deployment diagram

Deciding which UML Diagrams to Use

Each of the nine UML diagram types provides a different view of a system. Just as a portrait artist, psychologist, and neurosurgeon each prefer a different conceptual view of your head, the users, managers, designers, and technicians of computer and business systems each prefer specific system views. Very few systems require diagrams of all nine types; you can illustrate the objects and activities of many systems by using a single diagram, or perhaps one that is a hybrid of two or more basic types. No view is superior to the others; you can achieve the most complete picture of any system by using several views. The most important reason you use any UML diagram is to communicate clearly and efficiently with the people for whom you are designing a system.

Chapter Summary

❑ System design is the detailed specification of how all the parts of a system will be implemented and coordinated. Good designs make systems easier to understand. The UML provides a means for programmers and business people to communicate about system design.

❐ The UML (Unified Modeling Language) is a standard way to specify, construct, and document systems that use object-oriented methods. The UML has its own notation with which you can construct software diagrams that model different kinds of systems. The UML provides nine diagram types that you use at the beginning of the design process.

❐ A use case diagram shows how a business works from the perspective of those who approach it from the outside, or those who actually *use* the business. The diagram often includes actors, represented by stick figures, and use cases, represented by ovals. Use cases can include variations such as extend relationships, include relationships, and generalizations.

❐ You use a class diagram to illustrate the names, attributes, and methods of a class or set of classes. A class diagram of a single class contains a rectangle divided into three sections: the name of the class, the names of the attributes, and the names of the methods. Class diagrams can show generalizations and the relationships between objects. Object diagrams are similar to class diagrams, but they model specific instances of classes at one point in time.

❐ You use a sequence diagram to show the timing of events in a single use case. The horizontal axis (x-axis) of a sequence diagram represents objects and the vertical axis (y-axis) represents time. A collaboration diagram emphasizes the organization of objects that participate in a system. It is similar to a sequence diagram, except that it contains sequence numbers to represent the precise order in which activities occur.

❐ A state chart diagram shows the different statuses of a class or object at different points in time.

❐ In an activity diagram you show the flow of actions of a system, including branches that occur when decisions affect the outcome. UML activity diagrams show simultaneous activities using forks and joins.

❐ You use a component diagram when you want to emphasize the files, database tables, documents, and other components that a system's software uses. You use a deployment diagram when you want to focus on a system's hardware.

15

❐ Each of the nine UML diagram types provides a different view of a system. Very few systems require diagrams of all nine types; the most important reason to use any UML diagram is to communicate clearly and efficiently with the people for whom you are designing a system.

Exercises

1. a. Develop a use case diagram for a convenience food store. Include an actor representing the store manager and use cases for `orderItem()`, `stockItem()`, and `sellItem()`.

   b. Add more use cases to the diagram you created in Exercise 1a. Include two generalizations for `stockItem()`: `stockPerishable()` and `stockNonPerishable()`. Also include an extension to `sellItem()` to `checkCredit()` when a customer purchases items using a credit card.

   c. Add a customer actor to the use case diagram you created in Exercise 1b. Show that the customer participates in `sellItem()` but not in `orderItem()` or `stockItem()`.

2. Develop a use case diagram for a department store credit card system. Include at least two actors and four use cases.

3. Develop a use case diagram for a college registration system. Include at least three actors and five use cases.

4. Develop a class diagram for a `Video` class describes objects that a video store customer can rent. Include at least four attributes and three methods.

5. Develop a class diagram for a `Shape` class. Include generalizations for child classes `Rectangle`, `Circle`, and `Triangle`.

6. Develop a class diagram for a college registration system. Include at least three classes that cooperate to achieve student registration.

7. Develop a sequence diagram that shows how a clerk at a mail order company places a customer `Order`. The Order accesses `Inventory` to check availability. Then the `Order` accesses `Invoice` to produce a customer invoice that returns to the clerk.

8. Develop a statechart diagram that shows the states of a `CollegeStudent` from `PotentialApplicant` to `Graduate`.

9. Develop a statechart diagram that shows the states of a `Book` from `Concept` to `Publication`.

10. Develop an activity diagram that illustrates how to build a house.

11. Develop the UML diagram of your choice that illustrates some aspect of your life.

12. a. Develop the UML diagram of your choice that best illustrates some aspect of a place you have worked.

   b. Develop a different UML diagram type that illustrates the same functions as the diagram you created in Exercise 12a.

A

A DIFFICULT STRUCTURING PROBLEM

In Chapter 2 you learned that you can solve any logical problem using only the three standard structures—sequence, selection, and looping. Often it is a simple matter to modify an unstructured program to make it adhere to structured rules. Sometimes, however, it is a challenge to structure a more complicated program. Still, no matter how complicated, large, or poorly structured a problem is, the same tasks can *always* be accomplished in a structured manner.

Consider the flowchart segment in Figure A-1. Is it structured?

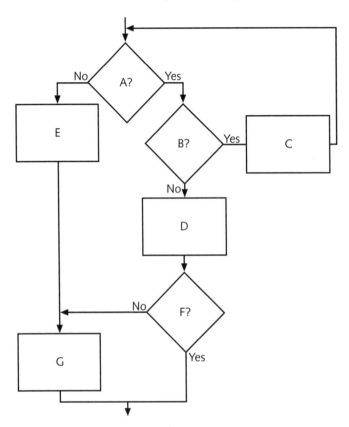

Figure A-1 Unstructured flowchart

No, it's not. Let's straighten it out. You can use the "spaghetti" method to enforce struc-ture. Start at the beginning with the decision labeled A, shown in Figure A-2. This must represent the beginning of either a selection or a loop, because a sequence would not contain a decision.

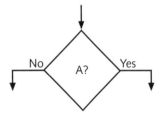

Figure A-2 Structuring Step 1

If you follow the logic on the "No" or left side of the question, you can pull up on the left branch of the decision. You get process E, followed by G, followed by the end, as shown in Figure A-3.

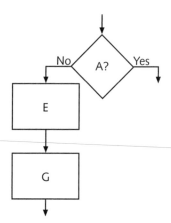

Figure A-3   Structuring Step 2

Now continue on the right or "Yes" side of decision A. When you follow the flowline, you encounter a decision symbol, labeled B. Pull on B's left side, and a process, D, comes up next. See Figure A-4.

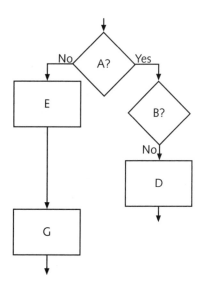

Figure A-4   Structuring Step 3

After D, a decision labeled F comes up. Pull on its left side and get a process, G, and then the end. When you pull on F's right side, you simply reach the end, as shown in Figure A-5.

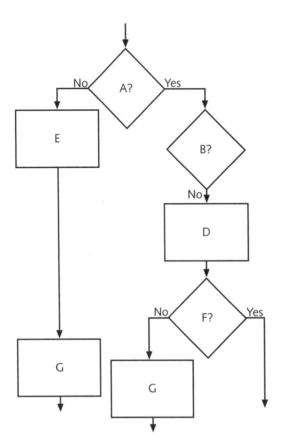

Figure A-5 Structuring Step 4

The biggest problem in structuring the original flowchart segment lies on the right side of the B decision. Pull up and get process C, as shown in Figure A-6. This looks like a loop because it doubles back on itself, up to Decision A. However, the rules of a structured loop say that it must have the appearance shown in Figure A-7: a question, followed by a structure, returning right back to the question. If the arrow coming out of C returned right to B, there would be no problem; but as it is, Question A must be repeated. The spaghetti technique says if things are tangled up, start repeating them. So bring another A decision down after C, as Figure A-6 shows.

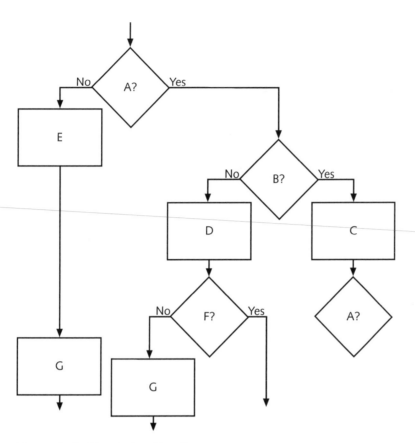

Figure A-6   Structuring Step 5

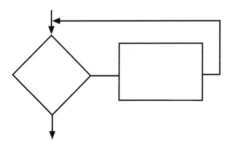

Figure A-7   A structured loop

Now, on the right side of A, B repeats. On the right side of B, C repeats. After C, A occurs. On the right side of A, B occurs. On the right side of B, C occurs. After C, A occurs again. Soon you should realize that you will repeat these same steps forever. See Figure A-8.

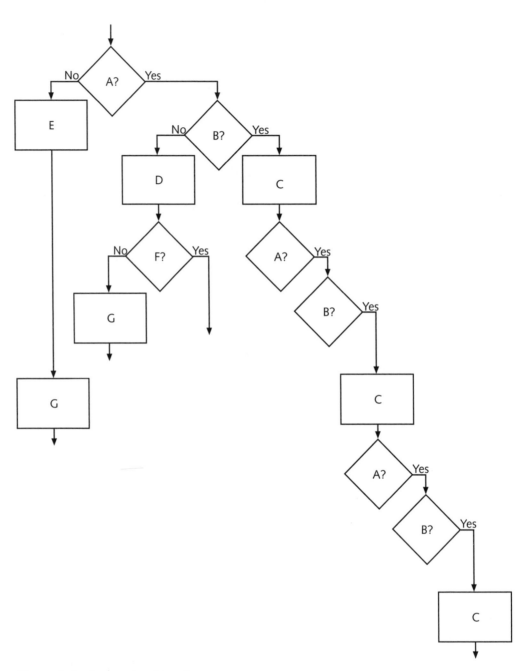

Figure A-8 Structuring Step 6

Sometimes, in order to make a program segment structured, you have to add an extra flag variable to get out of an infinite mess. A flag is a variable that you set to indicate a true or false state. Typically, a variable is called a flag when its only purpose is to tell you whether some event has occurred. You can create a flag variable named `goBackToA` and set the value of `goBackToA` to "Yes" or "No," depending on whether it is appropriate to "go back" to Step A. When A is no, the `goBackToA` flag should be set to "No" because in this situation, you never want to go back to Question A again. See Figure A-9.

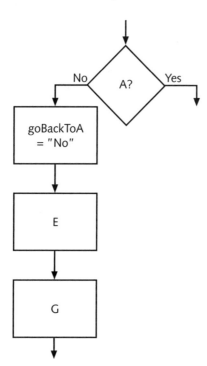

Figure A-9   Structuring Step 7

Similarly, when B is No, you never want to go back to A again, either. Figure A-10 shows that you set `goBackToA` to "No" when the answer to B is No.

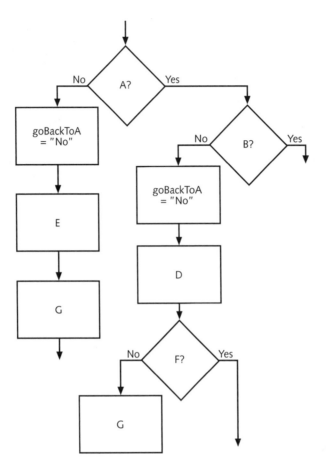

Figure A-10   Structuring Step 8

When the B decision result is Yes, however, you *do* want to go back to A. So when B is Yes, perform the process for C and set the **goBackToA** flag equal to "Yes", as shown in Figure A-11.

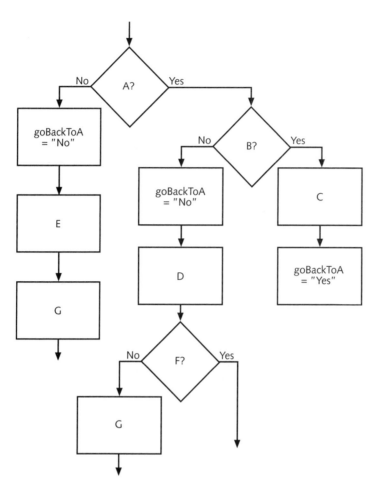

Figure A-11   Structuring Step 9

Now all paths of the flowchart can come together at the bottom with one final question: Is **goBackToA** equal to "Yes"? If it isn't, exit; but if it is, extend the flowline to go back to A. (See Figure A-12.)

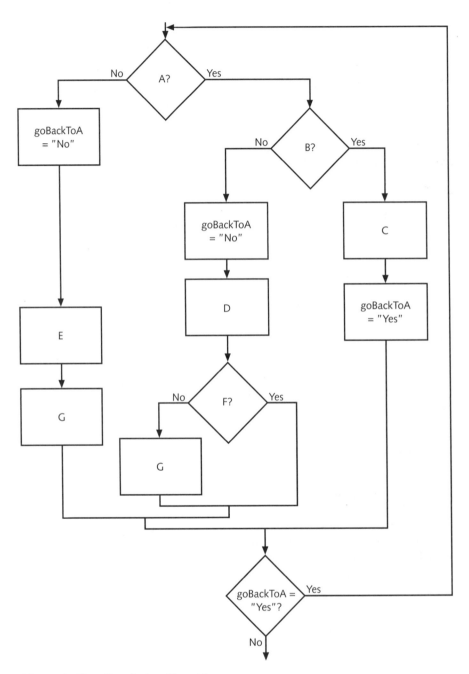

Figure A-12   Structuring Step 10

Is this flowchart segment structured now? There is so much information here that it is hard to tell. You may be able to see the structure more clearly if you create a module named `aThroughG()`. If you create the module shown in Figure A-13, then the original flowchart segment can be drawn as in Figure A-14.

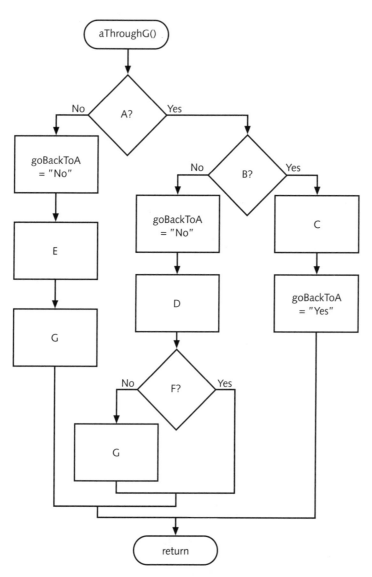

Figure A-13   The aThroughG() module

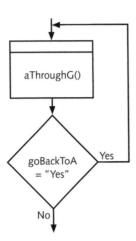

Figure A-14   Original segment using aThroughG() module and do until loop

Now you can see that the flowchart segment is a do until loop. If you prefer to use a while loop, you can redraw Figure A-14 to perform a sequence followed by a while loop, as shown in Figure A-15.

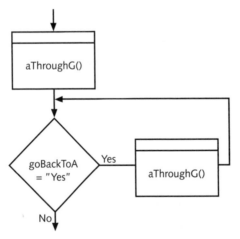

Figure A-15   Original segment using aThroughG() module and while loop

It has taken some effort, but any logical problem can be made to conform to structured rules. It may take extra steps, including using some flag variables, but every logical problem can be solved using the three structures.

B

USING A LARGE DECISION TABLE

In Chapter 5 you learned to use a simple decision table. Real-life problems often require many decisions; a complicated decision process is represented in the following situation. Suppose your employer sends you a memo outlining a year-end bonus plan with complicated rules. Appendix B will walk you through the process of solving this problem by using a large decision table.

To: Programming staff
From: The boss
I need a report listing every employee and the
bonus I plan to give him or her. Everybody gets
at least $100. All the employees in Department 2
get $200, unless they have more than 5 dependents.
Anybody with more than 5 dependents gets $1000
unless they're in Department 2. Nobody with an ID
number greater than 800 gets more than $100 even
if they're in Department 2 or have more than 5
dependents.
P.S. I need this by 5 o'clock.

Drawing the flowchart or writing the pseudocode for the mainLoop() for this task may seem daunting. You can use a decision table to help you manage all the decisions, and you can begin to create one by listing all the possible conditions. They are:

- empDept = 2

- empDepend > 5

- empIdNum > 800

Next, determine how many possible Boolean value combinations exist for the conditions. In this case, there are eight possible combinations, shown in Figure B-1. An employee can be in Department 2, have over five dependents, and have an ID number greater than 800. Another employee can be in Department 2, have over five dependents, but have an ID number that is 800 or less. Since each condition has two outcomes and there are three conditions, there are 2 * 2 * 2 , or eight possibilities. Four conditions would produce 16 possible outcome combinations, five would produce 32, and so on.

Condition	Outcome							
empDept = 2	T	T	T	T	F	F	F	F
empDepend > 5	T	T	F	F	T	T	F	F
empIdNum > 800	T	F	T	F	T	F	T	F

Figure B-1   Possible outcomes of bonus conditions

Next, list the possible outcome values for the bonus amounts. If you declare a numeric variable named **bonus** by placing the statement num bonus in your list of variables at the beginning of the program, then the possible outcomes can be expressed as:

- bonus = 100

- bonus = 200

- bonus = 1000

Finally, choose one required outcome for each possible combination of conditions, as shown in Figure B-2. Place Xs in the **bonus = 100** row each time empIdNum > 800 is true, no matter what other conditions exist, because the memo from the boss said, "Nobody with an ID number greater than 800 gets more than \$100 even if they're in Department 2 or have more than 5 dependents."

Condition	Outcome							
empDept = 2	T	T	T	T	F	F	F	F
empDepend > 5	T	T	F	F	T	T	F	F
empIdNum > 800	T	F	T	F	T	F	T	F
bonus = 100	X		X		X		X	
bonus = 200								
bonus = 1000								

Figure B-2   Decision table for bonuses, Part 1

Place an X in the **bonus = 1000** row under all remaining columns in which **empDepend > 5** is true unless the **empDept = 2** condition is true, because the memo stated, "Anybody with more than 5 dependents gets \$1000 unless they're in Department 2." Only the sixth column in Figure B-3 meets these criteria.

Condition	Outcome							
empDept = 2	T	T	T	T	F	F	F	F
empDepend > 5	T	T	F	F	T	T	F	F
empIdNum > 800	T	F	T	F	T	F	T	F
bonus = 100	X		X		X		X	
bonus = 200								
bonus = 1000						X		

Figure B-3   Decision table for bonuses, Part 2

Place Xs in the **bonus** = 200 row for any remaining columns in which **empDept** = 2 is true and **empDepend** > 5 is false because "All the employees in Department 2 get $200, unless they have more than 5 dependents." Column 4 in Figure B-4 satisfies these criteria.

Condition	Outcome							
empDept = 2	T	T	T	T	F	F	F	F
empDepend > 5	T	T	F	F	T	T	F	F
empIdNum > 800	T	F	T	F	T	F	T	F
bonus = 100	X		X		X		X	
bonus = 200				X				
bonus = 1000						X		

Figure B-4   Decision table for bonuses, Part 3

Finally, fill any unmarked columns with an X in the **bonus** = 100 row because, according to the memo, "Everybody gets at least $100." The only columns remaining are the second column and the last column on the right.

Condition	Outcome							
empDept = 2	T	T	T	T	F	F	F	F
empDepend > 5	T	T	F	F	T	T	F	F
empIdNum > 800	T	F	T	F	T	F	T	F
bonus = 100	X	X	X		X		X	X
bonus = 200				X				
bonus = 1000						X		

Figure B-5   Decision table for bonuses, Part 4

The decision table is complete. When you count the Xs, you'll find there are eight possible outcomes. Take a moment and confirm that each bonus is the appropriate value based on the specifications in the original memo from the boss. Now you can start to plan the logic. If you choose to use a flowchart, you start by drawing the path to the first outcome, which occurs when **empDept** = 2, **empDepend** > 5, and **empIdNum** > 800 are all true, and which corresponds to the first column in the decision table. See Figure B-6.

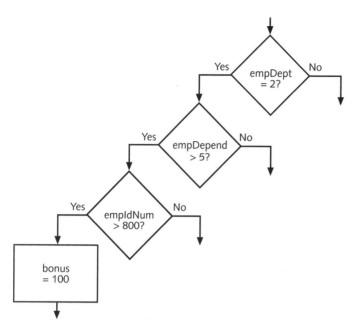

Figure B-6   Flowchart for bonus decision, Part 1

Add the "false" outcome to the `empIdNum > 800` decision, which corresponds to the second column in the decision table. See Figure B-7.

Add the "false" outcome when the `empDepend > 5` decision is No and the `empIdNum > 800` decision is Yes, which is represented by the third column in the decision table. See Figure B-8.

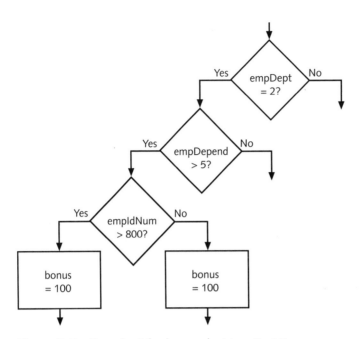

Figure B-7   Flowchart for bonus decision, Part 2

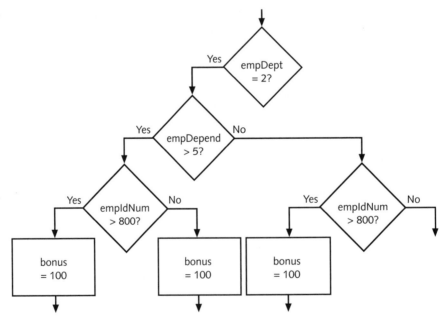

Figure B-8   Flowchart for bonus decision, Part 3

Continue until you have drawn all eight outcomes, as shown in Figure B-9.

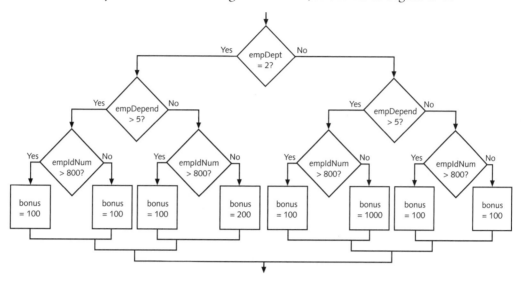

Figure B-9 Flowchart for bonus decision, Part 4

Next, eliminate any decision that doesn't make any difference. For example, if you look at the far left side of Figure B-9, you see that when `empDept` is 2 and `empDepend` is greater than 5, the outcome of `empIdNum > 800` does not matter; the `bonus` value is 100 either way. You might as well eliminate the selection. Similarly, on the far right, the question `empIdNum` makes no difference. Finally, many programmers prefer that the True or Yes side of a flowchart decision always appears on the right side. The result is Figure B-10. The pseudocode appears in Figure B-11.

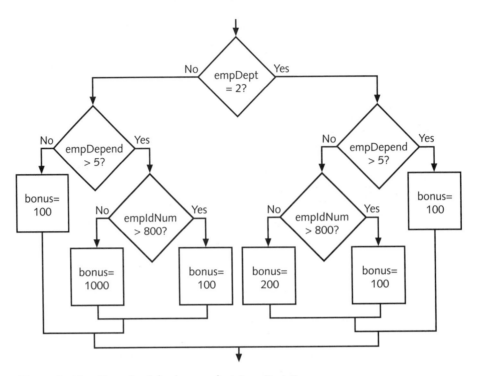

Figure B-10 Flowchart for bonus decision, Part 5

```
if empDept = 2 then
      if empDepend > 5 then
            bonus = 100
      else
            if empIdNum > 800 then
                  bonus = 100
            else
                  bonus = 200
            endif
      endif
else
      if empDepend > 5 then
            if empIdNum > 800 then
                  bonus = 100
            else
                  bonus = 1000
            endif
      else
            bonus = 100
      endif
endif
```

Figure B-11 Pseudocode for bonus decision

INDEX